British Cabinet Ministers

British Cabinet Ministers

The Roles of Politicians in Executive Office

by
BRUCE HEADEY

London · George Allen & Unwin Ltd
Ruskin House · Museum Street

First published in 1974

© George Allen & Unwin Ltd 1974
ISBN 0 04 320098 2

Printed in Great Britain
in 10 point Times Roman type
by Alden & Mowbray Ltd
at the Alden Press, Oxford

To Martha

Preface

Despite its title this study does not pretend to be a definitive work on the tasks of the twenty or so Ministers who, at any given time, constitute the Cabinet. Nor, by any stretch of the imagination, does it purport to be a manual for Ministers. What it does try to do is present a Minister's-eye view of his job. It is largely based on interviews with a sample of fifty contemporary Ministers (and a smaller sample of civil servants) who were asked to record their task priorities and the problems they face in achieving their objectives in office. It was discovered that the great majority of Ministers see their departmental work – their work in Whitehall rather than in Cabinet or in Parliament – as the most important aspect of their job. Accordingly, this study focuses primarily on Ministers in Whitehall and their relationship with senior civil servants. There is almost nothing here about non-departmental Ministers and less than a comprehensive study would require on the Cabinet and Parliament.

The use of interview data has both important advantages and important disadvantages. The principal advantage is that it does not require an enormous investment of time to question a significant number of informants about their interpretation of the roles of leading actors in government. Furthermore, respondents can be selected on the basis that they have held jobs which give them markedly different perspectives. Thus the tendency of some Ministers to exaggerate their contribution to policy making may be set against the equal and opposite bias of those (relatively few) civil servants who believe that ministerial influence on policy is minimal. This is not to deny, however, that interview data are qualitatively less satisfactory than data on actual behaviour. Whatever the size and composition of the sample, one is still collecting verbal reports about government and the policy-making process rather than observing the process itself. The author is acutely aware that, at many points in the study, the ratio of 'hard' evidence to assertion, of case studies to statements about what generally occurs in government, is not as high as ideally it should be. The fact is, however, that case studies of the activities of Ministers and their relationship with civil servants are extremely difficult to carry out in Whitehall. The Official Secrets Act and the convention that advice to Ministers is confidential mean that sufficiently detailed evidence cannot normally be obtained. A few excellent case studies have been produced but, unless the laws and conventions of British government change, the case study method is not likely to pay high dividends.

The study was originally suggested by Professor Richard Rose who has been extremely generous in his interest and encouragement. He made a constructive suggestion for each criticism offered and gave an enormous amount of help with problems of outline and organisation as well as with more detailed points. Professor Anthony King of the University of Essex made many valuable comments which, I believe, strengthened the logic of the argument and enabled me to relate this study more closely to other work on the roles of political executives. I would also like to thank Anthony Barker of the University of Essex, Professor Maurice Kogan of Brunel University, Malcolm Punnett of Strathclyde University and Charles L. Taylor of Virginia Polytechnic Institute for their comments on earlier drafts. The Nuffield Foundation funded the project under its Small Grant Scheme and my thanks are due to the foundation for this assistance. Finally I am extremely grateful to the Ministers and civil servants who found time to answer my questions and gave permission for their remarks to be quoted.

Bruce Headey
Politics Department
University of Strathclyde
Glasgow
August 1973

Contents

Tables

Part I

The Job of
Cabinet Minister

Chapter 1

Cabinet Ministers and Executive Political Leadership

The British Constitution is unwritten but this has never deterred commentators wishing to cite its provisions. According to the Constitution, then, the principal task of Cabinet Ministers is to decide the policies which civil servants administer and from which the public either benefits or suffers. Individually, Ministers are assumed to decide policies emanating from their own departments and together, as a Cabinet, their duty is to resolve inter-departmental disputes and arrive at decisions for which they accept collective responsibility. Civil servants exist purely to advise on policy alternatives and to implement the decisions of their political masters. Constitutional doctrine thus treats the Minister–civil servant relationship as a constant. No distinction is recognised between the priorities and skills of individuals, the demands of different departments, situational constraints, or historical periods. Political observers, on the other hand, have long recognised that performance in office is highly variable and have distinguished between 'strong' Ministers who dominate their departments and significantly influence public policy and 'weak' Ministers who are, in effect, run by their officials and influence policy only in detail, if at all. This distinction introduces some degree of realism but is still inadequate as a basis for analysing the variance in ministerial performance. The objectives of this study are to propose a more precise five-category typology of Ministers based on their different approaches to their job, to analyse the factors affecting performance in office, and to review the consequences for British government of Ministers being better qualified to perform some of their tasks than others.

The study is not written, however, solely from the viewpoint of a student of British government. It is also intended to reflect a broader social science concern with classifying the roles of politicians in the executive branch of government and analysing the opportunities and constraints of office. Conceived in these terms it is something of an exploratory venture. Our present understanding of the tasks and problems of executive political leaders – by leaders we shall mean, simply, office-holders[1] – is minimal, despite the high annual output of biographies, autobiographies and memoirs, and studies of such institutions as the American Presidency and the British Cabinet. Political scientists have always been fascinated by differences between active and passive Presidents and Prime Ministers, brutally repressive and plainly laughable dictators, or simply between dominating and dominated committee members. However, most empirical and theory directed research has been concentrated on the, in many ways, less important tasks of legislators and Parliaments. The study of politicians in executive office has been relatively neglected and there has been no attempt to generalise or develop a theory about the causes and consequences of variance in executive leadership performance.

Where can we turn for ideas about developing such a theory? The single most stimulating work in this area is Richard E. Neustadt's *Presidential Power*.[2] Neustadt begins by posing the basic problem of American Presidents which is that their power to achieve their objectives by command is strictly limited with the consquence that they have to rely principally on their 'power to persuade'. The President's power to persuade depends on the 'credit' he has built up with the 'Washington community' of influentials and media men. If a President is perceived to possess a high order of 'political will and skill' his credit-rating will be favourable. If, on the other hand, he has appeared irresolute in his efforts to get others to accede to his publicly stated wishes (for example, in pressing Congress to enact his legislative programme), or if his decisions have turned out badly (the Bay of Pigs invasion, for example), then his credit-rating will sink low. In order to be perceived as having political will and skill, what must the President do and what attributes must he possess? First, Neustadt suggests he must constantly view issues from 'the presidential perspective', which means assessing how his involvement or non-involvement, and any decisions he might take, are likely to affect his 'credit'. If an issue has low priority for him, if he cares little how it is decided, he should not risk getting involved, and even on issues of high priority he must be selective and only use his credit when the chances of achieving his objectives seem reasonably good. Secondly, a President must avoid hierarchical staffing arrangements and act as his own director of intelligence, ensuring

[1] The words leader and leadership are ambiguous in social science as in colloquial usage. Political scientists and social psychologists often define a leader as an influential – someone who gets others to do what they would not otherwise do – and leadership as the exercise of influence. See Robert A. Dahl, 'Power' in David L. Sills (ed.), *International Encyclopaedia of the Social Sciences* (New York: Crowell Collier, 1968), XII, 405-15.

[2] (New York: John Wiley, 1960.)

that a wide range of decisional options are presented to him. Only then will he be in a position to judge how best to build up, conserve, or use his credit. Finally, Neustadt indicates what kind of personality and background an effective President will generally have. Self-confidence is more important than intelligence, and a professional politician, with some experience in the executive branch of government is most likely to have the appropriate skills.[1]

It should be noted that Neustadt thought of his work as relating only to American Presidents and that his propositions about the conditions of effective presidential leadership are mostly implicit rather than being stated as formal hypotheses.[2] However, much of what he says can plausibly be generalised to other politicians in executive office and, without quite aspiring to do a Neustadt for Ministers (his father worked as an aide to Roosevelt and he worked for Truman and Kennedy) it is appropriate here, to acknowledge a debt to his seminal work.

Suppose we did have an explicit theory of executive political leadership, what would it look like, what would be its constituent elements? Presumably, in the last resort our concern should be with the consequences for government of variance in political leadership performance. To put it more precisely, we should seek to discover the conditions under which different types of political leaders contribute, positively or negatively, to the performance of governmental tasks. We may appropriately ask three questions:

1. What roles do political leaders intend to perform? In so far as their priorities (or *role conceptions*) differ, *what are the main types of leader?*[3]

2. What factors (conditions) influence leaders' ability to perform their intended roles and act in accordance with their role conceptions?

[1] The book draws on the experiences in office of Roosevelt, Truman and Eisenhower. Roosevelt appears to have been Neustadt's model President and to have had the personality and background, working methods and 'presidential perspective' that Neustadt advocates.

[2] A thoughtful attempt to state Neustadt's implicit propositions as formal hypotheses and to set out the linkages between them is made in Peter W. Sperlich 'Bargaining and Overload: An Essay on *Presidential Power*' in A. Wildavsky (ed.), *The Presidency* (Boston: Little, Brown, 1969).

[3] Ultimately, of course, a typology of political leaders in the executive branch of government should be based on their *behaviour* rather than their role conceptions. However, since this study relies on interview data (role data) it is appropriate to phrase Question 1 as in the text. Questions 2 and 3 would also be phrased differently if one had sufficiently detailed evidence of ministerial behaviour in office.

3. What are the consequences for government of variance in political leadership performance?

These are the questions we shall try to answer in respect of one group of political leaders in executive office, British Cabinet Ministers. It must be recognised at the outset that our answers are bound to be tentative and provisional. The data available are not sufficiently detailed for us to measure and systematically compare the effectiveness with which Ministers perform their roles (question 2) or to establish reliably linkages between the performance of specific ministerial roles and specific dimensions of governmental performance (question 3). It was felt to be worthwhile, however, to state our research questions in the most general terms so that readers are in a position to see what objectives we are driving at and how much remains to be done.

1. WHAT ROLES DO CABINET MINISTERS INTEND TO PERFORM? IN SO FAR AS THEIR PRIORITIES (ROLE CONCEPTIONS) DIFFER, WHAT ARE THE MAIN TYPES OF MINISTER?

It would be hard to quarrel with the statement that the Prime Minister, Cabinet Ministers and senior civil servants are the most influential office-holders in British government. Tomes have been written about the Prime Minister and the Civil Service has in recent years been the target of a series of highly critical reports by government appointed committees.[1] Yet despite the fact that Cabinet Ministers are twenty times as numerous as the Prime Minister and ostensibly responsible for the actions of civil servants, there has been no book-length study describing their principal roles and analysing variance in ministerial performance. In particular, there has been little systematic research on the departmental tasks of Ministers and their relations with civil servants. For the most part we have to rely on the memoirs and biographies of many politicians and a few officials.[2] Ministers claim,

[1] For evaluations of the Civil Service and reform proposals see *Control of Public Expenditure* (The Plowden Report), Cmnd 1432 (1961); *The Civil Service* (The Fulton Report), Cmnd 3638 (1968); *Committee on Overseas Representation* (The Duncan Report), Cmnd 4107 (1969). The literature on the Prime Minister is sampled in Anthony King (ed.), *The Prime Minister: A. Reader* (London: Macmillan, 1969).

[2] Memoirs often provide fascinating insights into the working methods of individual politicians. See, for example, H. Dalton, *Memoirs* (London: Frederick Mullar, vol. I, 1953, vol. II, 1957, vol. III, 1960); H. Macmillan *Memoirs* (London: Macmillan, 6 vols 1967-73); G. Brown *In My Way* (London: Gollancz, 1971); R. A. Butler, *The Art of the Possible* (London: Hamish Hamilton, 1971). Civil

and their biographers tend to accept, that whatever was decided in the Minister's day was the Minister's decision.[1] An uncritical approach is especially unfortunate in this area because, as we shall see, Ministers themselves believe that the departmental side of their job deserves top priority.[2]

There are certain basic difficulties in collecting evidence about the actual behaviour of Ministers in office. The much discussed and deplored secrecy of British government presents a real barrier to the student of politics. Departmental and cabinet papers cannot, under the terms of the Official Secrets Act, be made available without official clearance, and civil servants are not permitted to pass on information which, to use the vague official phraseology, might be prejudicial to the public interest. This has always been interpreted as precluding discussion with outsiders about the specific content of advice to Ministers. In recent years, however, the secrecy barrier has been to some degree lifted and research on Ministers has become correspondingly more feasible. Some government documents – notably the new Green Papers and the Treasury's annual 'forward look' at public expenditure over the next five years – are now more forthcoming about the policy alternatives Ministers are considering.[3] The greatest gain for political scientists has not, however, resulted from formal decisions to publish a bit more and file away a bit less, but from a more informal change of attitude to outside research. The Fulton Report on the Civil Service recommended greater openness in government and closer links with the universities and, in all fairness, it has to be said that Ministers and civil servants appear now to be a great deal more willing to discuss their main duties and even, in general terms, their relations with each other.

Given that one can now obtain interviews with members of British government, the obvious method to employ in studying the tasks of Ministers is *role analysis*.[4] Roles may be defined as 'regularly

servants' rather different perspectives and work patterns are reflected in Lord Salter, *Memoirs of a Public Servant* (London: Faber, 1961); Lord Strang, *Home and Abroad* (London: Deutsch, 1956). See also the ministerial (Sir Edward Boyle) and the civil servant's (Sir Edward Playfair) contribution in 'Who are the Policy Makers?', *Public Administration*, 43 (1965), pp. 251-87.

[1] More critical and analytic approaches are employed, however, in Sir E. Boyle, A. Crosland and Maurice Kogan, *The Politics of Education* (Harmondsworth: Penguin, 1971) and Jeremy Bray, *Decision in Government* (London: Gollancz, 1969), ch. 3.

[2] See Chapter 3.

[3] The first five-year 'forward look' to be published was *Public Expenditure 1968-9 to 1973-4*, Cmnd 4234 (1969). Similar publications have appeared in each subsequent year.

[4] For an up-to-date and detailed discussion of role analysis see Theodore R. Sarbin and Vernon L. Allen, 'Role Theory', in G. Lindzey and E. Aronson

recurring patterns of social interaction (or modes of behaviour) that can be described by (1) who expects (2) whom (3) to do what (4) in what situation'.[1] A basic assumption of role analysis is that one can find out more about how office-holders behave from discovering the expectations that attach to their offices than from studying the biographies and personalities of the individuals themselves. In this study the expectations which attach to the office of Ministers were discovered through interviews with fifty Ministers and twenty-five civil servants.

The interviews were conducted by the author, mainly in the summer of 1969. The fifty ministerial respondents were divided roughly equally between the two major parties (twenty-three Conservatives, twenty-seven Labour) and in experience ranged from long-serving Cabinet Ministers to relatively inexperienced junior Ministers.[2] Most of them were recent office-holders or were currently in office, but a few had served in the wartime coalition or in Mr Attlee's Labour Government. The author was also conscious of the need to interview politicians from different social and occupational backgrounds and with varying reputations for effectiveness in office. It must be conceded immediately, though, that the respondents do not constitute the large statistically representative sample of contemporary politicians, which would have been ideal but which was beyond the resources of this study.

Little difficulty was experienced in obtaining interviews; just over two-thirds of those contacted were actually interviewed. Very senior Ministers currently in office were somewhat more likely than lower ranking or former Ministers to decline. In a few cases Ministers were out of the country, or a convenient time proved impossible to arrange. On average the interviews lasted an hour to an hour and a half, but respondents, of course, differed in the amount of time they could spare. Accordingly, it was felt that the best procedure was to begin with standard questions, the answers to which could be tabulated to provide basic information on such topics as role expectations and satisfaction with departmental advisory machinery, and then to proceed with a more general discussion of points suggested by answers to the standard questions, or on which the interviewer believed the respondent might have something particu-

(eds), *The Handbook of Social Psychology* (Reading, Mass.: Addison-Wesley, 1969), I, pp. 488-567.

[1] This definition of the concept of 'role' comes from Andrew S. McFarland, 'Role and Role Conflict', in Wildavsky (ed), *The Presidency*, pp. 3-17.

[2] The Civil Service sample is described later in this chapter. A more detailed breakdown of both samples and notes on interviewing procedures are given in Appendix 2.

larly interesting to say.[1] In this way it was possible to explore different topics with different respondents and to take advantage of individuals' special knowledge and greater frankness on some subjects than others.

Potentially quotable responses were noted at the time and full notes were taken as soon as possible after the end of each interview. The exact wording of some answers must have been lost, but since the interviews were 'not for attribution' it was felt that a procedure which ensured that substantive points were noted was adequate. Alternative methods of making a record were scarcely feasible. A tape recorder might well have precluded frankness, even if it had not led to an outright refusal to be interviewed, and the business of taking full notes in the course of an interview led, on the couple of occasions it was tried, to a rather disjointed question and answer session.[2]

The first of the standard interview questions was directed towards our initial objective of discovering Ministers' own role conceptions, the roles they expected to perform and intended to give priority:

What are the most important tasks a Minister has to perform? In other words what is a good Minister actually good at doing?

On the whole Ministers gave very full and interesting – and widely divergent – answers to this question. The variance in their answers gives us a basis for constructing a typology of Ministers. Previous classifications have simply referred to 'strong' and 'weak' Ministers – which begs the question ' 'strong' or 'weak' at what?' – or borrowed the social psychologists' distinction between instrumental (ends-means orientated) and affective (morale orientated) leaders.[3] Here we classify Ministers into five types. Policy initiators and policy selectors intend to perform rather different roles in the process of policy formulation, Executive Ministers give priority to departmental management roles, Ambassador Ministers to public relations roles

[1] Interview schedules for ministers and civil servants are given in Appendix I.

[2] Alternative methods of interviewing and recording information are discussed in Lewis A. Dexter, *Elite and Specialised Interviewing* (Evanston, Ill.: Northwestern University Press, 1970).

[3] The pioneering research on instrumental and affective leaders was carried out by R. F. Bales. See R. F. Bales and P. E. Slater, 'Role Differentiation in Small Decision-Making Groups', in C. A. Gibb (ed.), *Leadership* (Harmondsworth: Penguin, 1969) pp. 255-78. Research on political leadership has tended not to confirm the social psychologists' finding that different persons are normally found performing instrumental and affective roles. See James D. Barber *Power in Committees* (Chicago: Rand, McNally 1966) and John F. Manley, 'Wilbur D. Mills: A Study in Congressional Influence', *American Political Science Review*, 63.2 (June 1969), pp. 442-64.

and Minimalists are concerned only to retain office and some degree of credibility in Whitehall and Westminster (see Chapter 3).

A second approach to analysing the tasks of Ministers, which we might term 'activities analysis', is employed to a limited extent in this study. The object of activities analysis is to discover how the working week is actually spent. There are three methods of doing this: direct observation, interviews and collecting diaries.[1] Direct observation is the ideal method and has been used in studies of business managers.[2] Clearly, however, it is out of the question for most ministerial activities; the day is not about to dawn on which political scientists will be allowed to attend cabinet meetings and meetings between Ministers and civil servants for no better reason than to find out what goes on. In this study a combination of the second and third methods was used. Seven Ministers made available to the author copies of their appointments diaries. These diaries are kept by their Private Offices and list all appointments made for the Minister except unscheduled 'office meetings' with civil servants.[3] They include cabinet and cabinet committee meetings, appointments with deputations, journalists, Members of Parliament and so forth. They also remind the Minister when he is required at the House of Commons to vote. They are thus extremely useful in providing an outline picture of the Minister's working week. Their limitation is that they do not record what a Minister did at times when he had no definite appointment. It is not possible from the diaries alone to estimate, for example, how much time in a given week a Minister spent in the Palace of Westminster, or how much time he devoted to reading and discussion of papers dealing with policy issues. It was therefore necessary to supplement the information in the diaries by asking Ministers and officials about the length of time spent on unlisted activities. Ministers were also asked which activities they felt absorbed too much time and which they wished they could devote more time to.

2. WHAT FACTORS INFLUENCE THE ABILITY OF MINISTERS TO PERFORM THEIR INTENDED ROLES AND ACT IN ACCORDANCE WITH THEIR ROLE CONCEPTIONS?

We shall regard a Minister's ability to perform an intended role as a function of the following: his own skills and attributes (including his

---

[1] These methods are discussed in Rosemary Stewart, *Managers and Their Jobs* (London: Macmillan, 1967), ch. 1.

[2] See, for example, Sune Carlson, *Executive Behaviour: A Study of the Workload and Working Methods of Managing Directors* (Stockholm: Strombergs, 1951).

[3] 'Office meetings' are meetings held with departmental civil servants normally in the Minister's Private Office.

'personality'), the advice and expectations of civil servants, the favourableness of the situation and the department he is assigned to, and, in the case of a Minister who intends to act as a policy initiator, the extent to which his policy objectives can be translated into administratively feasible policy programmes. It must be made clear that these factors will be assumed and not proven to influence ministerial performance. Hopefully, the list seems plausible; it is derived partly from *Presidential Power* and partly from a review of the extensive social psychology literature on small group leadership.[1]

ability to perform a ministerial role	=	ministerial skills	+	advice and expectations of civil servants	+	the favourableness of the situation and the department

(+ feasibility of policy objectives)

It is popularly thought that certain individuals are 'born leaders' specially fitted to hold office in any group or organisation. If this were so, there would be no special problem finding out what skills, attributes and personality traits contribute positively to ministerial role performance. Sadly, however, social psychologists who have studied leadership in a wide variety of settings are agreed that the born leader is a myth. As Cecil A. Gibb, reviewing these findings writes, 'a leader is not a person characterised by any particular and consistent set of personality traits'.[2] Individuals with widely different personalities and skills attain leadership positions in different types of groups and organisations, and new leaders often emerge as groups needs change. It follows that it is by no means straightforward to determine what skills are appropriate for particular roles in particular situations. Common sense is not an adequate guide and it is necessary either to discover empirically what skills assist role performance or, as a substitute, to obtain the assessments of qualified judges including, where possible, leaders themselves. For this study the Ministers and civil servants interviewed were asked what skills are required for the performance of ministerial roles and whether requirements vary from department to department. In some cases disagreement arose over the skills required to perform particular roles. More interesting, however, were differences that related to alternative role conceptions and expectations. We shall find that

[1] For an up-to-date summary of this literature see C. A. Gibb 'Leadership' in G. Lindzey and E. Aronson (eds.), *The Handbook of Social Psychology* (Reading, Mass: Addison-Wesley, 1969), IV, pp. 205-82. References to specific hypotheses and findings are contained in the footnotes to this chapter.

[2] Gibb (ed.), *Leadership*, p. 11.

Ministers who see their jobs in a different light have markedly different views about the abilities and skills required.[1]

To some extent the information we need to assess the skills Ministers bring to office is already available in books and articles about ministerial recruitment.[2] The defect of these studies from our point of view, however, is that they are concerned with social origins and evidence of linkages between political and other elites rather than with assessing ministerial skills. We learn that in Britain, as elsewhere, politics is mainly a middle-class job with a declining number of aristocrats on the Conservative side and working-class politicians on the Labour side. We also know that for a good many MPs in both parties politics is the family business; they have or had relatives in Parliament and tend to marry girls brought up in political homes and hence accustomed to a rather residual private life. Above all, we are inundated with information about family, school tie, Oxford Union and Pall Mall Club connections between politicians and men in senior positions in other public and private institutions. What we lack, however, is a systematic attempt to assess the previous occupational, parliamentary and junior office experiences of Ministers as preparation for cabinet office. The question of whether future Ministers acquire the skills which will enable them to perform in accordance with their own or others' expectations is not even posed, let alone answered.[3] This may appear extraordinary in view of the enormous amount of attention given to recruiting, training and career planning designed to develop the right skills in civil servants, businessmen, army officers and members of other professions. One problem with Ministers, however, arises from the difficulty we have already noted of deciding what their most important tasks are and hence what skills it is necessary to develop.

Political leaders in executive office do not need to rely solely on their own skills and abilities. They also depend on organisational resources and support to aid them in role performance. British Cabinet Ministers (non-departmental Ministers excepted) are the

---

[1] See Chapter 3.

[2] Harold J. Laski, 'The Personnel of the English Cabinet,' *American Political Science Review*, 23.1 (Feb. 1928), pp. 12-31; J. F. S. Ross, *Parliamentary Representation* (London: Eyre & Spottiswoode, 2nd edn., 1948); W. L. Guttsman, *The British Political Elite* (London: MacGibbon and Kee, 1963); P. W. Buck, *Amateurs and Professionals in British Politics* (Chicago: University of Chicago Press, 1963); J. Bonnor, 'The Four Labour Cabinets', *Sociological Review*, 6.1 (1958), pp. 37-48; F. M. G. Willson, 'The Routes of Entry of New Members of the British Cabinet, 1868-1958', *Political Studies*, 7.3 (1959), pp. 222-32, Willson, 'Entry to the Cabinet, 1958-69', *Political Studies*, 18.2 (1970), pp. 236-38.

[3] See, however, Richard Rose, 'The Making of Cabinet Ministers', *British Journal of Political Science*, 1.4 (Oct. 1971), pp. 393-414.

political heads of Whitehall departments and it is the job of civil servants to advise and assist them in the performance of their duties. The larger departments have a staff running into tens of thousands, including numerous specialist advisers, a research capability and contacts with a range of outside experts and pressure groups in the fields they are concerned with.[1] The Ministers interviewed for this study were asked:

Are you generally satisfied with the range and quality of advice available in the department?

Ministers' answers to this question provide a focus in Chapter 5 for our review of the Whitehall advisory structure. We shall find that, although the overall satisfaction of Ministers with the services provided by departments is quite high, they are concerned about the expertise (subject matter competence) of their most senior advisers and about the possibility that, under the guidance of Permanent Secretaries, departments may tend to form a 'united view' on policy issues and hence tend to foreclose feasible policy options that Ministers need to be aware of.[2]

Apart from the expertise of civil servants and the size and structure of departments, the quality of advice a minister receives is also bound to be affected by the extent to which officials understand and approve of the way he approaches his job and the objectives he brings to office. The social psychologist E. P. Hollander, has analysed the implications of the fit (or misfit) between a leader's role conception and the expectations of his subordinates.[3] He has shown that an initial period of conformity to expectations is particularly vital to a leader's future performance. During this period a leader can build up what Hollander terms 'idiosyncrasy credits' (cf. Neustadt's analysis of Presidential 'credit') which can be cashed in at a later date to make changes in policy or procedure which would otherwise be resisted by subordinates. We shall argue in this study that, while there is a sense in which all Ministers are automatically assigned idio-syncrasy credits, those who act roughly in accordance with Civil Service

[1] The department with the largest number of non-industrial staff is Defence with 112,000, followed by the Department of Health and Social Security with 72,080, the Inland Revenue with 70,185, the Department of the Environment with 39,095 and the Department of Employment with 31,375. Some important departments have small staffs, however. The Treasury has 1,985 employees and the Civil Service Department 2,175. See *Whitaker's Almanack*, 1973, p. 608.

[2] Cf. Neustadt's observations on the danger of presidential foreclosed options and his advice that Presidents act as their own directors of intelligence. See *Presidential Power*, ch. 7.

[3] E. P. Hollander, *Leaders, Groups and Influence* (London: OUP, 1964).

expectations are likely to be more effectively advised and assisted.

Whitehall expectations regarding Ministers were reflected in interviews with twenty-five senior civil servants and Ministers' Private Secretaries. Clearly, this is a modest sample; essentially what we have are 'key informants' who provide us with some guidance on Whitehall reactions to different types of Minister but whose responses cannot reasonably be tabulated or regarded as statistically significant. Twenty-one of the respondents were career officials, four were temporary appointees in Mr Wilson's Labour Government. All but one of the career officials had worked in a Minister's Private Office and five were Private Secretaries to Ministers at the time. The sample included seven current or retired Permanent Secretaries, five Deputy- and two Under-Secretaries. The median Civil Service interview lasted just over two hours (rather longer than the median ministerial interview) and it was found to be useful to send a list of questions in advance. The initial question designed to elicit expectations regarding ministerial roles was:

From the point of view of the department what are the main tasks a Minister needs to perform well?

The remaining standard questions dealt with the skills required to perform these tasks, the demands different departments make on Ministers and the strengths and weaknesses politicians were found to have as heads of large complex organisations. Additional questions were concerned, *inter alia*, with the roles of Ministers in policy making. Did officials find that most senior Ministers had clear views on policy, or was it often a matter of selling the Minister whatever policy proposals the department had in the pipeline at the time of his appointment? Did they prefer a Minister with clear policy preferences of his own, or was there a disposition in some sections of the department in favour of the kind of Minister who concentrated mainly on being an adequate representative of the department in Cabinet, in Parliament and in public, but who did not greatly concern himself with the substance, as distinct from the presentation of policy. Finally, it was possible to broach with some respondents the question of the effects of Ministers' political ambitions. Had they known of instances when a desire for short term political kudos had a detrimental effect on policy decisions?

Next, the ability of a Minister to perform a role in accordance with his intention depends on the extent to which the situation, and the department he is assigned to, are favourable to the performance of that role.[1] Suppose, for example that a Minister believes that one of

[1] An interesting attempt to classify situational factors in terms of their favour-

his most important roles is to impose his own or his party's policy objectives on his department and initiate the search for appropriate policy programmes. There is likely to be less scope for such a Minister, at least in spending departments,[2] during a period of economic stringency than when public expenditure is being allowed to rise. It may also be true that fewer policy initiatives are possible for a Minister appointed towards the end of a Government's term of office than for a Minister in a newly elected Government. Departmental and situational variance also affect Ministers who concentrate less on policy formulation and more on generating publicity and ensuring that relevant groups are aware of the programmes and services provided by their department. In Chapter 7 we shall illustrate the point that in some departments and with some programmes it is easy to catch headlines and broadcast one's aims, whereas in other departments little arises to catch the imagination of newspaper editors and their readers.

In the final chapter on factors affecting ministerial role performance we deal with a matter of serious concern only to those Ministers who are determined to influence the substance of policy. On *a priori* grounds it seems reasonable to assume a Minister is more likely to influence policy if, at the time of his appointment, he has well defined objectives which are capable of being translated into administratively workable policy programmes. If he initially lacks personal or partisan objectives in the policy areas he is responsible for, he is likely simply to adopt measures already in the departmental pipeline. We shall find in this chapter that many of the Ministers interviewed, especially those appointed in mid-term, conceded that they had either no conscious policy objectives or only the vaguest of general commitments at the time of taking office. This finding prompts an examination of the non-Civil Service sources of ideas and programmes for future policy available to 'Shadow' Ministers in Opposition and actual ministers in office.

3. WHAT ARE THE CONSEQUENCES FOR GOVERNMENT OF VARIANCE IN MINISTERIAL PERFORMANCE?

In trying to answer the final question raised in this study, which

ableness to different types of leader has been made by the social psychologist F. E. Fiedler. See his *A Theory of Leadership Effectiveness* (New York: McGraw-Hill, 1967).

[2] All departments spend money, of course, but in normal Whitehall usage the phrase 'spending departments' refers to the domestic departments which provide expensive services, notably the Department of Health and Social Security, the Department of Education and Science, and the Ministry of Agriculture, Fisheries and Food.

concerns the consequences of ministerial role performance for British government, we shall change levels of analysis. Instead of considering the problems of individual Ministers in acting in accordance with their role conceptions, we shall be asking what the consequences are if it appears that, as a general rule, Ministers are well qualified to perform certain roles but ill-equipped to perform others. To what extent is it reasonable to attribute the successes and failures of British post-war Governments to the quality of ministerial leadership? An attempt to answer this question is bound to be somewhat speculative since, obviously, the successes and failures of Governments and policies (which are, in any case, hard to evaluate) may be a function of numerous sociological, organisational and situational factors, and of the skills and abilities of other persons besides Ministers. Nevertheless, it will be suggested that explanations in terms of ministerial performance have been neglected and have some significance, particularly in the more 'technical' policy areas in which the traditional British 'intelligent layman' Minister is not obviously the right man to take even formal responsibility. In this context it will be useful to provide international comparisons to show that the skills and experiences that Ministers bring to office differ widely from country to country; presumably, therefore, their performance in office and their effects on government and policy are variable also.

SYNOPSIS

The plan of this study is straightforward. Parts I, II and IV are concerned with the three crucial questions about executive political leadership, and ministerial leadership in particular, that have been posed in this chapter; Part III consists of case studies of ministerial performance in office. Chapter 2 sets the scene by outlining the potential roles of Ministers in relation to their own departments, the Cabinet, Parliament, their party and publics outside Whitehall. A Minister's working week is described and sheer pressure of work is seen as the basic reason why Ministers are forced, consciously or unconsciously, to give higher priority to some roles than others. Chapter 3 then analyses the role conception or priorities of Ministers and classifies them according to the type of leadership they intend to provide.

In Part II one chapter is devoted to each of the factors which we have reason to assume affect a Minister's performance in office: his own skills, the Whitehall advisory structure, the expectations of civil servants, situational factors and the feasibility of his policy objectives. Whenever possible, attention is drawn to problems of special concern to particular types of Minister. Part III illustrates some of these special problems and indicates how individual Ministers with ambitious role conceptions (policy initiators, Executive Ministers and Ambassador Ministers) have overcome them and registered considerable achievements in office. In Part IV cross-national comparisons are introduced to show that the criteria by which British Ministers are selected, the skills they bring to bear, and the roles they perform are characteristic of one political system rather than universal and inevitable. This is preliminary to the final chapter which considers the implications of our findings for individual Cabinet Ministers, for the Prime Minister appointing his ministerial team, for reform of the machinery of government – and, last but not least, for students of political leadership.

Chapter 2

The Demands of the Job

Time is a Cabinet Minister's scarcest resource. The creation of the welfare state, nationalisation of major industries and increased government involvement in the management of the economy have, since 1940, again transformed the Minister's job. All aspects of the job now make heavier demands. Some government departments have become giant organisations, as large as any private corporation, and Ministers are responsible for an enormous range of decisions on subjects which are often highly complex, technical and specialised. There are more cabinet and cabinet committee meetings to attend than before World War II and parliamentary sessions last longer. Consultation between departments, interest groups and professional bodies has also greatly increased and this, too, affects Ministers. This chapter is an attempt to assess the totality of demands on Ministers preparatory to the analysis in Chapter 3 of the roles to which they actually give priority. We begin here with an outline of their working week and a breakdown of the amount of time they might be expected to spend on different activities.

Like anyone else with an increasing workload a Minister has to choose his priorities. His implicit choice may be to attempt the impossible and seek to perform all his tasks equally conscientiously, in which case he is in danger of driving himself to physical or nervous exhaustion, if not an early grave. Alternatively, he may consciously decide to give higher priority to some tasks than to others. Thus, in the performance of a particular task a Cabinet Minister may be actively or only minimally involved, or may delegate the task entirely to a junior Minister or civil servant. The second part of the chapter reviews the potential roles of Ministers in relation to their own departments, the Cabinet, Parliament, their party and interest groups.

THE MINISTER'S WORKING WEEK

'The pattern of the Minister's day is fixed by the Private Office and the gulf with the outside world begins. The Minister is alone: the loneliness of the short distance runner . . . . You control every single ten minutes of the Minister's day and night. I would have to plead with my Private Office to get half-an-hour with my constituency secretary.'[1]

It is possible to get a fair idea of the work pattern of Ministers from their appointments diaries. The Minister's working day usually begins with instructions issued to his Private Secretary arising from papers read the night before. If he has doubts about proposals contained in any of these papers he may well want to question the civil servants concerned. Having given these instructions the Minister will then have a day full of meetings. Like top men in most organisations Ministers spend their day talking rather than reading or writing.[2] There may be a Cabinet or cabinet committee in the morning and later a deputation, a Member of Parliament with a constituency grievance, or a reception for a Minister from abroad. Quite often an influential individual – a union leader, industrialist, or well-known journalist – will ask to see him and it will be impolitic to refuse. Before most of these engagements the Minister will require briefing by his civil servants. His most profitable contact with civil servants, however, occurs at what are called 'office meetings' which are usually arranged at short notice so as not to interfere with other engagements. Some office meetings are held to help the Minister reach decisions on the major policy issues confronting his department. Others are held for less portentous reasons; to guess at supplementaries to Parliamentary Questions, for example.

At lunchtime the Minister may have an official engagement, or may, perhaps, go down to the House of Commons and take a leisurely meal during which he can be approached by Members of Parliament. In any case he will have to attend the House in the evening (most often at 10 p.m.) if a vote is expected and a three line whip is on. Parliamentary commitments are one reason why Ministers are forced into a rather fragmented pattern of work, subject to frequent interruptions. Another reason lies in the frequency with which even senior Ministers are obliged (or feel obliged) to attend receptions, luncheons, and other formal engagements. It is no exaggeration to say that one such engagement every day of the week is not unusual.

All day, whatever the Minister's engagements, papers are piling up in the department ready to go into his 'red boxes' (despatch boxes)

[1] Barbara Castle, 'Mandarin Power', *The Sunday Times* (10 June 1973).
[2] For comparison with work patterns of business managers, see Rosemary Stewart, *Managers and Their Jobs* (London: Macmillan, 1967).

which normally shut about 7 p.m. At that time he will leave his office knowing that he has reading material which may well keep him busy until midnight, or later. It is only in the evening, or in the early hours of the morning, that he can really get down to the paper work,[1] although even then it would be wrong to imagine that he is totally absorbed with major policy matters. There will be letters for signature and 'minutes' (memoranda written by civil servants) to be read for information only. These will simply be initialled and passed on to the next interested party. Also the Minister will have to master briefs prepared by his civil servants; briefs suggesting the line he should take in cabinet or cabinet committees, 'defensive briefs' to enable him to defend the department in Parliament, to deputations and so forth. Most papers, however, are submitted to a Minister for decision, or at least with the intention that he should 'take a view'. Civil servants require to 'know the Minister's mind' so that they can frame proposals in accordance with his objectives. They also seek backing for bargaining positions they want to strike, or have struck, on interdepartmental official committees. Other papers which take up a great deal of time are those concerned with individual cases ('casework'), which may be politically sensitive but are unlikely to be intrinsically all that important. Ministers do not just deal with broad policy questions, they are also, as Jeremy Bray writes, responsible for a great variety of executive acts: 'appointments, approvals of all kinds, planning appeals, research programmes, licences, charters, investment plans, references to public bodies and so on'.[2]

Most minutes written by officials are short, often only a paragraph or two. Matters of greater importance may be dealt with in four or five pages and 'perhaps once a week will come the 40 or 50 page memorandum requiring hours of study and a series of consultations and meetings'.[3] On these occasions, the advice of officials would normally be accompanied by previous minutes, records of committee meetings on the subject and tabulated statistical information. Departments, however, differ in the amount of background informa-tion and conflicting advice they present to a Minister. When Roy Jenkins was appointed to the Home Office he found that all the written advice he received was in the form of minutes written by the Permanent Secretary.[4] Jenkins felt that this procedure ran the

[1] In fact, not all evenings are free for paper work. If parliamentary votes are expected a Minister will often take his despatch boxes to his room at the House of Commons and work there.

[2] J. Bray, *Decision in Government* (London: Gollancz, 1969), p. 57.

[3] *Ibid.*, p. 52.

[4] Roy Jenkins, 'The Reality of Political Power', *The Sunday Times* (17 January 1971).

risk of foreclosing his policy options and, as any minister is at liberty to do, asked for changes to be made.

In addition to reading papers written by members of his own department, Ministers are also expected to prepare themselves for cabinet and cabinet committee meetings, although many in fact concede that pressure of work often forces them to neglect items on the agenda which do not directly affect their own department. A few Ministers keep abreast of party publications and most are avid newspaper readers. Overall, the burden of paper work and, more important, the pressure to reach decisions or 'take a view' is tremendous: 'What is unique about ministerial work is not its length but its momentum; it is highly organised and processed by others. . . . The result is a great easing of minor burdens, accompanied by a constant pressure to deal adequately with the strong flow of demanding work brought forward by others.'[1]

Some days, naturally, the pressure is heavier than on others and here a lot depends on Parliament. If the department happens to be first for Parliamentary Questions (once every four weeks) or if, worse still, the Minister is involved in a set piece debate, then policy considerations have again to take a back seat. On the other hand, if Parliament is in recess, life becomes almost tolerable.

A day away from London – 'visiting' is the expression used – may be even more gruelling. For example, on a recent visit to Glasgow one Cabinet Minister arrived in the city at 6.30 a.m., took a working breakfast and was ready for his first inspection at an engineering works by 9.15. This was the first of five organisations he visited during the day, including the regional office of his own department. He had meals with representatives of two other groups, gave a press conference, paid his respects to the Lord Provost and left Glasgow Central Station on the overnight sleeper, arriving London Euston at 6.55 a.m. His Private Secretary described this as a 'routine regional visit'.

Having obtained a rough idea of the work pattern of Ministers we can now construct a picture of a Minister's week. No Minister is entirely typical in his use of time; indeed Ministers may make a conscious effort to find extra time for what they regard as their most important tasks. It should also be noted that Table 2.1 is only supposed to be a guide to the working week of departmental Ministers who have to make regular 'visits' outside London. Non-departmental Ministers and Ministers who do not need to go on provincial 'visits' (the Prime Minister, the Chancellor, the Foreign Secretary, and the Chief Secretary to the Treasury) have a rather different timetable.[2]

[1] Roy Jenkins, 'In and Out of Power', *The Observer* (20 June 1971).
[2] The Prime Minister spends more time on cabinet matters and even more

The figures in Table 2.1 below are very approximate but give rise to several significant points. First, even if we suppose that

Table 2.1   A Cabinet Minister's Working Week

Activity	Hours
Cabinet	3– 5
Cabinet committees: 3–4 meetings	4– 6
Informal meetings with ministerial colleagues	1– 2
Parliament[a]	10–15
Party meetings	1– 2
Interviews: deputations, the Press, MPs with constituency problems, CBI, TUC etc.	8–10
Formal receptions, luncheons, meetings with Ministers from abroad	6– 8
Visits, inspections[b]	10–12
Constituency responsibilities	2– 3
Office meetings[c]	5–10
Papers[c]	10–20
	60+ [d]

[a] Includes all time spent in the Palace of Westminster except at party meetings. Some Ministers habitually work on their papers in the evening in their room in the House of Commons.

[b] Much 'visiting' is concentrated in the parliamentary recess in the summer. The figure given here includes travelling time.

[c] Reading papers and office meetings are to some extent alternatives. Some Ministers prefer to take advice orally, others optically.

[d] This figure excludes work done at the weekend. Most weekends a Minister would take home papers, or prepare or deliver a speech.

Ministers work sixty plus hours a week (and many work longer) they can still only spend a relatively small percentage of their time on major policy problems confronting their departments. At most about twenty hours a week are available for holding office meetings and reading papers and, as indicated, a good deal of this time would be devoted not so much to substantive policy questions as to reading defensive briefs, discussing tactics for cabinet committees and so

time than an ordinary Minister on public relations and attending formal engagements. The Chancellor, more than most Ministers, has an office job and so does the Chief Secretary except that much of his time is spent on cabinet committees arguing about public expenditure. The Foreign Secretary and other external affairs Ministers spend a good deal of time abroad but their 'visits', of course, often have real policy significance, unlike the visits of other Ministers.

forth. Too often policy decisions have to be fitted in between other engagements or taken late in the evening. It is unfortunate that Ministers can only give sufficient attention to what a majority of them regard as their most important task[1] by dint of putting in the kind of working week which is prohibited for long distance lorry drivers and others whose errors of judgement are recognised to have fatal consequences.

The explanation for this state of affairs is obvious from the Table. It cannot be too strongly emphasised that what might be called the purely parliamentary and public relations aspect of his job absorb a great proportion of a Minister's time. When Parliament is in session ten to fifteen hours a week are likely to be spent in the Palace of Westminster and maybe another six or eight hours would be spent at formal receptions of various kinds and rather more time (perhaps one full day a fortnight) on a routine regional visit. Not surprisingly, many Ministers wish they could spend more time on policy matters and regret the time-consuming nature of their parliamentary and public relations commitments.

The following two-part question was put to Ministers interviewed for this study:

> Obviously you are extremely busy in general, but are there any aspects of your job you particularly wish you could give either more or less time to? (See Table 2.2 below.)

A few Ministers appeared rather unselfconscious about their use of time. Several simply stated that their timetable was organised by their Private Secretary and they more or less carried out the engagements arranged by him, although they expected to be consulted. A few took the opportunity to say that they enjoyed every minute of their job ('It is a marvellous life – I highly recommend it') and that all their duties were important. Nevertheless, among those who chose to mention activities that required more time, there was a fair measure of agreement that major policy issues tend to receive insufficient attention. Often this view was coupled with a statement that forward-thinking is neglected. Several Ministers felt that intrinsically important long-term questions are crowded off their agenda by minor decisions which only need to be referred to a Minister because they are politically sensitive. 'Decision making is the greatest enemy of thought' was how one Minister expressed it. Home Secretaries, Secretaries of State for Scotland and Social Service Ministers particularly, have to spend much of their time handling political 'hot potatoes' (see Chapter 7). This problem is,

[1] See Chapter 3.

of course, a direct result of Ministers' accountability to Parliament. The institution of Question Time especially, provides an opportunity for Members of Parliament to make political capital out of any errors apparently committed by government departments. At times Ministers must envy business leaders and leaders in other organisations who do not have to worry too much about getting minor decisions right, provided their overall strategy holds good.

Table 2.2 *Problems in the Organisation of Ministerial Time: Ministers' Own Views*

Activities requiring more time	No. of Ministers (N = 43)[a]
Deciding major policy issues	15
Cabinet and cabinet committees	5
Parliament, contact with backbench MPs	3
Administrative decisions, casework	2
Constituency responsibilities	2
Relaxation and recuperation	2
	29 (N = 25)[b]

Activities which absorb too much time	
Parliament, MPs with constituency cases	13
Public relations activities, especially formal occasions	13
Minor decisions, especially political 'hot potatoes'	10
Deputations, pressure group representatives	9
Cabinet committees	5
Constituency responsibilities	2
Other	3
Not short of time, no problem	2
	57 (N = 44)[c]

[a] Seven of the Ministers interviewed were not asked this question due to lack of time.
[b] i.e. twenty-five Ministers cited activities requiring more time of whom four cited more than one activity, giving a total of 29.
[c] See note b.

Far more Ministers (forty-four as against twenty-five), had strong views on activities which took up too much time than were explicit about how they would use the extra hours if their timetable were reorganised. Parliament and MPs with constituency cases were most often mentioned as time wasters. There was some irritation among senior Ministers that MPs often insist on seeing them rather than junior Ministers. Predictably, also, visits and inspections were thought to be too time consuming. Several Ministers mentioned their efforts to reach an understanding with various associations that they could not attend annual luncheons every year, or said that they instructed their Private Secretaries to so arrange visits that they would meet people informally and learn things at first hand, rather than sit through a formal meal, make a speech and confer only with dignitaries. Several Ministers thought that time spent seeing deputations, particularly large deputations, was unfruitful. On this point, a former Conservative Minister mentioned good-humouredly that he always allowed an hour and a half for Welsh deputations. In general, it was felt many group representatives only appeared at the Ministry in order to reassure their members that everything possible was being done to safeguard their interests. Finally, it is worth noting that there was a division of opinion on the importance of Cabinet and more particularly cabinet committee meetings. Five Ministers regretted that they could not read their cabinet papers thoroughly but they were counterbalanced by five who thought that a lot of time was wasted on cabinet committees in discussion of matters which should have been resolved by the departmental Minister primarily concerned.

MINISTER'S POTENTIAL ROLES

Ministers have important tasks to perform in their own departments, in Cabinet, in Parliament, in their party and in relations with pressure groups and other sections of the public. In the performance of these tasks they may be relatively active and dominant, or relatively passive and uninvolved. Ideally, they might wish to be actively involved in all their main areas of activity. However, time constraints do not permit this and it is important to be specific about the potential range of variation in role performance.

Ministers and their departments: policy leadership and management roles

Up until the mid-nineteenth century it was possible for an exceptionally able and industrious Minister to be literally responsible for all decisions of any significance taken by his department.[1] At that time departments were not the large complex organisations they are

[1] See H. Parris, *Constitutional Bureaucracy* (London: Allen and Unwin, 1969), pp. 106ff.

today. In 1850 there were 39,147 civil servants working under the supervision of 14 Cabinet Ministers, or 2,796 per Minister.[1] By 1914 the ratio of Cabinet Ministers to non-industrial civil servants was 1 to 18,666 and 1 January 1971, there were 500,000 non-industrial civil servants to 17 Cabinet Ministers; a ratio of 1 to 29,271.[2] Even if we include non-Cabinet Ministers of whom there were 48 at the beginning of 1971, the ratio is still 1 to 7,692. It would be foolish to suggest that size of staff reflects the number of intrinsically important or politically sensitive decisions to be taken by departments; on this basis the Inland Revenue with a staff of nearly 70,000 would appear thirty-five times more 'important' than the Treasury with a staff of just under 2,000. However, the overall figures do suggest a number of important points.

First there can be little doubt that civil servants now take decisions which in the past would have been submitted to Ministers. As one of the senior civil servants interviewed remarked: 'When I first entered the Service in the thirties, one often used to hear officials say that they would have to refer back to their political masters. One hears that said far less these days.' Clearly, contemporary civil servants sometimes face difficult judgements in deciding what issues to refer to Ministers; and this discretion extends all the way down the hierarchy. Henry Parris was only romanticising slightly when he visualised a Minister's Private Secretary who, when he inserted 'his paper knife in each letter of the morning's mail could not know whether the envelope contained a routine request for a printed form which he could deal with himself in thirty seconds or the political scandal of the century'.[3] Senior officials, naturally, have much wider discretion. It is they, and particularly Permanent Secretaries, who finally decide which policy options to refer to Ministers. If they refer too little, Ministers may complain that feasible policy options were not brought to their attention, or even that major issues are being decided by bureaucrats instead of elected politicians. If they refer too much, Ministers may equally complain that they are prevented from giving due attention to the great issues of the day. It would be a mistake to suggest that merely because many decisions have passed out of the hands of Ministers, they automatically have less power. As H. E. Dale wrote on this subject, no one would suggest that the captain of the *Queen Mary* has less

[1] Figures on the size of the nineteenth-century Civil Service are given in K. B. Smellie, *A Hundred Years of English Government* (London: Duckworth, 1960), Appendix IV.

[2] For figures on the growth of the Civil Service in the twentieth century see David Butler and Jennie Freeman, *British Political Facts* 1900-1968 (London: Macmillan, 1969), pp. 173-74.

[3] Parris, *Constitutional Bureaucracy*, p. 112.

power than the captain of a rowing boat, so why should they suggest that a Minister in a big department has less power than a Minister in a small department.[1] Clearly, though, the size of departments and the press of business make it important to ask what criteria civil servants use in deciding whether to refer issues to Ministers.

In any department at any given time there are conventions and established practices which help officials decide what issues to refer to ministerial level and which mean that they do not, in every case, have to go back to first principles. These established practices are learned from one's colleagues and from going through one's predecessor's files. However, if an official were pressed to articulate the criteria, or questions he asks himself, in deciding whether to submit to Ministers, he might mention four:

1. Does the issue require primarily a normative judgement? Or have politicians already made their values, objectives and priorities clear so that only decisions about programmes, organisations, staffing etc., remain?

2. Is it obvious what the Minister would decide in view of his (and his party predecessors') past decisions – or would an official have to excercise an unduly wide margin of discretion in order to resolve the issue himself?

3. How intrinsically important is the issue? i.e. what quantity of resources would be committed by a decision, how many people would be affected, how serious would the consequences be if things went wrong, how great is the probability of error etc?

4. How politically sensitive is the issue, i.e. how likely is it that parliamentary controversy (debates, questions) will be aroused?

The last three criteria appear perfectly reasonable although, naturally, mistakes or deviations from the norm occur when civil servants apply them.[2] The result of such mistakes is unfavourable publicity when Parliament gets its teeth into a Minister who is revealed not to have known what his officials were doing. The

[1] H. E. Dale, *The Higher Civil Service in Great Britain* (London: OUP, 1941).
[2] Clearly there is no easy 'slide-rule' measure to be used in applying the first two criteria. For a discussion of criteria 3 and 4 in relation to inter-departmental differences see Chapter 7. Even if all four criteria could be easily operationalised there would still, of course, be problems of weighting them in deciding to refer specific cases to Ministers. As noted in the text, however, precedent is the usual guide. In practice an official will ask himself, 'Are issues relating to this subject usually referred to Ministers?'

rationale for the first criterion may be called in question, however. The traditional Whitehall view has always been that the role of elected politicians is to make normative, or 'ought' judgements and hence determine policy objectives which can then be used to guide the administrative process.[1] The corollary of this view is that if an issue is purely technical, if it is just a question of the policy programmes, organisation and staffing required to implement objectives, then civil servants probably should decide it. This divorce between 'policy', which is the politician's concern, and 'administration' which may be left to civil servants is repeatedly criticised in the academic literature and is much modified in practice both by the application of the other three criteria and by specific rules (e.g. ministerial approval is required for appointments at Assistant Secretary level and above). In general, it may be objected that it makes little sense for a Minister to pronounce on objectives and priorities if the programmes, organisation, and resources to achieve them are not available. Objectives have to be adjusted to suit the means available, as well as vice versa, and the risk is that if Ministers think of themselves solely as value setters they are likely to hinder rather than facilitate this adjustment. It should be added that in specific cases it can be difficult to judge whether an issue has a normative component, or whether it is purely technical. A former Ministry of Power official, wanting to illustrate the point that civil servants often take important technical decisions without reference to Ministers, cited the case of his having taken the final decision in the early 1960s to introduce larger electricity generating plants throughout Britain.[2] Subsequently, due to plant breakdowns, the Minister queried whether it was right for him not to have referred the matter. The official replied that he considered it a purely technical decision to be made on efficiency (cost per unit of output) grounds. In retrospect, though, he commented that he was perhaps mistaken in that the matter could have been politically sensitive (in the event MPs did not create a major fuss). He also added that nowadays a ministerial decision would definitely have been necessary due to the existence of an environmentalists' lobby (i.e. a normative judgement – efficient fuel production versus amenity – would have been required).

At the margin a Minister can alter the criteria or procedures for reporting issues to him. Despite the example just given, the temptation for Ministers is to concentrate on politically sensitive issues at

[1] For a lucid exposition of this Whitehall view and critique of it see Maurice Kogan, 'Modern Government Administration' (mimeo, paper given at Political Studies Association Conference, 1970).

[2] Interview with the author.

the expense of intrinsically important issues, especially if the latter involve highly technical, specialised considerations.[1] There are two reasons for this. First, Ministers hate to be caught out in Parliament, and Parliament normally seizes on issues with a high normative and human interest element – immigration, arms to South Africa, free contraception. A second reason is that Ministers' own backgrounds as career politicians who typically are laymen in the subjects covered by their departments, make them ill-equipped to take decisions which, although they may involve value judgements either explicitly or implicitly, also require, ideally, a sophisticated appreciation of technical matters.

Several of the Ministers interviewed were acutely aware of their deficiencies, and the consequent limitations on their control over policy, in relation to the increasing range of specialised subjects which governments deal with. As a former Labour Minister said, 'your political antennae are not much use to you when it comes to deciding whether to put Rolls-Royce engines in Hawker Siddeley aircraft'. In the same vein, another Minister who at one stage of his career was responsible for atomic energy policy confessed that 'in eighteen months I never understood a word on the subject'. Economic policy is another area in which Ministers who lack relevant specialised knowledge often find it difficult to evaluate advice. Everyone, including Ministers, claims to know what has been wrong with the management of the economy in the past. But it is only necessary to raise a contemporary problem to appreciate the difficulties a layman faces. To take one example, some academic economists advocate floating currency exchange rates while others argue for the system of fixed rates subject to change only by means of what are perceived as humiliating devaluations. A third group of economists believe that compromise arrangements under which frequent small changes in exchange rates ('the crawling peg' is one such system) could be made would work best.[2] The arguments are so technical and, in the absence of empirical data about any but the fixed-rate system, so abstract, that a Chancellor of the Exchequer who was not an economist would be bound to have difficulty in forming a view of his own, or in suggesting a compromise between competing sets of proposals. At least one student of policy making, Sir Geoffrey Vickers, has answered the question of whether policy makers must be either experts or rubber stamps with a bald 'yes'.[3]

---

[1] For examples given by officials of Ministers doing this see Chapter 6.

[2] For a review of the arguments see S. Brittan, *The Price of Economic Freedom* (London: Macmillan, 1970).

[3] Sir Geoffrey Vickers 'Planning and Public Policy', *Political Quarterly*, 38: 3 (July–Sept. 1967), pp. 253-65.

As well as deciding what types of issues he wants referred to him and how to handle technical or specialised issues, a Minister also has to decide at what stages of the policy-making process to intervene.[1] (Again, though, one possibility is just to accept the current practice of the department). It is necessary to specify Ministers' potential roles in policy making as closely as possible. The minimum, least dominant role for a Minister is that of *policy legitimator*. A ministerial policy legitimator permits civil servants to monopolise crucial stages of the policy-making process. He permits them to identify and define policy problems, stipulate objectives, priorities and criteria for decision, formulate alternative proposals and, in the end, arrive at a set of recommendations which he simply endorses or 'legitimates'. His 'decision' involves no more than taking political responsibility for the recommendations and committing himself to try to mobilise support for them within the government, in Parliament and, perhaps, among outside publics. In practical terms all a ministerial policy legitimator does is initial the top document in a file containing the advice of the most senior civil servant concerned. Of course in relation to minor matters all Ministers regularly act as mere policy legitimators. As R. G. S. Brown writes, 'most Ministers will initial most documents most of the time'.[2]

On issues which are highly normative, intrinsically important, or politically sensitive most Ministers at least go through the motions of being *policy selectors*. A policy selector considers alternative recommendations and makes up his own mind. Again the procedure is straightforward. A Minister who wishes to unravel the arguments that have been put forward in his department may ask to see the files and read through them. Alternatively he may hold an office meeting and encourage civil servants to air their views. He may also personally consult with outside experts, group representatives and party colleagues outside the department. The distinction between a policy selector and a policy legitimator is sometimes rather a fine one. If a Minister really prefers that his department arrive at a 'united

[1] There are of course, many alternative conceptualisations of the 'stages' of the policy-making process. Probably the best known is presented in Harold D. Lasswell, *Seven Categories of Functional Analysis* (Maryland University Bureau of Government Research, 1956). The stages of the policy process referred to in this and subsequent paragraphs are: identifying and defining a policy problem, stipulating policy objectives and priorities and initiating the search for alternative programmes designed to achieve objectives, plotting the consequences of these alternatives with the aid of an explicit or implicit model, selecting the programme best designed to achieve objectives (with or without an explicit decision criterion), mobilising support for the programme both within government and among outside publics, implementing the programme and defending it in Parliament.

[2] R. G. S. Brown, *The Administrative Process in Britain* (London: Methuen, 1970), p. 96.

view', or if he generally finishes by accepting the advice of the most senior official involved, then, *de facto*, he is acting as a policy legitimator. On the other hand, if he prefers to be apprised of a wide range of policy options and probes for weaknesses in the advice proffered by senior civil servants, he is genuinely acting as a policy selector.

Last, a Minister may be a *policy initiator*. Rather than accept his department's existing policy objectives and priorities, a policy initiator seeks to impose his own or his party's objectives. This is not easy. It is no use the Minister's relying on imprecise statements of objectives. If a Secretary of State for the Social Services does little more than say to his officials, 'we must have greater selectivity in the social services', or a Chancellor of the Exchequer says, 'higher priority should be given to economic growth as against protecting the balance of payments', or a Secretary for Employment tells civil servants that 'we must hold down the level of wage settlements', the effect on policy is unlikely to be very great. Imprecise objectives are less likely to be clearly communicated and understood by members of the department than objectives stated in measurable terms and less likely, in any event, to serve as guides to decision in specific cases. Government departments, after all, are long established organisations with long established objectives. Thus, to pursue the above examples further, officials in the Department of Health and Social Security, if left to themselves, would probably prefer to adhere to Civil Service norms of non-discrimination and even-handedness[1] rather than introduce greater selectivity in the social services. Similarly, Treasury civil servants have been accustomed to giving top priority to protecting the balance of payments and the Department of Employment, in its years as the Ministry of Labour, saw its role as one of preserving industrial peace by conciliation, rather than enforcing an incomes policy.

The first steps a policy initiator must take, if he is to make any impact, is to define his objectives in fairly precise terms. What criteria are to guide civil servants in formulating proposals for greater selectivity in the social services? What level of increases will be permissible under the incomes policy and what exceptions could be made? How big a balance of payments deficit is the Chancellor willing to risk in pursuit of economic growth and would he be willing to devalue the pound if the deficit persisted? It is unusual for even those Ministers who see themselves as policy initiators to come to office with adequately defined objectives, and a full scale policy review, usually leading to a White Paper, may be necessary.

[1] See A. Shonfield, *Modern Capitalism* (London: OUP, 1965), ch. 6.

As well as defining his objectives, a policy initiator will need to decide how his objectives are to be pursued. This involves not only reviewing policy options but also taking tactical decisions. Will legislation be required, or would a circular or statement of intent be less politically controversial and hence, perhaps, more effective? Will new administrative machinery be needed at either central or local level? If so, who should run it – career civil servants, outside experts or local representatives? As implied above, a policy initiator also needs to take great care over the enforcement of his policies. Continuous supervision rather than occasional one-off ministerial interventions may be called for. Unless the Minister consistently makes his priorities clear, civil servants, like members of other organisations, will tend to react to new problems in terms of old objectives. Thus, the Treasury will reach for the economic brakes at the first sign of a threat to the balance of payments, the Department of Employment will be anxious to set its conciliation machinery in motion if a major strike seems imminent, the *laissez-faire* Board of Trade will press for the removal of trade restrictions and the Department of the Environment will give in to local authority pressure.

Within his department a Minister may thus act as a policy legitimator, a policy selector or a policy inititator. In addition to performing these policy leadership roles some Ministers also seek to perform departmental management roles. As we have noted, management (or administration) is not always easily distinguishable from policy and some statements of the functions of managers include policy making. Thus Rosemary Stewart, in her widely used textbook *The Reality of Management*, states that managers engage in 'planning', 'organising', 'motivating' and 'controlling'.[1] By planning she means policy formulation: the manager, she writes, must 'set objectives, forecast, analyse problems and make decisions'. In Whitehall, on the other hand, it is usual to distinguish between policy formulation and management functions and we shall follow the Whitehall usage. A Minister who concerns himself with management, then, deals with questions of *departmental organisation*: appointments and promotions, the assignment of responsibility for different tasks, the introduction of new management techniques and so forth. Alternatively, or in addition, he may seek to *maintain departmental morale*, to 'motivate' civil servants, to exercise affective leadership. A third potential management role that Ministers may undertake is that of *controlling* departmental performance by setting standards and checking the extent to which objectives are being achieved.

[1] Rosemary Stewart, *The Reality of Management* (London: Pan Books, 1967), pp. 71-3.

Cabinet and cabinet committee roles

The growth of departmental business has been paralleled by a growth in cabinet business. The mid-nineteenth-century Cabinet discussed questions of policy and administration once a week over dinner.[1] No minutes were kept, cabinet committees were set up only occasionally and for special purposes, and some members enjoyed their usual postprandial snooze. These days, although according to the former Labour Foreign Secretary, Patrick Gordon Walker, Ministers sometimes still nod off, the conduct of the Cabinet 'is on the whole more businesslike'.[2] It meets on average twice a week, since the First World War minutes have been kept, the agenda and papers are supposed to be circulated forty-eight hours in advance and, most significant of all, an elaborate network of cabinet committees has been created.

Little is known about cabinet committees but a few introductory points may be made here. The first standing cabinet committee – the Committee of Imperial Defence – was set up in 1903 and there are now ten to fifteen such committees.[3] In addition there are numerous *ad hoc* committees which frame proposals to deal with a particular problem and then are abolished.[4] The important standing committees – including the Steering Committee on Economic Policy, the Public Expenditure Survey Committee, the Overseas Policy and Defence Committee, the Social Services, Home Affairs and Future Legislation Committees – are chaired either by the Prime Minister, or a senior Cabinet Minister and consist entirely of Cabinet Ministers. Other committees, however, although registered with the Cabinet Office and classified as cabinet committees, consist entirely of junior Ministers.

There can be little doubt that an increasing number of decisions which would formerly have been taken by the full Cabinet are now taken by cabinet committees. Matters of the highest importance, or matters which are likely to arouse acute political controversy automatically go to Cabinet, but all other questions are liable to be settled in committees. In 1967 Mr Harold Wilson decreed that only if committee chairmen agreed could inter-departmental disputes be taken to the full Cabinet.[5] The significance of this move is open to

[1] J. P. Mackintosh, *The British Cabinet* (London: Stevens, 1968), ch. 5. The weekly meeting to discuss parliamentary business, as distinct from policy, was held at Number 10 Downing Street.

[2] P. Gordon Walker, *The Cabinet* (London: Jonathan Cape, 1970), p. 108.

[3] ibid., pp. 176-7.

[4] Lists of cabinet committees are not published and it is not possible even to estimate how many there are.

[5] Gordon Walker, *The Cabinet*, pp. 45-6.

doubt. John P. Mackintosh, Richard Crossman and other observers see any accession of power to the committees as an accession of power to the Prime Minister in that he appoints their chairmen and members.[1] Patrick Gordon Walker, on the other hand, believes that the Cabinet's influence over major policy questions is increased by its being relieved of having to consider some of the more petty inter-departmental disputes.[2]

The question of the balance of influence between cabinet committees and committees staffed by officials is also of great significance. Since the 1930s a system by which all ministerial committees are serviced by parallel official committees has emerged. In so far as the latter simply clear the ground for Ministers they serve a useful function. There is a possibility, however, that agreements reached by officials may foreclose the options of Ministers. If officials seem agreed a Minister needs considerable self-confidence to press for reconsideration. Dr Jeremy Bray believes that 'an established Whitehall view' is sometimes worked out and that the problem of foreclosed options needs to be taken seriously by Ministers.[3] In general, however, a security blackout prevents scholarly investigation and the question of the relative influence of ministerial and official committees is one of the great unknowns as far as students of government are concerned. Even more mysterious is the meeting of Permanent Secretaries held weekly under the chairmanship of the head of the Civil Service. This is sometimes said to be 'for information only', but the merits of policy questions are also discussed and one wonders whether, in moments of crisis, Permanent Secretaries may not reach an understanding on how Ministers should be advised. The debate over whether to devalue the pound in July 1966 was mentioned to the author as an occasion on which such an understanding was reached.

These broader questions are only background to the main concern of this chapter, however. From the point of view of the individual Minister the Cabinet is a forum in which he fights for his department's policy proposals, for Treasury money and for Parliamentary time. Since many proposals affect the interests of more than one department, a sponsoring Minister is always likely to have to

---

[1] Mackintosh, *The British Cabinet*, ch. 13; Richard Crossman, Introduction to Walter Bagehot, *The English Constitution* (London: Fontana edn 1963). See also Colin Seymour, 'The Disintegration of the Cabinet' *Parliamentary Affairs*, XXIV: 3 (1971).

[2] Gordon Walker, *The Cabinet*, p. 48.

[3] Bray, *Decision in Government*, p. 55. Most civil servants would deny that the risk of foreclosed options is a real one. They would say that the norm of loyalty to their Minister and the duty of trying to implement his policy objectives overrides any other consideration. See Chapter 6.

defend his proposals against damaging amendments proposed by cabinet colleagues. Conflict between some departments are almost endemic. The *laissez-faire* Board of Trade (now part of the Department of Trade and Industry) and the protectionist Ministry of Agriculture rarely see eye to eye and conflicts between the main spending departments and the Treasury occur every year when the estimates are brought to the Public Expenditure Survey Committee and the Cabinet.[1] Parliamentary time is also a commodity much in demand. Every year departments want far more legislation than Parliament can possibly enact. As many as 300 bills may be proposed in January when the Cabinet Office asks for legislation for the next parliamentary session. Excluding Consolidated Fund Bills a maximum of about 55 measures can be enacted.[2] The Future Legislation Committee decides which shall go forward (although aggrieved Ministers can appeal to Cabinet) and the competition is intense.

The role of *departmental battle-axe*, fighting for policy proposals, for funds and parliamentary time is a Minister's main cabinet role. A second potential role is that of *cabinet all-rounder*. The concept of collective ministerial responsibility implies that Ministers shall seek to influence decisions on a broader range of matters than those directly affecting their own departments. However, it is almost impossible for Ministers to read all their cabinet papers or even 'skim them in the car on the way to No. 10'. In practice, therefore, the number of Ministers who regularly go beyond their departmental brief tends to be limited (see Chapter 3). Very senior Ministers (the Chancellor, the Foreign Secretary and the Home Secretary) might be expected to speak frequently and ambitious younger Ministers may be anxious to show that they have growth potential and deserve promotion. It is only on quite rare occasions that a Prime Minister obliges even the most departmentally orientated Minister to raise his eyes to broader horizons by going round the cabinet table asking for views.[3]

A Minister's effectiveness in Cabinet, his capacity to win battles, depends on both his personal standing and conduct in Cabinet and his tactics. A Minister who has 'political weight', that is high standing in the parliamentary party or in the country, and whose resignation would be a serious blow to the Government is clearly in a stronger position than a Minister whose disappearance would

[1] The reason for appointing a Chief Secretary to the Treasury and giving him cabinet rank was to prevent disputes over the estimates reaching the full Cabinet. It is doubtful whether this aim has been achieved. See S. Brittan, *Steering the Economy* (London: Secker and Warburg, 1969), ch. 4, 'The Control of the Public Purse'.

[2] This figure refers only to public and general acts.

[3] Gordon Walker, *The Cabinet*, p. 28.

scarcely cause a ripple. However, a Minister who constantly threatens resignation loses credibility and much also depends on the reputation a man has established in the Cabinet itself. If his colleagues believe that a Minister's judgement has proved right in the past they are more likely to accept new proposals he brings forward, or to take seriously his opposition to their own proposals. At the other extreme are Ministers who talk a great deal in Cabinet but whose judgement is suspect. Lord Attlee, the former Labour Prime Minister, enjoyed sacking such Ministers.[1]

Cabinet tactics can win or lose a few tricks. Clearly, Ministers have some discretion over what issues to take to Cabinet and when to take them. Some Ministers try to cover themselves with the cloak of collective responsibility by taking even minor issues to Cabinet and by testing out reactions at an early stage of policy formulation. Other Ministers prefer to present the Cabinet, if not with a *fait accompli*, at least with proposals already worked out in considerable detail and perhaps supported by an array of pressure groups who will be distressed if they fall through at the last minute. Ministers also vary in the skill and enthusiasm with which they lobby the Prime Minister and cabinet colleagues and use leaks to the press in their efforts to win cabinet battles.[2]

Parliamentary and party roles

As was indicated earlier in the chapter, Parliament makes enormous demands on a Minister's time.[3] It is not just that many hours a week are actually spent in the Palace of Westminster. Preparation and briefing for Parliamentary appearances also absorb precious time. Speeches prepared by the Minister's Private Office have to be mastered and the Minister and his officials are obliged to hold meetings at which the guessing game of spotting supplementaries to Parliamentary Questions is played. Also, in any given week, several MPs are likely to want to interview the Minister about problems raised by their constituents, or about subjects of special interest to them which are covered by the Minister's department.

It was largely increasing parliamentary commitments that in the nineteenth century first led Ministers to devote less attention to administration and the running of their departments.[4] Certainly, the pressure of parliamentary business has continued to increase. At

[1] Mackintosh, *The British Cabinet*, p. 432.

[2] On press leaks see Gordon Walker, *The Cabinet*, pp. 30-5.

[3] Administrative class civil servants are also obliged to spend over 20 per cent of their time on parliamentary matters. See *The Civil Service* (Fulton Report), V, 119.

[4] Parris, *Constitutional Bureaucracy*, ch. 4.

the beginning of this century parliamentary sessions still lasted from only February to July or August, with occasional summer sittings. Nowadays Parliament meets from October to July with the summer providing the only long recess. The amount of legislation passed has continued to increase and Ministers are liable to be asked over 20,000 Parliamentary Questions a year. (The long session from 18 April 1966 to 27 October 1967 set a record of 33,965 Parliamentary Questions.[1])

The pressure of Parliament, however, varies as between departments. The Scottish Office, the Department of Health and Social Security and the Department of the Environment receive the most Parliamentary Questions.[2] The Chancellor of the Exchequer, the Foreign Secretary and the Home Secretary, however, speak most often in debates. The Chancellor every year has to pilot his budgetary measures through Parliament and lead for the Government in economic debates, and Foreign Secretaries are liable to be called on for emergency debates of international crises. Home Secretaries, on the other hand, are particularly subject to sudden parliamentary storms. Gaol-breaks, allegations of cruelty in prisons, books alleging wrongful conviction for murder, make life difficult for the Home Secretary, or alternatively, give him an opportunity to shine. Again, some Ministers have more legislation to pilot through the House than others. Some departments like the Foreign Office and the Ministry of Defence rarely legislate. Others, including the Department of the Environment, the Home Office, the Scottish Office and the Board of Trade legislate in every Parliamentary session. Ministers in these latter departments require stamina and mastery of detail, particularly in steering bills through standing committee. (Increasingly, though, junior Ministers take the committee stage.)

As a Parliamentarian the minimum role a Minister is expected to perform is that of *political trouble shooter*. He needs to be able to spot the kinds of issues that may cause a parliamentary storm and to be capable of defending and explaining the actions of his department to the House. The worst kind of trouble a Minister can run into is trouble with his own party. Provided the majority party holds together the Opposition can always be defeated. However, if backbench members of the government party disagree with a Minister's actions (or proposed actions) it may be necessary to back down rather than risk defeat in the lobbies. It is a Minister's task, therefore, to defend his department sufficiently convincingly to win at least the acquiescence of backbenchers.

A more activist, less defensive parliamentary and party role than

[1] Butler and Freeman, *British Political Facts*, p. 125.
[2] See Chapter 7.

that of political trouble shooter consists of *piloting measures through Parliament and the party so as to maximise support*. Backbenchers are not necessarily aware of a Minister's reputation and ability as a 'doer' in his department; their main chance to observe him is as a speaker in the House of Commons and there is general agreement that upsurges and falls in morale depend quite largely on ministerial performances at the despatch box. Ministers who by common consent are parliamentary wizards and have the knack of persuading backbenchers that even their most mundane proposals represent the incarnation of higher party philosophy are a great asset to the Government.

Ministers, of course, do not encounter their supporters and seek to defuse opposition exclusively from the despatch box. They meet backbenchers informally in the smoking room and tea-room of the House and more formally at party meetings. Labour holds meetings of the parliamentary party twice a week, with one meeting being to discuss the following week's parliamentary business. Ministers are expected to attend reasonably frequently. Conservative Ministers, on the other hand, appear at meetings of the 1922 Committee (the Conservative backbench gathering) by invitation only. In both parties, however, there are backbench subject groups which meet Ministers regularly. In some cases the subjects covered by a group correspond to those covered by a department, in other cases they are more narrow. One has the impression that Labour groups are more active and make greater demands on Ministers than Conservative groups, but this is hard to substantiate.[1]

In short, Ministers are at the interface between government departments and political parties. It is their role to interpret their party to their department and their department to their party.

Public relations and brokerage roles

Ministers are also obliged and may even enjoy spending a good deal of time on what may be termed, non-pejoratively, their public relations roles. There is a long tradition in Britain that, before publishing policy proposals, government departments should consult fully with interested parties. The involvement of the Government in more areas of national life has naturally meant more consultation. Most departments now have an interest group clientele and advisory committees which expect to be consulted as a matter

---

[1] P. G. Richards, *Honourable Members* (London: Faber and Faber, 1959), pp. 94ff; Ronald Butt, *The Power of Parliament* (London: Constable, 1967), ch. 9; Hugh Dalton, *High Tide and After* (London: Frederick Muller, 1962), pp. 22-3.

of course on all matters which might remotely concern them. Some departments deal primarily with a few interest groups, others have a wider clientele. Thus, major groups attached to the Department of Health, the Ministry of Agriculture and the Department of Education and Science are, respectively, the British Medical Association, the National Farmers' Union and the National Union of Teachers and the Association of Education Committees. The Department of Employment works closely with both the TUC and the CBI. A department like the Home Office, on the other hand, deals with groups ranging from the Police Federation to members of the so-called 'race relations industry', the Department of Trade and Industry deals with a vast array of trade associations and the Department of the Environment deals with everybody from the Association of Municipal Corporations and the Royal Institute of Chartered Surveyors to tenants' associations and conservationists. The Scottish and Welsh Offices, naturally, are subject to influence from all Scottish and Welsh pressure groups.

Most of this consultation is carried out by civil servants, but a deputation or the leader of an interest group may ask to see the Minister and, unless the group were very inconsequential or eccentric, it would be unusual to refuse. In engaging in the normal round of *consulting groups and seeing deputations*, a Minister is performing his minimum public relations or brokerage role, a role he could scarcely avoid. Some Ministers, however, make special efforts to attract attention and 'sell' their values ('law and order', 'private enterprise'), policies, departments and selves to relevant publics. They give more than the usual number of interviews to journalists, they cultivate relations with important individuals (prominent businessmen and trade union officials, for example) and use the platforms provided by annual dinners or ceremonies to open exhibitions and factories, and routine regional visits to make speeches designed to attract maximum publicity. Publicity may promote a number of purposes. It may help a Minister to build up support and give encouragement to pressure groups who are backing policy proposals that he would like soon to introduce, provided he could get the necessary cabinet approval. A Minister of Transport for this reason may speak publicly about possible road safety measures. Similarly, a Minister of Housing may fly a kite in public for changes in legislation governing rents and the rights of tenants, or a Home Secretary may speak of liberalising the system of paroling prisoners. A second possible reason for a Minister seeking to attract publicity would be to make the public aware of the policies or services offered by his department, or to give help to his department's clients. Thus Ministers of Posts and Telecommunications usually try to gain publicity for a new service to be offered by the Post Office and Ministers responsible for civil aviation normally try to boost the sales of new commercial aircraft by singing their praises. A third reason for ministerial public appearances is to show concern and sympathy and offer symbolic reassurance to sections of the public in need of it. This is what a Minister is doing when he inspects a flooded area, the scene of a mining disaster, or, currently, a Northern Ireland city torn by riots. Last, a Minister may seek publicity to give his own career a lift.

CONCLUSION

Table 2.3 summarises the potential roles of Ministers. The minimum roles Ministers may perform are listed first in each category, with more activist or dominant roles listed later. The multiplicity of roles listed in Table 2.3 suggests a basic dilemma for Ministers. On the

Table 2.3   *The Potential Roles of Cabinet Ministers*

Classification of roles	*The Minister's roles*
I. Roles as head of department	Policy leadership roles: 1. policy legitimation 2. policy selection 3. policy initiation Management roles: 1. departmental organisation ('organising') 2. departmental morale ('motivating'; affective leadership) 3. 'controlling'; checking departmental performance
II. Roles as a member of the Cabinet	1. departmental battle-axe; fight for parliamentary time, Treasury money, etc. 2. Cabinet all-rounder
III. Roles as parliamentary and party leader	1. political trouble shooter 2. piloting measures through Parliament and the party so as to maximise support
IV. Public relations and brokerage roles	1. consult with department's interest group clientele 2. sell values, policies, department, self to relevant publics

one hand, their reputation in Whitehall and Westminster is bound to depend on appearing to perform a range of roles satisfactorily. A Minister's future career, never mind his future influence, is damaged if he gets a reputation as a loser in the tight little world of London SW1, where everyone knows everyone else's standing and where politicians are dismissed in cryptic single sentences: 'he is a light-weight'; 'he kicks the ball through his own goal every time he goes to Cabinet'. On the other hand, pressure of time, the totality of demands made on Ministers, make it well nigh impossible for them to be consistently active in the performance of all potential roles. Some kind of choice has to be made. A Minister has to decide his priorities, decide in which roles he will be really active and in which he will seek to achieve only a passing level in the eyes of the political world. In the next chapter the priorities, or role conceptions of the fifty Ministers interviewed for this study are analysed.

Chapter 3

A Typology of Cabinet Ministers

The purpose of this chapter is to present a typology of Cabinet Ministers based on their own conceptions of their job. The significance of Ministers' *role conceptions* can hardly be exaggerated. A Minister whose top priority is to initiate policy changes is likely to approach his job in a different way and face different problems from a Minister who is primarily concerned with, say, his management, or public relations roles. Of course, knowing an individual Minister's role conception will not necessarily tell us which roles he in practice devotes most attention to, let alone enable us to predict what he will achieve in office. It is essential, however, to the later analysis to make it clear that different Ministers have different priorities. An analysis of behaviour without reference to priorities would be meaningless.

For present purposes we treat the role conceptions of Ministers as mental guidelines they bring to office and, in general, intend to follow. This is not to imply, however, that role conceptions consist simply of personal predilections, or ego ideals, uninfluenced by exposure to the practical constraints of office or the expectations of other actors. On the contrary one would expect that some of the variance in ministerial role conceptions could be explained in terms of having held office in certain government departments rather than others, at particular periods of time and in harness with senior officials who, without lecturing on the subject, might influence a politician's view of his job. Given the sample size, however, it is not possible to investigate systematically relationships between role conceptions and previous office-bearing experience. We shall merely content ourselves in later chapters with suggesting how inter-departmental differences and situational factors influence role performance.

There are a number of difficulties associated with discovering Ministers' role conceptions. It would have been possible in the interviews to present Ministers with a list of roles similar to that given in Chapter 2 and ask them to rank the roles in the order of importance they personally attached to them. This method has been adopted in several role studies in political science and other fields.[1] It was rejected in this study for one specific and one more fundamental reason. The specific reason was that it was felt that public norms, or the conventions of British Government might inhibit some Ministers from expressing their private norms and implying that certain aspects of their job were relatively unimportant. For example, a Minister who in reality gave little time and thought to cabinet decisions other than those directly affecting his own department might nevertheless baulk at ranking his cabinet duties as the least important aspect of his job.

The more fundamental reason for not proffering a standard list of roles was that it is now generally agreed by social scientists with experience of what is fashionably termed 'elite interviewing' that the more fruitful procedure is to ask open-ended questions, which leave respondents free to describe their duties in their own words, define their own concepts and include or omit whatever they see fit.[2] Interviews with political leaders are quite different from interviews with the general public. In social surveys concerned with the general public, care is taken to draw a representative (random or quota) sample and the interviewers typically ask straightforward, easily understood questions and receive straightforward, relatively easily interpretable answers. The main interest lies in the *distribution* of 'yes–no', 'pro–anti' responses. In interviewing political leaders, on the other hand, the researcher typically does not have a strictly representative, let alone a random sample, and, in any case, he is often more concerned to discover new information, or the respondents' interpretations of events or political processes, than to discover distributions of opinion. The interviewer is relatively ignorant, the respondent relatively knowledgeable. It makes more sense, therefore, for the respondent to frame his own answers in his own terms, rather than be put in a strait-jacket by the terms of the questions.

One final remark about 'elite interviewing' concerns the interpretation of the data obtained. Although respondents are knowledgeable about the subjects they are asked to discuss, their statements need to be interpreted with a degree of imagination and, sometimes, scepticism. Each respondent holds, or has held, a particular political office and speaks on the basis of particular experiences which predis-

---

[1] For a review of the different methods employed in role analysis see Theodore R. Sarbin and Vernon L. Allen, 'Role Theory', in G. Lindzey and E. Aronson (eds), *The Handbook of Social Psychology* (Reading, Mass.: Addison-Wesley, 1969), I, pp. 488-567.

[2] See, for example, Lewis A. Dexter, *Elite and Specialised Interviewing* (Evanston, Ill.: North-Western University Press, 1970), pp. 55-6.

pose him to expectations and biases different from respondents whose experiences have been in other offices. Respondents are giving their version of what goes on in government and telling the interviewer, or maybe deceiving him, about what they personally try to accomplish. In interpreting these data, a social scientist has to act a bit like a judge who discovers that some witnesses are more reliable than others, who tries to perceive the implications of what is said to him and who, in summing up for the jury, tries to present a coherent reconstruction, or alternative reconstructions of the case, instead of just giving an edited version of the way it was reported to him.

The first part of the chapter reports data on the proportion of Ministers attaching importance to various roles. Party differences are analysed and we also see what skills Ministers believe to be necessary for role performance. In the latter part of the chapter, the data are interpreted more imaginatively (or, at any rate, less literally), individual roles are discussed more fully and a typology of Ministers, based on their role conceptions, is proposed.

ROLE CONCEPTIONS AND ROLE SKILLS: AN OVERVIEW

Two standard questions were used to elicit role conceptions. First, Ministers were asked:

> What are the most important tasks a Minister has to perform? In other words what is a good Minister actually good at doing?

Then, to get a fuller appreciation of how they viewed their job, they were asked:

> What skills and types of ability do Ministers need to carry out these essential tasks?

Table 3.1 tells us what Ministers consider their most important tasks to be.

An initial point emerging from Table 3.1 is that more Ministers attach importance to their policy leadership roles as heads of departments than to cabinet, parliamentary, party or public relations roles. Generally speaking, departmental roles were the first to be mentioned and some Ministers commented explicitly on the pre-eminent importance of this aspect of their job: 'The main thing is the department. This absorbs all your energies. There is not enough time to read cabinet papers – although admittedly I am a slow reader – and personally I always cut down on dinners and formal occasions and tell my officials that my job is here at the centre.' Only a few Ministers (ten out

Table 3.1 *Roles Cited as Important by Ministers* ($N = 50$)

Classification of roles	Number of Ministers
I. Roles as head of department	
Policy leadership roles:	
1. policy initiation	23
2. policy selection	21
3. no mention of policy leadership	6
	50 (N = 50)
Management roles:	
1. departmental morale ('motivating'; affective leadership)	14
2. departmental organisation ('organising')	8
3. 'controlling'; checking departmental performance	3
	25 (N = 20)[a]
II. Roles as a member of the Cabinet	
1. Cabinet battle-axe	19
2. Cabinet all-rounder	5
	24 (N = 22)[a]
III. Roles as parliamentary and party leader	
1. political trouble shooter	19
2. piloting measures through Parliament and the party so as to maximise support	26
	45 (N = 36)[a]
IV. Public relations roles	
1. consultations with department's interest group clientele	9
2. selling the department, policies, self to relevant publics	9
	18 (N = 15)[a]

[a] In each category of roles (except the 'policy leadership' category) several Ministers cited more than one role. The figures in brackets give the number of Ministers citing a role in that category.

of fifty) mentioned either cabinet or parliamentary roles first. This tends to confirm the view, endorsed by some academics and politicians, that in Britain we have departmental government rather than cabinet or parliamentary government.[1] Ministers presumably regard their departmental work as the most important side of their job because they believe that most policy proposals are put into near final form within departments rather than in Cabinet. In so far as the Cabinet is important to Ministers, it is seen as an inter-departmental battleground (by nineteen Ministers) rather than as a forum for collective deliberation on policy (by five Ministers). Ministers go to Cabinet hoping to persuade their colleagues that their departments' policies deserve priority or should not be altered to meet the objections of other departments.

Certainly the most interesting feature of Table 3.1 is the division of opinion it reflects among Ministers about their principal role in the policy-making process. Twenty-three Ministers saw themselves as policy initiators, while twenty-one Ministers could better be described as policy selectors. (Six Ministers did not mention a policy leadership role at all and may perhaps be put down, by default, as policy legitimators). The distinction between policy initiators and policy selectors is crucial and in most cases clear-cut. It does not, however, follow party lines in the way one might expect. Traditionally the Labour Party has been regarded as the party more likely to initiate change. In fact, however, this difference, if it still exists, is not reflected in the role conceptions of the Ministers interviewed for this study.

Table 3.2   *The Policy Leadership Roles of Conservative and Labour Ministers* ($N = 50$)

Role conception	Party	
	Conservative	Labour
Policy initiators	11	12
Policy selectors	9	12
No mention of policy leadership roles	3	3
	—	—
	23	27
	—	—

[1] See, for example, John P. Mackintosh, *The British Cabinet* (London: Stevens, 1968), ch. 13; L. Amery, *Thoughts on the Constitution* (London: OUP, 2nd edn, 1964), ch. 3; Ian F. Gilmour, *The Body Politic* (London: Hutchinson, 1969), ch. 6; P. Gordon Walker, *The Cabinet* (London: Jonathan Cape, 1970) takes the opposite view and believes that collective deliberation in Cabinet remains important on a wide range of issues. Additional points relating to this debate are made in the conclusion to this chapter and Chapter 7.

Labour Ministers were, if anything, slightly less likely than Conservatives to see themselves as policy initiators. Twelve out of twenty-seven Labour Ministers as against eleven out of twenty-three Conservatives fell in this category. It must again be recalled that we are dealing with a relatively small sample but, in general, it was remarkable how rarely in private conversation Ministers mentioned party differences or made party points. Only three Ministers stated explicitly that as policy initiators their role was to implement party policy or take decisions in accordance with party principles. This lends confirmation to the view that, at least at top levels, the parties have come closer together. It would be hard to imagine that thirty or forty years ago Labour leaders in particular would have omitted to mention as one of their main roles the implementation of party principles.[1] Several Ministers, in fact, went out of their way to state that party ideology was no guide at all to policy or to claim that they were 'not conscious of ever taking a decision on party grounds'. Furthermore, although election manifestos were referred to as a source of policy objectives early on in a Government's period in office, no Minister mentioned any other party publications or his party head office (or research department) as influencing his decisions.

Further light can be thrown on Ministers' role conceptions by asking what skills and types of ability they believe their job requires. A hundred years ago Ministers would probably have had no great difficulty in answering this question. They would probably have answered in terms given classic expression by Bagehot in *The English Constitution*: 'There is every reason to expect that a parliamentary statesman will be a man of quite sufficient intelligence, quite enough various knowledge, quite enough miscellaneous experience, to represent general sense in oppositon to bureaucratic sense.'[2] The traditional Bagehot view of the qualities required may be called the 'intelligent layman' theory. The modern layman Minister, however, often lacks the 'miscellaneous experience' which Bagehot recommended and which nineteenth-century politicians generally acquired through keeping up an outside career while sitting in Parliament. Nowadays, nearly all Cabinet Ministers are men who entered the House of Commons before the age of forty and many do not have an outside career.[3] They could as well be called 'professional parliamentary politicians' as 'intelligent laymen'.

[1] See, for instance, G. H. Thomas, *When Labour Rules* (London: Collins, 1920), especially ch. 1, 'The England of Tomorrow'; C. R. Attlee, *The Labour Party in Perspective* (London: Gollancz, 1937), ch. 7, 11.
[2] W. Bagehot, *The English Constitution* (New York: Dolphin Books edn, 1965, 1st edn, 1867), p. 232.
[3] See Chapter 4.

Whatever label we pin on Ministers with this type of background, one thing is clear; it is no longer immediately obvious that the qualifications they possess are those required for a Minister. At least two alternative viewpoints may be cited. First, it may be argued that the increasingly specialised and technical nature of the work of many departments makes it desirable that Ministers should be not laymen but specialists, or at least that they should be fairly knowledgeable in the subjects dealt with by their departments. According to this view if a Minister lacks some degree of specialised knowledge, one of two things may occur. Either he may simply rubber stamp proposals put forward by advisers who do understand what is at stake; alternatively, he may interfere in an erratic way, preventing the development of a consistent and sensible policy.[1]

A third view is that Ministers should be not specialists but experienced organisation men and decision makers. This view is based on an ascertainable fact and a more dubious theory. The ascertainable fact is that many government departments are large complex organisations. The dubious theory (so-called classical management theory) is that the basic principles of organisation and the qualities required to be a successful executive are the same in all types of organisation.[2]

Occasionally, the qualities associated with the intelligent layman, the specialist and the experienced executive may be found in the same individual. Also it is arguable and, as we shall see, some Ministers believe that different qualities are required by Ministers in different departments. Therefore it is not necessary to favour one of the three sets of qualifications to the exclusion of the other two. The views of Ministers regarding their role skills are given in Table 3.3.

Table 3.3　*The Role Skills Required by Ministers*

Skills, attributes	Number of Ministers
Intelligent layman/parliamentary politician	25
Knowledge of subjects covered by the department	16
Executive, managerial, administrative skills	15
N = 50	56[a]

[a] The total number of attributes mentioned exceeds the number of Ministers interviewed because six Ministers listed both 'knowledge of subjects' and 'executive skills'.

[1] See Anthony King, 'Britain's Ministerial Turnover', *New Society* 18 August 1966.

[2] For a contemporary assessment of classical management theory see Joseph L. Massie, 'Management Theory', in James G. March (ed.), *Handbook of Organisations* (Chicago: Rand, McNally, 1965), pp. 387-422.

The interesting finding in this Table is that half the Ministers interviewed believed that the attributes of the intelligent layman and Parliamentary politician are no longer ideal qualifications for holding office. One would have expected that, since most Ministers themselves could best be described as intelligent laymen, they would subscribe to the view that men of their own kind are best qualified. The fact that half believed that either executive ability, or knowledge of specific subjects, or both, are now relevant may be taken as a reflection of the pressures of modern government. It would be incorrect to imply, however, that Ministers are seriously worried about their capacity to tackle the job in hand. They are mostly self-confident men and some of those who mentioned the need for more modern skills thought of them as a desirable bonus rather than an essential qualification. Nevertheless, it is significant that the intelligent layman no longer has the field to himself.

Supporters of the traditional type of Minister place their main emphasis on qualities of 'judgement' and general intelligence. Intelligence or analytic ability was in fact the quality most frequently cited by all respondents (twenty-four out of fifty). 'Judgement' like its English public school fellow 'character' means different things to different people. Some respondents equated judgement with foresight. A Minister who possessed judgement was one who could foresee whether policy proposals which looked fine on paper would actually work out in practice. Other Ministers equated judgement more narrowly with political trouble-spotting. On this definition a Minister with good judgement was one who knew what kinds of decisions were likely to lead to a Parliamentary Question or a stormy party meeting. In general, supporters of the intelligent layman theory also placed a high valuation on parliamentary and human relations skills. It was sometimes implied that only a lifetime at Westminster could equip a man to manage Parliament, 'to get the feel of the House' and acquit himself well at the despatch box.

Taken to its logical conclusion, the intelligent layman theory implies that a Minister should be able to make any equally good job of running any department he is assigned to. In practice, however, it was widely recognised that departments do make different demands on their political heads and therefore Ministers need to some extent to be selected on a 'horses for courses' basis. It was said, for example, that departments like the Home Offiec and the Foreign Office, which handle a large number of politically sensitive issues, require Ministers with the traditional virtues of sound judgement and, in dealing with Parliament, 'safe hands'. But it was admitted that a few departments may benefit from having Ministers with either special knowledge or executive ability. The Treasury was frequently mentioned in the first category and the Ministry of Defence in the second.

Again, perceptions of the relevance of different skills do not follow party lines in the way one might expect. Labour rather than Conservative Ministers are somewhat more likely to be upholders of the traditional layman (see Table 3.4).

Table 3.4   *Perceptions of Ministerial Role Skills by Party*

Role skills	Conservative	Labour
Intelligent layman/parliamentary politician	10	15
Knowledge of relevant subjects	6	10
Executive skills	9	6
N = 50	25 (23)[a]	31 (27)[a]

[a] The total number of attributes mentioned exceeds the number of Ministers interviewed because six Ministers listed both 'knowledge of subjects' and 'executive skills'.

Over half the Labour Ministers but only ten out of twenty-three Conservatives believed the qualities of the intelligent layman to be necessary and sufficient. Conservatives were more likely to believe that executive skills are helpful and about equally likely to attach importance to relevant specialised knowledge. Not unnaturally, the judgement of some Ministers appears to have been affected by their own background. Nine of the fifteen respondents who mentioned executive skills had some experience in business and twelve of the sixteen Ministers who thought specialised knowledge valuable believed that their own academic (university degree) or previous experience in political office had made them to some extent specialists.

Even more significant is the relationship between Ministers' perceptions regarding role skills and their role conceptions. It may be hypothesised that Ministers who conceive of themselves as policy initiators are more likely to believe that their job requires either special knowledge, or executive skills, or both. On the face of it a thorough knowledge of the subjects involved appears to be a particularly necessary qualification for initiating policy changes; unless, that is, one believes that in government, as elsewhere, fools rush in where angels fear to tread. Executive skills based on experience in a large organisation might also be thought valuable to a policy initiator, since it would be no use his having worthwhile objectives if he lacked the ability to get his department to respond and formulate administratively practical programmes.

Table 3.5   *Relationship between Ministerial Role Conceptions and Role Skills*

Role skills	Role conception		
	policy initiator	policy selector	no mention of policy leadership roles
Intelligent layman/parliamentary politician	7	14	4
Knowledge of relevant subjects	12	4	0
Executive skills	10	3	2
N = 50	29 (23)[a]	21 (21)[a]	6 (6)[a]

[a] Figures in brackets indicate the number of respondents. The number of responses in the policy initiator column exceeds the number of respondents because six policy initiators perceived a need for both 'knowledge of relevant subjects' and 'executive skills'.

Table 3.5 confirms the hypothesis. Twelve out of twenty-three policy initiators thought special knowledge useful and ten valued executive skills. Only seven subscribed to the intelligent layman theory. In contrast, only four out of twenty-one policy selectors mentioned special knowledge, three mentioned executive skills and fourteen upheld the intelligent layman. It is particularly interesting that all six Ministers who mentioned both special knowledge and executive skills intended to be policy initiators.

A TYPOLOGY OF CABINET MINISTERS

Different Ministers have different priorities. The purpose of this section is to propose a typology of Ministers based on the roles they give high priority to and are most concerned to be active in performing. The typology is presented for its heuristic value and, hopefully, as having a reasonable fit with Whitehall and Westminster realities. It must be recognised, though, that by no means all Ministers fit neatly into one of the 'ideal type' categories. Some Ministers cite one particular role as being of overwhelming importance; they are easy to classify. A majority of Ministers, however, mention more than one role and, as the following pages make clear, there are some interesting *role sets* (i.e. 'bundles' of roles which respondents perceive as 'going together'). Finally, there were a few respondents who would not define their priorities at all: one said, 'all aspects of the job are important.

You can't afford to neglect anything. You just work longer hours.'
This statement may simply have reflected an unwillingness to be
pressed further. Taken literally, however, it would suggest that this
Minister and others like him, by not defining their priorities and
arranging their timetable accordingly, are in danger of performing
all roles relatively inadequately. The list of Ministers who have been
exhausted by office is quite long and any classification should,
perhaps, include the would-be all-rounder heading for nervous or
physical breakdown. For the purposes of the later analysis, however,
it seemed preferable to classify only Ministers whose priorities were
reasonably clear-cut, while recognising that important consequences
may follow if a Minister genuinely tries to tackle all aspects of his job
with equal assiduity.

A minister's minimum roles and ministerial Minimalists

There are three minimum roles which all Westminster politicians and
all Whitehall civil servants expect a Minister to try and perform
adequately;[1] though it cannot be said that instant dismissal is the
inevitable penalty of failure. First, if only to permit Her Majesty's
Government to be carried on, a Minister must get through an
enormous amount of paper work and accept responsibility for a
large number of decisions for which civil servants require a politician's
endorsement. Ministers often claim that they are 'snowed under with
paper' and readily concede that this is partly because they have to
spend a great deal of time dealing with matters which are politically
sensitive but which they know to be intrinsically trivial.

Second, a Minister is obliged to put up a fight in Cabinet to win
for his department parliamentary time to pass legislation (some departments pass little legislation, however),[2] and Treasury money to
finance the department's measures. Not to make an effort to win
cabinet battles would run flatly counter to the expectations of
ministerial colleagues, civil servants and the department's interest
group clientele. Ministers do, however, vary considerably in the
degree of concern they express about cabinet battles. This point
could be better illustrated than in the statements made to Maurice
Kogan by Sir Edward Boyle and Mr Anthony Crosland who were
both referring to their experiences as Minister of Education.[3] Boyle said:

[1] Almost all Ministers mentioned the three roles described in this section at
some stage of their interview. They did not all, as is clear from Table 3.1, mention
them in response to the opening question about their 'most important tasks'.
[2] See Chapter 7.
[3] Sir Edward Boyle was Minister of Education from July 1962 to April 1964
and Minister of State for Education until October 1964. Anthony Crosland was
Secretary of State for Education and Science from January 1965 until August 1967.

'The most difficult aspect of the job is that so many decisions rely on collective discussions with colleagues. There are few important educational decisions that don't involve money, don't involve discussions with the Treasury and deciding how to play the hand, at what moment to put on the greatest amount of pressure in your dealings with Treasury Ministers.'[1]

In terms of the sample interviewed for this study Boyle was quite atypical in his anxiety about inter-departmental relationships; an anxiety which presumably reflected his difficulties as a Conservative 'left-winger' on humanitarian and welfare issues. Crosland is the limiting case in the other direction. Replying to the question, 'What limitations from within the government were placed on your authority by the Prime Minister, or the whole Cabinet, or the Treasury?' he said, 'As far as the Cabinet is concerned again very little. I only recollect taking two matters to Cabinet – Circular 10/65 and the Public Schools Commission – and then the discussion was very brief.'[2]

The third minimum role is that of defending one's department adequately (preferably brilliantly) in the House of Commons. Any Minister with an instinct for self-preservation will try to act as political trouble spotter and trouble-shooter in dealing with issues likely to be taken up by Parliament. That is, he will try to spot in advance issues likely to cause a parliamentary storm and will prepare himself carefully for parliamentary set pieces; for debates and Question Time. Thus one senior Labour Minister referred to his 'twelve to one Parliamentary ratio'; 'twelve hours preparing a one hour speech, six hours for a half hour speech'. Other Ministers emphasise the value of frequenting the smoking-room (Conservative Party) or the tea-room (Labour Party) of the House of Commons in order to keep abreast of parliamentary gossip, discover what issues are troubling backbenchers and give oneself the opportunity of placating MPs who have a grievance against the department and might vent it in the Chamber if unable to get satisfaction in private. Referring to the danger of Ministers' becoming preoccupied with their departmental duties and getting out of touch with parliamentary life a Conservative Minister said that, 'It is essential to remain a House of Commons man. Remember you belong to this place. You've got to have a nose for matters that arouse Parliament's attention. I used to do as much paper work as possible in my room in the House.' A Labour Minister, in the same vein, said,

[1] E. Boyle, A. Crosland and M. Kogan, *The Politics of Education* (Harmondsworth: Penguin, 1971), p. 94.
[2] *ibid.*, p. 160. Crosland did say, however, that as President of the Board of Trade he took more issues to Cabinet.

'Never forget you are a Parliamentarian. I go down to the House for lunch and drinks in the evening most days. You can defuse back-benchers and prevent them going hammer and tongs for you at party meetings. You also meet informally with other Ministers. There is a table at the House at which Ministers and Privy Councillors sit. You talk shop and hear what is brewing in Parliament; it is vital.'

All Ministers, then, recognise the need to perform these minimum roles adequately. There are some Ministers, however – we shall term them *Minimalists* – who are concerned only with these roles. A crucial point about the Minimalists interviewed for this study is that, when asked about their most important tasks, they made no mention of setting policy objectives, or deciding between policy options. They do not openly state that their role is restricted to policy legitimation but by not referring to any more activist role thay leave this open to inference. The role conceptions of Minimalists may be illustrated as follows: 'First, you must get to know the substantive side of the department's work and the kinds of issues that are politically sensitive. When I was appointed to a new department I would ask to see all kinds of papers to discover whether they were liable to cause a storm. If not – then one would not see them again' (Conservative Minister). This respondent added that it paid to get to know which civil servants were good at political trouble spotting. He also placed emphasis on 'knowing what your colleagues in Cabinet will accept' and on being adequate in the House. His assessment of the skills necessary for a Minister followed quite logically from his role conception: 'you have got to have a barrister's ability to master a brief and argue a strong case in Cabinet. . . . Ideas and drive are really only necessary for a few senior Ministers in the Cabinet, except in wartime'. Another Conservative Minister asked about his main tasks said that: 'A new Minister has lunch with the outgoing Minister and asks about political hot potatoes and which MPs give trouble in the House – at Question Time and so forth. Then you meet the Permanent Secretary and find out what business the department has in hand and what you have to take decisions on forthwith.' This Minister thought that his experience in business and as a military staff officer had been useful preparation for office but noted that some of his colleagues had attributes that he lacked: 'the barrister's forensic skills are most valuable – I found that personally I had to take a lot of time preparing for parliamentary occasions'. On the question of policy, he stated that, 'I only actually overruled officials' advice once in eight and a half years – usually it was a matter of give and take.'

Last, a Minister in Mr Wilson's Labour Government, who was

much criticised but showed considerable survival capacity and held
three Cabinet posts, began the interview by saying that a Minister
needed 'stamina and the capacity to work anything up to sixteen or
eighteen hours a day. I never knew I could work so hard.' It became
clear that a good deal of this time was spent avoiding political trouble.
He took the unusual step of inviting interested MPs of both parties
to regular meetings in his department so that they could question
both himself and officials. In this way he hoped to forestall Questions
on the floor of the Houe. This Minister also claimed to read all the
newspapers every day, looking for items concerning his department.
He would question his officials on such items as a means of keeping
them alert to the political difficulties their decisions could provoke.
The main qualities he looked for in a Minister were 'the ability to
master papers and unfailing courtesy'.

To summarise: a Minister must achieve a 'passing level' in the performance of his minimum roles in order to maintain his overall standing and credibility in the Government. Because there is a universal
expectation in Whitehall and Westminster that he will try to perform
these roles adequately, he will be regarded as a failure if he is unable
to do so. The point about the ministerial Minimalist is that he is concerned only with minimum roles. The remaining types of Minister
described in this chapter regard other roles as worthy of higher
priority.

Policy selectors/intelligent laymen

The distinction has already been drawn between two types of Minister who intend to provide policy leadership in their departments:
policy selectors and policy initiators. Policy selectors themselves may
be divided into those who see the role as just one among several important roles but attribute no overriding significance to it and those
(eight in our sample of fifty) who see themselves as intelligent laymen
whose special task it is to bring an independent perspective to bear
on the affairs of the department and only to select or endorse policy
proposals after questioning assumptions, probing for weaknesses
and providing suggestions and ideas to be followed up by officials.
The former category of policy selectors tended to refer to the role
relatively briefly and as part of a role set. Their role conceptions may
be gauged from the following statements:

'First you call for the facts; the civil servants provide these. Then
you must make up your mind. If you can't do this you waste cabinet
time.'

(Conservative Minister)

'As Lord Attlee told me when I was first made a Parliamentary Secretary, the Minister's job is to go in and get decisions. Then you have to fight for them in Cabinet and sell them to Parliament.'

(Labour Minister)

Policy selectors of the less ambitious kind are broadly content to accept the objectives of the department as they find them. Their main emphasis is on the role of the Minister as a decision taker. They tend to see departmental policy making as falling into clear-cut stages: formulating policy options, decision taking and administration of policy. The Minister, in the view, should only be involved at the second of these stages. Thus the very senior Conservative Minister, whose role conception is quoted first, distinguished between 'the facts' and a decision based on the facts. He dismissed as unworthy the suggestion that there was a risk of being presented only with facts which supported one particular line of analysis, or which were relevant given one definition of a problem but not another. The Labour Minister quoted above clearly regarded policy selection as logically the first of a sequence of roles, or role set, that he was called upon to perform.

The above points do not apply to those ministerial policy selectors who attribute great significance to the qualities of the intelligent layman. Typical responses from the Ministers who fall into this category were:

'A Minister should be a good prober. Like the non-executive director it is his job to ask the damn fool question and expose shaky assumptions.'

(Conservative Minister)

'You must exercise your critical faculties in analysing papers put up by officials. You provide both an outsider's perspective and inject political judgement into the considerations of the experts.'

(Labour Minister)

The analogy between the layman Minister and a non-executive director on a board was drawn by more than one Conservative Minister with business experience and, among Labour Ministers, those with a background in academic life, like the Minister quoted above, were likely to see themselves playing an intelligent, or even an intellectual layman's role in their departments. Several Ministers spoke of the need to expose inconsistencies in compromise proposals arrived at by civil servants unable or unwilling to override each other or the organised groups affiliated to departments. A Conservative, who believed strongly in the value of office meetings for exposing such compromises, thought that on these occasions the layman Minister should sit opposite his civil servants and probe their views rather than have the Permanent Secretary sitting next to him, 'whispering in his ear'. Not until he fully understood a set of proposals and was persuaded in his own mind that they were right should he adopt them and throw the weight of his department behind them.

Policy initiators; setting departmental objectives and priorities

Like policy selectors, policy initiators may be divided into those who just mention the role as one among several and those who attach paramount importance to it. Some of the twenty-three Ministers who intended to be policy initiators appeared to be doing no more than paying lip service to a constitutional norm when they said that a Minister should 'decide his policy objectives', or 'dominate his department', or 'make an impact on policy – so that everyone knows he has been there [in the department]'. At least nine Ministers in the sample, however, regarded policy initiation as easily their most significant role and intended to play a more activist part in policy making even than policy selectors/intelligent laymen. Their role conceptions may be gauged from the following statements:

'A Minister must set objectives and then understand the motives that will lead people to implement these objectives. The main motive is self-interest. It is a question of changing a few vital nuts so that people will move in the direction you want.'

(Conservative Minister)

'The Minister should offer intellectual, philosophical leadership. He must think things through – the East of Suez role, the future of the Health Service, whatever it is. Only Ministers can make major changes; proposals generated by civil servants are bound to put safety first.'

(Conservative Minister)

'There are three kinds of Minister: creative Ministers, administrators and those who are no good at either. A really creative Minister can sometimes lead his department to reinterpret its functions. In this department we have tried to move away from the civil service habit of even-handedness in dealing with industry and to provide special incentives for firms which are efficient – particularly if they are strong on the export side.'

(A Labour Minister of State)

Several interesting points arise here. The first quotation gives a very Conservative view of change. The object should be to interfere with market forces only to the extent required to bring self-interest and the public interest into line. This Minister illustrated his point by referring to the goal of making landlording profitable. In his opinion legislation decontrolling rents, and incentives to carry out improvements and make more property to let available, had failed in their purpose because the tax structure continued to discrimate against landlords. 'Changing a few nuts' in the tax structure would do the trick.

The assertion made by the second Conservative Minister that 'only Ministers can make major changes; proposals generated by civil servants are bound to put safety first' may have been a conscious overstatement. He justified it, however, by stating that proposals initiated by civil servants were bound to reflect both intra- and inter-departmental compromises agreed on before they were put up to Ministers. This reflects the view of many critics who believe that all too often British government proceeds by 'directionless consensus' and that 'we spend so much time in being sure of keeping in step that we hardly advance at all . . . in other words, things that ought to happen do not happen while we are making sure that nobody will be upset if they do happen'.[1]

Last, the remark that a 'creative Minister' in leading his department to reinterpret its functions may have to override Civil Service norms hints at the possibilty of conflict between ministerial policy initiators and civil servants. In this connection it is pertinent that only two of the twenty-three policy initiators in the sample, as compared with eleven policy selectors, expected to act as affective leaders in their departments. It appears that policy initiators accept that in pressing changes on civil servants they are unlikely to be popular.

Executive Ministers and management roles

Textbooks on British public administration assert that the management of government departments is the responsibility of the Permanent Secretary. It was therefore somewhat surprising to find that

---

[1] The phrase 'directionless consensus' comes from Richard Rose, 'The Variability of Party Government', *Political Studies*, 17, 4 (December 1969), pp. 413-45. The second quotation, attributed to a Permanent Secretary, comes from Gilmour, *The Body Politic*, p. 14.

twenty out of the fifty Ministers interviewed attached importance to management roles (see Table 3.1). Fourteen Ministers believed that part of their job was to maintain or boost the morale of their department, eight concerned themselves with questions of departmental organisation and three with problems of controlling and evaluating the way in which existing programmes were being implemented. It was clear from the context of their remarks, however, that most respondents who cited a management role regarded it as of secondary importance only. On the other hand, three Ministers in the sample attached such importance to management roles, and clearly regarded policy and management as inseparable (as a role set) that they may reasonably be termed Excutive Ministers.

Most Ministers who attached importance to maintaining departmental morale were simply concerned to 'make the civil servants feel one is worth working hard for', or, 'to bring the best out of civil servants – after all you can't sack them!' It was said that R. A. Butler was outstanding in this respect: 'whenever you talked to RAB you were made to feel that you were awfully good at the subject'. As well as seeking to boost the morale of senior officials with whom they came in regular contact, several Ministers tried to encourage lower ranks of civil servants by taking an interest in even non-political aspects of their departments' work and by welcoming the opportunity in the Parliamentary summer recess to arrange a programme of inspections of departmental regional offices. One Minister went so far as regularly to hire a meeting hall in order to address and be addressed by all members of his department 'from the Permanent Secretary to the lift boys'. These meetings were to serve both a suggestions and complaints function and to communicate ministerial objectives to officials at all levels.

A more activist management role is played by those Ministers who concern themselves with departmental organisation, including promotions and appointments and decision-making methods:

'My rule was that if a young civil servant was being put up for promotion he was probably good. If it was an older man it might be a question of Buggin's turn next and it was best to interview him. With military appointments I tried to use "visits" to meet officers of Major-General and above who might be promoted in the coming year.'

(A former Conservative Minister of Defence)

'When I came to this department there were no economists and the level of economic thinking among civil servants was appalling. I have recruited a few economists at senior levels and a lot lower down. The only trouble with outsiders is that they don't know how Whitehall works.'

(A Labour economic Minister)

'The valuable thing about business experience is that it gives you a basis of comparison for running a department. You know when to "hive off", when to set up a project team, how to evolve a cost accounting system and so forth.'

(Conservative Minister)

Last, a Minister concerned with the control function of management said:

'In running a department one of the most important things for a Minister to do is introduce proper methods of control and management. You should have a regular check that things are moving forward and that bad trends are not being established. Government statistics are not always adequate and Ministers fail to observe unwelcome developments until they blow up in their face.'

(Conservative Minister)

The first two quotations illustrate ways in which a Minister may intervene in the appointments process. The former Conservative Minister of Defence quoted here was not content to leave departmental promotions in the hands of the Permanent Secretary where they normally rest and the Labour economics Minister was determined, presumably with Treasury approval, to improve the quality of advice available to himself by hiring economists as temporary civil servants. The last two Ministers quoted were both businessmen and at several points in the interview compared the tasks of a Minister with the tasks of a managing director. They both endorsed the Fulton Committee's criticisms of civil servants as managers and, while noting the duties of the Permanent Secretary, were anxious themselves to take steps to improve the machinery for programme evaluation and reviewing priorities in their departments.[1] They both favoured 'hiving off' to public agencies areas of departmental work which were essentially managerial and did not involve decisions of a controversial political nature. Finally, it may be noted that the Minister who believed that government statistics (he was speaking mainly of housing and welfare statistics) are inadequate had been much impressed by programme evaluation techniques employed by the Bureau of the Budget in

[1] See Chapter 5 for a review of some of the Fulton Committee's findings on Civil Service management.

Washington and wished to see similar techniques introduced in Whitehall.

Ambassador Ministers and public relations roles

It is not uncommon to read assertions to the effect that Ministers have 'day to day horizons and public relations obsessions'.[1] Implicit here is the view, no doubt widely held, that our rulers and betters should be concerned with nobler ends than mere public relatons. Some Ministers doubtless agree, others among those interviewed probably omitted to give their true assessment of the importance of public relations roles. In fact only fifteen Ministers mentioned such roles and most apparently placed them rather low in order of priority. Only three Ministers in the sample clearly regarded their activities as ambassadors for their departments, communicating its policies and projecting its image, as central to their job. They may be labelled Ambassador Ministers.

Ministers who attached importance to their consultative role (see Table 3.1) made it clear that they had more in mind than simply routine contact between their department and its established clientele of interest groups and advisory committees. In some cases they believed that as politicians they were especially well equipped to persuade interest group leaders to accept policies and co-operate in implementing them. In other cases their main motive for consultation was to increase their range of policy options, or at least to ensure that all feasible options and objections to possible courses of action had been considered. For this purpose it was said to be necessary to go beyond consulting the usual bodies and to seek a wider range of contacts. The comments of several Ministers on their consultative role are given below:

'It is more important for a political leader to be persuasive than for a business leader. You can't just give orders in politics as you often can in business. You have got to negotiate with the CBI, the TUC and other groups.'

(A Conservative Minister)

'Civil servants do not have the necessary outside contacts. They put up a proposal and *tell* industry what they are going to do. I would *ask* what was the best way of, for example, introducing and collecting a corporation tax.'

(A Conservative Minister)

[1] S. Brittan, *Steering the Economy* (London: Secker and Warburg, 1969), p. 30.

'To be effective a Minister must see propoasls at an early stage of policy formulation and personally discuss them with interest groups and advisers. It is a mistake to leave consultation to your civil servants.'

(A Labour Minister)

'Civil servants are sometimes too restrictive about whom they consult. I went round the casinos myself finding out how the gaming laws would work and found they would not work at all.'

(A Labour Minister of State)

The second ministerial public relations role – that of publicising the department and explaining its objectives and policy programmes – is performed to some extent by all Ministers through the programme of visits and speeches arranged by their Private Office. Ministers who attached particular importance to this role justified their concern in a number of ways. Two Ministers said that it was essential for the head of a new department to make a public impact and 'put the department on the map'. A Labour Minister, at that time in an economic department, believed that, 'Human relations are often what count. I have had a lot of negotiating experience as a Minister – pit closures at the Ministry of Power, constitutional conferences at the Colonial Office – and more explaining and trying to humanise decisions affecting declining industries and redundancies in this job.'

A former Minister of Labour saw his job as being primarily concerned with selling policy: incomes policy, industrial retraining policy and so forth. His role was to maintain and improve his trade union contacts and persuade union leaders to accept government policy and make use of the conciliation, industrial retraining and other services offered by his department. Finally, a Conservative Minister thought it important that as a member of the Cabinet team he should play an active part, principally through weekend speeches, in projecting government policies and refuting the Opposition. He thought this a particularly suitable role for a Minister who did not have a heavy current programme of legislation.

CONCLUSION

The purpose of this chapter has been to analyse Ministers' role conceptions, to ask where their priorities lie and what kind of leadership they intend to provide. Five main types of Minister have been distinguished:

1. Minimalists

2. Policy selectors
3. Policy initiators
4. Executive Ministers
5. Ambassador Ministers

Ministerial Minimalists give priority to their parliamentary tasks and to fighting their departmental corner in Cabinet and cabinet committees. All Ministers are hindered if they cannot achieve a passing level in these minimum roles. Their credibility in Westminster and Whitehall is undermined and they are unlikely to achieve much, even if they retain office. Most Ministers, however, aim to be more than Minimalists. Policy selectors and policy initiators intend to provide policy leadership but whereas the policy selector generally restricts himself to probing for weaknesses in advice and choosing among alternative lines of policy submitted to him, the policy initiator thinks of himself as defining and setting his own objectives. A fourth category of Ministers – Executive Ministers – emphasises management roles and Ambassador Ministers emphasise public relations roles.

Critics might argue that whatever Ministers' intentions they lack the knowledge and skills required to perform in accordance with their role conceptions. We have seen that Ministers recognise this problem. Among those who conceive of themselves as policy initiators the majority (sixteen out of twenty-three believed that the attributes of the intelligent layman are no longer adequate. Some argued that previous knowledge of the subjects dealt with by their departments is required, others that Ministers need to be experienced organisation men and decision makers. Even among Ministers who, in general, defended the intelligent layman, there was widespread recognition that departments make different demands on their political masters and that some departments require abilities that an orthodox Parliamentary politician could not be expected to have.

Several findings in this chapter may surprise some observers and it is worth considering alternative interpretations. First, consider the finding that most Ministers attach priority to departmental policy leadership roles and show relatively little concern for cabinet and inter-departmental relations. One explanation for this would be that ministerial perceptions accurately reflect the realities of British government in that the majority of policy programmes are initiated within Whitehall departments and are neither a response to Cabinet, Treasury or other central directives, nor are they likely to be significantly amended as a result of inter-departmental discussions. An alternative interpretation, more likely to be adopted by observers who believe we still have cabinet government rather than a government of departments, is that Ministers attribute overriding importance to departmental policy making partly out of egotism – they like to think they run their own empires relatively free from outside control – and partly out of a failure to perceive the multiple constraints imposed, not just by the Cabinet, but by the Treasury, the Civil Service Department and understandings reached on inter-departmental committees of civil servants. On this view Ministers who believe that departments are in a position to formulate policy objectives and programmes independently of central economic and staff management are slightly naive. Finally, one might also suggest that Ministers concentrate on the departmental side of their job because they find it more agreeable to work in a setting where everyone is subordinate to them, than to face rivals and critics in Cabinet, in Parliament and on public platforms. The evidence does not permit any definitive assessment of these alternative interpretations of the interview responses but the reader is referred to Chapter 5 where the constraints imposed by the 'centre' of government on individual Ministers and their departments are analysed more fully.

Another finding which was perhaps unexpected was that the role conceptions of Conservative and Labour Ministers were very similar. Although Labour is generally thought of as the party of change, Labour Ministers were not more likely than Conservatives to see themselves as policy initiators. In general, Ministers appeared almost apartisan in their approach to their job. Only three explicitly stated that a priority task was to implement party policy objectives or frame policy in accordance with party philosophy. Others made the point that, except in the immediate post-election period when the manifesto might be a source of policy objectives, they received no guidance from party publications or research. A sceptical view would be that Ministers give apartisan responses because it fits their public image to appear concerned about the public interest rather than party commitments. An equally plausible explanation would stress the capacity of Whitehall departments to institutionalise their Ministers. Departments arrange Ministers' timetables, partially insulate them from their political grass-roots and so monopolise them that they readily accept departmental policy formulations and identify them with the public interest.

Last, it would be natural for Ministers in the interview situation to underplay ambitions to advance their own careers, and hence their concern with party standing, Parliamentary performance and attracting favonrable publicity. One can accept that many Ministers *want* to give priority to policy leadership roles without imagining that the Minister who referred to his 'twelve to one parliamentary ratio' was exceptional in anything but his frankness. Even those Ministers whose comments bore out Norman Macrae's assertion that, 'we have established in Britain a supposedly parliamentary system of government where the Ministers who are Parliament's sole creations are privately rather ashamed of what goes on in Parliament and much prefer to talk things over with civil servants instead',[1] almost certainly recognised that failure to prepare thoroughly for parliamentary occasions involves taking serious career risks.

This chapter has dealt with role conceptions. But role conceptions by no means perfectly predict role performance. Ministers may think of themselves as, say, policy initiators but in reality make no impact on policy whatever. In Part II we analyse the factors which determine whether they are able to live up to their role conceptions.

[1] Norman Macrae, 'The People We Have Become', *Economist*, 20 April 1973.

Part II

Factors Affecting Performance in Office

Chapter 4

The Skills of Ministers

To what extent do Ministers have the skills, ability and previous experience required to perform their roles effectively? In so far as they appear better qualified to perform some roles than others what are the consequences for British government? Questions about 'role skills' are inevitably raised by any recruiting agency, or interviewing board commissioned to fill any job. Yet, curiously, political scientists who have studied the recruitment of Ministers have raised them only obliquely, if at all. A great deal is known about the social origins, schooling, university education and acreage owned by past and present Ministers, but these data have been used to demonstrate the social exclusiveness of the political elite rather than to make inferences about their skills.[1] There are also valuable studies tracing the political careers of Ministers, telling us which junior offices lead to high office.[2] Again, however, the evidence has not been analysed from the point of view of establishing whether their previous experience adequately prepares Ministers for high office.

Probably the main reason why the 'role skills' perspective has been neglected in the study of ministerial recruitment lies in the difficulty of deciding precisely what skills, in practice, contribute to improved performance in office. The problem would be solved if the popular conception that there are certain people who are 'born leaders' were correct. It would then only be necessary to specify the person-

---

[1] W. L. Guttsman, *The British Political Elite* (London: MacGibben and Kee, 1963); J. F. S. Ross, *Parliamentary Representation* (London: Eyre and Spottiswoode, 2nd edn, 1948); Harold J. Laski, 'The Personnel of the English Cabinet', *American Political Science Review*, 22.1 (Feb. 1928), pp. 12-31; J. Bonnor, 'The Four Labour Cabinets', *Sociological Review*, 6.1 (1958), pp. 37-48; R. Rose, *Class and Party: Britain as a Test Case* (Glasgow: Strathclyde University, 1968).

[2] P. W. Buck, *Amateurs and Professionals in British Politics* (Chicago: Chicago University Press, 1963); F. M. G. Willson, 'The Routes of Entry of New Members of the British Cabinet: 1868-1958', *Political Studies*, 7: 3 (1959), pp. 222-32; Willson, 'Entry to the Cabinet, 1959-68', *Political Studies*, 18-2 (1970), pp. 236-8.

ality traits and skills of such leaders and then discover to what extent Ministers possessed them.[1] However, as noted in Chapter 1, if there is one finding on which social psychologists are agreed, it is that the 'born leader' is a myth and that different groups and organisations performing different tasks and with differing expectations regarding styles of leadership require leaders with radically different skills and personalities. In short, skills are role specific and the attributes required of a Minister cannot be decided by reference to a personality trait theory of leadership.[2] The strategy was therefore adopted of asking Ministers themselves what particular skills their job demands. The results, reported in Chapter 3, reflect a three-way division of opinion with some support for specialist Ministers, some support for Ministers with executive experience and rather more support for the traditional Minister who combines the qualities of the intelligent layman with those of an astute Parliamentary politician.

Ministers themselves recognised that different roles require different skills. Policy initiators believed that both specialised knowledge and executive experience are valuable (see Table 3.3). Policy selectors upheld the intelligent layman theory. Ministerial Minimalists hardly need to be more than astute parliamentary politicians and for Executive Ministers executive experience is clearly appropriate. Ambassador Ministers require a flair for publicity and this cannot be programmed, but parliamentary life develops forensic skills, and would therefore seem useful preparation.

In this chapter biographical information from newspaper files and standard reference works like *Who's Who?* and the *Dictionary of National Biography* is used to estimate the extent to which Ministers actually possess the skills they prescribe. Comparisons are made between the careers of contemporary Ministers and the careers of Ministers in earlier periods to see whether any change in skills can be detected which would reflect the changing demands of the Minister's job.

First, to what extent do Ministers possess the qualities ascribed to the intelligent layman in office?

THE ATTRIBUTES OF THE INTELLIGENT LAYMAN/PARLIAMENTARY POLITICIAN

As an intelligent layman a Minister is supposed to bring a fresh

---

[1] C. A. Gibb (ed.), *Leadership* (Harmondsworth: Penguin, 1969), pp. 9-15, Part III, 'Personality'; C. A. Gibb, in G. Lindzey and E. Aronson (eds), *Handbook of Social Psychology* (Reading, Mass.: Addison-Wesley, 1969), IV, pp. 205-82.

[2] For attempts to formulate alternative theories of leadership see Gibb (ed.), *Leadership*, Part IV, 'Interaction Theory'.

mind to the problems confronting his department and to probe weaknesses and assumptions which civil servants long immersed in those problems might otherwise miss. As an experienced parliamentary politician he is expected to have developed sensitive political judgement, adeptness at handling Parliament and a capacity to manage men whether individually, in small groups, or in large audiences. Logically, of course, there is no reason why the two sets of attributes should be associated but, in practice, they appear to be indissolubly linked in British political minds.

R. A. Butler (Lord Butler of Saffron Walden) may be taken as an example of a Minister who closely approximated to the ideal type. Born in Attoch Serai, India in 1902 he went to Marlborough and Cambridge University, taking a Double First in modern languages and history. Like a good many eminent politicians, past and present, he was President of the Union and thereafter graduated quite naturally to a parliamentary seat, entering the Commons at the unusually early age of twenty-seven. Three years later in 1932 he held his first ministerial appointment as Parliamentary Under-Secretary at the India Office. From then on he was in office continuously until 1964, except for the period of the Labour Government, 1945-51. The extent to which he remained a layman in relation to the policy areas he was concerned with may be gauged from the fact that he held office in seven different departments[1] and was only twice reappointed to departments (the Ministry of Labour and the Foreign Office) where he had previously been a Minister. The average length of time he spent in the twelve ministerial posts he held was only two years and two months, the post he held longest being, curiously, his Parliamentary Under-Secretaryship at the India Office. He twice narrowly missed being Prime Minister and held all three of the most prestigious and venerable offices of state, being Chancellor of the Exchequer 1951-5, Home Secretary 1957-62 and Foreign Secretary 1963-4. His career is thus an illustration of the belief of successive Prime Ministers that 'a good man can do anything' and that a first-class mind can readily get up a new subject in a few months.

The kind of contribution the intelligent layman Minister can make may be gauged from the description of Butler's methods given by a senior civil servant who worked closely with him at the Treasury. As Chancellor, Butler apparently never learned much economic theory. Nevertheless, his oral summaries of points raised at departmental office meetings were held to be extremely valuable. He could highlight remaining difficulties and bring the best out of civil servants with probing questions and suggestions. (It was said that he was

---

[1] The India Office, the Ministry of Labour, the Foreign Office, the Ministry of Education, the Treasury, the Home Office, the Central African Office.

particularly ready with novel suggestions after spending a weekend with his politically astute first wife). However, he never took major decisions at departmental meetings but preferred to think things over privately and later communicate with the Permanent Secretary. His decisions by no means always followed the balance of departmental advice and even after he had provisionally made up his mind he did not regard his contribution as ended. He believed that as an experienced politician he had developed an acute sensitivity to the political acceptability of proposals and to questions of political timing. So, after he had taken a decision provisionally, he would instruct his officials to make all preparations to implement it and to act entirely as if it were final. The decision might be communicated to close political friends, to his wife and possibly to interested groups but would not be made public. Then after several days, if Butler's own reactions to living with his decision were unfavourable, if, perhaps, it looked like causing unnecessary political or administrative difficulties, it would be reversed and the department would be told to cancel its preparations. Not surprisingly Mr Butler acquired the reputation among his colleagues of being something of a political divining rod and was regularly asked in Cabinet to give his prognosis of parliamentary and public reaction to proposals.

Although few Ministers have matched Butler's qualities as intelligent layman and parliamentary politician, the evidence suggests that the overall general intelligence and ability of Ministers has remained high and certainly few could be accused of parliamentary inexperience. One indicator of the general ability of Ministers is their level of educational attainment. Of the 355 Cabinet Ministers who have held office since 1885, 235 obtained a university degree, most of them at Oxford or Cambridge.[1] Of perhaps greater interest, since a place at Oxbridge has in the past been virtually guaranteed to male members of many political families, is the number of Ministers who have done well enough to obtain a First Class degree. If we take just the two most recent Cabinets we find that of the twenty-three Ministers in the Labour Cabinet (1964-70) who attended university, nine obtained First Class degrees and in the Conservative Cabinet (1970-4) five of the fifteen Ministers who attended university obtained Firsts.[2]

These data admittedly have limitations. A man may be a brilliant

[1] Figures for 1886-1955 are in Guttsman, *British Political Elite*, pp. 102, 106. For later years data were obtained from *Who's Who?* and *Who Was Who?*
[2] Ministers who obtained Firsts usually note the fact in their *Who's Who?* entries. If any Minister omitted to do so he has not been counted here.

classical scholar at the age of twenty-one or a historian of some promise and might by the time he reached the Cabinet in middle age have permitted his mind to addle. Nor should the data be taken to imply that Ministers who did not attend university lack the ability to function as intelligent laymen in their departments. Competition for senior ministerial office is severe and, although meritocratic criteria are not the only ones applied,[1] a politician would hardly attain senior office unless the Prime Minister and his parliamentary contemporaries believed him to be intellectually reasonably able. It is only necessary to read biographies of former Ministers like Ernest Bevin and Aneurin Bevan to be reminded that outstanding ability and administrative resourcefulness are not found only among Ministers who have received a prolonged formal education.[2] The probability is that less well educated Ministers will experience some difficulty in wading through the enormous amount of paper work that falls to them but, in exceptional cases, this difficulty can be overcome by taking oral advice and holding frequent office meetings to unravel policy problems. This, apparently, was Ernest Bevin's practice as Minister of Labour and Foreign Secretary and given his sharpness of mind and ability to probe and find the weaknesses of the advice he was being offered it seems to have worked perfectly well.[3]

The second string in the intelligent layman Minister's bow is his parliamentary and political experience. In practice, as noted above, those Ministers who stress the value of the intelligent layman's contribution also tend to stress the necessity for a Minister to be an experienced and shrewd politician and parliamentarian. Certainly British Ministers could not be accused of being politically inexperienced. As P. W. Buck has shown, Cabinet Ministers who may think of themselves as laymen in other respects are career professionals as far as politics is concerned.[4] Of the Cabinet Ministers who held office in the 1918-59 period, 63.9 per cent entered Parliament before the age of forty and 82.8 per cent before the age of forty-five.[5] Most of them held safe seats and hence were able to retain their

[1] See pp. 106-107 and Chapter 12.

[2] See A. Bullock, *The Life and Times of Ernest Bevin* (London: Heinemann, 2 vols, 1960, 1967); Michael Foot, *Aneurin Bevan* (London: MacGibbon and Kee, 1962).

[3] Bullock, *Ernest Bevin*, II, ch. 5.

[4] Buck, *Amateurs and Professionals*. However, many MPs, especially on the Conservative side, continue to have outside jobs until becoming Ministers. In some cases the 'jobs' consist only of non-executive directorships which bring in a steady but not hard earned income. See Andrew Roth, *The Business Background of MPs* (London: Parliamentary Profile Services Ltd, undated).

[5] Buck, *Amateurs and Professionals*, p. 118.

place in the queue for office and serve the long parliamentary apprenticeship which is almost a prerequisite for high office. The median Cabinet Minister in this period served, in the course of his career, between seventeen and twenty years in the House of Commons and fewer than one in ten served less than a decade.[1] The picture has certainly not changed in recent years. Of the thirty-seven Ministers who served in Mr Wilson's Cabinets, eighteen were aged thirty-five or younger when first elected to the Commons and only five were over forty. The median Minister in the Wilson Government was fifty-three years old at the time of his first Cabinet appointment and had already served sixteen years in the Commons. Ministers in Mr Heath's Cabinet (1970-4) entered the Commons even younger than their Labour counterparts but served a rather shorter backbench apprenticeship and reached the Cabinet at a younger age. Of the seventeen Ministers in the Heath Government who ever held a Commons seat (two were always in the House of Lords),[2] eleven were first elected at age thirty-five or younger, four were in the thirty-six to forty age group and only two were over forty. The median Minister served eleven years prior to his first Cabinet appointment which came at the age of forty-four.

Little significance should be attributed to the apparent tendency of Labour to attach even greater importance to seniority than the Conservatives. The difference between the parties is largely to be explained by the fact that a rather elderly Cabinet was initially appointed in 1964 in order to include men who had ministerial experience in the 1945-51 Labour Government. The point to be stressed is that Prime Ministers from both parties have seen fit to preserve the traditional *cursus honorum* of British politics which involves a prolonged sojourn on the backbenches and in the tea- and smoking-rooms of the House of Commons before it leads the ambitious politician to junior office and, perhaps, eventually to Cabinet office. The Minister brought in from outside Westminster to do a job he is specially qualified for remains a rarity, despite acceptance of a need for 'cross-fertilisation' in other branches of the government.[3]

Why do Prime Ministers continue to recruit Cabinets almost exclusively from among the senior men in their parliamentary

[1] ibid., p. 118.

[2] Lord Carrington and Earl Jellicoe (resigned 1973).

[3] Temporary transfers of staff ('cross-fertilisation') between the Civil Service and other organisations was recommended by the Fulton Committee on the Civil Service. See Chapter 5.

parties? One obvious reason, at least for the perpetuation of the practice, is that party leaders now automatically expect office when their party returns to government. Any change would give offence and make party management that much harder. Handing out patronage is for a Prime Minister like handing round the Indian pipe of peace. The more jobs that are filled from the party the less likely it is that a dissident leader will emerge on the backbenches to lead parliamentary revolts. Apart from considerations of party management, however, there is the entirely realistic judgement that a Minister benefits greatly from finesse in handling Parliament and this finesse can only be developed by experience. There is probably no other country in the world in which assessments of politicians are based so heavily on their parliamentary performances. At Question Time and in debates there are ample opportunities to attack Ministers and, although the number of MPs who attend debates is falling, a Minister still cannot afford to take parliamentary occasions lightly.

The fate that has befallen Ministers who have lacked parliamentary skills is instructive. Mr Frank Cousins, for example, who was Minister of Technology, 1964-6, was mercilessly harassed. As a trade union leader who was found a parliamentary seat only after his appointment to the Cabinet,[1] it was not surprising that initially his performances at the despatch box were rather inept and that he lacked the ability to ride synthetic Parliamentary storms. When his department was first for Parliamentary Questions (every four weeks) he regularly found that Opposition members had taken the unusual step of putting down enough questions to take up the entire hour. The Opposition also took the initiative in promoting a number of debates on subjects handled by the Ministry of Technology and the Select Committee on Estimates issued a report highly critical of the department.[2] Mr Cousins is reported to have made his position more difficult by not troubling to hide his irritation with some aspects of parliamentary life and procedure: late night sittings, almost irrelevant supplementaries to Parliamentary Questions and a certain male exclusiveness. Although he had policy disagreements with his cabinet colleagues as well, his lack of success in the House probably hastened his resignation in 1966.

Conversely, effective parliamentary performance can rapidly

[1] He became MP for Nuneaton in January 1965 three months after his appointment to the Cabinet.

[2] *Parliamentary Debates* (Commons), 716, 500-658 (14 July 1965); ibid., 720, 944-1070 (16 Nov. 1965); ibid., 727, 366-496 (25 April 1966). *The Select Committee on Science and Technology* (session 1966-7) also made heavy demands on the department.

advance a Minister's career. It seems to be widely considered by junior Ministers themselves that a reputation for parliamentary skill is the single most important factor that can win them promotion. One Minister, who between 1967 and 1969 advanced through the junior ranks to be a full Minister outside the Cabinet, having only been elected to Parliament in 1964, attributed his advance principally to the fact that as a Parliamentary Secretary he had badgered his Minister to let him take over parliamentary duties as much as possible and the Minister, who disliked the harsh criticism his policies were receiving from the Labour left wing, often consented. His performance at the despatch box, he felt, had given him the edge for a senior appointment over three or four other junior Ministers whom he named and felt had equal claims on other grounds. Even more compelling than this personal testimony was the overall judgement of a former Conservative Chief Whip, who had been instrumental in recommending many junior Ministers for promotion, that nine times out of ten it was parliamentary performance that gained a man his chance. In his view the administrative ability of a junior Minister was hard to assess, so that parliamentary ability was all that could differentiate one aspirant from the next. At senior levels, of course, this is not the case. A senior Minister needs to be competent in the House, but he can also be assessed in terms of administrative ability and policy achievements.

A further point concerns the parliamentary standing of the Government as a whole. It is often written, not least by lobby correspondents, that every Government needs a few parliamentary wizards to rally the backbenchers, maintain party morale and shore up its public image. The late Iain Macleod was frequently cited as a Minister who could brilliantly perform this role. It is just conceivable that parliamentary triumphs and disasters count for little in the eyes of God but in the Palace of Westminster they are the staple diet of conversation and any Prime Minister disposed to rely purely on his Government's reputation for administrative competence would be ignoring a plain fact of political life.

THE SPECIALISED KNOWLEDGE OF MINISTERS

In all, sixteen of the fifty Ministers interviewed and a majority of policy initiators believed that some degree of specialised knowledge is a relevant qualification for office, and indeed, expressed such regrets as that its absence means that 'it takes anything up to eighteen months before you really get to know your job'. Specialised knowledge is, of course, particularly relevant in departments like Defence,

Power, and Trade and Industry, commonly referred to in Whitehall as 'technical' departments.

Only a few Ministers in Britain could reasonably be termed specialists. Sir Anthony Eden was one of the few. After leaving Oxford where he took a First in oriental languages, he entered Parliament and soon embarked on a career in foreign affairs. He was Parliamentary Private Secretary to the Foreign Secretary, Austen Chamberlain, at the age of twenty-six and his first ministerial job in 1931 was as Parliamentary Under-Secretary at the Foreign Office. Seventeen out of his twenty years as a Minister were in foreign affairs departments and, indeed, until he became Prime Minister in 1955 he had never had any responsibility for domestic policy. The making of his career was his resignation as Neville Chamberlain's Foreign Secretary in 1938. This gained him a reputation as an opponent of appeasement and he was therefore a suitable choice as Foreign Secretary in Churchill's wartime and 1951-5 Governments. His critics might argue that his long experience in foreign affairs led him to make his greatest mistake. He explicitly drew a parallel between President Nasser of Egypt and the pre-war European dictators and, scorning appeasement, sent British troops to take key points on the Suez Canal in 1956.[1] However, not only specialists are prone to false analogies.

The usual level of specialisation among Ministers may be illustrated by again referring to the careers of members of the two most recent Governments. In the Labour Government (1964-70) seventy-one cabinet appointments were made. Twenty of these were to non-departmental posts in relation to which the question of special-isation does not arise. In the remaining fifty-one cases, perhaps five appointees could genuinely be termed specialists and another five or six would have some claim to be regarded as such. Among the former Mr Denis Healey, Minister of Defence 1964-70, had been employed in the Labour Party's international department from 1945 to 1952, had written numerous articles on defence and foreign policy and had been a Councillor of the Royal Institute of International Affairs and the Institute of Strategic Studies. As a Shadow Minister he had concentrated on external affairs and defence questions since 1959.[2] Mr Patrick Gordon Walker was another foreign affairs specialist. He had written extensively on European history while a don at Christ Church, Oxford, and

[1] Sir A. Eden, *Memoirs: Full Circle*, III (London: Cassell, 1960), pp. 482-3, 577-80.
[2] He was an Opposition spokesman on foreign affairs, 1959-61, and the main spokesman on colonies 1961-3 and defence 1963-4.

followed this by working for the BBC European Service broadcasting to Germany during World War II. He was Commonwealth Secretary 1950-1 and in Opposition from 1951-64 continued to write and speak mainly on foreign and Commonwealth affairs. In the event, however, his appointment as Foreign Secretary lasted only three months due to his failure to win a parliamentary seat. Another three Ministers were specialists in the field of economics and finance. Mr Anthony Crosland had been an economics don at Trinity College, Oxford and had written on a number of contemporary policy issues including, in *Britain's Economic Problem*,[1] the balance of payments. A second President of the Board of Trade, Mr Douglas Jay, who was in office 1964-7 had been a Principal Assistant Secretary at the Board of Trade during the War and was a junior Minister at the Treasury 1947-51. He had also been Shadow Board of Trade Minister prior to 1964. The third economic Minister who might be regarded as a specialist was Mr Jack Diamond, Chief Secretary at the Treasury, 1964-70, who was formerly a chartered accountant running his own firm. His job in the Treasury, appropriately, concerned the control of public expenditure. In other areas of government Lord Gardiner, the Lord Chancellor, and Mr Ray Gunter, Minister of Labour 1964-7, might also be regarded as specialists. Lord Gardiner was an eminent barrister and had for eleven years been a moving force on the Lord Chancellor's Law Reform Committee. Mr Gunter was a long serving President of the Transport Salaried Staff Association and as such had worked closely with Ministry of Labour officials and had acquired a thorough knowledge of the department's methods and great affection for its staff and traditions.

Several other Labour Ministers would have some claim to be regarded as more than laymen. Mr Richard Crossman, Secretary of State for the Social Services 1967-70, knew a great deal about alternative pensions schemes as a result of his active service in Opposition on Labour's superannuation policy group. Mr Roy Jenkins was successively Home Secretary and Chancellor of the Exchequer. He had long been interested in reform at the Home Office and, in 1950, had drawn up a checklist of reforms which he would like to see enacted.[2] He also had a relevant educational qualification for his job as Chancellor having taken a First Class degree in politics, philosophy and economics. Other Ministers with some relevant background were Mr Fred Peart who had been Parliamentary Private Secretary to the Minister of Agriculture, 1945-51, and Shadow Minister of Agriculture prior to 1964, and

[1] (London: Jonathan Cape, 1953.)
[2] See Chapter 9.

Mr Edward Short, who fulfilled what must be the dream of many headmasters in becoming Secretary of State for Education and Science. Mr Frank Cousins had served on several advisory bodies in the technology field before becoming Minister of Technology and Mr James Callaghan's sympathy for the police, which was evident as Home Secretary, had no doubt been nurtured in his role as consultant to the Police Federation between 1955 and 1964. If one were to scrape further for evidence of special knowledge it would only be to point out that the Secretaries of State for Scotland and Wales were, after all, Scottish and Welsh.

The same overall picture emerges if we examine appointments to the Conservative Cabinet in office since June 1970. Two Ministers were reappointed to departments where they had previous experience. Sir Alec Douglas-Home, Foreign and Commonwealth Secretary 1970-, had been Commonwealth Secretary 1955-60 and Foreign Secretary 1960-3. Lord Carrington, apart from having begun his career as an army officer, had been a junior Minister at Defence 1954-6 and First Lord of the Admiralty 1959-63 before returning as Minister of Defence in 1970. Several Ministers had relevant occupational backgrounds. Mr James Prior, Minister of Agriculture 1970-2, was a farmer and land agent who had taken a First Class degree in estate management at Cambridge. Mr John Davies, former Secretary of State for Trade and Industry, was a businessman and a former chairman of the Confederation of British Industry and Quintin Hogg, the Lord Chancellor, was a barrister. Finally, some Conservative Ministers had made considerable efforts to prepare themselves for office while in Opposition. Mr Robert Carr had been in charge of the party policy group which had produced the industrial relations proposals contained in the publication 'Fair Deal at Work', which formed the basis of Carr's Industrial Relations Act, 1971 and Mr Iain Macleod, as Shadow Chancellor of the Exchequer, although he certainly would not have claimed to be an economist, had initiated a good deal of work on tax reforms which was to bear fruit in the 1971 budget. Thus, at most, eight of the nineteen Ministers who have served in the Conservative Cabinet since June 1970 could lay claim to some degree of special knowledge or preparation for the offices to which they were appointed.

A point arising from this analysis which merits emphasis is that in the case of very few Ministers is there any evidence of what management textbooks call 'planned career development'. It would, after all, be possible for a Prime Minister, or successive Prime Ministers, to adopt a personnel policy which involved grooming potential Chancellors of the Exchequer by having them serve as junior Ministers in economic departments, grooming future social service Cabinet Ministers by putting them in social service departments and so on. Just how rarely this is done may be gauged from the fact that in only twelve[1] out of the ninety-three cabinet appointments made between October 1964 and April 1971 was a Minister appointed who had previous experience (including experience in junior office) in the same department or in a department in the same general policy area. This is hardly a greater number than might have occurred by chance and slight evidence of Prime Ministerial forethought.

Random promotion, at least in regard to the development of special knowledge, has not always been a feature of British government. Nineteenth-century Ministers were not infrequently reappointed to offices they had previously held and a few, indeed, must have come to expect that if their party were returned to office they would be returned to their old departments. Lord Palmerston, for example, was appointed Foreign Secretary on three separate occasions and held that office for fifteen years in all. Lesser offices were also sometimes held by the same individual in more than one government. Lord John Manners, Disraeli's friend from the Young England Party, was First Commissioner of Works in 1852, 1858-9 and 1868-72. He then went on to become Postmaster-General 1874-80 and 1885-6.

The infrequency with which Ministers in recent times have been reappointed to the same department would be less remarkable if posts were initially held for long periods. It is, of course, possible for sensible men to disagree about the ideal period for which a Minister should remain in post. Clearly the longer his tenure the more likely a Minister is to become more of a specialist, less of a

[1] The appointments were Mr G. Thomas as Secretary of State for Wales 1968, previously Minister of State 1966-7; Mr A. Crosland as President of the Board of Trade 1967-9, previously Minister of State, Department of Economic Affairs 1964-5; Mr D. Jay as President of the Board of Trade 1964-6, previously Economic and Financial Secretary, Treasury 1947-51; Mr A. Greenwood, Minister for Overseas Development 1965-6, previously Colonial Secretary 1964-5; Mr P. Gordon Walker, Foreign Secretary 1964-5, previously Commonwealth Secretary 1950-1; Mr P. Shore, Minister of Economic Affairs 1967-9, previously Under-Secretary 1967; Sir A. Douglas-Home, Foreign Secretary 1970, previously Foreign Secretary 1960-3; Lord Carrington, Minister of Defence 1970, previously First Lord of the Admiralty 1959-63. Two Ministers twice received appointments for which they had previous relevant ministerial experience. Mr George Thomson was Chancellor of the Duchy of Lancaster in charge of EEC negotiations 1968-70 and Secretary of State for Commonwealth Relations 1967-8, having previously been Minister of State, Foreign Office 1964-6 and 1967. Mr A. Bottomley was Secretary of State for Commonwealth Relations 1964-6 and Minister for Overseas Development 1966-7, having previously been Under-Secretary at the Dominions Office.

layman in the subjects dealt with by his department. Hence those who favoured ministerial specialisation favour long tenure. Upholders of the intelligent laymen tradition, on the other hand, believe that a long-serving Minister is almost a contradiction in terms:

> If he stays too long, a Minister becomes the creature of the department. He ceases to be a Minister at all and becomes a sort of second Permanent Secretary. When I found myself explaining the technicalities of a tariff agreement to a young civil servant I knew I had been there [the Board of Trade] too long.

Ministers who adopted this viewpoint believed that 'three years is the maximum length of time you should spend in one department – and about the optimum, too'.

When we examine the evidence on ministerial tenure an extraordinary picture emerges. Under Mr Wilson (1964–70) the typical (median) Cabinet Minister was in post for only nineteen months. If we exclude non-departmental Ministers on the grounds that their remit is usually too wide to permit the development of specialist knowledge, the picture is not much altered. The median departmental Minister, in fact, lasted twenty-one months. Only five Ministers – Mr Wilson himself, Mr Healey the Defence Secretary, the Lord Chancellor, Lord Gardiner, the Secretary of State for Scotland, Mr William Ross, and the Chief Secretary of the Treasury, Mr Jack Diamond – remained in the same job throughout the Government's period in office and there were thirty occasions on which a Cabinet post changed hands after the Minister had been in office less than eighteen months. Mr Wilson's Ministers were required to be more versatile than even the most fervent upholder of the intelligent layman tradition could reasonably expect.

Mr Wilson was the most addictive reshuffler of the ministerial pack to date but his practice only represented the continuation of a striking post-war trend, as Table 4.1 below illustrates.

Table 4.1 compares ministerial tenure in Cabinets since the first Reform Act of 1832. Coalition and wartime Cabinets are excluded as are Cabinets in which ministerial tenure was unavoidably short due to the fact that the Government lost office after less than three years. The significant finding here is that Ministers in the three post-war Governments served shorter periods in office before being reshuffled than in any of the other Governments listed, since the Grey-Melbourne Government, 1830-4. Grey and Melbourne changed their Ministers with almost exactly the same frequency as Conservative Prime Ministers in the 1951-64 period.

Table 4.1 *Ministerial Tenure in Cabinets since 1830*[a][b]

Cabinets	Prime Ministers	Median tenure of all Ministers (months)	Median tenure of departmental Ministers[c] (months)
Whig 1830-4	Grey – Melbourne	28 (25)[d]	28 (17)[d]
Whig 1835-41	Melbourne	49 (22)	46 (15)
Conservative 1841-6	Peel	32 (25)	32 (16)
Whig 1846-52	Russell	44 (25)	42 (18)
Whig 1859-66	Palmerston – Russell	33 (29)	26 (22)
Liberal 1868-74	Gladstone	35 (29)	35 (22)
Conservative 1874-80	Disraeli	48 (21)	48 (16)
Liberal 1880-5	Gladstone	31 (27)	31 (18)
Conservative 1885-92	Salisbury	64 (28)	57 (23)
Conservative 1895-1905	Salisbury –Balfour	42 (49)	52 (39)
Liberal 1905-15	Campbell – Bannerman – Asquith	29 (67)	29 (48)
Conservative 1924-9	Baldwin	50 (28)	56 (22)
Labour 1945-51	Attlee	20 (51)	24 (37)
Conservative 1951-64	Churchill – Eden – Macmillan – Home	28 (115)	28 (81)
Labour 1964-70	Wilson	19 (71)	21 (51)

[a] Wartime and coalition Cabinets are excluded as are Cabinets which lost office after less than three years.

[b] All figures are in months and are calculated from E. L. Woodward, *The Age of Reform* (Oxford: Clarendon Press, 1962), pp. 632-43; R. C. K. Ensor, *England 1870-1914* (Oxford: Clarendon Press, 1952), pp. 606-14; D. E. Butler and J. Freeman, *British Political Facts 1900-68* (London: Macmillan, 1969) pp. 1-50.

[c] This column excludes non-departmental Ministers: the Prime Minister, Lord President of the Council, Lord Privy Seal, Paymaster-General, Chancellor of the Duchy of Lancaster and Ministers without Portfolio.

[d] Figures in brackets indicate the number of cabinet appointments made during a Government's period in office.

Interestingly, Table 4.1 suggests that some Prime Ministers have taken the view that, barring accidents, a Minister should serve out an electoral term. Only thirteen changes were made in Salisbury's Cabinet between 1886 and 1892 and in his third Cabinet no changes were made between 1895 and 1900. Stanley Baldwin made only twenty-two appointments to eighteen departmental posts in his 1924-9 Government. The majority of Baldwin's departmental

Ministers in fact served throughout the Government's period in office which lasted fifty-six months. Disraeli appears to have been a third Prime Minister who believed that he should find the right men for the jobs and then leave them to it; the median departmental Minister in his 1874-80 Government lasted exactly four years. In short, not all Prime Ministers in the past were great reshufflers and, as Anthony King has shown, ministerial tenure in Britain is now considerably shorter than in other major Western countries.[1] France in the period of the Fourth Republic had slightly higher ministerial turnover but in the United States, West Germany and France under the Fifth Republic turnover was less rapid.

How is the British pattern to be explained? Several somewhat pausible hypotheses may be discounted. First, Prime Ministers are not vigilantes on the look-out for the slightest sign of weakness or incompetence and ready to sack any Ministers they suspect of these faults. Ministers are not sacked: they are reassigned. The same datum makes us reject a second hypothesis, namely that the pressures of modern government are such that after holding down a gruelling departmental job for a few years Ministers have to be rested. In practice, very few Ministers are deliberately given a sojourn on the backbenches or a dignified but undemanding non-departmental post in order to 'recharge their batteries', as the phrase is. A return to the backbenches would be too demeaning and non-departmental posts are nowadays often used for Ministers on short term special assignments.[2]

Reshuffles sometimes seem to be carried out for electoral reasons. Prime Ministers are subject to the temptation of believing that their Government is losing popularity because Ministers are thought to be tired or stale. One more reshuffle might just enable the Government to regain an image of freshness and efficiency. This is what Nigel Birch MP accused Mr Harold Macmillan of trying to do in July 1962 when 'he laid down his friends for his life'.[3] Other reasons for reshuffles include illness and death, the resignation of Ministers over policy differences, the need to change a Minister who has fallen out with his department's interest group clientele and a reorganisa-

---

[1] Anthony King, 'Britain's Ministerial Turnover', *New Society* (18 August 1966).

[2] Recent examples include Lord Shackleton, Paymaster-General 1968-70, who was in charge of Civil Service reform and Mr George Thomson (under Labour) and Mr Geoffrey Rippon and Mr John Davies (under the Conservatives) who as Chancellors of the Duchy of Lancaster have been concerned with Common Market affairs.

[3] In 1962, in fact, Mr Macmillan not only reshuffled his government, but carried out the only post-war mass sacking of Ministers. Seven Cabinet Ministers were dismissed from office.

tion of departments in Whitehall.[1] It is also a point of some significance that the number of Ministers moved in a reshuffle is increased by the existence of a rigid though only partly formalised (in terms of ministerial salaries)[2] hierarchy of departments. A Prime Minister will not normally fill a vacancy for, say, Foreign Secretary or Chancellor of the Exchequer by vertical promotion of a junior Minister. Instead he will appoint a Minister of equal rank, say the Home Secretary, or a Minister who is one rank lower, say the Secretary of State for Employment, or for the Social Services. Suppose the Secretary for Employment is chosen; he also has to be replaced by a Minister of equal rank or one rank lower, say the Minister of Transport. So the process goes on with dislocation all the way down the hierarchy. Abstractly, a Prime Minister could minimise this dislocation by ignoring the hierarchy but when Attlee tried this in 1950 and vertically promoted the Minister for Economic Affairs, Hugh Gaitskell, to be Chancellor of the Exchequer resignations followed and splits in the party opened wider.

Both rapid turnover in office and lack of prior specialist knowledge militate against Ministers having as thorough a grasp as they might of the policy problems and options confronting them. Of course, the knowledge of a wide range of subjects which an intelligent politician acquires through half a lifetime's immersion in the politics of Westminster and Whitehall is not to be discounted. But it can hardly be doubted that many decisions, especially in the more technical departments, cannot be taken wisely without somebody concerned having a specialist's understanding of the options involved. If the Minister is not that somebody then there is a risk that decisions will, for all practical purposes, be taken by his advisers with the Minister merely acting as a rubber stamp, or tinkering with the details. Alternatively, if the Minister exerts his authority, explores the options and decides contrary to the views of his advisers, his decisions are likely to be unwise.

A second danger, arising more particularly from high ministerial turnover, is that a Minister may be tempted to try to make a

---

[1] Mr Wilson's reshuffles in both 1968 and 1969 resulted in part from departmental reorganisations. In 1968 the Foreign Office absorbed the Commonwealth Office and the Department of Health and Social Security was created out of the Ministries of Health and Pensions and National Insurance. In 1969 the Ministry of Technology absorbed a large part of the Board of Trade and the Minister assumed overall responsibility for Power and a new Secretary of State for Local Government and Regional Planning was in overall charge of Housing and Transport.

[2] Ministerial salaries are as follows: Prime Minister £14,000, Lord Chancellor £14,500, most full Ministers £8,500, Ministers of State £7,625 or £5,625 and Parliamentary Secretaries £3,750.

splash and build up a great reputation in his early days in office. He knows he will probably not be in the same post long and may therefore not be personally held responsible for the consequences of his policies. A dramatic announcement on an issue of current public concern, or a promise to introduce a big bill, or an instant recipe for making some tenet of Conservative or Labour philosophy a living reality may be real temptations. Of course, his civil servants will try to restrain the Minister if they fear the consequences of his actions and it would be wrong to paint a picture of politicians concerned only with the advancement of their own careers. Nevertheless, as Anthony King has suggested, the discipline of knowing one has to live with the consequences of one's decisions is a valuable constraint.[1]

Thus the present pattern of recruitment entails clear risks in so far as it does not produce Ministers with a high degree of substantive knowledge of the problems they are dealing with and does not necessarily maximise Ministers' personal concern for the consequences of their policies. It is at least arguable that the demands of ministerial office and the skills of Ministers are getting more and more out of step. The job increasingly requires specialised knowledge but Ministers have less and less opportunity to acquire such knowledge through learning 'on the job'. As Anthony Crosland, who held his cabinet posts for two years and seven months, two years and one month and eight months respectively, told Maurice Kogan: 'I reckon it takes you six months to get your head properly above water, a year to get the general drift of most of the field, and two years really to master the whole of the department.'[2]

THE EXECUTIVE, DECISION-MAKING EXPERIENCE OF MINISTERS

We saw in Chapter 2 that government departments are large complex organisations and that Ministers are obliged to get through an enormous amount of paper work and take a wide range of decisions requiring the exercise of political, value and managerial judgement. It was therefore understandable, though surprising, that almost one-third of the politicians and civil servants interviewed expressed the heterodox, untraditional view that a Minister is better qualified for office if he has prior experience in an executive, decision-making position in a large organisation. Put more colloquially they believe that 'a man who has never in his life run anything is not likely to make a terribly good job of running a department of state'.

[1] Anthony King, 'Who Cares About Policy?', *Spectator* (10 January 1970).
[2] A. Crosland, E. Boyle and M. Kogan, *The Politics of Education* (Harmondsworth: Penguin, 1971), p. 155.

Prima facie, this is not an implausible belief. Broadly, there are two ways in which a Minister may acquire executive experience. First, he may hold an executive position, in say, a business or a trade union before going into politics, or in conjunction with his political career. Second, he may and, indeed, is likely to spend several years as a junior Minister before attaining cabinet status. Executive experience acquired prior to entering politics could be exceptionally valuable to a Minister. It could give him a basis of comparison for evaluating the performance and methods of government departments. It could also give him a sound knowledge of how large organisations operate at the working level from which most policy recommendations initially emanate and at which the practical problems of implementation have to be faced. Few Ministers, however, have these advantages. It has never been easy in Britain for a man to rise far up another hierarchy before turning successfully to politics. The need to serve a long parliamentary apprenticeship before attaining high office militates against such dual careers.

Wartime provides the exceptions which prove the rule. In World War I Field-marshal Kitchener and newspaper magnate Beaverbrook were brought into the Government and in World War II Beaverbrook again, a civil servant, Sir John Anderson, a trade union leader, Ernest Bevin, and two businessmen, Lords Woolton and Chandos, were appointed to the Cabinet. Their inclusion was justified in terms of a need to bring into Whitehall men with executive experience and drive at a time when the Government was taking wide responsibility for supervising industry and in some areas was directly involved in production tasks. The point to be made here, however, is that it was only feasible to have so many Ministers who lacked parliamentary *savoir-faire* because in wartime patriotism muted opposition and the formal Opposition consisted only of party rumps.[1]

Peacetime exceptions to the general rule that Ministers are men who have spent most of their adult lives in politics are rare. One thinks of the Duke of Wellington, ageing and deaf, Disraeli's great reforming Home Secretary, R. A. Cross, Sir Percy Mills who was in Mr Macmillan's Cabinet from 1957 to 1962 and, more recently, the trade union leader, Mr Frank Cousins, and the businessman and employers' leader, Mr John Davies. In the early 1960s the inclusion of men like Sir Keith Joseph and Mr Ernest Marples in the Cabinet led to talk of a new breed of 'manager Ministers' but the breed did

---

[1] This point was made repeatedly in the interviews with contemporary Ministers. It is certainly part of the lore of Westminster today that the wartime imported Ministers only avoided parliamentary slaughter because Opposition was suspended for the duration.

not prove particularly fertile. An examination of the careers of members of the most recent Labour and Conservative Cabinets dispels any impression that executive experience is coming to be regarded as an essential qualification for office.

The Labour Cabinet which demitted office in June 1970 had twenty-one members. Three Ministers had worked as wartime civil servants: Mr Wilson as Director of Economics and Statistics in the Ministry of Fuel and Power, Mr Crossman as Assistant Chief of Psychological Warfare at SHAEF and Mrs Castle as an official in the Ministry of Food. Mr Jenkins was a former Director of Financial Operations, John Lewis Partnership and the fact that Mr Diamond headed his own firm of chartered accountants has already been mentioned. It is only by stretching the phrase that it is possible to speak of other Ministers as having an executive background. Mr Shore had been head of the small Labour Party Research Department, Mr Short the Secretary for Education and Science was an ex-headmaster and several Ministers had served as army officers in World War II.

Conservative Cabinets are popularly believed to include more men with experience of 'running things' than Labour Cabinets and some Conservative supporters allege that this is why they run the country better.[1] The difference between the parties is easy to exaggerate, however. As in the Labour Cabinet three Ministers who served in the post 1970 Conservative Cabinet were formerly civil servants. Mr Heath was a junior official in the Administrative Class, 1947-50, and Mr Gordon Campbell and Earl Jellicoe (resigned 1973) were both formerly in the Diplomatic Service. In contrast to the Labour Cabinet, however, several Ministers have considerable business experience. Sir Keith Joseph was Chairman of Bovis Ltd and Mr Robert Carr and Mr Peter Walker both headed their own businesses. A number of other Ministers, prior to their appointment in 1970, had held directorships and been chairmen of boards but their posts were non-executive and they had been appointed as a result of, rather than prior to, establishing themselves as prominent politicians.

Neither party can claim that its leaders, collectively, have much executive experience outside Government. It can be argued, however, that the principal way in which future Cabinet Ministers acquire such experience is through 'on the job' learning in junior office. In the following pages we ask how long a period is typically spent in junior office and attempt to assess the value of the ex-

[1] For a full discussion of categories of so-called deferential voters see R. T. McKenzie and A. Silver, *Angels in Marble* (London: Heinemann, 1965); E. Nordlinger, *The Working-Class Tories* (London: MacGibbon and Kee, 1967).

perience as preparation for cabinet office. First, it may be noted that in British government, in contrast to most European governments, there are a large number of posts to be filled by Ministers below cabinet rank. At present there are, in fact, three levels below the Cabinet. There are full Ministers not in the Cabinet, some of whom like the Minister for Posts and Telecommunications and the Minister of Public Buildings and Works are heads of departments. Others, like the Ministers of Defence for Equipment and Administration, are subordinate Ministers in a department headed by a Cabinet Minister. Next are Ministers of State, who are found in all but the smallest departments and whose title was originally coined because, it was said, foreign governments objected to dealing with men with so humble a designation as Parliamentary Secretary.[1] Parliamentary Secretaries, then, of whom there is one or more in each department, form the lowest rank of Ministers.[2] Originally, as the title implies, they were only expected to help Ministers with their parliamentary duties (reply to MPs letters etc.).

The number of sub-Cabinet appointments has been growing over the years. Throughout the nineteenth century it rarely exceeded twenty,[3] but grew rapidly in the twentieth century, particularly after World War II. The high point was reached in 1964-5, in Mr Wilson's premiership, when the total of a hundred Ministers was reached, seventy-eight of whom were outside the Cabinet.[4] The largest departments had as many as six Ministers. Thus the Ministry of Technology by 1970 had two Ministers of State and three Parliamentary Secretaries. Other departments with a large complement of Ministers included the Ministry of Defence with six and the Scottish Office with five. At the other end of the scale the Welsh Office had only one Minister of State and one Parliamentary Secretary.

In view of the increased number of jobs and ranks it is a little surprising to find that contemporary Cabinet Ministers are not

[1] For an analysis of the reasons for creating the office of Minister of State see D. N. Chester, 'Double Banking and Deputy Ministers', *New Society* (11 June 1964).

[2] Parliamentary Private Secretaries help Ministers with their parliamentary relations. They are paid only an MP's salary, however, and are not members of the Ministry.

[3] In comparing nineteenth- and twentieth-century Ministries some fairly arbitrary decisions have to be made about which offices to include. Irish and Scottish law officers, members of Her Majesty's Household and Junior Lords of the Treasury and the Admiralty are excluded from the figure given here.

[4] In the later years of Mr Wilscn's Government and in Mr Heath's Government the number of Ministers declined. There were, in fact, only seventy-eight members of Mr Heath's Government appointed in June 1970. The decline is, in large part, due to the creation of the 'giant' unitary departments. See Chapter 7.

spending any longer in offices below Cabinet rank than their predecessors. F. M. G. Willson found that the average Cabinet Minister
between 1868 and 1958 had spent three and a half years in subordinate
posts with no significant increase over the period as a whole.[1] The
figures given in Table 4.2 relate to the 'apprenticeship' of Ministers
in the Conservative and Labour Cabinets of October 1964 and June
1970. The Cabinets in office at these times were selected as providing
examples of an unusually experienced and inexperienced Ministry
together with two more normal ones.

Table 4.2. *Experience of Cabinet Ministers 1964 and 1970 in*
Sub-Cabinet Office

Cabinet	Number in Cabinet	Period in junior office of median Minister (*months*)
Conservative October 1964	23	53
Labour October 1964	23	19
Labour June 1970	21	27
Conservative June 1970	18	41.5

[a] All figures are in months and are calculated from Butler and
Freeman, *British Political Facts*, 1900-68, pp. 1-50.

The Conservatives in October 1964 had been in office for thirteen
years and all members of the Cabinet, except Mr R. A. Butler and
Mr Peter Thorneycroft, had had to work their way up the hierarchy
since 1951. Not many Ministers voluntarily demit office and progress
is slow for the ambitious politician who belongs to a party which
enjoys a long period in office. If, on the other hand, a party is
doing badly at the polls this means that some ex-Ministers and some
potential Ministers are losing their parliamentary seats. Also a
few MPs decide that life in Opposition is tedious and leave politics
for other careers.[2] The ambitious politician, always provided that
he has a safe seat, can therefore make rapid strides up his party's
hierarchy and, when it is finally re-elected, find himself in the
Cabinet without ever having held junior office. This occurred to

[1] Willson, *Political Studies*, 7:3 (1959), pp. 222-32.
[2] During Labour's period in Opposition, 1951-64, Mr Alfred Robens, a former
Minister of Labour, was the most prominent politician who, without losing his
seat, gave up his political career. He became Chairman of the National Coal
Board. Since 1970 Mr Richard Marsh, former Minister of Transport, has
accepted the post of Chairman of British Railways. After the Conservatives lost
the general election of 1964 several ex-Ministers who were young enough to
hope for future office accepted life peerages and ceased to be active in politics.

ten Labour Ministers in the exceptionally inexperienced Cabinet formed in October 1964. The two 1970 Cabinets reflect a more normal range of experience (cf. F. M. G. Willson's figures) and indicate that politicians are usually judged to have cabinet potential, or to lack it, after a relatively short period in junior office. Deviations from this pattern are not all that rare but, generally, a politician who remains in office for more than five years without reaching the Cabinet has missed the boat.

How valuable to a future Cabinet Minister is time spent in junior office? This is not a question to which a snap answer can be given. Junior office appears better preparation for some roles than for others. Experience is obtained in defending one's department in Parliament and before party colleagues. Junior Ministers also attend cabinet committees, although, if the committee is one which a Cabinet Minister would normally attend, they are confined to speaking to their departmental brief, which only covers matters of direct interest to the department. Further, they make their share of visits, inspections and speeches. They see deputations and represent their Minister at social functions. Junior office is thus good training for the performance of the cabinet, parliamentary, party and public relations roles of a Cabinet Minister. The harder question is whether it provides adequate experience of decision making and a sufficient insight into how large organisations in general, and Whitehall departments in particular, operate.

Ministers below Cabinet rank report highly variable experiences. A Minister of State may be given *de facto* responsibility for the preparation and passage of a quite important bill, or for managing a large segment of departmental business. Thus, Mr Edmund Dell, Minister of State at the Board of Trade 1968-9, was said to have been largely responsible for the Industrial Expansion Act,[1] and Mr Gerry Fowler, a Minister of State at the Department of Education and Science 1969-70, apparently dealt with much of the business relating to higher education. Subordinate Ministers who were charged with major tasks in Mr Heath's post 1970 Conservative Government include the late Richard Sharples, who had a rough passage steering the 1971 Immigration Act through the House of Commons, and Mr Christopher Chataway who, as Minister for Industrial Development subordinate to the Secretary of State at the Department of Trade and Industry, appears to have been given

---

[1] The Act (1968) made additional funds available to industry for new plant, for research and development and, generally, for attempts to improve efficiency and productivity. For these purposes the powers of the National Research Development Corporation and the Industrial Reorganisation Corporation were extended.

responsibility for the Industry Act 1972.[1] Less frequently, a Parliamentary Secretary may be invested with real authority. Thus one Minister who had formerly been Parliamentary Secretary in the Dominions Office reported that his Secretary of State was an elderly man who preferred to concentrate on cabinet matters and 'two days after my appointment told me he was looking for someone to run the department'. Another Parliamentary Secretary who was concerned at the Home Office with immigration cases, also felt his experience was worthwhile. Some cases were politically controversial, 'intensely human problems' were involved and he was permitted considerable discretion in applying the law. These two Parliamentary Secretaries were exceptionally fortunate. Equally common were expressions of frustration with the business of 'processing routine cases', or 'translating civil servants' letters into ordinary English'. One Parliamentary Secretary even said that he did not feel that he was even in politics any longer because he had so much administrative routine to handle that 'I can hardly get down to the House to see my friends.'

The variability in the experiences of sub-Cabinet Ministers is to be explained by a large number of factors. The practice of assigning them specific areas of the department's work rather than reserving them for *ad hoc* duties tends to increase their influence. So also does the pressure on ministerial time produced by the growth of government business. Indeed, in some departments like the Scottish Office, where the burden on Ministers has long been particularly heavy, there is a tradition that junior Ministers exercise a fair degree of *de facto* autonomy. The Scottish Office, in fact, deals with a range of subjects covered by five equivalent English departments and, since 1962, a Minister of State has been responsible for economic development questions, with individual Ministers of State, or Parliamentary Secretaries, respectively covering education, home affairs and health, and agriculture and fisheries. Pulling against these decentralising tendencies, on the other hand, is the continued insistence of Parliament that senior Ministers answer for all matters dealt with by their departments. Thus, if a serious controversy, or at any rate a parliamentary storm arises, there is a clear expectation that the senior Minister will personally appear to defend his department and not send a lesser figure in his stead. Junior Ministers' lack of formal authority is symbolised by the fact that in answering all Parliamentary Questions they speak as if a senior Minister were responsible. A junior Minister does not say, 'I decided . . .' or

[1] On Mr Sharples's difficulties with the Immigration Act 1971 see *Parliamentary Debates* (Commons), vol. 819, pp. 400ff. (1970-1). On the Industry Act 1972 see ibid., vol. 837, pp. 1085ff. (1971-2).

'I believe that . . .'; instead he says 'My Rt Hon. Friend decided . . .' and 'My Rt Hon. Friend believes that . . .'. Clearly the knowledge that their reputation in Parliament will suffer if things go sour is one factor influencing senior Ministers not to delegate to their juniors. The pressure in this direction must inevitably be greater in departments like the Home Office which are particularly liable to political storms.

A second pressure on senior Ministers not to delegate comes from civil servants. Civil servants naturally prefer to deal with their political master. It is no use to them 'getting the junior Minister's mind' on an issue only to have a Cabinet Minister overrule him. Questions of personal status may also be involved. Very senior civil servants, it is said, sometimes regard junior Ministers as rather small fry. There are stories of former Permanent Secretaries refusing to make themselves available to see a junior Minister unless specifically instructed by the senior Minister, and, probably, no Permanent Secretary would accept being overruled on an issue by a junior Minister without feeling free to take it up with the senior Minister.[1] Deputy- and Under-Secretaries may also tend to look down on junior Ministers and to consider that informally they outrank them.

Last, apart from Civil Service pressure and awareness of his own answerability to Parliament, a senior Minister may hesitate to delegate extensively because he has reservations about the competence of his junior Ministers. Recent Governments have contained from seventy to just over a hundred Ministers. Even if appointments were made solely on the basis of a Prime Minister's assessment of MPs abilities, one might still have doubts about the ability of the man who filled the seventieth or hundredth post. However, as has already been pointed out, considerations of party management (the need to balance left and right wings and so forth) make for some surprising inclusions. Able men also have to be excluded, or in some cases, exclude themselves. Some MPs refuse to give up lucrative outside jobs in order to start on the bottom ministerial rung at £3,750 a year. Others are too old. A fair number are too new in the sense that, having just been elected to Parliament, they have not served a backbench apprenticeship. A few are too deviant in their personal predilections or too extreme politically to be considered. In all, Professor Richard Rose has calculated that these restrictions probably mean that over half its MPs are likely to be

[1] See R. S. Milne, 'The Junior Minister', *Journal of Politics*, 12, 3 (1950), pp. 437-50. The relative status of Permanent Secretaries and Junior Ministers is indicated by the fact that a Junior Minister would normally come to the Permanent Secretary's office for a meeting instead of vice versa – unless the Minister were a Privy Councillor!

ineligible for office when a party enters Government.[1] Given that the total complement is likely to be less than 350 and that 70-100 Ministers are required, this means that between a half and two-thirds of those not obviously ineligible must be in harness at any one time. Some observers see no cause for anxiety in this situation. A former Chief Whip who advised his Prime Minister on junior appointments expressed the view that:

'Basically any MP ought to be able to do the job . . . . You have to keep the party happy. We got most Members who wanted to be Ministers in at some stage. Sometimes you would put someone in because there was feeling that he'd been hard done by in previous reshuffles. Geographical balance counts too . . . you try to put someone in from Lancashire. When it is all done you have still kept a few good men out and put a few bad ones in.'

Fair enough in patronage terms, but the other side of the coin is that if a senior Minister does not feel, at least initially, that he can delegate decisions of importance to a junior Minister he may have some justification. A further point is that a senior Minister has little influence over the appointment of his junior colleagues. Apparently it is quite usual for a Prime Minister to telephone and say 'I'm thinking of sending you so and so', and if the senior Minister objects strongly he may succeed in exercising a veto. However, the Prime Minister will then simply propose the next man on his list and there is no guarantee in the end that senior and junior Ministers will be *en rapport* either personally or politically.

In sum, there are powerful pressures against the delegation of extensive authority to junior Ministers and a risk that those who eventually reach cabinet office, roughly one in three, lack significant executive experience. Of course, the Cabinet as a whole is not likely to be short of executive experience because there are usually some Ministers who have headed several departments and been in high office for years. However, the point remains that when first appointed to the Cabinet many Ministers are in the position of having never before 'run anything' and are presumably expected in middle age to demonstrate abilities and aptitudes which they have previously had no chance to develop.

CONCLUSION

One point regarding ministerial recruitment is certain; no Cabinet

[1] R. Rose, 'The Making of Cabinet Ministers', *British Journal of Political Science*, I, 4 (Oct. 1971), pp. 393-414.

could be made up of men who possessed all the qualifications which a critical commentator might think their jobs demanded. It is hard to see how Ministers could be at the same time past masters of the politician's art, specialists in the policy areas they are concerned with and experienced organisation men and decision makers. The crucial question posed in the concluding chapters of this study concerns the gains and losses to British government from having intelligent laymen/parliamentary politicians in office, rather than specialists or experienced executives. Here we simply ask which of their self-prescribed roles Ministers appear personally well or ill equipped to perform and leave out of account questions about who else in government may substitute for, or improve on the performance of Ministers.

First, let us make the working assumption that the politicians and civil servants interviewed were right in their assessment of the skills required to perform particular roles. If they were, it would appear that British Ministers are well equipped to act as policy selectors, Minimalists, or Ambassador Ministers. As policy selectors they possess, in the words of the classic Bagehot formula, 'sufficient intelligence, quite enough various knowledge, quite enough miscellaneous experience, to represent general sense in opposition to bureaucratic sense'. The only doubt here concerns their 'miscellaneous experience', since most contemporary Ministers are full-time politicians for most of their careers rather than, as in Bagehot's day, combining politics with outside activities. As Minimalists their experience in Parliament and as junior Ministers stands them in good stead. They have ample opportunity to learn what kinds of issues Parliament seizes on and how to fend for themselves at the despatch box. After many years of inter- and intra-party warfare they should also know which policies their party regards as sacrosanct and which as negotiable. In selling departmental decisions to the party they should generally be able to evoke the right symbols and battle cries and build support out of the coalition of interests the party represents. As for Ambassador Ministers, they have been accustomed since the time they entered Parliament to dealing with all kinds of sectional groups as well as with members of the ordinary public. They also have had the opportunity to observe how favourable – and unfavourable – publicity is obtained.

It is really in their capacity to act as policy initiators or as Executive Ministers that doubts arise about British Ministers. One suspects that, at least in the more 'technical' departments, Ministers who report that they only need a layman's understanding of issues, 'because the technical details have been taken out before they reach my level', may be living in a fool's paradise. In some cases it appears that their belief that they are on top of their job is only possible because the job itself has been doctored. Policy papers and briefs are written in terms that laymen can comprehend, even if it means that options are obscured, or only stated in tabloid form. Certainly the words of the former Permanent Secretary of one 'technical' department are hard to dismiss: 'In effect, it was always just a question of getting my Ministers to take on board policies we had in hand, anyway. Of the six Ministers I worked with closely it would be hard to say that any of them made even a minor contribution to policy.'[1]

A British Minister who lacks previous experience of decision making in a large organisation may also be under-qualified to perform some of the roles Executive Ministers attach importance to. While he may be successful in motivating officials and maintaining departmental morale, problems associated with the division of responsibilities in his department, the introduction of new decision-making techniques or a structural reorganisation, are not likely to be his *metier*. Nor, in more general terms, may he be sensitive to the capabilities and limitations of a large, complex organisation and to what the organisation expects from him as its head.

Inevitably, British Ministers are better equipped to perform some roles than others. The functioning of government and the formulation and execution of policy do not, however, depend on the unaided ability and skills of Ministers. An elaborate advisory structure exists to assist them in the performance of their duties and, to a degree, to compensate for any deficiencies they may possess. In the next chapter we discuss some key aspects of relations between Ministers and their advisers.

[1] Interview with the author.

Chapter 5

Ministers and their Departments   I
The Range and Quality of Advice

It is obvious that the quality of advice and assistance available to Ministers must greatly affect their performance in office and their ability to act in accordance with their role conceptions. It may be, as Machiavelli wrote, 'a general and infallible rule that the prince who has no wisdom of his own can never be well advised',[1] but presumably even the wisest 'prince' cannot check all the assumptions and data on which advice is based and so runs the risk of gross error through no fault of his own. For Ministers the provision of good advice is partly a function of the organisation of Whitehall departments. In this chapter we shall discuss a number of organisational questions to which the Civil Service has recently given a great deal of attention and to which new answers are gradually being evolved:

How can the need to despatch an enormous amount of business, which is most easily secured with a hierarchical organisational structure, be reconciled with the need to preserve effective ministerial choice, which would suggest a collegiate structure in which numerous advisers have access to the Minister?

What are the most appropriate management procedures that departments can adopt to clarify and co-ordinate objectives and to allocate resources to programmes designed to achieve objectives?

What provision is and could be made in government departments for forward thinking and innovation?

Are arrangements for communicating ministerial objectives and 'transmitting the political impulse' in departments satisfactory?

Just as important as these organisational questions, though rather more familiar, are questions about the qualifications appropriate for Ministers' advisers. In the past, administrative class civil servants have prided themselves on being intelligent laymen, amateurs, or 'generalists' rather than 'specialists'. Or, to be more accurate, they specialised not in particular subjects or policy areas but in their knowledge

[1] Nicolò Machiavelli, *The Prince* (London: Routledge and Sons, 1883, 1st pub. 1513), ch. 23.

110

of the government machine and, in C. H. Sisson's well-known phrase, 'in the awareness of ministerial responsibility'.[1] Needless to say, critics have not been wanting to argue that the administrative class is outmoded. The Fulton Committee recommended that the administrative class be abolished and that senior civil servants be referred to as a 'senior policy and management group'. In future all civil servants should be trained as managers and should also specialise in particular policy areas.

There is an enormous literature on the Civil Service and Civil Service reform, so some editorial principle was necessary to keep this review within manageable limits. The chapter is therefore based on Ministers' own criticisms and observations about their advisers. These observations relate mainly to the senior career officials (Under-Secretaries and above) with whom Ministers have most contact, although some points are made about temporary 'outsiders' or 'irregulars' in the Civil Service and about the advisory committees attached to Whitehall departments.

MINISTERIAL OBSERVATIONS ON THE CIVIL SERVICE

Ministers were asked:

Are you generally satisfied with the range and quality of advice available in the department?

If this question was answered rather briefly, a follow-up question asked for comment on the Fulton Report and, in some cases, the reference to the 'range' of advice was made more explicit by asking if the Minister had ever felt that he was not apprised of all feasible policy alternatives, or that it would have been desirable to obtain more advice from non-departmental sources.

Table 5.1   *Overall Satisfaction with Advice*

	Number of Ministers
Civil Service excellent: no criticisms	14
Generally satisfied: favour specific reforms	19
Some major criticisms: lack of expertise, policy options foreclosed etc.	12
Very critical: need for radical changes	5
	50

[1] C. H. Sisson, *The Spirit of British Administration* (London: Fulton and Faber, 2nd edn, 1966), p. 3.

In recent years civil servants have more than ever fulfilled their destiny as national scapegoats. It was therefore noteworthy that customer satisfaction among Ministers was reasonably high. Fourteen out of fifty said civil servants were excellent or 'dedicated' and had no doubt about the genuineness or ability with which they sought to implement ministerial policy objectives. Another nineteen were generally satisfied and made only specific criticisms (see Table 5.2). Only five Ministers (of whom three had held only junior office) echoed some of the more trenchant criticisms of the Service made in recent years. Of these, two said that Ministers were sometimes misled about advice offered by interest groups and outside experts and one that the level of economic thinking in his department was appalling. The remaining two contradicted each other: one saying that officials are extremely weak in the face of interest group pressure and the other that policy suffers because they simply tell outside bodies what they intend to do and consult only on matters of detail.

Table 5.2 categorises the principal criticisms and proposals for reform made by the thirty-six Ministers whose comments on the Service were not entirely favourable.

Table 5.2 *Specific Ministerial Criticisms of the Civil Service (N = 36)*[a]

	Number of Ministers
1. *Range of options presented to Ministers inadequate*	
Options foreclosed by desire for a 'united department view'; Permanent Secretary over-centralises; collegiate structure needed	10
Civil servants too conservative, cautious, lacking in ideas	8
Lack of forward thinking; 'planning units' needed	4
Options foreclosed on inter-departmental official committees	3
	25 (N = 18)[b]
2. *Lack of expertise*	
Outside experts should be brought into the Civil Service	18
Civil servants are not expert enough	7
	25 (N = 20)[b]

3. *Getting the Minister's mind known*
   Problems in communicating ministerial
   objectives; Private Office needs strengthening; more political aides needed   9
                                                            ___
                                                             9
                                                            ___

[a] Fourteen Ministers made no specific criticisms of their advisers
   or departmental organisations.
[b] Figures in brackets indicate the number of Ministers making
   one or more criticisms under each head.

Lack of expertise was a criticism expressed by twenty Ministers, eighteen thought that policy options were foreclosed, or at least felt a wider range of options could be presented and nine experienced some difficulty in communicating their objectives and 'getting their mind known' in the department. These are all criticisms which would most naturally be voiced by Ministers who attach high priority to their policy leadership (policy initiation and selection) roles. In the following pages we shall concentrate on these criticisms and reserve to the end of the chapter points of particular interest to ministerial Minimalists, Executive and Ambassador Ministers.

THE RANGE OF POLICY OPTIONS PRESENTED TO MINISTERS

Precedent and established objectives

The belief that civil servants consciously resist or go slow in the implementation of ministerial objectives is almost certainly false. This belief is particularly widespread in some sections of the Labour Party and is propagated in the party's evidence to the Fulton Committee.[1] It finds little support, however, in the memoirs of Ministers, or in the interviews carried out for the present study. Among post-war Labour Ministers, Lords Attlee and Morrison have paid notably fulsome tributes to the loyalty and hard work put in by officials in carrying through reform programmes, and Mr Harold Wilson is on record as stating that the Civil Service had prepared in advance for a Labour election victory in 1964 and already had in hand proposals to imple-

[1] *The Civil Service* (Fulton Report), V (2), pp. 652-73.

ment commitments made in the party's manifesto.[1] Ministers who imply that officials consciously baulked at implementing their objectives are definitely in a minority. Among these, Barbara Castle writes of the 'atmosphere of ill-concealed hostility' that she found at the Ministry of Transport in 1965 when she moved to introduce an 'integrated transport policy'[2] (see Chapter 9) and Aubrey Jones contents himself with some general remarks:

'I had been a Minister; but what was a Minister? The occupant for a couple of years of a department of State, numerous in its layers of staff, tenacious in its traditions, and massive to move. One scarcely in fact moved it. An apparent shift could be made on the surface for an odd year or so, but the changes were soon shrugged off and the department reverted to its ways'.[3]

If we accept the majority ministerial view that civil servants normally do seek to implement stated ministerial objectives, it does not follow that in doing so they necessarily provide Ministers with a sufficiently wide range of policy options. In so far as options are foreclosed, the basic problem in a Whitehall department, as in any organisation, is likely to be a tendency to build on precedents, to rely on 'official' figures, to consult with the usual advisory committees and interest groups, and propose programmes which have been tried before in circumstances at least superficially similar. The press of business leads a department to rely on its collective memory, on what is sometimes described as its storehouse of wisdom and experience, rather than commission a fresh analysis and consider alternative objectives and programmes. To put the matter more mundanely, old files are dusted off rather than new files opened. Thus, to quote one well documented example, M. J. Barnett has shown how in framing the 1957 Rent Act the Ministry of Housing and Local Government relied on misleading and deficient official figures regarding the existing stock and demand for housing, consulted only its usual interest group clientele (the Association of Municipal Corporations, the Royal Institute of Chartered Surveyors and so forth) and finally produced an Act in which most clauses closely followed precedents in the 1954 Housing Repairs and Rents Act.[4] The Rent Act is notorious in that, instead of increasing

[1] F. Williams, *A Prime Minister Remembers* (Heinemann: London, 1961), p. 91; H. Morrison, *Government and Parliament* (London: OUP, 2nd edn, 1964), p. 320; Wilson, *The Labour Government* (London: Weidenfeld and Nicolson, and Michael Joseph, 1971), pp. 4, 20.

[2] Barbara Castle, 'Mandarin Power', *The Sunday Times*, 10 June 1973.

[3] Aubrey Jones, *The New Inflation* (Harmondsworth; Penguin 1973), p. x.

[4] M. J. Barnett, *The Politics of Legislation* (London: Weidenfeld and Nicolson, 1969), pp. 40-4.

the supply of working class housing for rent by making landlording more profitable, it achieved the opposite effect.[1] In general, however, the tendency of large organisations to foreclose options by a process of selective perception and precedent-bound analysis is well documented.[2] The eight Ministers who complained that civil servants are conservative, cautious, or lacking in ideas were pointing to a tendency which is to some degree inevitable.

THE MINISTER–PERMANENT SECRETARY RELATIONSHIP AND THE DESIRE FOR A 'UNITED DEPARTMENTAL VIEW'

It would be more serious if the way the Civil Service machine works magnified the risk of policy options being foreclosed. As Table 5.2 indicates, ten Ministers believed that the desire to obtain a 'united departmental view' has this effect. Of course, like other individuals Ministers vary in the way they prefer advice to be served up. Some prefer to receive a 'united departmental view'. Thus a Conservative Minister said that 'the essence of advice is that it should be unitary, polished'. Most Ministers, however, claim that, when they are faced with a major decision, they prefer to be presented with a range of options and are more concerned to exercise effective choice than that advice should be 'unitary' and 'polished'. They are therefore concerned about the fact that, before presenting proposals to Ministers, the usual Whitehall procedure is to try to reach agreement within the department and sometimes inter-departmentally as well.

Apart from a general 'dispositon to seek agreement' in the Civil Service, it may be assumed that the task of attempting to fashion a 'united departmental view' normally devolves on the Permanent Secretary. Mr Roy Jenkins has described the procedure employed in 1965 (but then altered) by the Permanent Under-Secretary of the Home Office and the dangers inherent in it:

'All advice to the Secretary of State was submitted in the form of a single co-ordinated minute under the initials of the Permanent Secretary. I admired the speed of comprehension and decisiveness of expression on the part of the Permanent Secretary which made the system possible, but feared that the system effectively removed the point of decision from the Home Secretary. It also produced a certain re-

[1] ibid., ch. 13.
[2] For an interesting discussion of those points with 'political' examples see R. G. S. Brown, *The Administrative Process in Britain* (London: Methuen, 1970), ch. 7. A somewhat contradictory view, indicating that departmental objectives and priorities can be rapidly modified is presented by Sir Edward Boyle in E. Boyle, A. Crosland and M. Kogan, *The Politics of Education* (Harmondsworth: Penguin, 1971), p. 84.

luctance, on the part of officials, to disagree with each other at meetings within the department. Co-ordinated views on paper tended to
produce co-ordinated silence round the table.'[1]

There can be no doubt that until quite recently many Permanent
Secretaries saw fit to centralise advice-giving in their own hands. They
jealously guarded their access to the Minister and exercised the right
to approve all papers submitted to him. Indeed, stories are still current in Whitehall of retired Permanent Secretaries who even rewrote
answers to Parliamentary Questions and it appears that just a few
Permanent Secretaries, described by one frustrated Deputy Secretary
as 'the last of the brontosauri', still prefer to be the main if not the
sole confidant of their Ministers.

It may be that for less able Ministers there are advantages in having
a brontosaurus as Permanent Secretary. If a Minister lacks the capacity to evaluate complicated options, the existence of a dominating
Permanent Secretary may at least prevent a bottleneck and increase
the chance that decisions will be taken and the department's business
despatched. The Permanent Secretary can regulate the flow of papers
across the Minister's desk and see that he is not overburdened.
Through knowing the Minister well he can learn what kinds of
points he will need to have explained and make the necessary
arrangements. As Sir Edward Playfair said, many a Minister wants
to have 'one man at his side, whom he knows thoroughly, whose
reactions he can gauge and to get his views on everything'.[2]

Assuming, however, that the presence of a poorly endowed Minister does not provide an acceptable rationale for centralising advice,
the large majority of contemporary Permanent Secretaries would appear to take the view that it is not desirable to conceal divisions of
opinion within the department. A moderate stance, typical of several
Permanent Secretaries who were interviewed was that, 'Ministers
should not be bothered with issues that can be settled lower down.
It is the Permanent Secretary's duty to try to lick things into shape.
On the other hand if disagreements persist you display those disagreements to Ministers.' This respondent added that in some departments
differences of opinion are almost endemic and could not possibly be
concealed. He instanced conflicts between the home and overseas
divisions of the Board of Trade and the Treasury.

Nevertheless, it is hard to feel entirely reassured. The position of
Permanent Secretary is characteristic of British government. In most

[1] R. Jenkins, 'The Reality of Political Power', *The Sunday Times* (17 January
1971).
[2] Sir Edward Playfair, 'Who Are the Policy Makers?' *Public Administration*,
43 (1965), 251-87.

European countries and the USA the heads of various sections or bureaux of departments are equal in rank.[1] The pre-eminence of the Permanent Secretary's position and the fact that officials below the rank of Deputy Secretary, in practice, depend on him for promotion may, to some extent, make his subordinates unwilling to press hard for proposals he is known to disagree with. Permanent Secretaries are not normally petty tyrants and the Civil Service more than most organisations has a reputation for tolerating plain speaking and a diversity of views. Even so, it cannot be easy for most officials to disagree openly with their boss and press their views on Ministers.

It should be noted, however, that in some departments the hierarchy with the Permanent Secretary at the top, alone in his eminence, is definitely considered outmoded. These departments have adopted a more collegiate or 'management team' type of organisation.[2] A clear example is the Ministry of Defence where the Chief Scientific Adviser and the Chief of the Defence Staff sit alongside the Permanent Under-Secretary in the Defence Council. The Ministry of Technology (founded in 1964, and in 1970 absorbed into the Department of Trade and Industry) was also working towards a management team concept with its system of 'controllers' in charge of various aspects of the department's work. Even in departments where no formal steps have been taken, it appears to be increasingly common for Permanent Secretaries to meet with their senior colleagues about once a month, or even once a week, for what one Permanent Secretary called a *tour d'horizon*.

Ministers themselves can certainly encourage the development of a management team. Several Ministers remarked that, in so far as their colleagues might feel that policy options were foreclosed as a result of not seeing middle and junior level officials, this was their own fault. If a Minister wants to hold large office meetings with numerous officials and specialist advisers present, he has the authority to summon them. In any event the trend to a management team arrangement seems likely to continue. It is the logical corollary of the Fulton Committee's recommendation that specialist advisers be given more influence in Whitehall, and that those equivalent or higher in rank than Under-Secretaries should be regarded as part of a department's senior policy and management group.[3] There is limited point at lower levels in doing away with the system by which reports written by specialists can only reach their superiors with the approval of admin-

[1] For a comparison of British, French, Swedish, Australian and American departmental organisation see F. F. Ridley (ed.), *Specialists and Generalists* (London: Allen and Unwin, 1968).

[2] L. Gunn, 'Ministers and Civil Servants: Changes in Whitehall' *Public Administration* (Australia), (March 1967), 78-94.

[3] See pp. 124-128.

istrative class civil servants, if the system is to be preserved in the higher reaches of the department with all advice being channelled to the Minister through the Permanent Secretary.

Before leaving the subject of the crucial relationship between a Minister and his Permanent Secretary, it is worth discussing what happens if the two fall out. The job of Permanent Secretary imposes considerable strain. In the words of Sir Edward Playfair, it involves 'total subordination' because, whatever his own view, a Permanent Secretary is expected to swing the department loyally behind the policies of each new Minister.[1] For a man with strong convictions this task may occasionally prove intolerable and, in fact, Sir Edward considers that Permanent Secretaries should be compulsorily retired after five years because 'no man of spirit' could stay in post for a longer period without showing signs of deterioration.

Leaving aside disagreements over policy, Ministers and Permanent Secretaries sometimes disagree about the latter's main role. Occasionally a Minister will make it clear that he does not intend that the Permanent Secretary be chief policy adviser. One Minister told the author that, apart from 'encouraging him to go abroad as often as possible' he tried to restrict his Permanent Secretary to management tasks. On the same theme a retired Permanent Secretary said that his last Minister rarely asked him for policy advice and that the two of them would sometimes not meet for weeks on end. More rarely, a Permanent Secretary who regards himself primarily as a manager may regret the extent to which a Minister relies on him for policy advice. Thus, a former Permanent Secretary at the Ministry of Power said he was 'flattered but not pleased' with a Conservative Minister who, being accustomed as a businessman to centralisation, called him in most evenings to discuss cabinet as well as departmental business.

In view of the importance of the relationship, it is not surprising that Ministers sometimes attempt to select their own Permanent Secretary, or replace the incumbent Secretary. Several Ministers mentioned that they had influenced the choice of a new Permanent Secretary for their department by indicating a preference for one of the candidates known to be on the shortlist. More seriously, Mr Richard Crossman is believed to have produced his own candidate for Permanent Secretary at the Ministry of Housing and Local Government in 1966, and Mrs Barbara Castle was reported in the *Guardian* in January 1966 to be trying to remove the Permanent Secretary at the Ministry of Transport.[2] Such attempts are bound to fail. As H. E. Dale wrote, it is an unwritten rule of the Service that:

[1] Playfair, *Public Administration*, 43 (1965).
[2] Gunn, *Public Administration* (Australia, March 1967), 82-4.

'If the public interest require that a junior clerk be removed from his post no regard need be paid for his feelings; if it is a case of an Assistant Secretary they must be carefully considered, within reason; if it is a Permanent Secretary, his feelings are the principal element in the situation, and only imperative public interest can override their requirements.'[1]

Cabinet committees and official committees

A second way that policy options may be foreclosed is through the operation of the inter-departmental Civil Service committees which run parallel to cabinet committees. Almost all cabinet committees are in fact serviced by an official committee registered with the Cabinet Office. To take one example, the main economic policy committee of the cabinet is SEP (the Steering Committee on Economic Policy). Parallel to it and including officials (in this case Permanent Secretaries) of all the departmental Ministers concerned is SEPO, the equivalent official committee. Official committees are supposed only to reach agreement on matters not considered intrinsically important or politically sensitive enough to refer to Ministers. The agenda prepared for a ministerial committee should therefore provide for discussion and set out options in relation to all issues that Ministers might wish to decide themselves. However, official committees normally meet far more frequently than ministerial committees and, as one civil servant interviewed said, 'might take six months preparing proposals which Ministers would pass in a single meeting'.[2] The time factor alone means that there is a *prima facie* risk that options may be foreclosed:

The Labour Party in its evidence to the Fulton Committee was in no doubt that ministerial options are foreclosed:

'Inter-departmental committees of officials are a particularly effective way of undermining the authority of Ministers. The Minister may not be consulted until the officials have arrived at an agreed compromise: and if he then wants to disagree he can only do so at the cost of telling the officials to go back and put forward a different view from the one they have been arguing for against other departments.'[3]

---

[1] H. E. Dale, *The Higher Civil Service in Great Britain* (London: OUP, 1951), p. 126.

[2] This is not always the case, however; the author was told that the Prices and Incomes ministerial committee met far more often in the period of the Labour Government 1964-70 than the equivalent official committee.

[3] *The Civil Service*, V (2), p. 655.

Barbara Castle has written even more trenchantly and believes that official committees undermine the whole system of cabinet government:

'In my innocence when I went into cabinet government in October 1964, I still believed that governments work this way: that Cabinets were groups of politicians who met together and said, these are the policies we are elected on, now what will be our political priorities? And they would reach certain political decisions and then they would refer those decisions to an official committee to work out the administrative implications of what they had decided.'

'I was soon disabused of that . . . The official net is terrific, the political net is non-existent. I wonder if you realise.

'I suddenly discovered that I was never allowed to take anything to cabinet unless it had been processed by the official committee. In the official committee the departments had all their inter-departmental battles, and probably made their concessions to each other. The departments did the horse-trading and having struck their bargains they then briefed their Ministers on it, and so at cabinet meetings I suddenly found I wasn't in a political caucus at all. I was faced by departmental enemies.'[1]

Few of the Ministers interviewed were anything like so critical of official committees. A Conservative Minister thought that officials occasionally gave away a Minister's case without consulting him in order to get a *quid pro quo* from another department. He had the impression that officials at the Department of Technical Co-operation had done this in 1963 in agreeing not to press the Treasury to transfer all economic aid questions to the department.[2] A Labour Minister said that all too often in cabinet committees he was met with the cry 'Oh, I thought our officials were agreed', in regard to a compromise that he found unacceptable. In the same vein Dr Jeremy Bray has written that:

'In the process of consultation between departments officials may make accommodations which more often weaken the original proposal than strengthen it. Ministers in other departments are briefed to the weak view, and told that officials generally find it acceptable. The sponsoring Minister can then find himself having to start by rebut-

---

[1] Castle, *The Sunday Times* (10 June 1973).
[2] When the Ministry of Overseas Development was set up in 1964 economic and technical aid were under the same roof.

ting what has become an established Whitehall view of which his colleagues have been persuaded.'[1]

Another former Labour junior Minister believed that, 'Occasionally civil servants gang up on you and you find that other Ministers are all briefed the same way. If that happens it is pretty fatal.'

Many other Ministers, including some with a reputation of being extremely able, were adamant that in their experience officials had never conceded points which should have been referred back: 'any civil servant who did so would be taking a grave risk with his career'. A Labour economic Minister said jokingly that, although 'basically I regard all civil servants as spies of the Treasury, it is up to me to convince my ministerial colleagues that I am right, regardless of what officials think'. Last, one Minister dismissed the question and the questioner brusquely: 'Foreclosed options – what are you talking about? Ask me about something else.'

It is not surprising that the experiences of Ministers should differ, As we shall see in Chapter 6 civil servants have conflicting views about the tactics which it is proper for them to pursue on official committees. Some apparently think it right to withold or pass on information depending on whether it will further the interest of their own Minister. Others, no doubt equally genuinely, deplore departmentalism, claim to pass on information to all interested departments as a matter of course and seek to reach agreement before taking matters to Ministers.

Ensuring effective ministerial choice

A Minister who is chronically suspicious of his officials and always imagines that they are taking decisions out of his hands produces a situation in which far too much is referred up to him. This will only ensure that he examines details in detail; he won't have time to deal with major matters adequately. If, on the other hand, a Minister feels that there are particular issues that he would prefer to go into more fully the remedy lies partly in his own hands. Obviously, his first step should be to make clear to his Private Secretary and Permanent Secretary what these issues are. They can be asked to arrange that he see the full files, including records of committee meetings. Office meetings at which all officials the Ministers wishes to be present are present, can also be arranged. At these meetings it would be up to the Minister to try to bring out any points of difference between his officials and ensure that all feasible options were freely discussed. In the same

[1] J. Bray, *Decision in Government* (London: Gollancz, 1969), p. 55.

way, if a Minister believes that the Permanent Secretary has too pronounced a tendency to vet proposals before they are submitted, he can order that Deputy- or even Under-Secretaries and certain specialist advisers be given direct access to him. If he further chooses to formalise this arrangement and give his department a collegiate, or management team advisory structure, and to hold weekly or monthly meetings to review current business, no one can gainsay him.

In addition to these remedies which lie in the Ministers' own hands, certain other recent developments in Whitehall may help to preserve effective ministerial choice. First, there were a limited number of occasions during Mr Wilson's Government on which junior Ministers were asked to act as chairmen of departmental committees. Mr John Morris, while Joint Parliamentary Secretary at the Ministry of Transport, was in 1966-7 chairman of a committee on the Finances and Management of British Railways and Mr Arthur Skeffington, Parliamentary Secretary at the Ministry of Housing and Local Government, chaired the Committee on Public Participation and Planning which reported in 1969.[1] This is a development which could be carried much further. If junior Ministers sat on departmental and inter-departmental committees now staffed entirely by civil servants, it would be both an educative experience for them as prospective Cabinet Ministers and would provide some assurance that feasible policy options were not foreclosed.[2]

It is useful here to distinguish between ministerially and departmentally initiated proposals. In the case of ministerially initiated proposals, a junior Minister could ensure that they were not watered down and could refer back to his Cabinet Minister for guidance on doubtful points. But civil servants are supposed to do this anyway and the presence of junior Ministers might make little difference. The latter would, perhaps, make a more worthwhile contribution in cases where proposals were initiated by the department. It is surprising for an outsider to learn that such proposals are often only submitted to Ministers in more or less final form and after lengthy discussions both internally and with other interested departments. Junior Ministers would be in a position to brief the senior Minister as proposals were formulated and the latter could at any stage decide to throw his political weight behind them. Unresolved inter-departmental disputes would then be fought at ministerial rather than official level. The results might be the same or different but at least Ministers would have

[1] *Railway Policy*, Chairman: J. Morris, MP, Cmnd 3439 (HMSO 1967); *People and Planning: Report of the Committee on Public Participation and Planning*, SBN 750128 X (1969).

[2] Other advisers of the kind that might be appointed to a ministerial *cabinet* could also be put on departmental and inter-departmental committees. See pp. 128-131.

the choice of fighting for unmodified proposals rather than being presented only with an inter-departmentally acceptable version. One qualification is in order; junior Ministers could only be invited to sit on official committees formulating proposals judged to be of major intrinsic or political importance. There would not be enough of them to go round if they were invited to sit on all committees.

Last, recent developments connected with central resource allocation and planning may help Ministers to see policy options more clearly.[1] Concern about resource planning was focused by the 1961 Plowden Report on the Control of Public Expenditure.[2] Plowden's recommendations were accepted and in the course of the 1960s the Public Expenditure Survey Committee (PESC) system was evolved. The basis of the system lay in five-year projections of the gross domestic product and hence tax revenue. Correspondingly, departments were instructed to project the cost of their current programmes five years ahead and also to work out alternative sets of programmes based on assumptions about increases or decreases in their financial allocation. This to some extent obliged departments to rank their priorities, particularly as the idea was that detailed Treasury inquiry into costs should be relaxed and departments left free to budget as they saw fit, provided they stayed under their expenditure ceiling. The final allocations were made annually by the Cabinet through its Public Expenditure Survey Committee.

In practice the main focus of PESC thinking was on the allocation of resources between departments rather than between different programmes of the same department. As the Government White Paper on 'The Reorganisation of Central Government' (1970) stated:

'It [the PESC system] does not call for explicit statements of the objectives of expenditure in a way that would enable a Minister's plans to be tested against general government strategy; nor can it regularly embody detailed analysis of existing programmes and of major policy options on them.'[3]

Programme Analysis Review (PAR) instituted in 1970 is supposed to remedy this deficiency. The White Paper justifies PAR in terms of improving central control over policy strategy. Each year departmental PARs will have to be submitted to the centre (in the first instance to the Central Policy Review Staff) before PESC decisions are taken. However, it is hoped that PAR will be equally significant as a manage-

[1] The following account relies heavily on Sir R. Clarke, *New Trends in Government* (London: HMSO, 1971), and Brittan, *Steering the Committee*, ch. 4.
[2] Cmnd 2342 (1961).
[3] Cmnd 4506 (1970), para. 50.

ment tool for individual Ministers in their departments. Annual statements of objectives and priorities are to be prepared by departmental management services divisions, the cost-effectiveness of existing programmes is to be evaluated and Ministers should be afforded an overview of their departments' activities. Experience with the PESC exercise suggests that, realistically, it might still be hard for Ministers to make changes to take effect less than three years ahead but, overall, PAR/PESC developments hold out promise of enabling them to exercise more effective choice.[1]

Certainly PAR/PESC is likely to be of far greater practical utility to Ministers that the 'planning units' proposed by the Fulton Committee.[2] Fulton believed that these units should consider long-term policy questions and should be headed by senior policy advisers. (Permanent Secretaries would be restricted to management tasks.) To date ten departments have created planning units, but without senior policy advisers.[3] There was a clear risk of conflict between the latter and Permanent Secretaries and the Civil Service Department may well have decided that policy and management questions are best examined together rather than in separate divisions of departments. In any case PAR/PESC requires that departments look five years ahead and some departments are already accustomed to taking decisions the main results of which will not be seen for ten years.[4] There may be some point in having planning units operating on an even longer time scale but their prophecies are unlikely to be of much interest to Ministers whose time scale, or at least period in office, is rarely more than three years.

THE EXPERTISE OF ADVISERS

So far we have been concerned with the range of options open to Ministers. However, the most common criticism made of Whitehall departments by their political masters was that policy advice was insufficiently expert. Seven Ministers stated directly that senior civil servants lack specialised knowledge and eighteen saw a need for the importation of more outside experts into the Service on either a temporary or permanent basis. In making these points many Ministers endorsed the Fulton Committee which believed that administrative class generalists were too often 'unable to grasp the complex subjects with which they are dealing' and were 'not capable of evaluating the

[1] Brittan, *Steering the Economy*, p. 87.
[2] *The Civil Service* I, paras 175-6.
[3] A staff of four to ten officials headed by an Under-Secretary or Assistant Secretary seems to be usual. See G. K. Fry, 'Policy Planning Units in British Central Government', *Public Administration*, 50 (Summer 1972), 139-56.
[4] Clarke, *New Trends in Government*, p. 9.

success of the policies they administer' with the result that 'the drive for innovation' was inhibited.[1] Fulton's criticisms and recommendations will serve as a basis for the following discussion.

First, Fulton noted that civil servants are recruited on the basis of general academic ability rather than specialised knowledge relevant to the tasks they are destined to perform. The largest number of successful candidates in the entry examination continue to be classics and history graduates. Fulton believed that more weight should be attached to the subject in which the first degree was taken (social science preferred) and that, in any case, all entrants to the Service should take courses lasting 'up to a year' in management and in subjects appropriate for either 'economic' or 'social' administrators. None of these recommendations has been fully implemented. The Government rejected the idea of giving preference to social science graduates and the distinction between social and economic administrators has been found too blurred to apply.[2] The standard period of training for Assistant Principals has been increased; but only to twenty-eight weeks, not a year. Furthermore the core subject, taken for twenty-two weeks, is not management but economics, with additional six-week courses in one of the following: project appraisal and control, international economics, industrial growth, environmental planning and social administration.[3]

Some steps are also being taken to give civil servants above the level of Assistant Principal training in management and in subjects relevant to their jobs. The first annual report of the Civil Service Department notes that in 1968-9 1,663 Principals and Assistant Secretaries took management courses at the new Civil Service College; nearly double the previous year's figure.[4] In 1968-9 also, Principals were offered courses in economics, decision techniques and the use of computers, organisation and staff management and social administration, which together lasted sixteen weeks instead of, as previously, two weeks.[5] Seminars were held for Assistant Secretaries and Permanent Deputy- and Under-Secretaries were invited to half-day talks.

Overall, it is clear that for better or worse the amount of specialised training received by civil servants is only going to increase gradu-

---

[1] *The Civil Service* II, para. 67.

[2] *First Report of the Civil Service Department* (London: HMSO, 1970), p. 42.

[3] Curiously, in view of the rejection of the distinction for the purposes of training and career specialisation, the title of the twenty-two week course is economic *and* social administration. In substance, however, the course is mainly economics.

[4] *First Report of the Civil Service Department*, p. 32.

[5] Unlike the Assistant Principals' course, the courses for higher ranks are not compulsory.

ally. It is also important, from the point of view of the present study, to remember that today's Assistant Principals who have received more training than their predecessors will not begin to reach Under-Secretary level – and hence have regular access to Ministers – until about 1990.

In addition to highlighting training deficiencies, Fulton also pointed out that the Civil Service concept of career planning prevents specialisation:

'The ideal administrator is still too often seen as the gifted layman who, moving frequently from job to job within the Service, can take a practical view of any problem, irrespective of the subject matter in the light of his experience and knowledge of the government mach-ine. . . . The cult [of the generalist] is obsolete at all levels and in all parts of the Service.'[1]

The management consultancy group appointed by the committee was even more outspoken: 'We found that much of the movement of staff from job to job arranged by establishment officers masqueraded as career planning. This was because in the Civil Service all movement is thought of as good and contributing to the development of a career . . . '[2]

Research commissioned by the committee itself does not entirely bear out theses assertions. Admittedly job rotation was quite rapid – on average officials were found to be spending only 2–8 years in post – but transfers were mainly made within the same department.[3] Thus career patterns in three departments – the Home Office, the Min-istry of Housing and Local Government and the Ministry of Power – were analysed and it was found that only 28 per cent, 36.4 per cent and 35 per cent of officials respectively had ever switched departments. However, although the Fulton Committee may to some extent be guilty of projecting a stereotype instead of sifting its own evidence, the stereotype does fit the advisers with whom Ministers have most direct contact. In contrast to other officials, the so-called 'high fliers' of the Service – future Permanent and Deputy-Secretaries – do generally serve in a number of departments[4] and could not possibly be consid-ered subject matter experts. The pattern in Whitehall is thus for intel-ligent laymen (senior civil servants) to predigest the advice of relative

[1] *The Civil Service* I, para. 15.
[2] ibid., II, para. 240.
[3] ibid., IV, 583-91.
[4] The majority of Permanent Secretaries have served in the Treasury at some stage of their career, often for a total of ten years or more. See John S. Harris and Thomas V. Garcia, 'The Permanent Secretaries: Britain's Top Adminis-trators', *Public Administration Review*, 26: 1 (March 1966), 31-44.

experts (lower ranking civil servants) for the benefit of other intelligent laymen (Ministers).

The Fulton Committee believed that experts should have more direct influence on Ministers. Several recommendations were designed to secure this end. Members of the specialist classes – accountants, legal experts, scientists, engineers – should no longer automatically have their advice summarised, simplified and, perhaps, deliberately or accidentally modified by administrative class officials. Fulton recommended that in future specialists and administrators – indeed all civil servants – should be graded in a single hierarchy with the same opportunity to reach the top.[1] As implemented, this recommendation has not eliminated 'high fliers' but it has meant that specialists can now reach Permanent Secretary and other senior posts and have direct access to Ministers.

Fulton also recommended that, in future, senior posts in the Service should be advertised and hence be open to outside experts.[2] Indeed, the trend established by the Labour Government after 1964, of hiring outside experts as permanent or temporary civil servants, was welcomed. Most of Labour's 'irregulars' (as they were christened by Mr George Brown)[3] were economists and a number of them were Labour party supporters appointed at senior levels with access to Ministers.[4] In 1964 there had been only twenty-five 'economist' posts in the entire government and these were mainly in the economic section of the Treasury. By 1969 there were over 150 such posts with a high concentration in the Ministry of Transport, the Department of Economic Affairs, the Ministry of Overseas Development and the Board of Trade, as well as the Treasury.[5] It appeared that under the Conservative government in office since 1970 the fashion for economists was replaced by a fashion for businessmen.[6]

The difficulty with the 'irregulars' on secondment to the Civil Service is to fit them satisfactorily into the existing hierarchy. The Fabian Society, volunteering evidence for Fulton, interviewed 'irregulars' appointed since 1964 and found that many felt that their abilities had been wasted.[7] They had not been given access to vital information or

[1] The administrative, executive and clerical classes were merged on 1 January 1971. The merger with the specialist classes has not been formally carried out but specialists are already being recruited for the most senior posts. See *First Report of the Civil Service Department* (London: HMSO, 1970).

[2] *The Civil Service* I, para. 125-7. It was also recommended that civil servants should take up temporary appointments in industry, local government, banking, etc.

[3] Brittan, *Steering the Economy*, p. 29.

[4] ibid., pp. 55-6.

[5] ibid., p. 16.

[6] See *The Reorganisation of Central Government*, Cmnd 4506 (1970), pp. 13-14.

[7] *The Civil Service*, V (2), 559-68.

to Ministers. They attributed their difficulties partly to an ignorance of Whitehall, its committees and circles of influence (they felt an introductory course would have helped) and partly to a desire on the part of career civil servants to 'freeze them out'. In some departments the solution may be for 'irregulars' to band together and appoint a co-ordinator to communicate directly with the Minister. This was done by the industrial advisers in the Department of Economic Affairs.[1] It seems inevitable, however, that career civil servants should feel some resentment towards 'irregulars'. One Minister went so far as to say that the Civil Service 'rejects them like heart transplants'.

To summarise: the pre-Fulton theory was that final responsibility for formulating a department's considered advice to Ministers should rest in the hands of the administrative class officials, except in rare cases in which the issues involved could safely be regarded as 'technical' and politically non-controversial. Only in dealing with these other issues did chief medical officers, research controllers, solicitors and legal advisers and the like come into their own. The post-Fulton theory is that specialists should have the chance to reach the highest posts hitherto reserved for generalists and that administrative class civil servants should specialise rather more, at least to the extent of being 'economic' administrators or 'social' administrators. The Fulton Committee itself perhaps underestimated the value of the administrative class 'high flier' who, with experience spanning a range of departments, acquired an intimate knowledge of the government machine and a capacity to evaluate policy proposals in the light not only of administrative feasibility, but of the Whitehall and Westminster realities which would govern their prospects of being accepted. However, in implementing the committee's recommendations, the Civil Service Department appears to have struck a reasonable balance. In future years generalist-specialists and specialist-generalists will both have direct access to Ministers.

GETTING THE MINISTER'S MIND: THE PRIVATE OFFICE

'The whole machine is geared to finding out and acting on the Minister's mind.' This statement made by a Permanent Secretary expresses perfectly the norm that civil servants should prepare proposals, resolve individual cases and react to other departments' initiatives, in the way they believe their Minister would, if he were in their seat. It follows that the Minister's Private Office, which is the instrument, the radio receiver for 'getting the Minister's mind' and transmitting it to the department, plays a crucial role. The Private Office of Cabinet

[1] Campbell Adamson, 'The Role of the Industrial Adviser', *Public Administration*, 46 (Summer 1968), 185-91.

Ministers consists of a Private Secretary of the rank of Assistant Secretary or Principal and up to three Assistant Private Secretaries, who are usually Assistant Principals. Private Secretaries of Senior Ministers are civil servants marked out for rapid promotion. They are thus extremely able men and sometimes wield a degree of influence far greater than is normal for officials of their rank.

Private Secretaries would all agree that they have a difficult dual role as both the servant of the department in regular touch with the Permanent Secretary and as the personal assistant of the Minister. One experienced Private Secretary described this as an 'oil-can, a lubricating function', communicating the views of the Minister to the department and vice versa. A Private Secretary must judge which civil servants the Minister may want to see during the day and ask them to stand by. More delicately, he may be asked by the Minister to indicate to, say, an Under-Secretary that a particular project is urgent and that it would be appreciated if proposals could be with the Minister shortly. Conversely, a Private Secretary will himself be telephoned by members of the department to ask whether he has yet 'got the Minister's mind' on such and such a subject, or whether such and such a minute has yet been drawn to the Minister's attention. Clearly, to perform these tasks successfully a Private Secretary needs to have the confidence of both the Minister and of officials who outrank him. If he is not entirely satisfactory to his Minister he should, as Fulton said, be moved to another post without detriment to his career.[1] If he is unpopular with senior officials he is likely to be met with frequent minor rebuffs: 'If the Minister has specifically asked to see me, all well and good; if not, I can't promise to sit by the telephone all afternoon.'

Private Secretaries differ to a remarkable degree in their willingness to act as ministerial advisers. Some become personal confidants and do not hesitate to give their own views on policy. Thus, Harold Wilson has recorded that his Private Secretary, the late A. N. Halls, invariably criticised as insufficiently radical Civil Service Department submissions on machinery of government reform.[2] As an extreme instance, Lord Salter in his *Memoirs of a Public Servant*, claims that when he was Private Secretary to C. F. G. Masterman, who was in poor health, he regularly took urgent decisions himself, confident that the Minister would later endorse them[3]. More common are Private Secretaries who are willing to suggest to a Minister that he might consult Under-Secretary X whose views on a particular proposal are known to be at variance with those submitted by Under-Secretary Y. It is unfortunate if such tips are not treated as confidential. One

[1] *The Civil Service* I, para. 286.
[2] Wilson, *The Labour Government*, pp. 540-1.
[3] Lord Salter, *Memoirs of a Public Servant* (London: Faber, 1961), p. 65.

Private Secretary explained that he had stopped giving private information to his Minister who had 'twice blurted it out giving me as the source'.

Private Secretaries who act as confidants clearly lean towards the Minister's side in performing their dual role between the Minister and the department. Most Private Secretaries are more cautious, however. For every one who feels confident or arrogant enough to comment on advice submitted by his superiors, there are probably several who, if asked, simply paraphrase the 'departmental view'. Junior officials depend mainly on their Permanent Secretary for promotion and Permanent Secretaries presumably prefer Private Secretaries who do not interfere. Indeed, one Permanent Secretary complained of regularly having to tell his Minister: 'I know where that advice is coming from and it is no damn good.'

Nine of the Ministers interviewed felt that Private Offices needed strengthening and that it would be useful to have a somewhat larger staff, including a few personally and politically sympathetic individuals who knew the way their Minister's mind worked and could give him a second opinion on departmental submissions. A few Ministers in recent years have, in fact, made personal appointments in their Private Office. Mr Roy Jenkins, for example, kept the same Private Secretary while at the Ministry of Aviation, the Home Office and the Treasury and the same Special Assistant, largely employed as a public relations officer, in the latter two departments.

A more radical proposal is that, instead of merely strengthening their Private Office, Ministers should be permitted to form a French style *cabinet*. In France a ministerial cabinet may have as many as ten members. The chief political adviser is the *chef de cabinet* who is usually a political friend of the Minister.[1] The *directeur de cabinet*, on the other hand, is usually a career official and it is his task to impose the Minister's policy priorities on the department. Ridley and Blondel describe the members of the *cabinet* as 'administrative bully boys', and write that 'they clearly strengthen the Ministers' influence in their departments, both in matters of policy and in more routine administration'.[2] In its evidence to the Fulton Committee the Labour Party proposed a similar system in Britain.[3] According to Labour a *cabinet* would have three functions. It would transmit Ministers' views to the machine and perform a progress-chasing function, it would maintain

[1] See F. F. Ridley and J. Blondel, *Public Administration in France* (London: Routledge and Kegan Paul, 1964), pp. 65-7; A. Dutheillet De Lamothe, 'Ministerial Cabinets in France', *Public Administration*, 43 (1965), 365-81; 'Letters from Across the Channel: I. Ministerial Cabinets', *Public Administration*, 50 (Spring 1972), 79-86.

[2] Ridley and Blondel, *Public Administration in France*, p. 67.

[3] *The Civil Service*, V (2), p. 655.

liaison with other *cabinets* and it would engage in research and the planning of future policy.

The case for ministerial *cabinets* is hard to evaluate. It is only fair to say that few Ministers want them; for every respondent who was critical of the Private Office there were several who stated that they were well satisfied and doubted if comparably good arrangements existed in business and other organisations.[1] On the other hand, the general point that departments are not at present so constituted as to facilitate or at any rate maximise ministerial and party impact on policy also seems a strong one. Assuming, for the sake of this argument, that increased ministerial impact on policy is desirable, it does not seem unreasonable that Ministers should make a few appointments of their own to their Private Offices. The ideal appointee would be one who both shared the Minister's political views and who was relatively expert in at least one of the subjects covered by the department. Not all Ministers, perhaps, particularly if they themselves were serving in their third or fourth department in five years, would know people with these qualifications whom they could appoint; and there would be risks in recruiting strangers who might turn out to be personally or politically unsympathetic. However, in cases where suitable *cabinet* members could be found, they would help the Minister to think through and define his policy objectives (particularly necessary in mid-term, when election manifesto commitments may already have been fulfilled) and sit on departmental and inter-departmental committees and project teams with a brief to ensure that these objectives were adhered to as closely as possible in the formulation of policy programmes. Along with junior Ministers, who, it was suggested, might also sit on official committees, they would break the present monopoly of career officials in the process of policy formulation. The party political impulse (and perhaps the prospects of policy innovation) would thus be strengthened at the expense of the influence of civil servants.

EXECUTIVE MINISTERS AND MANAGEMENT ROLES

The problems we have dealt with so far in this chapter – ensuring that a reasonably wide range of policy options are presented to Ministers, the expertise of advisers and 'getting the Minister's mind known' in his department – all affect Ministers primarily in the performance of

---

[1] The following advertisement appeared in *The Times* (25 August 1969): RETIRED CIVIL SERVANT? Attractive opening for a retired civil servant of senior rank as personal assistant to public man with wide ranging financial and industrial interests . . . Having been Principal Private Secretary to a Minister would be a great advantage.

their policy initiation and selection roles. In the last part of the chapter we consider problems of special concern to Executive and Ambassador Ministers and Minimalists.

Executive Ministers are liable to face special difficulties in their relationship with their departments. First, most civil servants do not expect Ministers to devote much attention to management tasks. Secondly, they lack what social psychologists term 'power of position' (or formal authority) and before taking quite ordinary management decisions are obliged to obtain the agreement of central departments (the Treasury, the Civil Service Department or the Cabinet Office). The creation of 'giant' unitary departments, however, of which there are now five (Defence, Environment, Foreign and Commonwealth Office, Health and Social Security, Trade and Industry) makes effective management more than ever necessary and, just as officials influence policy decisions, there is a growing body of opinion which believes that Ministers should exert greater influence on management decisions. As Sir Richard Clarke puts it:

'One might see the total work of a department as a spectrum at one end of which is the formulation of objectives and priorities (which is the responsibility of the Minister) and at the other end of which is what might be called the permanent foundation of the administrative structure (which is normally left to the Permanent Secretary). Near the one end of the spectrum, in the decisions how to carry out the Minister's objectives, the officials will be heavily involved: near the other end, in the determination of senior appointments or the working system of the department it would be unwise for the Minister not to be involved.'[1]

A Minister cannot, like the heads of some organisations, hire and fire staff, arrange promotions and demotions, or unilaterally decide to reorganise his department or institute new systems of planning and controlling the use of resources. His authority in these matters is widely shared, subject to many constraints. First, man management: a Minister is, of course, at liberty to try to 'bring the best out of civil servants' and exercise effective leadership in his department. Appointments and promotions are not entirely his responsibility, however. Permanent and Deputy-Secretaries are in effect appointed by the Senior Appointments Selection Committee chaired by the Head of the Civil Service and consisting mainly of Permanent Secretaries.[2] The committee reports to the Prime Minister. Occasionally, an individual Minister might indicate his preference from a shortlist of

[1] Clarke, *New Trends in Government*, p. 100.
[2] *First Report of the Civil Service Department*, para. 154.

candidates but, as we have seen, any attempt to get a Permanent Secretary removed or nominate his successor is likely to be rebuffed. Appointments at Under-Secretary and Assistant Secretary level are submitted for ministerial approval, but only exceptionally, in the case of a promotion from Assistant to Under-Secretary, would a Minister be likely to know an individual's work well enough to question the Permanent Secretary's advice.

To arrange an increase in departmental staff (including appointing 'irregulars') has generally, in the past, presented difficulties. The Treasury, responsible for 'establishment' questions until 1968 when the Civil Service Department took over, scrutinised individual appointments closely, begrudged high salaries and itself set an example of parsimony and under-staffing.[1] Under Mr Wilson's Labour Government, however, it appears that control over establishments was relaxed. The overall size of the non-industrial Civil Service increased by over 50,000 and, more important, government policy decreed that the appointment of 'irregulars' was desirable. However, under the Conservative Government in office since 1970, the policy has been to reduce Civil Service manpower. The machinery for detailed control still exists and departments can still not make their own appointments (subject, say, to a cost ceiling) but must have Civil Service Department approval.

Responsibility for departmental organisation and resource management (excluding human resources discussed above) is also shared by the Minister with other agencies. A reorganisation of the department involving, say, the amalgamation of divisions, or an attempt to create what Fulton called 'accountable management units' (that is units working to a specified objective which they are held accountable for achieving) would require discussions with the Civil Service Department, which is in overall charge of machinery of government questions. Departmental resource management, on the other hand, is subject to control through the PAR/PESC exercise, by the Treasury, the new Central Policy Review Staff located in the Cabinet Office and, of course, the Cabinet itself. Thus the PESC returns will still be made to the public sector divisions of the Treasury and the PAR returns will initially be made to the Central Policy Review Staff.

In short, it is clear that a major difficulty for Executive Ministers

[1] See Sir Herbert Brittan, *The British Budgetary System* (London: Macmillan, 1959); Lord Bridges, *The Treasury* (London: Allen and Unwin, 1964); H. Roseveare, *The Treasury* (London: Allen Lane, 1969); H. Wright, *Treasury Control of the Civil Service, 1854-74* (Oxford: Clarendon Press, 1969): Brittan, *Steering the Economy*. The Fulton Committee found that many applicants for specialists posts withdrew their applications because selection procedures and the business of approving a starting salary took so long. *The Civil Service*, II, para. 224.

and their departments is the number of agencies with which they have to deal at the centre of government and the degree of detailed control imposed by these agencies. At a time when the tendency is to create 'giant' unitary departments it seems inconsistent to have three different departments at the centre – the Treasury, the Civil Service Department and the Central Policy Review Staff in the Cabinet Office – all concerned with reviewing departmental management. Sir Richard Clarke's proposal that all such review tasks should be performed by a Central Management Department which would include the present CSD, the public sector divisions of the Treasury and the CPRS seems entirely sensible.[1] Following this proposal the Treasury, shorn of its public sector divisions, would become a National Economic and Finance Department and the Cabinet Office would be restricted to servicing the Cabinet and its committees. Clarke also emphasises that, subject both to expenditure ceilings and to the Central Management Department's satisfying itself that systems for resource management were working properly, departments should be left to manage their own affairs. Item by item control of expenditure, which has been on the way out in the 1960s, would finally expire.[2]

The corollary of more rational and strategic but less detailed control from the centre would be greater departmental provision for the performance of management tasks. Organisation and management divisions have tended in the past to be worthy but unambitious, dealing with such matters as staff grading, the welfare of civil servants, accommodation, reprographic services and the installation of computers.[3] Fulton's management consultancy group found 'no evidence that top level organisation and procedures were ever scrutinised by departmental O & M', and 'little evidence of a systematic management review of the relative priorities and continuing justification of departmental activities and thus the staff needed'.[4] What is required in place of traditional O & M is a management services division which would be concerned with PAR/PESC resource management, forecasting and long term policy 'planning' and economic and financial appraisal of existing policy programmes. An Executive Minister, by definition, would take a close interest in the work of a management services division of this kind. He would have an extremely important, although, for a Minister, unconventional job on his hands.

AMBASSADOR MINISTERS AND PUBLIC RELATIONS ROLES

In performing the roles they attach highest priority to, Ambassador

[1] Clarke, *New Trends in Government*, pp. 65-71.   [2] ibid., p. 52.
[3] *The Civil Service*, II, paras 205-302.   [4] ibid., II, paras 218, 286.

Ministers have to rely less than other Ministers on the advice and assistance of their departments. In general, they tend merely to impose extra demands on fairly routine departmental services. Their speeches have to be written by the Private Office and they may require extensive briefing before embarking on consultations with interest group leaders, or before press and television interviews. A somewhat more difficult task, however, concerns the arrangement of programmes of 'visits' designed to attract maximum publicity for the Minister, or bring him into contact with people whom it would be worthwhile, from the point of view of the department and its policies, for him to try to influence.

In a few departments special committees have been set up to plan the 'visits' and other outside engagements of Ministers. At the Ministry of Transport in the late 1960s, the Deputy Secretaries and the Minister's Private Secretary met weekly to consider what appointments the Minister should accept. Similarly, at the Department of Employment and Productivity when Mrs Barbara Castle was Minister (1968-70), a 'speech committee' was instituted. For its own guidance and for the Minister's Private Secretary, it developed criteria about the kinds of invitations that would be accepted, or in some cases, manufactured. Would a visit by the Minister be likely to build support or reduce opposition to departmental policies? Would it be useful to suggest to a particular organisation that the Minister would appreciate an invitation? Would favourable publicity be likely if the Minister opened a particular exhibition, or spoke at an annual dinner?

Most departments, however, do not have a committee which meets regularly to plan the Minister's timetable. Matters are settled informally by the Private Secretary in consultation with senior officials and, when there is doubt about accepting a particular engagement, with the Minister himself. The danger with this informal method is that the Minister will simply attend the same annual dinners and conferences, meet the same dignitaries and consult the same advisory committees as last month or last year. Ministers of Defence tend to visit an establishment of each of the military services once a month, Secretaries of State for the Social Services inspect the regional offices of their departments every summer, Home Secretaries make the annual round of prisons, Ministers of Power descend coal mines in tin hats and Labour Ministers attend the Durham Miners' Gala.

Not surprisingly some Ministers are critical of the arrangements made for them. Several Labour Ministers claimed to have reduced the formality of visits and to have insisted on meeting 'fewer dignitaries and more people at the working level'. An Education Minister always tried to meet lecturers and students as well as vice-chancellors on university visits, a Minister in an industrial sponsoring department

preferred to address factory workers than meet only boards of directors, and a Home Office Minister regularly visited areas with large
immigrant populations to discuss their problems with the people
affected. In some cases the purpose of introducing greater informality
was for the Minister to learn more, judge how current policy
programmes were working and give him first-hand knowledge to help
him in future policy formation. A Conservative, at the time
Shadow Minister of Housing, said that:

'Ministers are ruled by invitations. Instead, one can make one's own
invitations and let the Private Office know that one would welcome
an invitation to visit such and such a place. A Minister of Housing
should go to several conurbations each year and arrange a full programme to find out at first hand what progress is being made.'

This respondent also believed that the parliamentary summer recess
could be better used and that Ministers would derive more benefit
from visiting other countries and studying their policies than from
touring regional offices. Another Conservative Minister, referring to
his period at the Department of Education and Science, believed that
visits were valuable mainly as a means of meeting individuals to whom
he could later turn for a second opinion on departmental advice.

If a Minister is critical of the format of 'visits' and the arrangements
his department makes for his other public relations activities, he can
readily make changes. Whether his department has a commitee to
plan engagements, or relies on informal discussions between the
Private Secretary and senior officials, a Minister is always at liberty
to make his priorities clear and instruct that his timetable be re-
arranged accordingly. If he wishes to cut down on public relations
activities, he will be told that this may give offence to the department's clientele and, if he wishes to increase such activities, officials
may be anxious about his capacity to keep up with paper work
and take decisions that the department needs in order to proceed
with its business. Once a Minister has indicated the value he attaches
to various kinds of engagement, however, there is no reason to
believe that his Private Office will fail to respond.

MINIMALISTS AND MINISTERS' MINIMUM ROLES

Few of the Ministers interviewed were critical of the assistance provided by their departments for performing their minimum roles. As
far as the role of clearing the in-tray and accepting responsibility for
decisions is concerned, it is generally agreed that the Minister's burden is considerably eased by the lucidity and conciseness of Civil

Service minutes. The mechanics of ensuring that the right minutes and supporting documents are ready for the Minister's 'red boxes' each evening are also efficiently handled. Urgent matters are distinguished from those which are less pressing, most minutes contain a specific recommendation and precisely what the Minister is expected to decide is clearly stipulated. In general, Ministers were satisfied that if, acting through their Private Office, they asked for fuller advice or more supporting documents the department was responsive. As we have seen, they also believed that, once decisions were taken, civil servants did not go slow in preparing measures, or executing decisions with which they disagreed.

A second minimum role for Ministers consists of fighting their department's battles in Cabinet. None of the Ministers interviewed for this study expressed criticisms of the quality of the briefing they received for cabinet meetings. A point was made by Sir Edward Boyle in *The Politics of Education* which is worth noting, however.[1] Boyle suggested that Ministers were more likely to represent their own department effectively in Cabinet if their colleagues were impressed by the standard of their contribution to discussions on a wide range of issues. It followed that any department which set up 'an organised system for briefing Ministers on general cabinet issues' would be doing itself a considerable service.

In relation to a Minister's role as political trouble spotter and trouble shooter, a distinction is made between defending the policies and actions of one's department at party meetings and performing the same task in Parliament. Party business is a Minister's own concern; to assist him would infringe the convention of Civil Service political neutrality. 'They [civil servants] expect you to manage party meetings by the light from heaven' was the comment of a former Chancellor of the Exchequer. On the other hand, a great deal of advice and briefing is supplied for parliamentary duties. Civil servants of the rank of Principal, Assistant Secretary and Under-Secretary spend, on average, just over 20 per cent of their time on Parliamentary work: on Parliamentary Questions, legislation, writing ministerial speeches for debates, correspondence with MPs etc.[2] Discovering the true answers to Parliamentary Questions, preparatory to framing an answer which will satisfy the House, is extremely time consuming. According to a well-known formula the aim is to draft an answer 'that is brief, appears to answer the question completely, if challenged can be proved to be accurate in every word, gives no opening for awkward "supplementaries", and discloses really noth-

[1] E. Boyle, A. Crosland and M. Kogan, *The Politics of Education* (Harmondsworth: Penguin, 197), p. 98.
[2] *The Civil Service*, V (1), p. 119.

ing'.[1] Oral supplementaries to Questions, which are, of course, asked without prior notice, present the main difficulties. But if a Minister is weak at these, it is not uncommon for his senior officials to meet with him before he is due at the despatch box and play an agreeable guessing game.

The criticism has been made that civil servants are too concerned about defending their Ministers from political criticism and that the costs of parliamentary accountability, measured in Civil Service man hours, are too high. A former Home Office civil servant remarked that it was 'an odd paradox but officials there were more politically jumpy than Ministers' and Dr Jeremy Bray writes that,

'Because Ministers are political animals, and will react and decide as such, there is a tendency for civil servants to tee up issues as political issues . . . . This is not to say that civil servants are not concerned with objective analysis. It is rather that the results of this analysis, to be acted upon, have to get through the political mill. There is a tendency therefore for the senior civil servant to act as a kind of politician's politician. This really is dangerous.'[2]

Ministers who intend to serve only as Minimalists could not, of course, be expected to endorse this criticism. So far as they are concerned, the more 'politician's politicians' there are in the department the better.

CONCLUSION

The purpose of this chapter has been to consider what resources are available in government departments to assist Ministers in the performance of their duties. It bears repeating that most Ministers are well satisfied with their advisers. They are not among those who attribute grave weaknesses to the Civil Service, or believe that it represents 'the apotheosis of the dilettante'.[3] Over a quarter of the Ministers interviewed made no criticism whatever of Whitehall personnel and procedures and most of the remainder advocated, not root and branch reform, but only specific changes to meet specific problems.

The latter part of the chapter was concerned with problems of

[1] Quoted by W. J. M. Mackenzie and J. W. Grove, *Central Administration in Britain* (London: Longmans, 1957), p. 374.

[2] Bray, *Decision in Government*, p. 66.

[3] 'The Apotheosis of the Dilettante' was the title of Thomas Balogh's critique of the Civil Service in Hugh Thomas (ed.), *The Establishment* (London: Anthony Blond, 1959), pp. 83-128.

special significance to Executive and Ambassador Ministers and Minimalists. The problems most frequently mentioned, however, were those affecting Ministers in their performance of policy initiation and policy selection roles. A significant number of Ministers saw a need either to obtain more expert advice, or to minimise to risk that feasible policy options may not be brought to their attention. The first problem could be, and is being mitigated by giving outside experts temporary Civil Service appointments in cases where it appears that their particular knowledge and skills will be useful either for special projects or, more generally, to lend impetus to 'the drive for innovation'.[1] The latter problem is more intractable and may require organisational changes. In so far as policy options are foreclosed on departmental or inter-departmental official committees, the presence of junior Ministers, or ministerial *cabinet* members might be helpful. In so far as the difficulty arises because the Permanent Secretary centralises advice-giving in his own hands, the Minister may insist on a more collegiate structure. This can be created either informally, by giving a number of advisers direct access to him, or by holding regular meetings of the 'management team' as is the procedure in the Ministry of Defence. Last, future options can be explored, and grounds for decision clarified, by a regular review of departmental objectives and programmes such as should be encouraged by the PAR/PESC system when it comes into full operation.

[1] *The Civil Service*, II, para. 67(b). Fulton's management consultancy group considered that one of the principal consequences of the shortage of experts in the 'line management' of the Service was a reduction in 'the drive for innovation'.

Chapter 6

Ministers and their Departments II

The Expectations of Civil Servants

'I am their leader and must follow them.'

This quotation, attributed to a leader of the French Revolution who caught sight of his followers charging off to another gory execution, expresses the important truth that leaders who fail to conform to the expectations of their followers run the risk of forfeiting the latter's esteem and hence their co-operation and assistance. Therefore Chapter 1 indicated that one of the principal factors for analysis would be the fit between the role conceptions of Ministers and the expectations of civil servants. There are, in fact, considerable pressures on Ministers to act in accordance with Civil Service expectations. First, Ministers almost never act without taking Civil Service advice. Indeed, decisions are often formally taken in the actual presence of officials. As one Minister said, when asked about possible conflicts between political pressures and the advice of officials:

'You have got to have the courage to resist the politically easy way out. Courage may come from great conviction of the public good, such as Gladstone had. In my case a more squalid motive suffices. Decisions are taken in a room full of intelligent civil servants. I am not going to have them saying, "what a weak-kneed bastard!" – so I try to do the sensible thing.'

Ministers as compared with the heads of other orgasniations are unusually dependent on the assistance and advice of their subordinates. Unlike, for instance, managing directors and military leaders, Ministers do not generally rise to the top after serving a long apprenticeship on lower rungs of the organisational ladder. As the short term heads of government departments, they are rarely expert in the subjects they are responsible for and hence in order to avoid disaster, let alone achieve any substantial policy objectives, they are highly reliant on Civil Service advice. They need to establish a close co-operative working relationship with senior officials and this relationship is more likely to be engendered if they broadly conform to expectations and provide the department with the kind of leadership it desires. At the very least there is likely to be some initial misunderstanding if a Minister's role conception is greatly at variance with the expectations of civil servants and, even if the passage of time erases such misunderstanding, civil servants are less likely to support their Minister by actions above and beyond the call of duty if he tackles his job in a manner they disapprove of.

However, countervailing arguments have to be set against the view that there are special pressures on Ministers to conform to expectations. First, the top man in any organisation has, almost by definition, a degree of discretion over which roles he gives priority to. The job specification of the boss is bound to be less rigid than those of his subordinates. In the case of Ministers there is some suggestion that expectations regarding the roles they should perform are even less fixed than usual. Civil servants regard themselves as duty bound to be responsive to Ministers' priorities and working methods to a degree which would probably be exceptional among officials of, say, a business organisation or trade union. Thus, one Permanent Under-Secretary interviewed for this study said that, 'A department must really and deeply get to know how its Minister works and sustain him in every way it can. The approach of Ministers to their tasks varies a great deal.' Another Permanent Under-Secretary (retired), Sir Edward Playfair, addressing the Royal Institute of Public Administration, said, 'That is the way I think a Permanent Secretary should behave, with a rather consistent attempt to consider what the Minister really needs. But I think no man of spirit can do this for long.'[1] Translating these statements into the language of social psychology one may say that Ministers are automatically assigned the 'idiosyncrasy credits' (the right to tackle their job in an unorthodox manner) which other organisational leaders have to earn by means of conforming to expectations and enduring a probationary period of good behaviour.[2]

It is extremely difficult to judge the balance between the arguments and counter-arguments about the pressures on Ministers to conform. The most that can be asserted is that, since Ministers themselves recognise the existence of some pressure, it is worthwhile asking

[1] Sir Edward Playfair, 'Who Are the Policy Makers?', *Public Administration*, 43 (1965), 251-87.
[2] E. P. Hollander in C. A. Gibb (ed.), *Leadership* (Harmondsworth: Penguin, 1969), pp. 293-306.

precisely what the expectations of civil servants are and how closely they accord with Ministers' role conceptions. Do civil servants prefer a ministerial policy initiator, a Minimalist, an Ambassador Minister – or what?

THE CIVIL SERVICE MINISTERIAL IDEAL

There is no perfect consensus among civil servants about the ideal Minister. Nevertheless, there are certain tasks which all civil servants want their Minister to perform well and certain abilities which they hope he will possess. The opening question put to the twenty-five civil servants interviewed for this study was:

> From the point of view of the department what are the main tasks a Minister needs to perform well?

As with Ministers this question was followed by several about skills:

> What skills and types of ability would you say Ministers need to carry out these essential tasks?

> Do the skills needed by a Minister vary from department to department? Are any special skills needed by a Minister in your department?

> In your experience do senior Ministers generally have most of the necessary skills and abilities? What are their main strengths and weaknesses?

Due to the small sample size the data must be interpreted cautiously and findings can only be regarded as suggestive and more or less plausible. Apparently, however, the type of Minister civil servants favour is the policy selector/intelligent layman. There seems to be no truth in the assertion that they prefer a Minister who is content to review only 'a bowdlerised version' of policy alternatives (a phrase used in the Labour party's evidence to the Fulton Committee[1]) and generally comes down in favour of the view endorsed by his most senior officials. Almost to a man civil servants claim to prefer a Minister who puts them on their mettle, annotates their papers, poses shrewd questions in office meetings, disputes received departmental assumptions and throws out ideas for further consideration. In part, they are happier with a Minister who is 'an intelligent prober' and who makes a contribution to policy, 'because that is

[1] *The Civil Service* (Fulton Report), Cmnd 3638 (1968), II, 655.

the way the Constitution is supposed to work'. Sir Stafford Cripps, Labour's Chancellor of the Exchequer from 1947 to 1950, was mentioned by several more senior civil servants as fulfilling his constitutional role to perfection. He would appear in the office each morning by 9 a.m. with all his papers read and annotated. He also wrote papers himself and these served as a means of effectively 'getting his mind known' in the department. It was said of him that 'he mastered advice and briefs like a good barrister and then let his mind play on things and expanded on what the department had given him'.

If they cannot have a policy selector who serves as an intelligent layman in the department, civil servants will settle for the type of policy selector who puts a premium on decisiveness, who believes in making up his mind quickly and sticking to it. 'Decisiveness' was a quality said to be important by nineteen of the twenty-five officials interviewed[1] and, as M. J. Barnett has remarked, might almost be termed the ideology of the Civil Service.[2] The great bogey of the Service is a Minister who cannot make up his mind, who vacillates, who delays decisions. Such Ministers constitute a bottleneck in the department. Civil servants need to 'get the Minister's mind' both in the course of formulating a set of proposals (a fairly general statement of intent might serve here) and to endorse more specific decisions and recommendations. As one very senior official said: 'the machine is geared to finding out the acting on the Minister's mind; and also to deciding which issues must go up to Ministers and which don't need to'. A Minister who fails to make his mind known poses problems both intra-departmentally and inter-departmentally on official committees. Intra-departmentally delay forces officials either to proceed along the lines they were already following, leaving contentious points unresolved and hoping to get decisions from the Minister at a later stage, or to do nothing and run the risk that the situation they hoped to deal with will reach crisis proportions. An Under-Secretary gave an example of the consequences of taking the first option. He reported that his Minister had kept him waiting for several weeks on decisions relating to a major bill. The result was that the bill would either not be passed in the current Parliament or would be 'a botched job containing somewhat conflicting provisions inserted by different divisions'. (In the event this particular bill was lost as a result of the dissolution of Parliament prior to the general election of June 1970.) Inter-

---

[1] The figure of nineteen includes two officials who said that, realistically, most Ministers simply endorsed advice submitted to them.

[2] M. J. Barnett, *The Politics of Legislation: The Rent Act 1957* (London: Weidenfeld and Nicolson, 1969), p. 29.

departmentally, officials representing a Minister whose views on a particular issue are unknown are at an acute disadvantage. Only after the Minister has made his view known can the department swing its weight behind him, write briefs and press arguments home with conviction. Officials can, of course, bluff ('I'm sure my Minister would not stand for this') or reserve their Minister's position but, even so, battles are likely to be lost for want of a ministerially sanctioned viewpoint.

Clearly, a Minister is more likely to display the quality of decisiveness if he is capable of reading and comprehending rapidly complicated policy submissions prepared by civil servants. It was generally agreed that most senior Ministers perform adequately in this respect but that the consequences of slow reading comprehension could be serious. As the private secretary to a Labour Minister said, 'A Minister who can't master paper can't be master of his department'. He went on to explain that his current Minister lacked this ability and that it was necessary to prepare précis of all complicated documents. The Minister thus only saw policy alternatives expressed 'in tabloid form' and his margin of real choice was inevitably curtailed. Even so, the Private Secretary continued, it was often necessary, in order to avoid intolerable delays to the department's business, 'to invent the Minister's mind', to pretend that he had taken a view on issues which he was scarcely aware of. 'Inventing the Minister's mind' was not something a Private Secretary could generally do on his own responsibility, so the time of more senior officials was wasted also. Another former Private Secretary pointed out that all a Minister who cannot master his files can do is engage in 'ritual assertions of control'. This may involve, for example, inserting a minor clause in a bill and then hailing it as a major Socialist or Conservative measure. This generally attracted scorn since 'everyone knows it is really the department's bill'.

In addition to taking decisions and despatching the business, civil servants also hope that their Minister will serve the department well as its representative in Cabinet. The second most frequently mentioned ministerial task after decision taking was winning cabinet battles. It is extremely frustrating for a department to spend six months or a year preparing proposals only for the Minister to fail to obtain sufficient money to finance them, or parliamentary time to enact them. The Minister will normally be carefully briefed but if he lacks party standing and committee skills and is representing a department which does not automatically weight (as, say, the Treasury does) he is likely to lose most of his battles. In these circumstances there is a danger that the flow of new proposals will dry up. There is no point in putting forward new proposals if the

Minister is likely 'to kick the ball through his own goal in Cabinet'. By contrast, a Minister who stands high in Cabinet induces euphoria in his department and the result may be a rash of innovations. It was said, for example, that for part of Mr Callaghan's period at the Treasury (1964-7) his standing was such that complicated tax changes went through without much Cabinet opposition.[1]

It is also of considerable benefit to his department if a Minister can handle Parliament and his party without undue difficulty. This is partly a matter of the Minister's being able to spot in advance and hence warn his department of issues and decisions which may cause trouble and partly a matter of presentation. If a Minister is accident prone in the House he is liable to attract an unusually high number of Parliamentary Questions and debates on his subjects and this puts an added burden on the department.[2] As it is, the Fulton Committee found that civil servants typically spend between 20 and 25 per cent of their time on parliamentary business.[3] Any further addition to this is not appreciated.

Finally, although only a few civil servants mentioned the role, it was noticeable that some Ministers were singled out as being especially popular with their department partly because they concerned themselves with departmental morale. They complimented and encouraged officials in their work and maintained morale in all divisions of the department by taking an interest in their business. Affective leadership was said to be particularly significant in the eyes of junior and middle-level civil servants (Assistant Principals to Assistant Secretaries) whose contact with Ministers is normally slight. It would be surprising, however, if even senior officials did not prefer a boss who was responsive and appreciative of their efforts.

CIVIL SERVICE CRITICISMS OF MINISTERS

To complement the discussion of the civil servant's ministerial ideal we may also review some of their more common criticisms of Ministers. An obvious area of criticism concerns the effects of Minister's political ambitions. In general, civil servants well understand the desire of politicians to avoid measures which will make them unpopular with their party or with important sections of the public. They claim to be not unsympathetic if a Minister tells them frankly that, although a particular measure may be administratively sound,

[1] The major tax changes of the 1966 Budget, particularly the introduction of Selective Employment Tax are generally attributed to Mr Nicholas Kaldor, the economist, then attached to the Treasury.

[2] See pp. 88-90.

[3] *The Civil Service* (Fulton Report), V, 119.

it would be politically damaging and that he consequently is not willing to take responsibility. Up to a point it is accepted that it is the Minister's role to inject a political and even a party political element into the considerations of the department. On the other hand, some civil servants fear that the ambitions of Ministers may produce measures contrary to the long-term public interest. Sir Edward Playfair writes that,

'They [civil servants] are growingly – to an extent that is hardly realised – the guardians of some form of public interest. . . But do not forget that Ministers are all men interested in power and they will tend, whatever their party, to what I might call inter-ventionist solutions . . . When I was concerned with overseas finance I found that Ministers of all parties were terribly ready and willing to break the letter or the spirit of international agreements; it was our job to say: "You cannot do that – the country's good name counts." '[1]

Several examples were given of Ministers whose desire for political kudos had allegedly caused them to take actions which civil servants perceived as not being in the national interest. Mrs Barbara Castle who held three cabinet posts (the Ministries of Overseas Develop-ment and Transport and the Department of Employment and Productivity) in Mr Wilson's Labour government was criticised as having 'a big bill mentality'. One view of her mammoth Transport Act (1968), the Equal Pay Act (1970) and her abortive Industrial Relations Bill (1969) was that they indicated a desire on her part to make a splash without sufficient regard to long-term consequences. Mr Harold Macmillan's housing drive in the early 1950s was said to have retarded development in other fields by consuming a high proportion of scarce resources.[2] Thus the housing boom of the early fifties had to be followed by an education boom in the late fifties. A more balanced programme of development might have been preferable. It was also alleged that some policy questions suffer from more or less constant ministerial neglect because they are not politically attractive, while other questions receive too much atten-tion. An official at the Ministry of Transport said that, in his ex-perience, Ministers concerned themselves mainly with road safety and neglected long-term questions of transport policy and planning. Similarly, an official at the Ministry of Power believed that ambitious Ministers tended to despair of his department because it offered so

[1] Playfair, *Public Administration*, 43 (1965), 251-87.
[2] See Chapter 9 where Mr Macmillan's housing drive is cited as an example of successful ministerial policy initiation.

few opportunities to catch the public's or the Prime Minister's eye.

A Deputy-Secretary advanced the interesting argument that the system of parliamentary control of the Executive could be better designed to prevent Minister's political ambitions running away with them, or rather to ensure that private ambitions and the public interest were more often in accord. If specialised parliamentary committees were set up, MPs would be better informed about the 'real' needs and priorities of departments and could judge Ministers accordingly. Ministers would be able to gain a reputation 'as wise policy makers and sound administrators' and would not have to rely so much on attracting immediate publicity. It was important that the 'insider' (inside Whitehall) and 'outsider' reputations of Ministers should be brought more into line.

In general, it is difficult to evaluate assertions about the effects of Ministers' political ambitions because perceptions of the public interest are usually at variance and points of analytic significance are hard to separate from personal prejudices. Civil servants are on less disputed ground when they say that it is important that Ministers realise the implications of the fact that they are heads of large complex organisations. One characteristic of large organisations, which their heads must take account of, is that branches of the organisation are likely to form, if not contradictory, at least competing goals. The most cited example in British government is in the Treasury. Some divisions of the Treasury are primarily concerned with international economic matters and the strength of the pound sterling. Other divisions attach higher priority to economic growth. Since contradictory policies are likely to emerge from these divisions the Chancellor must make up his own mind, not merely by arbitrating or splitting the difference, but in such a way as to arrive at a coherent economic strategy. It was no surprise to hear civil servants with experience in the Treasury say that few Chancellors succeeded in doing this.

Another significant characteristic of large organisations is that most of the time and in most areas of their work precedents are bound to be followed. It is easy to laugh at bureaucratic methods of decision making, but an important point is that they are designed to take advantage of the normally high correlation between consistency and equity. Several civil servants complained that Ministers who lack experience of the methods of a large organisation are sometimes far too ready to overturn precedents. Thus a former Minister of Housing and Local Government who frequently stated that 'I don't believe in precedents', was said to have caused a rash of appeals against planning decisions by overturning existing precedents without putting any new principles in their place.

A more open question is the extent to which Ministers can and should ignore the Civil Service hierarchy and take advice from officials of whatever rank they please. It is an almost universally accepted dictum among Labour Ministers that it is useful to obtain the advice of Assistant Secretaries and Principals as well as Under-Secretaries and above. There are arguments for and against this procedure. One civil servant, referring expressly to studies of organisational behaviour, thought it desirable that a Minister should be in direct touch with the middle-level officials among whom it has been found that innovative proposals are most likely to originate. Most senior civil servants, however, probably prefer Ministers not to sidestep the hierarchy. Not only reasons of vanity are involved. It is pointed out that, if the Minister sees middle-level officials alone, their superiors lose the advantage of hearing the arguments on which decisions are reached and hence may not implement them fully in accordance with intentions. On the other hand, if the senior and middle level officials are called in together, the result is a large meeting. Large meetings are not ideal for decision making and tend to be inordinately time consuming.

However, the point made most vehemently in regard to Ministers as the heads of large organisations relates back to the Civil Service ideology of decisiveness. Ministers must realise that decisions are often urgent, that delay may be worse than sub-optimising and that it is unavoidable that many decisions are somewhat unfair and in any case have to be taken on the basis of inadequate data. 'All too often', as one official put it, 'Ministers delay. They don't do this consciously but they set up a sub-committeee or take refuge in one of the other fifteen ways of postponing decisions.'

Somewhat different from the criticisms of Ministers as heads of large organisations were criticisms of failure to understand how Whitehall operates. Some Ministers apparently doubted the loyalty of their officials. Their suspicions were not normally of a partisan nature, though some Labour Ministers new to office in 1964 feared that having served a Conservative Government for thirteen years civil servants would be Conservative themselves.[1] However, these suspicions soon died. Longer standing and hence more serious were the suspicions some Ministers were said to have of inter-departmental official committees. They suspected that information was exchanged and compromises worked out contrary to their wishes. The result was a loss of trust between themselves and their department. Officials became unwilling to take decisions at all and

---

[1] One Minister went so far as to set up an advisory committee the existence of which was supposed to be secret from his department. Alas, a member of the committee telephoned the Minister's office and the secret was blown.

far too much was referred to Ministers, further burdening them with trivia.

There does appear, however, to be some ambiguity and disagreement about the proper role of civil servants on official committees. On the one hand, civil servants assert that the norm is 'total loyalty to one's Minister so that one decides issues as one believes the Minister would decide if he were present, or reserves the department's position if the issue is important and the Minister has not pronounced'. On the other hand, loyalty to the Minister does not generally seem to be interpreted as meaning that information about proposals being prepared by one's department is withheld from other departments, even if there is a risk that opposition will be given time to build up. As a former Permanent Secretary put it, 'Whitehall is a unity. Civil servants should not behave too departmentally. You do consult your opposite numbers (in other departments) even without ministerial approval and even perhaps if the Minister would not wish it. Contacts go on at the working level whatever Ministers think.' He elaborated on this by saying that if his Minister instructed him not to inform other departments about proposals he would interpret this simply as meaning that other Ministers should not be told. Contacts would be made on the official network, however, but with the injunction 'don't refer it to Ministers yet'.

So far it appears that a crucial distinction lies between the exchange of information on official committees and the taking of decisions. Decisions should not be taken contrary to the Minister's wishes, but information is a free good. However, it turns out that this distinction is not always observed. Contradicting the Permanent Secretary quoted above, an Under-Secretary said that 'of course departments keep secrets from each other'. As chairman of official committees he would not normally hesitate to use his position to further the interests of his department and might not summon meetings if he believed that opposition to his proposals would develop. Very occasionally, however, if he thought his Minister was planning a policy which was flatly contrary to the public interest, he would give other departments exceptionally early warning. He regarded this last practice as 'admittedly unconstitutional' in that if flouted the norm of loyalty to one's Minister. His final point was that discretion to tell all or conceal all could not be exercised in relation to issues of first importance, because then the Cabinet Office exercised some control and would instruct any department that was suspected of concealment to make its proposals known. Even allowing for this last important qualification, it is not surprising that, as we saw in Chapter 5, some Ministers are anxious about proceedings on official committees and suspect that both substantive and tactical points may be lost.

CIVIL SERVANTS' EXPECTATIONS: THEIR 'FIT' WITH MINISTERIAL ROLE CONCEPTIONS

The expectations of civil servants and some of their main criticisms of Ministers have been reviewed. We have seen that they favour a Minister who is a policy selector and possesses the qualities associated with the intelligent layman, who can win cabinet battles and conduct himself with aplomb at the parliamentary despatch box. The purpose of this section is to discuss their attitudes to Ministers who, not being policy selectors, have one of the alternative role conceptions outlined in Chapter 3.

The ministerial Minimalist who is generally content to legitimate official advice finds little favour with civil servants. Many such Ministers do not want to hear conflicting advice. They prefer to be presented by their Permanent Secretary with the 'united view' of the department. Sir Charles Cunningham, former Permanent Under-Secretary at the Home Office, believes such Ministers are in a majority:

'Some Ministers are not content unless a case presented to them sets out not only the facts which have to be taken into account but every step in the argument leading to the conclusion reached. Others prefer a consise and cogent statement of the grounds which lead the department to make a particular recommendation. With the press of business with which a Minister has to deal in these days of intense governmental activity, the latter course is usually preferred.'[1]

Be this as it may, the standing of a department depends, in part, on the reputation of its Minister, and if he is known to be a rubber stamp in the hands of officials he loses prestige, the standing of his department in Whitehall falls correspondingly and it starts to lose inter-departmental battles. In short, if the Minister suffers the department suffers with him.

Attitudes to ministerial policy initiation appear cautious and perhaps ambivalent, although again it is right to point out that the officials interviewed for this study could have been atypical. It was accepted that policy initiation was a proper constitutional role for a Minister and various metaphors were used to describe the

[1] Sir Charles Cunningham, 'Policy and Practice' *Public Administration*, 41 (1963), 229-38.

role. The Minister, it was said, is the macsuline principle and the department the feminine principle in policy making. The Minister must act as a dynamo, he must display 'fervour and enthusaism' to drive through proposals which inevitably are greeted with caution by civil servants who have seen previous attempts at reform run aground. Another civil servant spoke approvingly of the way his Minister, having been defeated in Cabinet on one major measure, 'sulked in his tent for a week' and then returned to lay a piece of paper on the Permanent Secretary's desk with the words, 'these are my next five initiatives'. Altogether, twelve of the twenty-five officials interviewed regarded ministerial policy initiation as desirable.

Inevitably, however, civil servants are acutely aware of the difficulties in the way of ministerial policy initiation. Some are of the opinion that it rarely, if ever, happens. We have already quoted the former permanent secretary of an admittedly highly technical department who said, 'In effect, it was always just a question of getting my Minister to take on board policies we had in hand anyway. Of the six Ministers I worked with closely it would be hard to say that any of them made even a minor contribution to policy.' Other officials, particularly of the older generation, tend to the view that 'wise policy does not differ much from Government to Government so the margin for initiation is not all that great'. These officials tend to be suspicious of ministerial initiatives and emphasise that if Ministers do make an impact on policy it is often for the worse. Examples given were Mr Wilson's ban on even official discussion of devaluation of the pound in 1966-7, and Mr Maudling's 'growth experiment' in 1963-4 which was based on the theory that an initial period of rising imports and balance of payments deficit, while industry stocked up, would give way to payments equilibrium coupled with sustained growth, provided that the Treasury did not intervene and deflate the economy in the meantime. A more trivial example of ministerial impact which in his opinion was harmful was given by a former Assistant Under-Secretary in the Home Office: 'Quite a lot of Ministers have some influence but generally in minor ways. Chuter Ede's decision not to permit graduate entrants to proceed straight to senior levels in the police force was a case in point. As a Labour man his view was that they should all serve their time on the beat.'[1]

Civil Service attitudes to Executive Ministers depend to some extent on precisely which management roles they emphasise. A Minister who encourages officials and gives praise where praise is due is bound to be welcome, although, in fact, only three of the officials interviewed listed maintaining departmental morale as one

[1] Chuter Ede, Home Secretary in Mr Attlee's Labour Government, 1945-51.

of a Minister's more important tasks. Civil servants are also content that a senior Minister should concern himself with organisational matters in so far as these affect the allocation of duties between himself and his subordinate Ministers. In the past the allocation was easily made; junior Ministers were regarded as dogsbodies and assigned those tasks which the senior Minister did not want to perform himself.[1] Civil servants probably preferred that delegation should be strictly limited, if only because they could not be sure that the decisions of a junior Minister were authoritative; but the matter assumed little importance. More recently, however, with the trend towards 'giant' unitary departments like the Ministry of Defence, the Department of Trade and Industry and the Department of the Environment, it is obvious that subordinate Ministers are bound to be given much wider responsibilities.

There is little evidence to judge how civil servants react to a Minister who concerns himself with a broad range of management questions: departmental appointments, the provision of management services, the introduction of new decision-making techniques and so forth. Such Ministers are rare, although again the trend towards 'giant' departments may bring changes. Initially, however, one might guess that there would be some resentment on the part of officials accustomed to regard most management questions as being within the province of the Permanent Secretary, the Treasury and the Civil Service Department.

In general, civil servants do not regard ministerial public relations activities, and hence Ambassador Ministers, in a particularly favourable light. Inevitably, they tend to see such activities through departmental eyes. If a Minister spends an hour reading the press in the morning or if he spends an unusual amount of time on visits, making speeches, or consulting with interest group leaders, civil servants tend to regard this as time off from the real business of government which consists of getting through the paper work and taking decisions. The Minister may have good reasons of his own for giving public relations work high priority but civil servants cannot be expected to share this perspective. An exception, however, was a former Permanent Under-Secretary whose first comment in reply to the question about Ministers' essential tasks was,

'A Minister must be good with people. I have known many an able Minister fall down because he rubbed people up the wrong way. Domestic Ministers have to get on well with local authorities. I remember one Minister who made it obvious that he considered a deputation from a large corporation stupid. He was very much at

[1] See Chapter 4.

fault; his department had to work with local authorities year in, year out.'

More typical in his assessment of appropriate ministerial priorities was a civil servant who, remembering his period as a Private Secretary, said that one of his main tasks was to see that the Minister got through the paper work and did not spend all his time 'glad-handing'. Or, as Barbara Castle wrote, 'The demands of the department must always be paramount – that seems to be the good private secretary's tenet.'[1]

CONCLUSION

In an average week a Cabinet Minister is likely to see at least two civil servants – his Permanent Secretary and his Private Secretary – far more frequently than he sees the Prime Minister or any of his party colleagues. The significance of this simple fact should not be under-estimated as a source of pressure on Ministers to conform to Civil Service expectations. It is not pleasant even for a self-confident politician to act according to his own role conception and run the risk of losing the esteem of his closest working colleagues. More important, the general Civil Service desire for a Minister who falls into the policy selector and intelligent layman mould means that Ministers with different role conceptions are likely to receive less support from officials. There is no suggestion that civil servants tend to reject nonconforming Ministers like the body tends to reject transplanted organs; the norms of loyalty in the Service are too strong for that. But in the highly competitive worlds of Westminster and Whitehall a Minister needs all the support he can get and it seems reasonable to conclude that policy selectors are at an advantage over policy initiators, Executive and Ambassador Ministers.

[1] Barbara Castle, 'Mandarin Power', *The Sunday Times* (10 June 1973).

Chapter 7

Differences between Departments and Situations

In the previous two chapters we have considered some general problems relating to the range and quality of advice to Ministers and the expectations of civil servants. No distinction has been made, however, between different departments or time periods. The purpose here is to analyse inter-departmental differences which significantly influence ministerial role performance. In which departments are Ministers who seek to exercise policy leadership (policy initiators and policy selectors) likely to flourish, and where in Whitehall will Executive and Ambassador Ministers perform satisfactorily? It will also be useful in this chapter to discuss situational factors affecting Ministers. By 'situational factors' are meant opportunities and constraints which are beyond a Minister's control but which fortuitously happen to be present during his period in office. Some civil servants believe that such factors explain almost all the variance in ministerial behaviour. Thus one recently retired Permanent Secretary said, 'Previous commitments often count for little. Incoming Ministers are frequently quite unaware of the real situation. Considerations which they have hardly noticed can be overwhelming and opportunities can open up which they had no idea existed.' Without necessarily accepting all the implications of this statement, it is worth reviewing some of the more common situations which arise.

One preliminary point is in order. When we say that a particular department, or a particular situation, presents favourable opportunities for a particular type of Minister, all we shall mean is that the Minister is likely to be able to act in accordance with his role conception. This is not at all the same as saying there is a definite *need* for this type of Minister in the sense that he will do most to further the department's interests (as perceived by, say, civil servants or competent outside observers) or resolve the policy issues of the day. To take one example, which will be more fully discussed below, an Ambassador Minister may find himself in a department which deals with subjects which are highly newsworthy and may, as a result, find it easy to live up to his role conception and attract a great deal of publicity for his policies, his department and himself. From his point of view, therefore, his appointment is highly favourable; but he may achieve nothing in the way of resolving issues and the publicity he generates may even be counter-productive from this standpoint.

POLICY INITIATION

First, what inter-departmental differences and situational factors affect the prospects of ministerial policy initiation? Probably the most crucial distinction for intending policy initiators lies between *fragmented departments*, which deal with a diversity of more or less unconnected subjects, and *single subject departments* in which the policy problems confronting Ministers are highly interrelated. In a fragmented department it is less difficult for a Minister to formulate his objectives and carry through a policy initiative because, at the cost of ignoring other issues, or rather delegating them to junior Ministers and civil servants, he can concentrate on what he regards as the key issues confronting him. In the single subject departments, on the other hand, Ministers who wish to introduce policy changes are obliged to work out a new *policy strategy* which takes account of interconnected problems. Their task is much less manageable, much less likely to be within the capacity of any single individual, let alone a layman Minister.

Following this distinction, one would expect significant ministerial policy initiatives to be relatively rare in single subject departments like the Treasury, the Ministry of Power, or the Ministry of Defence and much more common at the Home Office, the Scottish Office or the Department of the Environment.[1] At the Treasury, for instance, a Minister seeking to contribute to policy has to review the trade-offs between economic growth and a balance of payments deficit, and between full employment and inflation. It makes no sense to seek to promote, say, economic growth without considering the effect on other objectives. Similarly at the Ministry of Power, it makes no sense to boost, say, the oil industry without considering the implications for coal, gas and nuclear power and at the Ministry of Defence it is, on the face of it, foolish (although it was done for a long time)[2] to permit weapons duplication and fail to co-ordinate the capabilities of the Navy, Army and Air Force. At the Home Office, by contrast, a Minister is relatively free to concentrate on, for example, improve-

[1] This proposition would be hard to test systematically but see Chapter 9 for case studies of the problems of policy initiators in different departments.
[2] See Chapter 10.

ments in the prison service, or reform of the criminal law, or race relations and ignore other subjects. In the same way, a Secretary of State for the Environment could concentrate on transport, pollution, housing or even sport, while the Secretary of State for Scotland has the equivalent of five Whitehall departments under his command and hence has the widest choice of all in deciding his priorities.[1]

In addition to the distinction between fragmented and single subject departments, two other inter-departmental differences influence the chances of ministerial policy initiation. It was suggested in Chapter 4 that layman Ministers would be at a disadvantage in specialised or 'technical' departments like the Ministry of Aviation Supply, the Ministry of Power and, to a lesser extent, the economic policy departments. A layman Minister is almost by definition better equipped to serve as a policy initiator and contribute to the formulation of policy priorities and programmes in departments in which political sensitivity is at least as important as a feel for technical possibilities and an understanding of technical terms and jargon. This is not to suggest that a working knowledge of the business at hand in less technical departments like Health and Social Security is not an asset. Nevertheless, it is probably easier for the non-expert to come to grips with decisions about pension changes than it is to decide on the technical merits and likely profitability of aircraft that have yet to be built, or on the return to be expected from research to improve nuclear power stations.

A second point implicit in Chapter 4 is that Ministers are more likely to carry through policy initiatives in departments in which it is possible to make an impact in the short term than in departments in which results can only be seen ten years hence. This is partly a matter of career incentives. Ministers are short term appointees and there is less incentive for a Minister to inaugurate changes from which benefits will accrue long after his departure from office than to extract short-term kudos from initiatives which take effect more or less instantaneously. There is no implication here that Ministers are motivated solely by ambition but it may sometimes be difficult for them to work up much enthusiasm for subjects like reafforestation, the supply of scientific manpower in the 1980s and the improvement of government statistical services.

As well as inter-departmental differences, we also need to consider the effect of situational factors on policy initiation. It is often said that policy initiatives and, indeed, radical or even autocratic leadership

[1] The equivalent English departments are the Home Office, Ministry of Agriculture, Department of Health and Social Security, Department of Education and Science, and the Department of Trade and Industry in so far as it is concerned with regional development.

are more readily accepted in a crisis, (i.e. a threat situation) than in normal times.[1] There is no doubt some truth in this and examples of wartime leadership (Lloyd George, Churchill) and leadership during an economic slump (Roosevelt) are often cited. An important factor is that in a crisis public opinion and even vested interests will accept changes and risks that would normally encounter serious opposition. A leader who possesses self-confidence and apparently has solutions to offer may be welcomed with open arms.

The implications of a crisis situation for a Cabinet Minister who intends to act on a policy initiator are, however, more problematical. If a crisis situation exists, or blows up shortly after he attains office, he will have to devote most of his attention to the crisis, instead of selecting issues on which he has definite views, or on which his party, perhaps in its election manifesto, has made policy pronouncements. The Minister may be unprepared for and relatively ignorant of the problems engendered by the crisis and his prospects of exercising policy leadership in his department may be reduced. It is, of course, not uncommon for Ministers to be overtaken by crises which disrupt their plans and several examples were provided by respondents interviewed for this study. A former Labour Commonwealth Secretary, who believed that a Minister's primary task was to 'make an impact on policy so they [civil servants] know you have really been there', told the author that his priority on taking office was to try to improve Indian-Pakistani relations but that, in the event, he was obliged to devote most of his time to the Rhodesian crisis arising from that country's unilateral declaration of independence in 1965. In the same vein, a Conservative Minister of Agriculture believed that one of his annual farm price reviews, to which he had given a great deal of thought and in which he believed he had made significant innovations, was drastically amended in Cabinet largely because he was forced to attend international conferences on fish which were hastily summoned when Iceland extended its territorial waters. The policy initiatives he had taken were largely lost. As a further example of a crisis situation limiting a Minister's choice of subjects, one might suppose that whatever priorities two recent Home Secretaries – Mr James Callaghan and Mr Reginald Maudling – may have had at the time of their appointment, they were obliged to devote much of their time to the troubles of Northern Ireland.[2]

Numerous other situational factors influence a Minister's capacity

[1] See Fiedler in Gibb (ed.), *Leadership* (Harmondsworth: Penguin, 1969), pp. 230-41; Graham Tayar (ed.), *Personality and Power: Studies in Political Advancement* (London: BBC Publications, 1971), especially ch. 8.

[2] In 1972 Northern Ireland became the responsibility of a Secretary of State for Northern Ireland and ceased to be a Home Office concern.

to carry through policy initiatives. If his predecessor carried through a formidable list of reforms a Minister may be more or less obliged to concentrate on sorting out administrative problems and ensuring that the new programmes function as intended. To give just one example, Mr Richard Marsh was made Minister of Transport in April 1968 as his predecessor's mammoth Transport Bill was going through the committee stage in the House of Commons. Having piloted the bill through, he had to make appointments to the large number of transport authorities and consultative bodies which it set up and had to try to ensure that these bodies did a useful job of work rather than simply existed on paper or as talking shops.[1] Whatever Marsh's policy predilections, the Ministry could not have coped with any more major initiatives; a period of reform needs to be followed by a period of consolidation.

The stage of a Government's life at which a Minister is appointed can also affect his capacity to act as a policy initiator. A newly elected Government generally possesses, in some indefinable way, a degree of authority which a Government on its last legs lacks.[2] Back-benchers rarely rebel in the first year of a Government but disappointed with the party's record and disappointed of office, they not infrequently give trouble towards the end of an electoral term. Pressure groups also are likely to be less amenable as an election draws near. They may feel that they will get a better deal if the other party is elected or, regardless of this factor, simply resist being pushed around by a Government which has indefinite tenure but may have lost credibility. Both post-war Labour Governments have run into trouble of this kind at the end of their terms. The non-co-operation of the steel industry in the face of nationalisation in 1951 was doubtless partly motivated by the expectation that a Conservative Government would soon be elected.[3] In 1969, on the other hand, the trade unions, in resisting industrial relations legislation, could not have hoped for more favourable treatment from a Conservative Government but nevertheless were not going to knuckle under to a Government which was extremely unpopular.[4] It is fashionable in academic circles to belittle the significance of a Government's mandate from the people; after all, popular ignorance of politics is such that a Government cannot realistically claim that every measure it enacts, which was foreshadowed in its election manifesto, is willed by the people. However, Governments find to their cost that, once their

[1] See Chapter 9.

[2] For illustrations of this point see P. Jenkins, *The Battle of Downing Street* (London: Charles Knight, 1970); and the review by R. Hattersley, MP of Richard Crossman, 'Inside View' in *The Sunday Times* (7 May 1972).

[3] See George W. Ross, *The Nationalisation of Steel* (London: MacGibbon and Kee, 1965).   [4] Jenkins, *The Battle of Downing Street*.

diffuse popularity falls, it becomes difficult to enact controversial measures.

A final point concerning policy initiation is that a situation occasionally arises in which there is no opportunity for a Minister to make a significant contribution because all his advisers and most outdide observers are agreed on what the objectives of policy should be and on the means available for their attainment.[1] Thus when Mr Roy Jenkins, who undoubtedly believes that policy initiation is a Minister's most important role, was appointed Chancellor of the Exchequer in November 1967, all his advisers were agreed that, following devaluation of the pound, he would have to reject most proposals to increase public expenditure and use fiscal and monetary means to deflate the domestic economy in order to achieve the objective of diverting resources to the export market and hence correcting the balance of payments deficit. It may be that such situations rarely occur in relation to policy matters referred to Ministers – after all, if a subject is uncontroversial for a long period, it is usually dealt with by civil servants – but occasionally the reason for an intending policy initiator failing to make an impact on policy may simply be that he has little room for manoeuvre.

POLICY SELECTION

Several points registered in the preceding section apply equally well to Ministers who seek to perform an intelligent layman/policy selector role. Thus the policy selector will find it more difficult to select policy strategies in single subject departments than key issues in fragmented departments. All too often in the former departments he will simply find himself, as a layman, rubber stamping, or amending only the minor details of strategies proposed by civil servants and specialist advisers. Again, like intending policy initiators, Ministers who see themselves as policy selectors probably tend not to make much of a contribution in technical departments in which decisions are mostly politically non-controversial. They would appear more likely to intervene usefully in departments in which political judgements about the reactions of cabinet colleagues and Parliament are frequently required.

Probably the ideal situation for a policy selector is one in which there is a large number of proposals in the departmental pipeline. These proposals may be evaluated both in terms of their intrinsic use-

[1] This point is taken from Fiedler in Gibb (ed.), *Leadership*, pp. 230-41. Fiedler refers to situations in which both objectives and means to their attainment are widely agreed as highly 'structured'. 'Unstructured' situations are those in which either ends or means are problematical.

fulness and the extent to which sponsoring them is likely to enhance the Minister's and the Government's political standing. Thus a Minister who sees himself as a policy selector is likely to perform a non-trivial role in such departments as the Home Office, the Scottish Office, the Ministry of Housing and the Department of Health and Social Security which, between them, are largely responsible for the fact that when each January the Cabinet Office calls for proposed legislation for the next parliamentary session, as many as 300 bills are sometimes proposed.[1] Out of these 300 only 50 to 70 can be accommodated. It is up to Ministers as policy selectors to decide which bills are intrinsically worth sponsoring and (which may not be the same thing) which they have most chance of persuading the Cabinet and its Future Legislation Committee to endorse.

EXECUTIVE MINISTERS AND MANAGEMENT ROLES

Executive Ministers who are concerned with 'organising', 'motivating' and 'controlling', as well as with policy questions, are also significantly affected by inter-departmental differences. They are likely to find their tasks more formidable in those Whitehall departments which, by any standards, are large complex organisations. A rough guide to the complexity of an organisation is the number of senior staff required to run it. On this criterion, the most complex government departments are the Ministry of Defence and the Department of Trade and Industry which both have 91 civil servants of Under-Secretary rank and above and the Department of the Environment with 84 senior officials.[2] The least complex departments are Customs and Excise (12 senior officials), the Cabinet Office (19), Education and Science (20) and Employment (21).

In the case of Executives, more than other types of Minister, they appear least likely to perform satisfactorily at times when they are most needed. Let us envisage some of the most difficult management tasks with which a Minister might be faced. He might be responsible for converting his department from a federal structure to a unitary structure, as occurred at the Ministry of Defence in the 1960s. He might have to take over a large segment of another department and integrate it with his current departmental organisation. He might decide to reorganise his department on functional rather than subject lines. Hardest of all, he might have to set up an entirely new

---

[1] Information about the Cabinet Office 'trawl' was given in interviews with officials who had served as Private Secretaries to the Leader of the House and the Chief Whip.

[2] These figures were correct as of 1 January 1971 and are given in Sir R. Clarke, *New Trends in Government* (London: HMSO, 1971), Annex. II.

department to take over responsibility for areas of policy to which the Government intended to give higher priority. If an Executive Minister decided to take the lead in these matters, rather than leave them to his Permanent Secretary, he would have to concern himself with senior appointments and promotions, with problems of morale and, above all, with creating the right structure at the top of the department for dealing with policy priorities, allocating resources and co-ordinating programmes.

In a small department an Executive Minister might accomplish such tasks satisfactorily. In large, complex departments, on the other hand, he would find it harder to make a substantial contribution. First, he could not possibly become sufficiently familiar with the candidates and their work to make personally the large number of senior appointments required. Next, his cabinet, parliamentary and other outside engagements would probably prevent his devoting enough time to personnel problems and departmental morale. Finally, even if he made a major initial effort to create appropriate top level co-ordinating machinery in the department, he would be unlikely to stay in office long enough to iron out faults and ensure that it was working satisfactorily.

Several other points deserve mention. A Minister is particularly unlikely to be able to carry out organisational reforms if circumstances oblige him to take major policy decisions. His own time and attention would be pre-empted by policy matters and civil servants would, in any case, find it difficult and morale-sapping to get themselves accustomed to a new departmental structure, or a new budgeting system, in a period when they were also formulating a series of complicated submissions on policy. Civil servants, indeed, are acutely sensitive to the dangers of constant re-organisation in Whitehall. Sir Richard Clarke, for instance, who could not be accused of a lack of interest in organisation and management problems, felt obliged to preface a recent lecture series with the remark that 'I shall not be trying to awaken reforming zeal. The view of the former Permanent Secretary of the Ministry of Technology is bound to be that "enough is enough".'[1] The point he was making is that the Ministry of Technology, created in 1964 went through two major amalgamations before Labour left office in 1970, and another one after the election of a Conservative Government.

One possible compromise between avoiding policy questions while carrying out management reforms and the reverse pattern of concern only with policy is for a Minister to introduce changes in management which directly further his immediate policy objectives. We shall see in Chapter 10 that this was Mr Denis Healey's approach at the Min-

[1] Clarke, *New Trends in Government*, Introduction.

istry of Defence (1964-70) where new cost control systems (as well as cuts in military commitments) were introduced in order to reduce the proportion of GNP spent on defence.

A further consideration concerns the management function of controlling departmental performance. In a manager's utopia all organisations would be broken down into sub-units each charged with attaining specified objectives. Performance would be reliably and validly measured and managers promoted or demoted on measured merit. The Fulton Committee on the Civil Service and two Conservative Executive Ministers interviewed for this study indicated that in principle and where possible they would like to see such a system adopted in Whitehall.[1] The problem is that the degree to which some government objectives are being attained cannot readily be measured. It will hardly do, for instance, to give Civil Service industrial relations conciliators a quota of strikes to avert each month or measure the performance of parliamentary draftsmen by the number of bills they produce each year.[2] However, the problems in some areas of policy are less severe than in others. Specific targets could be set for Home Office civil servants concerned with the prison service (a reduction of x per cent recidivism and of y per cent in jailbreaks) and the effectiveness of weapons systems, if not of defence policy, can also be calculated.[3] It is much less easy, on the other hand, to obtain valid indicators of performance in the field of social policy. The performance of the National Health Service, or the value of services to the elderly, or primary education, cannot be readily measured, although valiant attempts are currently being made to develop 'social indicators'.[4] It follows that an Executive Minister who sought to perform a 'controlling' function in a social policy department would face an even more formidable task than a similar Minister in the Treasury or the Ministry of Defence.

AMBASSADOR MINISTERS AND PUBLIC RELATIONS ROLES

The most favourable departments for an Ambassador Minister are those in which it is easy to attract publicity. The Ministry of Trans-

---

[1] *The Civil Service* (Fulton Report) I, ch. 5.

[2] See John Garrett and S. D. Walker, *Management by Objectives in the Civil Service* (London: HMSO, 1969), Centre for Administrative Studies, Occasional Paper No. 10.

[3] For a discussion of problems of measuring the effectiveness of weapons systems and defence strategies see E. S. Quade and W. I. Boucher (eds), *Systems Analysis and Policy Planning Applications in Defence* (New York: American Elsevier, 1970).

[4] See C. A. Moser, *Social Trends* (London: HMSO, 1970), pp. 7-11; Raymond A. Bauer, *Social Indicators* (Cambridge: MIT Press, 1966).

port is a gift in this respect because everyone uses the roads and many people use public transport. Consequently, new safety measures (pelican crossings, or drink and drive laws, for example) or decisions regarding rail closures inevitably attract a large share of praise or abuse. The motoring organisations are particularly vocal pressure groups and also help to ensure that even the least newsworthy of Transport Ministers receives some publicity. Some departments, in contrast to MOT, are desperately dull. Ministers of Agriculture, Ministers of Power and Ministers of Defence all deal with subjects in which the general public has little interest as long as things go well. The pressure groups they have to deal with realise that it is futile to appeal for public support, and instead have a semi-private clientele relationship with their department. The National Farmers' Union is not in the habit of appealing to the public over the head of the Ministry of Agriculture, the oil companies prefer private consultation with the Ministry of Power, and it caused a sensation when, after the publication of the 1957 Defence White Paper, military chiefs took steps to publicise their differences with the Minister over reliance on nuclear deterrence at the expense of conventional weapons. They decided that, to quote one observer, 'the pattern of closed debate and service reticence was being exploited to impose unsound policies while concealing from the public and Parliament and even the full view of the Cabinet, risks that were being taken. . . .'[1]

Situational contingencies can also help an Ambassador Minister to publicise himself, his policies and his department. If a flock of seagulls are killed by oil in the ocean, a Secretary of State for the Environment can make play of his programmes for combating pollution. If a new airliner is launched, a Minister of Aviation can give himself and the aircraft industry a boost by being photographed at the controls of the plane as it breaks the sound barrier. If a planeload of illegal immigrants are proved, or even rumoured, to have landed in lonely fen country, a Home Secretary who coincidentally happens to be sponsoring an Immigration Bill should be able to exploit the opportunity. In the same way any strike which inconveniences the public enables a Minister who wants to introduce industrial relations legislation to identify himself with the public interest.

MINIMALISTS AND MINIMUM ROLES

Inter-departmental differences also affect the performance of a Minister's minimum roles: legitimating decisions and clearing his in-tray,

[1] Laurence W. Martin, 'The Market for Strategic Ideas in Britain: The Sandys Era', in Richard Rose, *Policy Making in Britain* (London: Macmillan, 1969), p. 259.

fighting cabinet battles and parliamentary trouble shooting. First, some departments impose a much heavier workload on their Ministers than others. The Treasury is particularly onerous, as an anecdote about Mr James Callaghan told by a former Treasury civil servant illustrates. After ceasing to be Chancellor of the Exchequer and becoming Home Secretary in 1967, Mr Callaghan was ill for about six weeks and hardly saw any papers. Eventually he asked for a few despatch boxes as 'light refreshment'. By dint of proceeding at his Treasury work rate he got through three weeks' work in a few hours. Such stories in Whitehall, as elsewhere, lose nothing in the telling but this one illustrates a genuine point. A similar point was made by a Minister whose cabinet posts were at the Ministry of Power and the Board of Trade. At the Board of Trade, he said, he took perhaps ten significant decisions a day; decisions on such matters as fraud cases, appeals against regulations and import levies. At the Ministry of Power, by contrast, he had months to reflect on proposed pit closures or plans to erect a new type of power station.

As far as fighting cabinet battles and building support for one's policy programmes is concerned, the theory is that all departments headed by a member of the Cabinet are equal in rank. In practice, however, the status of departments in Whitehall varies greatly. A Minister's capacity to win battles is partly a function of his own 'political weight' (see Chapter 4) but even more of his department's status. At one extreme is the Treasury, the stature of which is such that, if the Chancellor of the Exchequer loses even minor interdepartmental battles, he is clearly on the slide and may soon resign. When Mr Peter Thorneycroft resigned as Chancellor in January 1958, it was widely regarded as astonishing that he had gone into the political wilderness because he was defeated over a 1 per cent increase in the Estimates.[1] But defeat is almost unthinkable for a Chancellor and it was interesting that Mr Roy Jenkins, who was Chancellor a decade later during another period of public expenditure cuts, let it be known that he would have resigned over a similar sum. At the other extreme from the Chancellor are Ministers who head departments with precious little standing in Whitehall. If they want to legislate they are likely to get little joy out of the Cabinet's Future Legislation Committee, and if they want to spend money their programmes may well be successfully opposed by the Treasury. Traditionally, the Ministry of Works, now no longer a separate entity, was regarded as the Cinderella department but other spending departments like the Ministry of Agriculture and the welfare departments are also under the Treasury's thumb. It is no coincidence

---

[1] S. Brittan, *Steering the Economy* (London: Secker and Warburg, 1969), p. 135.

that former Treasury civil servants, who are found in senior posts throughout Whitehall, are particularly common in the spending departments.[1]

Cabinet endorsement of a Minister's proposals depends, in part, on the amount of interest group support he has obtained. A Labour Minister said that the need to consult interest groups made Whitehall 'a pluralist nightmare' and numerous observers have commented on the interminable delays as consultations and negotiations proceed.[2] In some departments it is easier to win over interest groups than others. Several Ministers commented that it was preferable to be able to play off one group against another and arrange compromises between them. This is, for instance, possible at the Department of Employment (unions versus employers) and the Department of Trade and Industry where proposals often reflect a compromise between the demands of different industries, or different regions of Britain. Far more difficult, it was said, are those departments in which a single dominant interest group can use its unopposed authority and expertise to fight proposals. Thus one Conservative Minister said, 'God help you if you are sent to Pensions, Agriculture or Education. You are subject to one way pressure – pensioners, farmers, teachers. If they are determined, they will do you down. No other pressure group can be brought to bear against them.'

Transient situational factors also affect a Minister's capacity to win cabinet battles. A Minister of Defence is unlikely to see the Defence Estimates cut if he can plausibly speak of the threat of war. Similarly, if the country is running a balance of payments deficit, expenditure proposals are more likely to go through if they hold out prospects for increasing exports (trade fairs) saving imports (British computers) or attracting foreign currency (tourism).[3] Needless to say, though, most proposals to increase public expenditure are foredoomed if advanced during a period of payments crisis and consequent economic stringency. The cause is especially hopeless if no powerful lobby exists to lend support. To give one example, successive Labour Ministers of Overseas Development were condemned to frustration in the 1964-70 period because the lobby in

[1] John S. Harris and Thomas V. Garcia, 'The Permanent Secretaries: Britain's Top Administrators', *Public Administration*, 26.1 (March 1966), 31-44.

[2] See particularly I. Gilmour, *The Body Politic* (London: Hutchinson, 1969). It is the main thesis of Mr Gilmour's book that 'the separation of powers has gone underground' (p. 6) and the failures of British government to take 'quick, difficult and unpopular decisions' (p. 2) result from habits of compromise between departments and with pressure groups.

[3] S. Brittan, *The Price of Economic Freedom* (London: Macmillan, 1970), exposes the costs of giving top priority to maintaining a balance of payments equilibrium and a fixed exchange rate. See especially ch. 5.

favour of increasing foreign aid to 1 per cent of GNP was hopelessly feeble.

If a Minister heads a department which lacks status in Whitehall, or in which a single dominant interest group opposes his proposals, there are still one or two eventualities which may save him. His cabinet colleagues may feel obliged to support proposals, even against their better judgement, if it is a question of honouring an election pledge. The crash housebuilding programme between 1951 and 1954 and the Land Commission set up by Mr Wilson's Labour Government were almost certainly supported for this reason.[1] When election pledges are at stake the party in Parliament, party activists in the constituencies and the desire of Ministers not to lose face all prompt action. Another circumstance which may save a Minister from defeat in Cabinet is the support of the Prime Minister. Most Prime Ministers put their reputation on the line several times during their period in office and, indeed, may be every bit as responsible for some policies as the Ministers who nominally sponsor them. Thus, of recent Prime Ministers, Macmillan was instrumental in initiating Britain's first application to join the Common Market and in ordering decolonisation in East and Central Africa. Wilson, at different times, staked his reputation on industrial restructuring as a substitute for devaluation of the pound and on industrial relations legislation; and Heath, like Macmillan, committed himself personally to Common Market entry. Even when the Prime Minister does not commit himself publicly there are presumably occasions when his support is crucial to a Minister carrying his proposals through Cabinet. Whether these occasions are frequent or rare is the backbone of the 'Prime Ministerial government' controversy.[2] This controversy cannot be resolved here, though one relevant if minor point may be noted. Three of the Ministers interviewed mentioned that, in their experience, Prime Ministers often backed colleagues serving in departments which they had previously headed themselves. The implication was that in those circumstances the Prime Minister knew the arguments; otherwise he could not be expected to intervene.

Finally, we come to differences between departments which affect a Minister's ability to perform his role as a parliamentary trouble

[1] On the housing programme of 1951-4 see H. Macmillan, *Tides of Fortune* (London: Macmillan, 1969), ch. 13. As far as the Land Commission is concerned, it was widely predicted before the commission was set up that it would fail to keep down land prices and hence house prices. The Permanent Secretary of the Ministry of Lands and Natural Resources resigned in 1965 probably because he did not want to be further implicated in the commission's creation. The Land Commission Act was finally passed in 1967.

[2] See A. King (ed.), *The Prime Minister: A Reader* (London: Macmillan, 1969).

shooter. The political, or to be more exact, parliamentary sensitivity of a department may be measured in several ways; the days of debate its Ministers are involved in, the amount of legislation they sponsor and the number of Parliamentary Questions they are asked. The figures below relate to the parliamentary session of 1969-70. No session is entirely typical, because the workload of a Minister increases or decreases depending on whether his department is putting through controversial legislation, and whether contentious and hence debatable issues arise within his area of responsibility. Also, if the Opposition believes that a particular Minister is shaky at the despatch box, it may deliberately choose for debate subjects covered by his department and may ensure that he is plagued by a surfeit of Parliamentary Questions. However, all observers would agree that some departments tend to impose a heavier parliamentary burden than others and the 1969-70 figures will be satisfactory for illustrative purposes.

Table 7.1   *Days of Debate by Department during Session 1969-1970*[a]

Department	Days	Department	Days[b]
Treasury	8	Education and Science	1
Foreign and Commonwealth Office	5	Transport	1
		Housing	1
Home Office	4	Public Building and Works	1
Technology	3	Overseas Development	1
Local Government and Regional Planning	3	Scottish Office	0
		Welsh Office	0
Posts and Telecommunications	3	Agriculture, Fisheries and Food	0
Employment and Productivity	2		
Health and Social Security	2	Defence	0
Board of Trade	1		
Total days of debate = 36	31		5

[a] Source: R. Oakley and P. Rose, *The Political Year 1970* (London: Pitman, 1970).
[b] These figures exclude adjournment debates and second reading debates on bills.

The figures in Table 7.1 cover major debates instigated by the Government, by the Opposition on their supply days and by private members under the Standing Order Number 9 (emergency debate) procedure. They do not include either adjournment debates held at the end of the day's session from 10 p.m. to 10.30 p.m., or debates on the second and third readings of bills, which are dealt with separately below. The Table indicates that subjects covered by the three most venerable departments of state – the Treasury, the Foreign Office and the Home Office – attracted the most attention in debates. The high Treasury figure each year is largely the result of the four days' debate on the budget. Foreign Secretaries, on the other hand, are always liable to be called for debates on international crises – in 1969-70 these included Nigeria and Biafra and the invasion of Cambodia from South Vietnam – and Home Secretaries can always count on several highly emotive issues arising during the session. Among these issues in 1969-70 were capital punishment, the proposed South Africa cricket tour and the troubles in Northern Ireland.

Piloting bills through Parliament also makes substantial demands on Ministers in those departments which have a heavy legislative programme. Second and third reading debates require a Minister to do some preparation (although his speech will be written by the Private Office) but most time-consuming of all is the committee stage of bills which the Opposition decides to fight clause by clause.

Table 7.2   *Legislation Introduced by Departments in Parliamentary Session 1969-1970*[a]

Department	Number of bills	Department	Number of bills[b]
Scottish Office	8	Agriculture, Fisheries and Food	3
Technology	8	Transport	2
Board of Trade	6	Lord Chancellor's Department	2
Employment and Productivity	5	Education and Science	2
Home Office	4	Defence	1
Health and Social Security	4	Public Building and Works	1
Treasury	4	Welsh Office	0
Foreign and Commonwealth Office	4	Posts and Telecommunications	0
Housing	3	Local Government and Regional Planning	0
		Overseas Development	0
N = 57	46		11

[a] Sources: *Public General Acts 1969, 1970* and *Parliamentary Debates (Commons) 1969-70*.
[b] Consolidated fund bills and private members' bills are excluded.

Most Opposition amendments are rejected out of hand, partly because they are received at short notice, often because they would defeat the main purpose of the bill.[1] Nevertheless a Minister's

[1] On this point see M. J. Barnett, *The Politics of Legislation* (London: Weidenfeld and Nicolson, 1969), ch. 9.

reputation suffers if he displays ignorance of his own legislation in committee and he must therefore be carefully briefed to withstand his opponents' arguments. Table 7.2 lists the number of bills introduced by departments in 1969-70.[1]

The Scottish Office always has a substantial legislative programme and so, usually, does the other domestic catch-all department, the Home Office. The Ministry of Technology's and Board of Trade's heavy programme in 1969-70 reflected the Labour Government's interventionist industrial policies. In other years one might have expected more activity from the Ministry of Housing and Local Government and the Department of Health and Social Security. Also, it should be noted that Table 7.2 understates the legislative burden on Treasury Ministers who, each year, have to pilot the Finance Act, giving effect to the budget provisions, through the House.

Answering Parliamentary Questions, preceded by briefing sessions with civil servants, is a third time-consuming House of Commons activity that Ministers undertake. The number of Questions a department has answered during the year may be measured by the

Table 7.3   *Parliamentary Questions, 1969-1970* [a]

Department [b]	No. of cols in Hansard	Department [b]	No. of cols in Hansard
Scottish Office	22	Education and Science	14
Health and Social Security	19	Defence	11
Housing and Local Government	18	Foreign and Commonwealth Office	9
Transport	17	Agriculture, Fisheries and Food	8
Technology	17	Wales	6
Treasury [c]	16	Public Building and Works	4
Home Office	15	Posts and Telecommunications	4
Employment and Productivity	15	Overseas Development	3
Board of Trade	14	Local Government and Regional Planning	3

[a] Source: Hansard, *Parliamentary Debates 1969-70*.
[b] All Whitehall departments with a separate ministerial head are listed.
[c] The Hansard index lists entries under names of departments. The Treasury's entries are an exception, however, and come under the heading 'national finance'.

---

[1] The figure of 'bills introduced' is used here rather than 'Acts passed' because, due to the fact that an election was called in June 1970, twenty-two out of fifty-seven bills did not receive the royal assent.

number of columns in the index of Hansard taken up by its entries.[1] Table 7.3 indicates that the domestic policy departments receive far more Questions than the external affairs departments. Thus, the

Table 7.4 *Departmental Differences Affecting Ministerial Role Performance*

Type of Minister	*Type of department favourable to role*[a]	*Type of department unfavourable to role*[a]
1. Policy initiation and selection	*Fragmented depts:* Home Office, Scottish Office, Board of Trade*[b]*, FCO	*Single subject depts:* Treasury, Defence, Power*[b]*
	Non-technical depts: FCO, DHSS, Employment, DES	*Technical depts:* Treasury Defence, Power
2. Management roles	*Non-complex organisations:*[c] DES, Employment, Home Office	*Complex organisations:*[c] Defence, DTI, DOE, DHSS, FCO
3. Public relations roles	*Newsworthy depts:* Treasury, DHSS, Home Office, MOT*[b]*	*Publicity difficult to obtain:* Power, Civil Service Dept, Defence, Agriculture
4. Minimum roles a. Legitimating decisions, clearing in-tray	*Light-workload:* Power, Agriculture	*Heavy workload:* Treasury, FCO and 'giant' unitary depts
b. Mobilising cabinet support	*High status depts:* Treasury, Home, Office, FCO	*Low status depts:* Agriculture, Works,*[b]* Scottish Office, Welsh Office
c. Parliamentary trouble shooting	*Politically safe depts:* Defence, Agriculture, Civil Service Dept, Power	*Politically sensitive depts:* Home Office, Scottish Office, Transport, DTI, Treasury, FCO

[a] FCO = Foreign and Commonwealth Office; DHSS = Department of Health and Social Security; DES = Department of Education and Science; DTI = Department of Trade and Industry; DOE = Department of the Environment; MOT = Ministry of Transport.
[b] Certain departments are cited for illustrative purposes in this Table which until recently were separate entities but are now merged in 'giant' unitary departments.
[c] Organisational complexity is measured by the number of civil servants of Under-Secretary rank and above in the department.

[1] Entries for debates and ministerial statements are not given in the departmental listings used for preparing this Table.

Scottish Office again heads the list and is followed by two other departments whose activities MPs often probe into on behalf of their constituents: the Department of Health and Social Security and the Ministry of Housing and Local Government. Constituents are not usually much interested in external affairs and the Foreign Secretary, the Minister of Defence and Minister of Overseas Development were accordingly not overburdened. One other interesting point in Table 7.3 is that several departments whose Ministers were not in the Cabinet in 1969-70 – notably Transport and Housing – were subject to more questions than some cabinet departments, including (in addition to the external affairs departments) the Ministry of Agriculture and the Welsh Office.

CONCLUSION

The purpose of this chapter has been to advance some fairly tentative propositions about the effect of inter-departmental differences on ministerial role performance. Table 7.4 opposite provides a summary. Most departments provide a favourable setting for the performance of some ministerial roles but an unfavourable setting for others. Thus the Home Office is a relatively favourable department for a ministerial policy initiator but a horrific department for a Minimalist anxious to avoid parliamentary controversy. The Ministry of Power is just the opposite. A further point is that what one Minister finds attractive about a department another Minister is likely to regard with dismay. For instance, an Ambassador Minister might rejoice at being appointed to the Ministry of Transport because it is easy there to generate publicity. But, by the same token, the department is not politically safe, and the Minimalist would be liable to find himself the target of more Parliamentary Questions than most of his colleagues.

One point bears repeating. There may be no relationship between a department's requirements and the type of Minister who is likely to flourish there. The Prime Minister's problem of appointing the right Ministers to the right departments at the right time is reserved for the concluding chapter in which a more prescriptive approach is adopted.

Chapter 8

Ministerial Policy Objectives

This chapter deals with a problem affecting all Ministers but of principal concern to those intending to initiate policy changes. Policy initiators believe that their main task is to secure the implementation of policy objectives which they themselves, or their party have formulated. They do not intend simply to adopt whatever proposals civil servants have 'in the pipeline'. Twenty-three out of fifty Ministers interviewed cited policy initiation as their most important role and it is a fair guess that, if interviews were held with the general public, let alone party activists or writers of constitutional textbooks, the proportion prescribing this role would be considerably higher. It has to be recognised, however, that a Minister may cast himself as a policy initiator but in reality make no contribution to policy whatever. He may think of himself as taking an initiative if he merely says to his officials 'something is wrong here, we must see what can be done about it'. At the other extreme he may, at the time of his appointment, have in hand draft legislation embodying an accurately costed, administratively feasible policy programme based on well defined and mutually compatible objectives. The initial question posed in this chapter concerns the extent to which contemporary politicians in fact come to office with well defined objectives. Where do they fall on the continuum between having no policy at all at the time of their appointment and having draft legislation ready to hand? Is there any difference between Ministers appointed at the beginning of Government's term of office and those appointed in mid-term: is it true that newly elected Governments are bursting with novel plans and proposals but that as their term progresses they 'run out of ideas'?

If a Minister merely intends to serve as a policy initiator but lacks well defined objectives his impact on policy may be nil. Furthermore, it is only a very exceptional politician who could hope to initiate policy changes by dint of relying exclusively on his own knowledge, experience and inspiration. It follows that, if Ministers are not just to adopt whatever proposals are in the Whitehall pipeline, they require sources of analysis and advice *external* to the Civil Service. The greater part of the chapter is concerned with the non-Whitehall policy sources available to Ministers. Where, to put it crudely, can policy initiators get their policy objectives from?

THE POLICY OBJECTIVES OF MINISTERS

Most policy initiatives of any significance take considerable time to bear fruit. Professor Richard Rose has suggested, as a rough guide, that it takes a year to prepare proposals, a year to carry them through Parliament and a year to ensure that they are being administered in accordance with intentions.[1] Given that contemporary Ministers typically spend only eighteen months to three years in a post before being reshuffled,[2] it follows that they need to propose policy initiatives almost as soon as they are appointed if they are to carry things beyond a formative stage. Indeed, if a Minister fails to make his intentions known at the time of his appointment, the risk that he will not act as policy initiator in his department is considerably increased. The pressure to do something, to have some proposals to take to the Future Legislation Committee and the Cabinet will probably mean that he simply adopts whatever proposals are in the departmental pipeline. His time will then be taken up piloting these proposals through the various stages of the policy-making process.

In view of this dilemma, the Ministers interviewed for this study who had served as heads of department (for junior Ministers the question was omitted) were asked:

When you were first appointed to the Ministry of . . . did you have definite policy objectives in mind, or did you have to generate your own objectives at a later stage?[3]

If necessary a follow-up question asked the Minister to specify what his objectives were. The answers in Table 8.1 are divided into those given by Ministers appointed to their department when the Government was new to office and those appointed in mid-term. The hypothesis here was that the former would be more likely to come to

---

[1] Richard Rose, 'The Making of Cabinet Ministers', *British Journal of Political Science*, 1 (1971), 393-414.

[2] See Chapter 4.

[3] The question was asked in respect of the last department which the Minister had headed.

office with definite policy objectives in mind as a result of work done by their parties in Opposition. By contrast, Ministers in Governments longer in office might be expected to have 'run out of ideas'.

Table 8.1   *The Policy Objectives of Ministers at the Time of their Appointment*

| | Time of appointment | |
Policy objectives	new government	mid-term
Claimed definite objectives	9	9
No objectives	2	13
	—	—
N = 33	11	22
	—	—

There may have been some tendency for Ministers to have claimed to have had objectives in mind at the time of their appointment which, in fact, they only adopted at a later stage. In the case of former Ministers who had been out of office for a number of years the risk of this occurring was, perhaps, quite high. This being so it was especially significant that 15 out of 33 Ministers questioned and 13 of the 22 who had come to office in mid-term stated that they had no objectives at the time of their appointment. Four Ministers attributed their lack of objectives specifically to the fact that they had inherited their offices in mid-term and two others, with equal frankness, said they were surprised by their appointment ('I didn't want the job') and therefore had not given prior thought to policy.

Among the eighteen Ministers who claimed to have come to their departments with definite views on policy at least half only stated them in non-specific terms. Thus one Minister was concerned with 'the modernisation of the trade unions' and another with 'establishing a closer working relationship between the department and industry'. Two Ministers went no further than to say that as a result of being in Cabinet they had formed general ideas about the lines of policy that should be followed in departments to which they were later appointed. In short, the interview data suggest that the majority of Ministers do not come to office with policy objectives sufficiently well defined to give their civil servants useful guidance in drafting legislation and devising administratively practical programmes. Why this is so may be inferred from a review of the sources of advice on policy available outside Whitehall. We shall consider separately policy formulation in Opposition, the fruits of which are available to Ministers in a newly elected Government, and the sources available to Ministers appointed in mid-term.

POLICY FORMULATION IN OPPOSITION

R. A. Cross, a hard-headed Lancashire businessman but a political innocent, was appointed Home Secretary in the Conservative Government elected in 1874. He had been a fervent, if distant admirer of the new Prime Minister, Disraeli, and was therefore disturbed to find on closer acquaintance that Disraeli had no policies to offer:

'From all his [Disraeli's] speeches I had quite expected to find that his mind was full of legislative schemes, but such did not prove the case; on the contrary he had to rely entirely on the suggestions of his colleagues and, as they themselves had only just come into office, and that suddenly, there was some difficulty in framing the Queen's speech'.[1]

In the 1870s there was no formal machinery for formulating policy in Opposition. Nowadays such machinery exists, but whether policy objectives and programmes which are sufficiently well defined, detailed and administratively feasible are produced, is open to question.

In the Labour Party policy formulation in Opposition is the responsibility of the Home Policy Committee of the National Executive Committee (NEC).[2] The Home Policy Committee sets up study groups to tackle particular subjects and these groups report back to the committee which itself reports to the annual party conference. The membership of the study groups includes Members of Parliament, non-parliamentary members of the NEC and, in some cases, outside experts who are party sympathisers. No attempt is made to cover all major areas of policy. Thus, shortly before the party's election in 1964, the annual conference report listed the following topics as having been singled out for special study: regional planning, mobility and security in industry, teacher supply, the proposed Land Commission, security and old age, an incomes guarantee, the health service, interest rates charged to owner occupiers, the appointment of a Parliamentary Commissioner, leisure, the honours system, Commonwealth immigration, crime prevention and penal reform, the air transport and aircraft industries, and advertising.[3] There are some notable omissions here, particularly in regard to economic management, prices and incomes policy and

[1] Robert Blake, *Disraeli* (London: Eyre and Spottiswoode, 1966), p. 543.

[2] See A. Barker and M. Rush, *The Member of Parliament and his Information* (London: Allen and Unwin, 1970), pp. 236ff.

[3] Labour Party, *Conference Report* (1964) pp. 36ff. There were also financial and economic policy, science and industry and local government committees but there is no indication in the conference report of specific subjects they studied.

industrial relations, subjects which were to absorb so much of the attention of the Labour Government. As far as the immediate prospect in 1964 was concerned, there was no guidance from party sources on how to respond to a balance of payments crisis and a run on the pound. Members of the staff at Labour headquarters, Transport House, believed in retrospect that the failure to anticipate these immediate problems discredited the NEC, the Research Department and the 'party' as sources of policy in the eyes of some Ministers.[1]

The working methods, duration and thoroughness of the study groups set up in Opposition varied a great deal. At one extreme Mr R. H. S. Crossman kept his security and old age group working throughout the 1955-9 and 1959-64 Parliaments. The group included well-known academic experts on welfare matters, notably Professor R. M. Titmuss, Mr Brian Abel-Smith and Mr Peter Townsend. Its members prepared detailed position papers and its report, *New Frontiers for Social Security*, contained a lengthy list of proposals which were intended to form the basis of legislation.[2] Other groups, however, were apparently in existence for less than a year and relied for their discussions and final reports on papers written by the Research Department officials attached to them. Inevitably they produced prescriptive documents rather than detailed guides to action.

Overall, it is difficult to judge how valuable the work of the study groups proved to be. The author was told that in introducing a Land Commission and a Parliamentary Commissioner, and in the policies on racial discrimination and wage related unemployment benefits, the Labour Government based itself on detailed work done by study groups. On the other hand, the Civil Service clearly had difficulty in making other proposals administratively practical. Mr Crossman's pensions plan is an instructive case. It took actuarial experts five years to make the necessary modifications and the plan was not introduced in Parliament until 1969 and was finally lost as a result of the dissolution of June 1970. Proposals put forward by the incomes guarantee, owner-occupier interest rates and health service study groups were also not implemented.

In addition to reviewing the extent to which study group reports were implemented, we may also consider the fate of Labour party election manifestos. Election manifestos are commonly thought of as containing pledges which Ministers bind themselves to refer to and

[1] Interviews were held with several members of the Transport House and Conservative Central Office staffs.

[2] (London: Labour Party Publications, 1963). Hugh Heclo, 'Pension Politics', *New Society* (23 September 1971) discusses Crossman's pensions plan briefly.

implement in office. Historically, the Conservatives have never accepted this doctrine and have asked the electorate for something akin to 'a doctor's mandate'. Their 1970 manifesto claimed to 'provide a programme for a Parliament' but, in reality, like previous manifestos, it contained very few specific pledges. The Labour Party, by contrast, has always prided itself on being 'a programmatic party in power'[1] and on implementing its manifesto pledges in a systematic way. Its manifestos read like shopping lists and there is evidence that attempts are made in Government to check the items off one by one. The post-war Labour Government is generally believed (by scholars as well as party supporters)[2] to have adhered to the pledges made in its 1945 manifesto 'Let Us Face the Future'. Herbert Morrison, who as Lord President of the Council was chairman of the Future Legislation Committee of the Cabinet wrote that, '. . . it was on the basis of this policy document that the majority Labour Government set about shaping both its legislative programme and its work of administration.'[3] The post-war Labour Government was in an unusually favourable position, however, in that detailed programmes to implement some of its pledges were already in existence when the Government took office. The wartime Coalition Government had made extensive preparations for peacetime through its Reconstruction Committee; and the Beveridge report on the social services was virtually the draft legislation required to create the welfare state. The 1964-70 Government was in a much less favourable position and, not surprisingly, it adhered to its manifestos less closely. Lewis Chester has calculated that twenty-one of the thirty-seven fairly specific pledges in the 1964 and 1966 manifestos were fulfilled, a proportion which, perhaps, should inspire neither congratulation nor cynicism.[4]

The record is patchy and certain weaknesses in Labour's policy-making machinery in Opposition may be mentioned. First, the fact that the NEC is responsible for policy grates on some Shadow Ministers. Relations between the NEC and the parliamentary party have not been uniformly good since the days when Ernest Bevin and Arthur Deakin kept the trade union members steadfastly in line behind the leadership. Nowadays, it is only in a minority of cases that Shadow Ministers are asked by the NEC to chair study groups and there may be a tendency for them to discount the groups'

[1] See S. H. Beer's description of Labour in office 1945-51 in his *Modern British Politics* (London: Faber, 1965), pp. 179-87.
[2] loc. cit.
[3] Herbert Morrison, *Government and Parliament* (London: OUP, 1954), p. 222.
[4] Lewis Chester, 'What's a Manifesto Worth?', *The Sunday Times* (24 May 1970).

reports when returned to office.[1] A second weakness results from lack of adequate co-ordination of proposals made in Opposition. In 1964, before the general election, meetings of the Shadow Cabinet and members of study groups were held in London to provide an element of co-ordination but, as noted above, little consideration was given to some of the major problems which were to confront the Labour Government and, without Civil Service advice, it was difficult to work out the opportunity cost of proposals. Thus it was later argued that increases in public expenditure arising from the implementation of promises to increase welfare payments were partly responsible for the failure to achieve faster economic growth which the party was also committed to try to achieve. This argument was perhaps implicitly accepted in Mr Roy Jenkins's period as Chancellor (1967-70) when it was decreed that public expenditure must rise no faster than national income.[2]

A final doubt concerns the capabilities of the Labour Party's Research Department. The department has an important role to play in Opposition. As mentioned earlier its officials act as secretaries to the study groups and are often, in practice, largely responsible for initiating proposals and drafting final reports. Difficulties arise, however, because, in addition to its policy research duties, the department performs numerous day-to-day tasks. It is responsible for three regular publications: *This Week*, *Economic Brief* and *Information Series*. It processes annual conference resolutions and it gives some help to party spokesmen with weekend speeches. Overall, Mr Terry Pitt, the present head of the department, estimates that only 20 per cent of the time of his staff of twelve research assistants is spent on policy research.[3]

Most of the staff are recent university graduates and only one of them besides Mr Pitt has been there more than five years. In the circumstances it is remarkable that the department maintains a flow of ten to twenty policy statements a year.[4] The conclusion must be, however, that its resources are seriously overstretched and that, if the Labour Party wished to improve its policy formulation in

[1] Mr R. H. S. Crossman seems to have been in great demand as a chairman. He chaired the teacher supply and security and old age study groups and also the Science and Industry sub-committee of the NEC.

[2] It would be wrong to imply, though, that by the end of the 1960s all Labour leaders took the view that public expenditure should not absorb a larger proportion of national income. See, for example, A. Crosland, 'Social Objectives for the 1970s', *The Times* (25 September 1970).

[3] Barker and Rush, *The Member of Parliament and his Information*, p. 244.

[4] *Labour Party Bibliography* (London: Transport House, 1967). Also see D. E. Butler and M. Pinto-Duchinsky, *The British General Election of* 1970 (London: Macmillan, 1971), pp. 58-61.

Opposition, one of the first things it would do would be to strengthen the Research Department.

In the past the Conservatives in Opposition have displayed a divided mind on the wisdom of detailed policy planning. In the 1945-51 period, R. A. Butler, who provided the impetus for the framing of the Industrial (and other) Charters had only the lukewarm support of the leader, Sir Winston Churchill.[1] However, under Mr Edward Heath, the Conservatives in Opposition, 1964-70, made a more substantial effort to prepare for office than any party previously. Twenty-nine groups were set up to prepare reports on all major areas of policy and elaborate procedures were undertaken to co-ordinate and cost their proposals (see below). The groups were variously described by a Shadow Minister as 'an educational exercise for Ministers' and by a senior Research Department official, closely concerned with the work of co-ordination, as 'revolutionising the relationship between the party and prospective Ministers'.

The typical group had twelve to fifteen members, about half of whom were MPs and half party sympathisers from business, insurance, the City, farming, the universities and other fields. Mr Heath took direct charge of appointments and, in selecting MPs for the groups, tried to balance 'ideas men' with opinion leaders from all sections of the party. For this task his experience as Chief Whip was invaluable, having given him an unrivalled knowledge of the interests and viewpoints of MPs. The chairmen of the groups were in most cases Opposition spokesmen and the secretaries were the Research Department desk officers whose normal work covered the subjects in hand. The groups tended to meet about every month, or in a few cases every two weeks, and to take eighteen months or so to prepare a report for submission to the Advisory Committee on Policy. As in the Labour Party study groups, papers would be written by the secretaries if other members were not particularly enthusiastic, but in the more active groups members prepared their own submissions.

The provisions made to co-ordinate the proposals of the policy groups were in many ways the most novel feature of the whole exercise and represented something of a breakthrough in the techniques of Opposition. Since Shadow Cabinet meetings were mainly taken up with parliamentary tactics and other day-to-day matters, it was decided to hold three-monthly meetings of policy group chairmen. Even more significant were meetings held annually from 1965 onwards at Swinton Conservative College to which all members of the policy groups were invited. A couple of major subjects were covered at each conference (economic policy, social

[1] See J. D. Hoffman, *The Conservatives in Opposition* 1945-51 (London: MacGibbon and Kee, 1964), ch. 6.

policy etc.) and an attempt was made 'to get the interfaces right'. The much publicised Selsdon Park Conference in January 1970 was really a final attempt to co-ordinate all the main policy proposals and decide priorities. From a public relations point of view it turned out badly, in that continuing differences over policy prevented the announcement of some policies, and the policies that were announced were mainly 'hardliner' statements on law and order, selectivity in the social services, and the reduction of state aid to industry.[1]

In addition to the policy groups, two other new organisations – the Conservative Systems Research Centre and the Public Sector Research Unit – were created. The Systems Research Centre further promoted co-ordination by costing proposals and working out interrelations between them. The idea was that members of the Shadow Cabinet should be able to see the effects of, say, building more houses on transport requirements, or of alternative tax packages on the standard of living of families in different income groups.[2] For these purposes a sophisticated computer model of public expenditure was developed. The Public Sector Research Unit, on the other hand, was concerned with machinery of government reform. Its director was the former Minister of Transport, Mr Ernest Marples, and its secretary was David Howell, MP. The published result of the unit's work was David Howell's *A New Style of Government*, in which he advocated the introduction of output budgeting and the 'hiving-off' of some activities of government either to private enterprise, or to project managers (preferably businessmen specially recruited for the purpose) in charge of semi-autonomous government agencies.[3]

Most of the reports made by the Systems Research Unit, the Public Sector Research Unit and the policy groups remained confidential. However, five reports were published and the Conservative Government since June 1970 has implemented some of the proposals framed in Opposition. It is therefore possible to make at least a preliminary estimate of the value of the whole exercise. The two most thorough of the published reports were *Fair Deal at Work* and *A Better Country*, which dealt with the subject of leisure. The proposals put forward in *Fair Deal at Work* are outlined in Chapter 9. It is sufficient to note here that they were detailed and cast in the form, if not of draft legislation, at least as instructions to parliamentary draftsmen. Existing industrial relations law was reviewed as was law in other countries and the proposals were translated

---

[1] See 'The Stainless Steel Tories', *The Economist* (7 February 1970).
[2] See Butler and Pinto-Duchinsky, *The British General Election of 1970*, p. 83.
[3] David Howell, *A New Style of Government* (London: Conservative Political Centre, 1970).

almost *in toto* into the Industrial Relations Act, 1970.[1] The report on leisure, *A Better Country*, written by Christopher Chataway, MP, ran to seventy-two pages and was a rather scholarly production with appendixes on leisure and recreation in the United States and Holland.[2] It recommended the creation of a number of new bodies, including a Coast and Countryside Commission.[3] The other three published reports were rather less impressive. The coverage of *Coping with Emergencies in War and Peace* and *Crime Knows No Boundaries* was probably too wide for useful proposals to emerge, and the topic of *Fair Share for the Fair Sex* is a Conservative perennial due to the fact that the women's section of the party is so formidable.

Other proposals made in unpublished policy group reports have been implemented by the present Conservative Government. The autumn 1970 mini-budget and the 1971 and 1972 budgets contained proposals on a Value Added Tax (to replace Selective Employment Tax) and a negative income tax that were based on recommendations made by the Economic Policy Group of which Mr Arthur Cockfield, a director of Boots and formerly of the Inland Revenue, was a prominent member. It was a vindication of the group's work that the 'package' they proposed was accepted by a Chancellor, Mr Anthony Barber, who had not been chairman of the group.[4] Another group which saw its proposals implemented was the Agricultural Policy Group which had advocated the introduction of import levies to supersede the system of deficiency payments for farm products.[5] The Agricultural Policy Group was, in fact, atypical in that its members, instead of reflecting a broad range of interests and opinions like the other groups, were all landowners and farmers.[6] However, they succeeded in persuading the Shadow Cabinet that the Common Market import levy system was preferable, regardless of whether Britain entered the Market. Reforms in Whitehall proposed by the Machinery of Government Group and the Public Sector Research Unit were also implemented. The creation of the Departments of the Environment and Trade and Industry was broadly on the lines suggested in *A New Style of Government*.[7] The founding of

[1] See Chapter 9.

[2] *A Better Country* (London: Conservative Political Centre 1966).

[3] In the event the Labour Government stole the Conservative Party's clothes and set up a Countryside Commission under the Countryside Act, 1968.

[4] Mr Iain Macleod, who was appointed Chancellor of the Exchequer in June 1970, had been chairman of economic policy study groups. However, he died on 20 July and Mr Barber replaced him as Chancellor.

[5] Deficiency payments could still be made as a fall-back guarantee if the levies failed to maintain farm prices at a level considered satisfactory.

[6] See footnote 1, p. 176.

[7] See Howell, *A New Style of Government*, pp. 27-9.

a central policy review staff, 'relating individual departmental policies to the Government's strategy as a whole',[1] and the instructions given to individual Ministers to investigate the possibilities of hiving-off and the reorganisation of their departments to ensure that, 'wherever possible, at all levels, responsibility and accountability are clearly defined and allocated'[2] also reflected plans laid in Opposition.

An assessment of Conservative policy formulation in Opposition, 1964-70, must recognise that the three main weaknesses of the Labour Opposition in the pre-1964 period were at least partially avoided. First, the Leader and Shadow Ministers, who would have to implement proposals, were prominent in their formulation, whereas in the Labour Party responsibility lay with an extra-parliamentary body, the NEC. Second, attempts were made to co-ordinate and work out the opportunity cost of proposals; this represented an innovation in the methods of Opposition. Finally, the Conservative Research Department with its thirty full-time research officers, including several long-serving senior men, is much better equipped than its Labour counterpart to play a major role in Opposition.

There were dissenting voices in the Conservative Party in the 1964-70 period, saying that the policy exercise was both politically unwise, in that published commitments provided hostages to fortune, and that proposals framed without Civil Service advice would have to be drastically revised anyway. A detailed review of the record of Mr Heath's post 1970 Conservative Government would be required to resolve these arguments; meanwhile the least that can be said is that new techniques of Opposition were developed and a significant attempt made to provide incoming Ministers with the ammunition required for them to act as policy initiators.

SOURCES OF POLICY FOR MINISTERS APPOINTED TO OFFICE IN MID-TERM

The longer a Government lasts the less Ministers can draw on policies proposed in Opposition. Most election pledges, if they are implemented at all, are implemented in a Government's first few years in office. Most Ministers, however, are not appointed during this period. In the 1964-70 Labour Government, for example, there were twenty-three initial Cabinet appointments and forty-eight appointments were made subsequently and in the 1951-64 Conservative Government there were twenty-one initial appointments and ninety-four subsequent ones. As we saw earlier, the majority of

[1] *The Reorganisation of Central Government* (London: HMSO 1970), p. 14.
[2] ibid., p. 15.

Ministers appointed in mid-term readily concede that they do not come to office with definite policy objectives in mind. To what sources can they turn in their quest for policy?

Before answering this question in respect of British Ministers it will be instructive, and will give us a basis of international comparison, if we consider briefly the sources available to Swedish Ministers. Sweden is a particularly interesting case because the same party, the Labour Party, has been in office since the early 1930s, and has been acutely aware of the danger of 'running out of ideas'. The danger has, however, been avoided by a quite remarkably extensive and systematic programme of research on future policy.[1] At any one time about a hundred *ad hoc* commissions are in existence, dealing with all major aspects of government policy.[2] Commissions are normally set up as a result of a proposal for legislation from a public authority or interest group. The typical commission contains between two and seven members, although one-man commissions are not uncommon. Civil servants from government departments and administrative agencies whose remit includes the subject under investigation usually form a majority of commission members, but academics and politicians from all parties are often included. The terms of reference of commissions are normally fairly broad and are prepared in consultation with the Ministry of Finance (the equivalent of the Treasury) to try and obviate the risk of a commission putting forward impossibly costly proposals. The most impressive aspect of the commissions' work is the research they undertake. The staff are full-time and mainly consist of junior civil servants. Over a period of two to three years (the average length of time a commission takes to report) extensive consultations take place with interest groups and public authorities and a great deal of original research data is accumulated. For example, the commission on the constitution, which reported in 1963, undertook studies of the effect that alternative electoral systems would have had on the distribution of party support in the legislature in the 1950s and commissioned an analysis of the parties' procedures in nominating election candidates. There were also studies of opinion formation in referendum campaigns, interest group behaviour and legislative decision making. The

---

[1] This section on the Swedish commissions is largely based on Hans Meijer, 'Bureaucracy and Policy Formulation in Sweden', *Scandinavian Political Studies* (1969), 103-116; Lars Foyer 'The Social Sciences in Royal Commission Studies in Sweden', *Scandinavian Political Studies* (1969), 183-203; Joseph B. Board, *The Government and Politics of Sweden* (Boston: Houghton, Mifflin, 1970); · D. A. Rustow, *The Politics of Compromise* (Princeton: Princeton University, 1955).

[2] The commissions are officially known as royal commissions but in view of the British connotation the term is misleading. See below.

analysis and collection of the data were carried out by academic political scientists as well as by the commission's staff.[1]

Even after a report has been presented there remains the 'remiss' procedure under which it must be despatched for comment to all public authorities and pressure groups whose interests may be affected. The whole exercise, as well as being thorough, is thus designed to bring as many alternative proposals to light as possible. In making their final decisions Ministers may be reasonably certain that neither civil servants nor any other single group of advisers have foreclosed their options.

An important advantage of the Swedish commissions is that they are well equipped to produce proposals which are innovative, or at least reflect the latest research, and at the same time, due to the presence of Civil Service members, are not likely to be regarded in official circles as wildly radical and impractical. In Britain, by contrast, it is difficult to achieve this balance. Proposals formulated by departmental officials, and only shown to Ministers at a relatively late stage of development, are likely to reflect existing priorities and to contain few innovations.[2] The same lack of innovation will probably occur if a Minister decides what measures to sponsor after consulting only his department's usual interest group clientele. Such bodies as the National Union of Farmers at the Ministry of Agriculture, the British Medical Association at the Department of Health and Social Security, the National Union of Teachers at the Department of Education and Science and the Association of Municipal Corporations at the Department of the Environment have such routine access to officialdom that their preferences are already taken account of in policy formulation. On the other hand, if a Minister, in his quest for policy turns to a group, or institution, or independent advisers who lack close ties with his department, there is an evident danger that the proposals which emerge will fail to take sufficient account of the department's experience and knowledge of what is administratively feasible.

However, despite the difficulties, Ministers frequently do seek advice outside Whitehall. The most traditional method is to appoint a royal commission, although these are now used rather sparingly. In fact only fifteen commissions[3] reported during the 1960s and four of them were concerned with historical monuments and manuscripts. Others, however, dealt with more politically sensitive, dare one say

[1] Foyer, *Scandinavian Political Studies* (1969).

[2] See Chapter 13.

[3] The six commissions not referred to in the text were concerned with doctors' and dentists' remuneration, local government in Greater London, tribunals of inquiry, the penal system in England and Wales, medical education and assize and quarter sessions.

more important topics: the police, the press, trade unions and employers' associations, and local government reform in England and Scotland. The procedures followed by royal commissions have been sharply criticised in recent years. Jenifer Hart, for example, basing her views on an analysis of the methods of the Royal Commission on the Police (1960-2) criticises commissions for failing to carry out adequate research and relying instead on the evidence of supposedly authoritative witnesses.[1] She argues convincingly that the data collected by the Government Social Survey on relations between the police and the public (the only piece of original research that was carried out) were seriously misinterpreted and that a commission report must, in any case, be either a compromise between the fifteen or so individual members representing divergent interests or else, 'it must be vague, general, ambiguous, or perhaps even express conflicting views in different corners'.[2] Other critics have alleged that royal commissions are often appointed to postpone action and that their members are selected from too restricted a circle of people whose names are found on a Treasury list sometimes referred to as the 'Book of the Great and the Good'.

It may be that royal commissions have been too harshly criticised; the publicity they receive lures academics to fire a blast at their findings. Certainly not all commissions could be criticised for being short on research, or for producing reports which are the embodiment of ambivalent compromise. The recent Redcliffe-Maud Commission on local government and the Roskill Commission on the third London airport could reasonably plead 'not guilty' on both counts.[3] For many purposes, however, and particularly when it is not necessary that a commission should be publicly seen to represent a diversity of interests, smaller independent committees of inquiry are preferable. Between ten and twenty such committees are set up each year. Again, as with royal commissions, some deal with politically important subjects, others are extremely specialised.[4]

---

[1] Jenifer Hart, 'Some Reflections on the Report of the Royal Commission on the Police' in Richard Rose (ed.), *Policy Making in Britain* (London: Macmillan, 1969), pp. 238-55.

[2] ibid., p. 255.

[3] *The Royal Commission on Local Government in England* (Redcliffe-Maud Commission), Cmnd 4040 (London: HMSO, 1969), vol. III; *The Commission on the Third London Airport* (Roskill Commission), SBN II 510171 3 (London: HMSO, 1971).

[4] Taking 1967-8 as a sample year one finds committees dealing with such intrinsically important subjects as the Civil Service (the Fulton Committee), the personal social services (the Seebohm Committee) and manpower resources for science and technology (the Swan Committee). At the other end of the spectrum were committees on civil judicial statistics, eggs, herbage seed supplies, trawler safety and maintenance grants.

Their potential advantage over larger royal commissions is that a small group may be able to meet more often, agree on the main lines of analysis and produce a report which reflects pooled ideas, rather than a compromise between individuals who started and finished as the representatives of disparate groups. The Geddes Committee on the Shipbuilding Industry will serve as an example of a committee which produced what was widely regarded as an innovative report.[1] The committee recommended that shipyards should form groups in order to combine their resources and improve their market research, shipyard plant, ship design, the competitiveness of their tenders for large contracts and other aspects in which the British industry was inferior to some of its international rivals. It also recommended that a Shipbuilding Industry Board be set up and given government funds to assist rationalisation and the formation of groups of shipyards. These funds would only be paid out for specified purposes (for example to pay management consultants, modernise plant, or provide tiding-over loans in cases where huge ships were being built and the group could not expect to be paid for its work for several years) and only then to groups which had already shown evidence of following the committee's recommendations. The Board of Trade welcomed the Geddes report to the extent of deciding that the principle of providing government funds to meet modernisation and rationalisation costs should be extended to other industries besides shipbuilding. The Industrial Expansion Act, 1968, was the result.

Independent committees of inquiry have, of course, long been a favourite Whitehall device. A more recent development, also of potential value to Ministers seeking outside advice, is the creation of research centres and institutes which are independent of government but whose officials in practice have excellent contacts in Whitehall. The National Institute of Economic and Social Research (which in practice has concentrated solely on its economic remit) is probably the most influential of these bodies. It receives a government grant, its staff includes many former Treasury men and its quarterly *Economic Review* contains analyses and forecasts which are widely publicised. Its pre-budget forecasts are of special interest and connoisseurs were delighted when in 1972, using a different model of the economy from the Treasury's, it recommended a reflationary boost of £2.5 billion, as against the Treasury's £1.2 billion, in order to achieve an agreed target of 5 per cent growth in gross domestic product in 1972-3.[2] Less influential than the NIESR and less willing

---

[1] The Shipbuilding Inquiry Committee 1965-6, *Report*, Cmnd 2937 (London: HMSO, 1966).

[2] *National Institute Economic Review*, No. 59 (February 1972).

to endorse alternative programmes are the foreign and defence policy institutes: the Royal Institute of International Affairs and the Institute of Strategic Studies. A few politicians and civil servants attend for seminars and the institutes maintain close links with international relations and strategic studies departments in the universities. Until the 1960s no comparable centres existed in the fields of environmental and social policy but the founding of the Centre for Environmental Studies, the Institute of Race Relations and the Centre for Studies in Social Policy indicate that these gaps are being filled.[1]

CONCLUSION

The paradox we have encountered in this chapter is that a high proportion of Ministers see it as their role to initiate policy changes but, in practice, come to office without well defined policy objectives and priorities. A principal reason for this state of affairs is that there are few sources of well informed advice outside Whitehall to which they can turn. They may find it distasteful to rely solely on civil servants to define objectives and submit policy proposals but often enough they have little choice. There are, however, several possible ways in which the range of options open to Ministers might be increased. In particular, small independent committees (as distinct from more cumbersome royal commissions) have a useful role to play in reporting on all but the most politically controversial subjects. There are obstacles, however, in Britain to increasing their coverage to quite the extent that has occurred in Sweden. The crucial constraint here is that the close relationship established in Sweden between investigating bodies and government departments could not be achieved in Whitehall when politically sensitive subjects were under review. In Sweden departmental files are accessible not only to government appointed committees and commissions but also to the general public: in Whitehall special permission has to be given before files can be inspected and officials would always have to be circumspect in revealing how the Minister's mind was working and what kinds of recommendations would be acceptable to him.

Whitehall secrecy is in part explained by the convention of Government versus Opposition. Government policy is treated by the Opposition as party policy and as such is opposed on partisan grounds in partisan rhetoric. If departments were to open their files, or otherwise reveal to outsiders the arguments against policies the government had adopted, or was thinking of adopting, this would

[1] Also the Department of Health now finances large scale research projects intended to evaluate the programmes it provides.

provide ammunition for the Opposition. In the Swedish political culture, on the other hand, partisan differences are played down and commissions and government departments behave as if it is possible to consult experts, compromise between interest groups and formulate recommendations which are widely accepted, if not quite universally regarded as in the public interest.

In addition to, or alternative to, expanding the role of committees of inquiry, it would assist British Ministers if an attempt were made to improve the quality of policy formulation by party sources. The Conservative Party, with its policy preparation in Opposition from 1964-70, has indicated what might be done. During the Opposition period, Shadow Ministers chaired policy groups consisting of outside experts as well as politicians and these groups received staff assistance from the party Research Department. After attaining office Ministers took a number of significant policy initiatives based on proposals formulated in Opposition. It seemed unlikely, though, that Mr Heath's Conservative Government would retain its momentum if it survived beyond its initial term.

Arguably, what Ministers who intend to act as policy initiators require is a flow of well informed proposals and recommendations from party sources, continuing throughout their period in office. In other words there needs to be a kind of Shadow Government even when a party is in Government. For this Shadow Government to function usefully the party research departments would have to be expanded.[1] Parallel to each government department, research departments would need a small staff of, say, four to six persons. (This is the complement of the more modest departmental planning units in Whitehall.) Cabinet Ministers would presumably be too busy to act as chairmen of these shadow departments and might therefore delegate the task to a junior Minister. One final point: the cost of running a permanent Shadow Government would be beyond the means of at least the Labour Party and would have to be met by an Exchequer grant. Subsidising political parties from public funds is contrary to post-eighteenth-century practice, but, if Ministers are seriously expected to serve as policy initiators, it may be necessary to pay a few thousand pounds a year to furnish them with policies to initiate.

[1] Anthony King, 'The Conservative Party and Policy', *New Society* (20 July 1972) discusses the links maintained by Mr Heath's Conservative Government with the party's Research Department.

Part III

Ministers in Office
Case Studies

Chapter 9

Policy Initiators

The Key Issues Approach

The object of this chapter is to present case studies of Ministers who exercised policy leadership in their departments and to discover the conditions which enabled them to do so. The most ambitious policy leadership role is that of policy initiation and the Ministers whose achievements are discussed here all instituted major policy changes. It will be recalled that nearly half the Ministers interviewed intended to perform this role. There is a world of difference, however, between intention and performance, between having a particular role conception and living up to it. In Part II factors influencing ministerial role performance were anaylsed in fairly general terms. The case studies serve to illustrate points raised in the earlier analysis and to suggest some rather more specific propositions about the conditions of policy initiation.

A preliminary point needs to be made about the Ministers whose performance of office is reviewed in the following pages. They all served as policy initiators in the sense that, instead of accepting the existing objectives and priorities of their departments, they succeeded in exacting policy programmes based on objectives defined by themselves or their party. There is no implication, however, that these Ministers 'succeeded' to the extent of producing the results (economic, social, military etc.) which were intended. It is notoriously difficult to assess and isolate the consequences of particular policy programmes and it therefore seems preferable, for present purposes, to include Ministers who made an 'impact' on their departments without necessarily having the intended impact on the 'real world' outside Whitehall.

The case studies cover Ministers in six different departments faced with problems as different as building 300,000 houses a year, decolonising in Africa and passing liberal (or libertarian) legislation for an erstwhile puritan society. The element these Ministers have in common is that they were all exponents of what may be termed the *key issues approach* to policy initiation. They believed that in order to make a significant contribution to policy a Minister must concentrate as much as possible on a single issue (or, at most, a few related issues) and seek to reduce other demands on his time. Like the other propositions in this chapter, however, the proposition that a key issues approach is essential to ministerial policy initiation can only be advanced tentatively. Evidence on the performance in office of individual Ministers is not as complete as one could wish and, in any event, there are bound to be many imponderables involved in assessing the impact of a particular person in a particular job at a particular time. The value of putting forward some reasonably specific propositions, however, is that they can then be tested in further studies and our knowledge of the factors influencing the role performance of political leaders gradually advanced.

HAROLD MACMILLAN: MINISTER OF HOUSING AND LOCAL GOVERNMENT 1951-1954

At the 1950 Conservative Party Conference a rather unseemly auction took place. The bidding stopped at 300,000 houses a year which thus became the party's general election pledge in 1951. Following the election Churchill appointed Mr Harold Macmillan, wartime Minister Resident in North-West Africa and future Prime Minister, to honour the pledge:

'On arrival at 3 p.m. I found him [Churchill] in a most pleasant and rather tearful mood. He asked me to "build the houses for the people". What an assignment! . . . Churchill said "it is a gamble— [it will] make or mar your political career. But every humble home will bless your name, if you succeed." More tears. I said I would think about it.'[1]

With amiable frankness Macmillan concedes that at the time of his appointment, 'I knew nothing whatever about the housing problem . . . I asked what was the present housing set-up. He [Churchill] said he had not an idea but that the "boys" [the civil servants] would know.'[2] His first step in taking office was to signal a change of priorities by changing the name of his department. The Ministry of Local Government and Planning became the Ministry of Housing and Local Government. It is clear from his memoirs that Macmillan devoted all his time to housing questions.

[1] Harold Macmillan, *Tides of Fortune* (London: Macmillan, 1969), p. 363.
[2] loc. cit.

He writes that 'it was essential to concentrate the whole of my thoughts and action upon the forcing of a narrow but heavily defended position'.[1] He had no time to read cabinet papers other than those affecting his department and his memoirs contain no reference whatever to local government, or any other subject except housing, that he was formally responsible for between 1951 and 1954.

Macmillan tackled the housing shortage with considerable ruthlessness. He found his department and its personnel ill-suited to supervising a production task.[2] Following the wartime Ministry of Supply model and against the opposition of his Permanent Secretary, he brought in a business and wartime colleague, Sir Percy Mills, to be Director-General in charge of the production effort. Mills set up regional housing boards to deal directly with local authorities, builders and building suppliers.[3] This was contrary to established departmental procedure; in the past the department had generally kept local authorities 'at arm's length', communicating with them by means of non-mandatory circulars. However, the regional housing boards appear to have worked well both as a means of identifying supply problems and as a forum through which builders could be reassured that the Government would meet its housing target and not leave them in the lurch with unused stocks.

As his Parliamentary Secretary Macmillan asked for and obtained Ernest Marples, who had made a fortune in civil engineering and real estate.[4] Marples was put in charge of designing a smaller standard council house which would require less materials. Marples succeeded in his task and produced the house which Macmillan referred to publicly as 'The People's House' and privately as 'The Boneless Wonder'.[5] Even with this house, however, Macmillan still had to fight in Cabinet for 'more than my fair share of the resources which the experts told me would be available'.[6] The Treasury was persuaded, for the benefit of Macmillan's department only, to break its practice of budgeting resources only one year ahead. Instead production and supply orders were placed three years ahead, so that the building industry could make its plans.[7]

Local authorities, too, required heavy subsidies to cover the rising interest rates they had to pay to finance house building; subsidies, in fact, quadrupled in the early 1950s.[8] In the end Macmillan's objective was achieved. The target of 300,000 houses a year was

[1] ibid., p. 377.   [2] ibid., pp. 375-6.
[3] ibid., p. 395.   [4] See Chapter 11.
[5] Macmillan, *Tides of Fortune*, p. 410.
[6] ibid., p. 375.   [7] ibid., pp. 408-9.
[8] D. V. Donnison, *The Government of Housing* (Harmondsworth: Penguin 67), p. 168.

actually exceeded in 1954. The building programme had been increased by 50 per cent and, for once in the post-war years, Britain was high up the European 'league table' of annual housing completions.[1]

IAIN MACLEOD, COLONIAL SECRETARY 1959-1961

Iain Macleod had made a considerable reputation as Minister of Labour by holding out against, and eventually defeating, the London busmen's strike of July 1958 and ushering in one of the few short periods since 1945 when wage rises did not exceed productivity increases. However, the Colonial Office was probably the department in which he made his greatest impact on policy. His key issue was African decolonisation. He came to office shortly after the general election of 1959 and after Mr Macmillan's famous 'wind of change' speech to the South African Parliament. In a sense, therefore, the initial impetus for the change of policy came from the Prime Minister but, equally, Macleod acted with great speed, decolonising more rapidly than large sections of the Conservative Party wanted or expected, formulating constitutions for newly independent African countries, installing African legislative majorities and Chief Ministers and incurring the lasting enmity of the white settlers and their leaders. He also had to overcome the opposition of his department in which the doctrine that political advance could only go in tandem with social and economic advance and the emergence of a native 'political class' had been accepted since the early 1940s. In the words of J. M. Lee's authoritative account of the post-war Colonial Office:

'The chief connection between the assumptions of the official classes and the policy for colonial development lay in the conviction that power could only be transferred legitimately if it were given to an experienced ruling class. The unexpected quickening in the speed of Britain's withdrawal from colonial responsibility in the late 1950s upset their plans to effect this operation, but not their intentions.'[2]

At the time of Macleod's appointment Kenya, Tanganyika, Uganda and Zanzibar were all still colonies in which white settlers dominated both the executive and legislative branches of government. In the Central African Federation also, comprising Northern

[1] Donnison, op. cit., p. 168.
[2] J. M. Lee, *Colonial Development and Good Government* (Oxford: Clarendon Press, 1967), p. 195.

and Southern Rhodesia and Nyasaland, whites were in charge both at the federal and the single state level. By the end of 1960 (only fourteen months later) the East African countries were clearly set for independence. The settlers in Kenya had, in February, accepted at the Lancaster House conference a constitution which they subsequently implied that Macleod had produced unexpectedly and insisted on making the sole basis of negotiation.[1] This constitution provided for an African majority in the legislature with an African Chief Minister in 1961. On Macleod's orders, and against the Governor's opposition, Jomo Kenyatta, the Mau-Mau terrorist leader, was released from goal in the expectation that he would take the post. Zanzibar, Uganda and Tanganyika (which already had an African Chief Minister) were also due to become independent in 1961 and 1962. Opposition in these countries, however, was less severe because there were fewer settlers.

Macleod enunciated his own view of the realities governing contemporary colonial policy in a widely reported speech delivered in January 1961. Drawing an analogy with policy towards Ireland in the nineteenth century, he argued that the doctrine that independence could only follow economic and social advance had always had disastrous consequences.[2] However, pressure was building up against him from both the Central African Federation, which had the largest settler population in colonial Africa, and the Conservative backbenches. Wary of the fate that had befallen their fellows in Kenya and alarmed by the Monckton Commission report that the Federation was hopelessly unpopular among Africans and would probably have to be broken up, the settlers formed a White Defence League. They also founded a lobby which worked with considerable effect at Westminster, where Macleod had angry meetings with the Conservative backbench colonial committee and where sixty-seven Conservative MPs signed a motion deploring the pace of political advance in Africa.[3]

The Colonial Secretary backpedalled a bit. The Central African Federation was ended and a constitution promulgated for an independent Nyasaland.[4] But the White Paper of February 1961, which appeared to promise an African legislative majority in Northern Rhodesia in the near future, was replaced by another White Paper in June, setting out constitutional provisions which

[1] The Kenyan settlers' views are reflected and endorsed in Lord Salisbury's attack on Macleod in the House of Lords, *Parliamentary Debates* (Lords), 229, cols 308-15.

[2] 'Political Advances in Kenya: Macleod Castigates Blimps', *Guardian* (4 January 1961).

[3] *The Times* (13 February 1961).

[4] Nyasaland actually became independent as Malawi in 1964.

would have given the Africans less than parity. It was left to Macleod's successors to find a workable constitution for Northern Rhodesia and to find that the problem of Southern Rhodesia, where the settlers were already threatening a unilateral declaration of independence (UDI), was intractable.

Like all Ministers Macleod did not achieve all he intended in office. But he directed, against the opposition of the settlers, a large section of his own party and senior officials of his department, the most significant instalment of decolonisation since India became independent in 1947. In the last year of his life Macleod said: 'It's quite true that in my Colonial Office period I did reach a level of political fulfilment that I never did before, and frankly, which I think I shall never attain again.'[1]

ANTHONY CROSLAND, SECRETARY OF STATE FOR EDUCATION AND SCIENCE, 1965-1967

In an interview in 1969[2] Anthony Crosland made clear his adherence to a key issues approach: 'It is necessary to concentrate on a limited number of crucial policy areas and take a few big decisions each year. In a sense everything else is a distraction and should be delegated, if at all possible.' Crosland initially decided to concentrate on two issues. His wife noted in her diary four weeks after his appointment that, 'in fact he does think only teacher supply and the comprehensive issue deserve priority at this moment'.[3] Crosland fully accepted the corollary of his key issues approach, namely that issues like teachers' pensions and much of policy regarding tertiary education, which had preoccupied some of his predecessors at the department, would, for six months at least, have to be dealt with by civil servants, or junior Ministers. He told Maurice Kogan that,

'The worst sort of Minister is the one who tries to control it all, and stays up till 3 a.m. each night going through endless red boxes and getting himself bogged down in detail. . . . But the price you pay for this is that occasionally you approve a decision you haven't gone into yourself in detail and you find you're landed in a political mess.'[4]

In regard to the teacher supply issue Crosland was in no way an originator or initiator of policy. He simply adopted and broadcast a

---

[1] 'One Nation, Which Macleod', *Guardian* (27 February 1970).

[2] Interviewed by the author.

[3] E. Boyle, A. Crosland and M. Kogan, *The Politics of Education* (Harmondsworth: Penguin, 1971), p. 155.　　　　[4] ibid., pp. 177-8.

fourteen-point plan to increase the number of teachers available, the details of which had been worked out by an Under-Secretary before his arrival.[1] The plan was eminently successful and the teacher shortage was largely eliminated but Crosland can claim only the credit for pressing matters along. In dealing with the comprehensive issue, on the other hand, he made major contributions in both the substance of policy and the tactics of getting his proposals accepted and implemented. His predecessor, Michael Stewart, although like Crosland committed to party policy on comprehensive reorganisation and the abolition of the 11-plus examination, had made little progress, having distressed officials by choosing 'to cloister himself with his papers'.[2]

Essentially, Crosland had to resolve two questions. First, he had to decide whether to make comprehensive reorganisation compulsory by Act of Parliament, whether to send out a mandatory circular to Local Education Authorities (LEAs) 'requiring' them to draw up plans, or whether simply to 'request' them to do so.[3] Secondly, he had to decide which of numerous alternative types of school he would recognise as 'comprehensive'. Several factors were bound to influence these decisions. The 163 LEAs were jealous of their limited autonomy and would certainly resent any appearance of dictation from the Department of Education and Science. On the other hand, most local authorities in 1965 were Labour controlled and might be expected to be co-operative so long as they were consulted. A further important constraint was that the authorities had limited funds and an existing stock of school buildings, which could not overnight be replaced in order to conform to a single comprehensive blueprint.[4]

In the event Crosland's famous circular 10/65 merely 'requested' LEAs to draw up reorganisation plans, but stipulated that they meet the request within one year. The adoption of the non-mandatory formula Crosland said, 'was strongly influenced by my meetings with the AEC and my judgement of the general mood of the local authority world.'[5] The second major decision – the designation of six alternative types of comprehensive school – also reflected extensive consultation with local authorities. Middle schools were to be permitted as well as the orthodox straight through eleven to eighteen-year-old schools, but two-tier systems with optional transfers to a senior school would only be accepted as a temporary ex-

---

[1] ibid., pp. 191-3.   [2] ibid., p. 49 n.
[3] The possibility of introducing a bill had been ruled out by Michael Stewart and Crosland apparently did not reconsider this option. See ibid., p. 188.
[4] ibid., p. 188.
[5] ibid., p. 189. The A.E.C. is the Association of Education Committees.

pedient.[1] In drawing up plans LEAs were themselves to consult with teachers and to keep parents informed.[2]

Crosland's tactics proved to be nicely judged. The Conservative Opposition was divided, partly due to the influence of the former Minister of Education, Sir Edward Boyle, who himself regarded the 11-plus examination as iniquitous and comprehensive schools as one among several satisfactory types of institution.[3] More important, by the end of 1967 (Crosland's last year in office) 134 LEAs had prepared schemes, 5 had formally declined to do so and 24 had taken no action.[4] With only a small number of recalcitrants to combat it was possible to invoke the 1944 Education Act. Authorities that refused to prepare schemes were threatened with having their school building funds cut off (circular 10/66) and in the case of Surrey the threat was made public. The extent to which Crosland's approach was well judged may be inferred from the difficulties encountered when his successor, Mr Edward Short, brought forward a bill to make comprehensive reorganisation compulsory.[5] The Conservative Party at Westminster united and Conservative LEAs (in a majority after the local elections of 1968 and 1969) took a more obstructionist line. Progress in extending comprehensive schooling slowed down. By the end of 1969 there were still twenty-two authorities which had not submitted schemes, or had their schemes declared unsatisfactory by the Minister.[6]

Crosland attracted some criticism within his own party both for his choice of key issues and also for his handling of comprehensive reorganisation. Some Labour MPs were opposed to his decision to, in effect, postpone Labour's attack on the public schools by setting up a Public Schools Commission.[7] One of Crosland's motives may have been to keep the political temperature down while comprehensive reorganisation took place. (Inevitably, public school Old Boys would have fought lustily in defence of their alma maters.) The main reason he gave to his supporters, however, was that the commission had a necessary role to play, since no practical proposals existed on

[1] *The Reorganisation of Secondary Education* (Department of Education and Science Circular, October 1965).

[2] Boyle, Crosland and Kogan, *The Politics of Education*, p. 190.

[3] Boyle's very moderate views on comprehensives, his disapproval of the 11-plus examination and his unwillingness to take a totally condemnatory line regarding circular 10/65 are explained in ibid., pp. 65-143, especially pp. 78-9.

[4] *Education and Science in 1967: Annual Report of the Department of Education and Science*, Cmnd 3564 (London: HMSO, 1968).

[5] The bill was lost because Labour failed to have a majority in a crucial committee stage division.

[6] *Education and Science in 1969: Annual Report of the Department of Education and Science* (London: HMSO, 1970).

[7] Boyle, Crosland and Kogan, *The Politics of Education*, pp. 196-7.

how to abolish the public schools, or integrate them with the state system.[1] As far as the comprehensive issue itself was concerned, his critics, who included his own Minister of State, believed that it would have been tactically shrewder to make reorganisation mandatory.[2] The ensuing political row, so it was argued, would have rallied public support and made it harder for any subsequent Government (as Mr Heath's Government did) to withdraw circular 10/65.[3]

ROY JENKINS: HOME SECRETARY 1965-1967

In a newspaper interview shortly after his appointment as Home Secretary Mr Jenkins was asked what he had learned from writing biographies of former Ministers. He replied: 'First, not to spread one's energy too widely but to concentrate on a limited number of major issues at any one time.'[4] One reason for this was to 'try to avoid being tired when major decisions are taken'. The extent to which Jenkins' concentration on key issues paid off, is more easily verified than in the case of most Ministers, because he had published his objectives in advance. In the Penguin special *The Labour Case* (1959), under the heading 'Liberalising the Home Office', he had written of the 'wholesale reform of which the Home Office is in urgent need' and went on to list the liberal reforms which a Home Secretary of his persuasion would seek to pass.[5] These included changing the law in relation to homosexuality, theatre censorship and race relations. In the event Mr Jenkins was able to initiate work on the Race Relations Act (although it received the royal assent in 1968 under his successor Mr Callaghan) and to give Home Office blessing to private member's bills on the other two subjects. The Race Relations Act set up a Race Relations Board to investigate complaints of discrimination, *inter alia* in housing and employment. The Sexual Offences Act made homosexual behaviour between consenting adults legal and the Theatres Act ended the Lord Chamberlain's reign as a special censor for theatrical productions.

The strategy of using private members' bills was quite deliberate. The primary aim, Jenkins claimed, was not to avoid the odium of making the world safe for homosexuals and pornography but to ensure that, on these matters of faith and morals, a free vote could be taken in the House of Commons. Had government bills been

[1] loc. cit.

[2] ibid., p. 189.

[3] Circular 10/65 was withdrawn by the Conservative Secretary of State for Education and Science in DES Circular 10/70.

[4] 'The Tolerant Community', *The Sunday Times* (26 April 1966).

[5] Roy Jenkins, *The Labour Case* (Harmondsworth: Penguin, 1959), pp. 136-7.

introduced convention would have dictated that the whips be on. When, instead, Jenkins persuaded individual MPs whose names came up on the ballot for private members' bills to sponsor measures drafted by the Home Office, the House could vote 'according to its conscience'. Most private members' bills, however, even if they command majority support, are lost because the Government pre-empts almost all the parliamentary time available for legislation. Jenkins made sure that this would not happen in the case of the bills he was supporting, by obtaining government time for them. Allocating government time to private members' bills was, in fact, an innovation in House of Commons procedure.

The longest piece of legislation introduced by Jenkins in his period as Home Secretary was the Criminal Justice Act, 1963. This was not a measure foreshadowed in *The Labour Case*, but it did contain several liberal provisions. The courts were empowered to give suspended sentences rather than send criminals to gaol immediately, very short gaol sentences were abolished, additional categories of prisoners became eligible for parole after one year and to receive one-third remission of their sentences, and drunks were in future to be committed to hostels not cells. Probably the action which most endeared Jenkins to professional liberals, however, did not involve legislation. This was the pardoning of Timothy Evans, convicted and hanged for murder several years before. Considerable doubt had arisen about the case but Home Office officials had succeeded in persuading previous Home Secretaries (notably Sir Frank Soskice, Jenkins' Labour predecessor who prior to taking office had demanded Evans' pardon) not to reverse the decision of the court.[1]

Jenkins certainly made a considerable personal impact on policy at the Home Office. If he had any regret about his time there, it was perhaps that he failed 'to create a climate of opinion which is favourable to gaiety, tolerance and beauty and unfavourable to puritanical restriction, to petty minded disapproval, to hypocrisy and to a dreary, ugly pattern of life'.[2] In the short run his reforms appeared to produce a puritan backlash and a climate of opinion which, at the end of the 1960s, may have been more antipathetic to liberalism than before.

BARBARA CASTLE: MINISTER OF TRANSPORT 1965-1968

The 1964 general election manifesto committed Labour Ministers of Transport to 'a national plan for transport', or what was usually

[1] On Soskice's *volte face* see H. Nicholson, *The System* (London: Hodder and Stoughton, 1967), p. 186.

[2] R. Jenkins, *The Labour Case* (Harmondsworth: Penguin, 1959), p. 135.

referred to as 'integrated transport planning'. The phrase was vague, but it least implied that road and rail services would not be in direct competition to carry all kinds of passengers and cargo. Investment and pricing policy would be used to direct extra business to the railways. The roads were overcrowded and the social benefit of diverting traffic to British Rail must be weighed against the financial cost. Statements by Labour leaders prior to the 1964 election also made it clear that railways in remoter parts of Britain which had been closed, or were due to close because of their un-profitability, might be reprieved for social reasons.

Whatever the precise meaning of the phrase his critics were agreed that Mr Tom Fraser (Mrs Castle's predecessor) had not achieved 'integrated transport planning'.[1] Newspaper reports suggested that officials at the Ministry were insisting that a national transport plan was impractical and that road, rail and water transport should continue to be administered separately by separate divisions of the department.[2] Mrs Castle was determined to overcome any resistance. At her first press conference as Minister she announced that it would be 'presumptuous' of her, after only three days, to lay down the law on transport policy. Nevertheless (she continued) the respective roles of public and private transport must be decided and an inte-grated plan for roads, railways, canals and ports worked out: 'We must decide the place of each of them and have criteria for deciding the level and the distribution of investment we can afford to make in giving the country a modern transport system.'[3]

Mrs Castle's transport reforms were embodied in the Transport Act 1968, the longest Act in parliamentary history. The principal feature of the Act, for which it was much criticised, was the setting up of a large number of new administrative bodies all concerned, in some sense, with planning.[4] There were to be Road Construction Units to co-ordinate the road building activities of county councils, a National Freight Authority to co-ordinate road and rail freight and produce a national freight plan, conurbation transport authori-ties for Birmingham, Liverpool, Manchester and Tyneside, a Transport Co-ordinating Council for London, and Transport Co-ordinating Committees in each region working under the direction of the existing Regional Economic Councils.

Some changes of substance were also introduced. The policy

[1] See, for example, 'Transport Victims', *The Scotsman* (24 December 1965).

[2] See, for example, 'Mrs Castle Brings in Economists', *Guardian* (6 January 1966).

[3] *Glasgow Herald* (7 January 1966).

[4] *Parliamentary Debates* (Commons), 756, cols 1281-440. The Opposition's main line of attack was that the Act involved backdoor nationalisation. Mrs Castle called it 'practical socialism'.

enshrined in the 1962 Transport Act, that British Rail must break even, was altered and it was stated that railways had a special role to play in saving road space by carrying heavy freight and inter-city and commuter passengers.[1] However, for accounting purposes, the railway lines which were expected to be profitable would be treated separately from those kept open for social reasons. The latter would be identified by a steering group (in effect a departmental committee) under the chairmanship of a junior Minister.[2] The committee reported within the year and a number of railway lines were reprieved.

In Mrs Castle's case, it is useful to distinguish between her impact on the department and the impact of her policy initiative on the real world. It would take an expert to tell whether her concept of 'integrated transport planning' made much practical difference to the transport industries of Britain, to the balance between road and rail, between social service and profitability criteria and so forth. However, there can be no doubt that she made at least a temporary impact on her department. Ministerial policy objectives were imposed and the 'departmental view' overborne.

ROBERT CARR, SECRETARY OF STATE FOR EMPLOYMENT 1970-1972

Robert Carr is a lucid exponent of the key issues approach to policy initiation. In an interview in the summer of 1969, a year before his appointment as Secretary for Employment, he stated that, 'As a Minister you must know your objectives. Pick out two or three things you want to do in your time at the department – that is all you will be able to manage.' Few Ministers, and certainly none of the others discussed in this chapter, have come to office with their objectives so specifically and publicly stated, and with a detailed policy programme already worked out. Carr had been chairman of the Conservative policy groups which in the period in Opposition prior to June 1970 had formulated the proposals contained in the party publication *Fair Deal at Work*.[3]

Fair Deal at Work was virtually draft legislation. So in its first parliamentary session the Conservative Government was ready to introduce the most controversial and, on paper, most radical reform of industrial relations in British history. The ten main proposals in *Fair Deal at Work* were all in the Act.[4] A Registrar

---

[1] *Transport Policy*, Cmnd 3057 (London: HMSO, 1966).   [2] ibid.
[3] *Fair Deal at Work* (London: Conservative Political Centre, 1968).
[4] ibid., 'Summary of Recommendations', pp. 63-4.

of Trade Unions and Employers' Associations was appointed with powers to examine rule books and ensure democratic procedure and the protection of individual rights; trade unions were assigned corporate legal status and were in future to be immune from civil suits only when pursuing an industrial dispute which did not involve a breach of agreement; an Industrial Court was set up to adjudicate, *inter alia*, on alleged breaches of collective agreements, on appeals against unjust dismissal and inter-union disputes and to arbitrate in disputes referred to it by the Secretary for Employment; a Code of Practice for industrial relations was promulgated; collective agreements became legally binding unless the parties themselves so decided; employers were legally bound to recognise a trade union if the majority of their employees wanted them to; employees could appeal against dismissal or penalties imposed by their own union; sympathy strikes, strikes over inter-union disputes, to enforce a closed shop or prevent the hiring of labour a union disapproves of became illegal; union shops were only to be permitted subject to special provisions, including majority approval; and finally the Secretary for Employment was given new powers to apply for an injunction to prevent or delay strikes which, in his view, would endanger the national interest, to refer such disputes to the Industrial Court for arbitration, and to order a secret ballot to discover whether a majority of the strikers favoured strike action.

One of the prime objectives of the Act, although this was not formally stated, was to prevent unofficial strikes. An individual shop steward who called a strike would not, like a registered union acting in furtherance of a lawful dispute, be immune from civil proceedings. Furthermore, any union which was tempted to give all shop stewards official status would be taking a major risk, because if a strike was called in breach of contract, or without following agreed procedures, or if any 'unfair industrial practice' was resorted to, then the union itself would be liable for damages.[1] The Act was thus intended to strengthen the senior officials in trade union hierarchies against unofficial leaders on the shop floor.

The only major provision included in the Act, but not in *Fair Deal at Work*, was designed to ensure that proper grievance procedures existed in industry and gave the Secretary of State and employers, as well as unions, the right to ask the Commission on Industrial Relations to draw up a set of procedures.[2] Even if the

---

[1] This provision was only confirmed in 1972 as a result of the House of Lords decision in the Heaton's Transport case. The Lords reversed the Appeal Court decision which itself had reversed the National Industrial Relations Court.

[2] The Commission on Industrial Relations was set up by the Labour Govern-

procedures were not acceptable to the parties, the CIR could apply to the Industrial Court for an order to put them into force. Further, once procedures had been laid down, action in breach of them would render a union or employer liable to be sued for damages. This change made the Act rather more 'hardline' as far as the unions were concerned. One other less important change was a concession. *Fair Deal at Work* had recommended that all closed shops should be illegal.[1] In the event the Government conceded that in certain industries, including entertainment and shipping, closed shops would have to be permitted.[2]

Robert Carr's Industrial Relations Act is a clear-cut example of a ministerially initiated policy programme. The Minister and the policy groups he had chaired in Opposition laid down the main lines of policy and his department was only left to frame the legislation. If senior officials at the Department of Employment were dubious of the wisdom of providing 'a framework of law' for industrial relations, their influence was certainly slight. In Robert Carr's case, however, the distinction between a Minister's impact on his department and his impact on the real world is again worth stressing. By now it is fairly clear that, if the unions continue to refuse to comply with the law, employers and future Secretaries of State will not be willing to enforce it.[3] Furthermore, the Act probably contributed to making 1971 and 1972 record post-war years for working days lost in strikes; hardly the improvement in industrial relations that was looked for. Problems of enforcing legislation in general, and the Industrial Relations Act in particular, are more fully discussed below.

MINISTERIAL POLICY INITIATION: SOME GENERALISATIONS

Clearly defined role conceptions, pre-selected key issues

Why did these six Ministers succeed in initiating policy changes? The first point to re-emphasise is that they all had clearly defined role conceptions; they had made up their minds what the Minister's

ment in 1969 as 'a disseminator of good practice and a focus of reform by example' in the industrial relations field. Industrial relations problems were referred to the commission by the Secretary of State but it deployed no legal sanctions except those required to obtain information required for its work. See *In Place of Strife*, Cmnd 388 (London: HMSO, 1969).

[1] A closed shop means that only union members can be recruited.

[2] In the entertainment industry, for example, the flood of volunteers to take minor film roles etc. would be so great that without the closed shop arrangement, which Equity (the entertainers' union) operates, wages would be forced down to absurdly low levels.

[3] The Labour Party is, of course, committed to repeal the Act.

job was all about. They intended to make a major contribution to policy by concentrating their attention on a key issue, or at most a few related issues. In addition to being exponents of the key issues approach as a matter of conviction, they all knew at the time of their appointment what their key issues would be, and four of them had their objectives defined with reasonable precision. Thus Macmillan knew that he must try to get 300,000 houses a year built, and Macleod intended to arrange for Britain's Central and East African colonies to become independent in the very near future.[1] In Roy Jenkin's case the objectives of race relations legislation, homosexual law reform, and relaxing theatre censorship were obvious and, in the latter two cases, it was basically a matter of repealing existing laws. Robert Carr in *Fair Deal at Work* had not only set out his objectives but also prepared a detailed policy programme. In the case of Mrs Castle her key issue was known in advance, but her precise objectives were uncertain; she had to define 'integrated transport planning' before putting it into operation. Anthony Crosland's objectives were initially less vague than Mrs Castle's but he still had to decide on targets for increasing the supply of teachers (in April 1965 the colleges of education were given the target of increasing their output of graduates by 20 per cent)[2] and on a timetable for comprehensive reorganisation.

It can hardly be overemphasised that a Minister who intends to act as a policy initiator has precious little time to get to know his department and reflect on future policy. The department always has policy proposals in the pipeline and suggestions about future measures. An incoming Minister will be told, quite correctly, that delay in deciding what he wants to do may mean a failure to obtain Treasury approval for expenditure, or the refusal of parliamentary time for legislation in the next session. Departments cannot hope to sponsor more than one major bill per session and they want their Ministers to fight hard for a place in the parliamentary queue. The problem from an incoming Minister's point of view is that if, to avoid delay, he decides to adopt measures which essentially reflect the department's priorities, he is likely to find that his time is taken up with these measures to the exclusion of others that he may later come to believe are more worthwhile. It is the department's measures that he will have to sponsor through Cabinet and cabinet committee, defend before Parliament and explain to his party and to interest group representatives.

Instead of sponsoring departmental measures, a policy initiator

---

[1] All the Central and East African colonies bar Southern Rhodesia were independent by 1964.

[2] Boyle, Crosland and Kogan, *The Politics of Education*, p. 192.

needs to devote as much time as possible to promoting the policy objectives he has selected. The corollary is that tasks which other Cabinet Ministers may perform themselves must be delegated to junior Ministers. Junior Ministers may be assigned to receive deputations and MPs, inspect regional offices of the department and attend formal luncheons and receptions. Routine legislation and letter signing can also be delegated. On a fair number of occasions it will be possible to let junior colleagues answer Parliamentary Questions and even take the committee stage of bills and deputise on cabinet committees.

This strategy clearly entails running certain risks but these have to be accepted. The greatest risk is that the Minister will run into parliamentary storms over decisions which he has merely rubber stamped. Crosland gives two examples of this occurring: Welsh MPs were angry over the decision to include the Welsh College of Advanced Technology in the University of Wales, instead of making it separate as Cardiff University, and the decision to increase overseas student's fee provoked an angry reaction on the Labour backbenches, as well as student demonstrations. Both decisions were ineptly announced in written answers to Parliamentary Questions.[1] The purpose of running parliamentary risks, however, is to permit the Minister to spend as much time as possible in his office dealing with policy matters. It is vital for him to explore a wide range of options on the key issues he has selected. A Macleod constitution for an African state, a Castle Act, or a Crosland strategy for introducing comprehensive schools cannot be formulated in a day. Papers written by middle level and junior as well as senior officials need to be read and departmental meetings held to explicate and evaluate policy options. In short, some of the most crucial decisions a Minister makes concern the allocation of his own time. Ministers who select key issues to concentrate on, and allocate their time accordingly, greatly improve their prospects of making a significant contribution to policy.

The favourableness of the situation

In the case of all six Ministers situational factors were reasonably favourable to policy initiation. First, although major initiatives

[1] ibid., pp. 177-8. A similar case of a Minister rubber stamping a decision without considering the parliamentary reaction may have occurred in spring 1969 when, without even warning his backbench subject group and on the eve of the year's main local government elections, Mr Richard Crossman, Secretary of State for the Social Services, announced increased charges on false teeth and spectacles. Health Service charges are always an emotive issue to Labour backbenchers and the increase could hardly have won votes.

invariably arouse controversy, there were important sources of support for their policies. Macmillan's housebuilding programme had widespread public support; indeed the promise of a major increase in house completions was widely believed to have won votes for the Conservatives at the 1951 election. In fighting for necessary funds in Cabinet, Macmillan, in fact, regularly reminded his colleagues of their public and collective commitment.[1] Robert Carr's Industrial Relations Bill also had strong public support because it was generally thought to be an anti-union measure and public opinion had, in the late 1950s and 1960s, became steadily more critical of the big unions and their conduct of industrial relations.[2] The support of public opinion was probably not an important factor for the other four Ministers. However, Labour Party opinion was solidly behind Mrs Castle's efforts to fulfil the 1964 election pledge and introduce integrated transport planning and had been critical of her predecessor for failing to do so. Mr Crosland, in his instructions to local education authorities to produce plans for comprehensive schools, also had the backing of Labour MPs. Mr Macleod and Mr Jenkins both lacked the support of a substantial section of their own party. As we saw, Macleod was at one stage faced with a critical motion signed by sixty-seven Conservative MPs, and Jenkins' liberal measures were presumably not supported, or not strongly supported, by the large number of Labour MPs who absented themselves for the free votes.[3] For these two Ministers crucial support came from the Prime Minister. In Macleod's case the impulse for decolonisation in Africa came from Prime Minister Macmillan's 'wind of change' speech, and he had Macmillan's support throughout. Similarly, Mr Harold Wilson's memoirs reveal that he warmly supported Mr Jenkins' plans for the Home Office and, indeed, had promised him the job eleven months before his actual appointment.[4]

Support in important quarters is always a prerequisite for policy initiation. It is also necessary to be lucky enough not to be blown off course by a crisis. The journalistic cliché that Governments often react to events rather than mould them is true enough. Had the insurrection in Northern Ireland broken out while he was Home Secretary, instead of under his successor, James Callaghan, Roy Jenkins' energies would have been pre-empted and he could probably not have passed his liberal reforms. Had Southern Rhodesia

[1] Macmillan, *Tides of Fortune*, p. 375.

[2] See also P. Jenkins, *The Battle of Downing Street* (London: Charles Knight, 1970), pp. xiii-xiv.

[3] The voting at the report stage of the Sexual Offences Act, for instance, was only 102 in favour, 23 against.

[4] H. Wilson, *The Labour Government* (London: Weidenfeld and Nicolson, and Michael Joseph, 1971), p. 66.

issued a unilateral declaration of independence while Iain Macleod was Colonial Secretary, instead of a decade later, his time would have been taken up in negotiations and flights to Salisbury, and the other African colonies might have been left to their own devices. Pre-selected key issues are always in danger of being pre-empted by crisis issues.

As noted in Chapter 7, it is easier for a Minister to take policy initiatives in some departments than others. None of our six Ministers was at the Treasury, the Ministry of Defence, or the Ministry of Power. The interdependence of the subjects dealt with by these departments is so great that policy initiation cannot be based on the selection of key issues but requires a complex reordering of priorities, the formulation of a new policy strategy. Policy initiation is more straightforward at a department like the Home Office which deals with a wide range of more or less unrelated subjects. Mr Jenkins was thus able to concentrate on liberalising specific laws governing public morality and not concern himself overmuch with the police, probation officers, local authority children's departments – and other subjects within his department's remit. It was also perfectly feasible, and not *prima facie* unwise, for Mr Crosland initially to concentrate on reform of secondary education rather than primary or higher education, for Mr Macleod to concern himself primarily with Central and East African colonies and for Mr Macmillan to build houses rather than, say, press for local government reform. Mrs Castle's reforms were in an intermediate category. Her proposals covered all the main sectors of the transport industry, except air travel, but it will be recalled that she mainly created new administrative machinery rather than introduced substantive changes. Mr Carr came closest to formulating a new policy strategy. The Industrial Relations Act was intended to embody a long-term strategy for improving management-union relations. Carr's ability to impose such a complicated set of reforms is largely to be explained by the fact that he was the only Minister of the six who came to office armed by his party with a detailed programme, rather than just stated policy objectives.

Policy initiators and their departments

Once a ministerial policy initiator has decided on his policy objectives, he may ask himself whether his department as at present constituted is a suitable administrative instrument for achieving them. In most cases the answer will be that it is, but if the achievement of ministerial objectives requires the adoption of administrative methods alien to the department's traditions, or the application of skills not possessed by its staff, then changes may have to be made. It is interesting that three of the policy initiators instanced in this chapter found it necessary to make changes in the departmental machinery.

When Mr Macmillan took over the department he rechristened Housing and Local Government, he found an organisation 'concerned with guidance, advice, supervision, sometimes even warning and reproof but never with positive action'.[1] This was no use for Macmillan's purpose. He wanted to build houses in record time and he could not do so with a department that had 'no production organisation central or local; no progress officers; no machinery for identifying and breaking bottlenecks'.[2] To advise him at the centre and co-ordinate the building programme he therefore set up a 'ministerial council', which included temporary civil servants as well as permanent officials.[3] More important, the Regional Housing Boards were charged to 'identify and break bottlenecks' and consisted of representatives of management and labour in the building industry, local government officials, and officials of the Ministries of Housing, Labour and Works.[4]

As well as the right machinery Macmillan wanted the right men to run it. Like later critics he believed that civil servants were not good at running things, at taking over direct responsibility for executive tasks. His Permanent Secretary, in particular, was not cut out to head a production drive. He was, Macmillan wrote,

' . . . a charming and cultivated man with a background of scholarship and the Church – he was the son of a bishop – and with agreeable manners. He had a wide knowledge of the Civil Service and a deep respect for its conventions. He was well liked by the local authorities and their organised bodies. But he knew nothing of the problems of industry or of production.'[5]

One of Macmillan's strengths was that he knew people in industry whom he could ask to assist him at the Ministry. As noted above, Sir Percy Mills, a businessman with whom he had worked in his period as a junior Minister of Supply during the war, was appointed with the title Adviser on Housing but in reality as director-general of production. Macmillan clearly believes that Mills played an indispensable role as his adviser and, in fact, the Regional Housing Boards were his brainchild. However, the appointment was initially opposed by the Permanent Secretary who was backed up by the head of the Civil Service.[6] The Permanent Secretary wanted to know

---

[1] Macmillan, *Tides of Fortune*, p. 375.   [2] loc. cit.
[3] ibid., pp. 397-8.   [4] ibid., pp. 389-99.
[5] ibid., p. 393.   [6] ibid., pp. 396-7.

what rank Mills would be and whether he would have executive or advisory status. Macmillan got his way but the civil servants remained suspicious of the outsider, 'particularly of the speed with which he worked'.[1] The Permanent Secretary even complained that it was 'unconstitutional' for a Minister to take advice from anyone other than himself. Macmillan noted in his diary, contrasting the situation with wartime, 'The "Trade Union" of officials is back in power. The Treasury planners are supreme. Ministers are treated very politely, but with firmness, as temporary nuisances.'[2]

Barbara Castle also found it necessary to make changes in her department. Some of the institutions she founded, like the National Freight Authority and conurbation transport authorities, implied no criticism of the department. In certain respects, however, she clearly was dissatisfied with the existing personnel and machinery. She probably tried to remove her Permanent Secretary[3] and she has since written of the 'atmosphere of ill-concealed hostility' with which she was confronted as a new Minister committed to integrated transport planning. At first, officials drafted replies to Parliamentary Questions which said, 'We do not believe in an integrated transport policy.' Later, the phrasing changed but, as Mrs Castle asked rhetorically, 'Does anybody really believe that an attitude of mind had changed?'[4] As far as departmental structure was concerned, it was unsatisfactory for the purpose of integrated transport planning that road, rail and water transport should be dealt with by separate divisions of the department. (The so-called Transport Policy Division which sounded as if it had a co-ordinating role was not empowered to deal with roads.) Like Macmillan, Mrs Castle turned to an outsider to make changes. A well known transport economist, Christopher Foster, was brought in as Director-General of Economic Planning and he, in turn, recruited about twenty more economists and also set up a mathematical advisory section to assist with investment analysis.[5]

The third Minister cited here who made organisational changes was Anthony Crosland. Against the wishes of some officials he set up a Planning Branch, taking the view that the separate operating branches of the Department of Education and Science were not performing the planning function adequately.[6] It may also be mentioned that, in addition to his Civil Service advisers and the local

[1] Macmillan *Tides of Fortune*, p. 399.
[2] ibid., p. 387.
[3] See L. Gunn, 'Ministers and Civil Servants', *Public Administration* (Australia, March 1967), 82-4.
[4] B. Castle, 'Mandarin Power', *The Sunday Times* (10 June 1973).
[5] 'Red-Head in Action', *The Observer* (2 July 1967).
[6] Boyle, Crosland and Kogan, *The Politics of Education*, p. 177.

authority and teachers' groups at the DES, Crosland had a private group of advisors who met regularly at his house to discuss issues on which decisions were imminent. This private group consisted mainly of academics who had written on educational topics and was intended to provide 'a check on the advice I was getting from the department'.[1]

It seems a plausible hypothesis that a ministerial policy initiator cannot expect to avoid conflict with his senior officials. The findings of social psychologists indicate that instrumental leaders generally tend to be unpopular with their subordinates,[2] and a policy initiator intent on changing established departmental priorities appears particularly liable to run into opposition. In addition to Mr Macmillan's and Mrs Castle's conflicts with their Permanent Secretaries which have already been mentioned, it appears that Mr Jenkins also had a somewhat strained relationship with his Permanent Secretary at the Home Office, partly as a result of the latter's tendency to co-ordinate all policy advice but partly, one suspects, because of such reversals of Home Office decisions as the pardon of Timothy Evans. It is also clear that the policy initiatives of Mr Macleod and Mr Carr were opposed by senior officials, although in these instances there is no suggestion that policy disagreements were embittered by a personality clash. It is not personally pleasant for a Minister to press on with policies opposed by officials with whom he is in almost daily contact. Some degree of unpopularity in the department may, however, be a penalty of policy initiation.

The skills of policy initiators

In Chapter 3 it was shown that most Ministers who intend to act as policy initiators believe that, as well as possessing the qualities associated with the intelligent layman in politics, it is also an asset to have some degree of relevant specialised knowledge. As far as intelligence goes all six Ministers cited here have the reputation of being intellectually extremely able. Macmillan, Crosland and Jenkins obtained First Class degrees. Macleod had a photographic memory and, at the time he gave up cards to go into politics, was one of the world's leading bridge players, having just led the British team to victory in the European Championships. Brilliance at bridge may be as good evidence as a First Class degree of high intelligence and, although an unusual qualification for a Minister, was one that his enemies believed stood Macleod in good stead.[3]

[1] ibid., p. 185.

[2] See Bales and Slater, 'Role Differentiation in Small Decision-Making Groups', in C. A. Gibb (ed.), *Leadership* (Harmondsworth: Penguin, 1969), pp. 255-76.

[3] See p. 195 and p. 213.

As well as being intellectually able, all six Ministers were experienced politicians who had the difficult to define but important quality of 'political weight'. Macmillan was a future Prime Minister and Macleod and Jenkins were both tipped as such. Mrs Castle had a fearsome reputation for successfully using histrionics to win cabinet battles and, after leaving Transport and moving to the Department of Employment and Productivity, she was generally ranked third in the ministerial 'pecking-order' behind the Prime Minister and Mr Jenkins. Anthony Crosland and Robert Carr at the time of their appointments at the Department of Education and Science and the Department of Employment were not, perhaps, political heavyweights. Carr's reputation in his own party rose rapidly in his first two years in office, however, and Crosland, although he lacked a large backbench following, was respected for his force in argument and economic expertise.

Other qualities which these Ministers appear to have possessed are self-confidence and a degree of ruthlessness.[1] It takes self-confidence to overrule officials presumed to be more knowledgeable than oneself, and Macmillan and Mrs Castle, in reorganising their departments, and Macleod, in his negotiations with the settlers, displayed considerable ruthlessness. Crosland's threat to withhold school building funds from the county of Surrey if it refused to draw up plans for comprehensive schooling also shows a streak of determination, if not ruthlessness, as does Jenkins's insistence at the Home Office that the Permanent Secretary should not co-ordinate all departmental advice and that he would employ in his Private Office a special assistant and a Private Secretary chosen by himself.[2]

The value of specialised knowledge for ministerial policy initiation is not conclusively confirmed by the case studies. Robert Carr had considerable knowledge of industrial relations. He had spent a lifetime in industry, written on industrial relations as early as 1950 for the Conservative 'One Nation' group and spent several years as a hyperactive Shadow Minister working with the policy groups which produced *Fair Deal at Work*. Before their appointment to office Anthony Crosland and Roy Jenkins had a special interest in education and Home Office affairs respectively, and had reviewed policy options in published writings. Neither would claim to be an expert, however. The other three Ministers were not, so far as one knows, especially interested in, or knowledgeable about, the subjects

[1] Cf. Neustadt's view that self-confidence is a vital personality trait of effective American presidents. *Presidential Power* (New York: John Wiley, 1960), ch. 7.

[2] See pp. 115–16, p. 130.

dealt with by their departments. Indeed, as we noted, Macmillan, who belongs to a generation that affects amateurism, claimed that, at the time of his appointment, he 'knew nothing whatever of the housing problem. . . '.

A note on tactics

Once a Minister's policy objectives have been defined he still has to decide how to translate them into practical policy programmes and what tactics to employ in persuading or obliging relevant publics (housebuilders, local authorities, trade unionists, white settlers . . .) to act as he intends. It is often thought that legislation is the principal method of enacting a programme and some Ministers are perhaps prone to believe that steering a major bill through Parliament is the way to enhance a political reputation. Legislation has the dubious advantage of introducing an element of compulsion, but the law may be unenforceable and legislation is not the only method open to Ministers. In fact only three of the six Ministers cited in this chapter sought to achieve their objectives and made their reputations by personally introducing legislation.

Macleod promoted decolonisation in Africa through intricate negotiations with white settlers and black nationalist leaders in a series of conferences held at Lancaster House and elsewhere. His admirers described him as a skilful negotiator and conciliator. His opponents, and notably Lord Salisbury, who made a well remembered attack on him in the House of Lords, thought him 'too clever by half' and accused him of using 'bridge tactics'.[1] The Kenyan settlers, in particular, claimed that they were expecting only preliminary talks in February 1960 but were bamboozled by Macleod into accepting a complicated new constitution the implications of which they did not fully understand.[2] Mr Crosland's main tactic was to avoid legislation. His circular of October 1965 to local education authorities contained only guidelines on comprehensive schooling which LEAs were requested to adhere to. Mr Macmillan, at the Ministry of Housing, concentrated first on getting the necessary allocations of materials in the Treasury's capital investment programme and, after that, it was a question of the Regional Housing Boards dealing with specific bottlenecks as they occurred. Occasionally risky assumptions had to be made as when Macmillan decided to press on with his programme even though assured by steel manufacturers that they could not supply the necessary steel.

[1] *Parliamentary Debates* (Lords), 229, cols 308-15.
[2] ibid., loc. cit.

He simply assumed the manufacturers were lying about the size of their stocks and was right.[1] His tactics and achievements were more those of a successful manager and entrepreneur than an orthodox politician. He did, however, also make use of his skills as a politician when he toured the country talking to builders, encouraging and exhorting them to bring their problems to the Regional Housing Boards and not let temporary difficulties cause long delays. For tactical reasons he took the line that, 'We must take housing out of politics. We must create a public opinion in support of . . . "The Housing Crusade".'[2]

Of the three Ministers who did seek to achieve their objectives by introducing legislation, Mr Jenkins adopted the unusual tactic of working through private members' bills. The experience of the other two illustrates some of the defects of legislation. When the Industrial Relations Act was going through the House of Commons, doubts were expressed as to whether its provisions could be enforced. At the time of writing the TUC order to its member unions not even to register under the Act is still in force. It is difficult to foresee what the Government or employers can do. It is hardly likely, though, that the unions will suffer the full consequences of losing their legal immunities, including immunity from suits for civil damages when they go on strike. Mrs Castle also found that the law was an irrelevance in relation to certain aspects of integrated transport planning. The Transport Act created a number of administrative and planning agencies, but one major barrier to the integration of road and rail transport was the refusal of the National Union of Railwaymen to accept the use of liner train terminals by private enterprise road haulage firms. It took twenty-eight hours of angry negotiation and a kiss for the union leader to get the ban rescinded.[3]

List of propositions

Ministers who are successful policy initiators enact a programme based on policy objectives and priorities defined by themselves or their party, rather than their department. The purpose of this chapter has been to derive from case studies some general propositions about the conditions of ministerial policy initiation. The propositions which have been advanced are listed below:

A minister is more likely to be successful as a policy initiator if he

[1] Macmillan, *Tides of Fortune*, p. 430. [2] ibid., p. 398.
[3] 'Why Barbara Castle Kissed the Signalman', *The Sunday Times* (5 March 1967).

consciously adopts a key issues approach. The approach entails delegating a wide range of duties often performed by Cabinet Ministers to junior Ministers.

A Minister is unlikely to be able to enact a policy programme during his short period in office unless his key issues and, preferably, his policy objectives are defined within a short time of his appointment (six months?).

Major policy initiatives invariably arouse opposition. An initiative is more likely to succeed, however, if there is a strong public feeling that 'something must be done'. Failing public support, a party commitment (election pledge etc) or the support of the Prime Minister may be sufficient.

The key issues approach is feasible in departments which deal with a range of relatively unrelated subjects. In departments which deal with highly interdependent subjects, policy initiation needs to be based on a new 'strategy'. As short term appointees Ministers are not well placed to formulate such strategies.

Policy initiators, in altering departmental priorities, must expect some conflict and unpopularity with their civil servants. Conflict is especially likely if, to press through his initiative, the Minister reorganises his department or recruits 'irregulars'.

The skills and attributes possessed by successful policy initiators appear to include intellectual ability, 'political weight' and self-confidence. Specialised knowledge of the issues under review may be an asset but is not a prerequisite.

The propositions are intended only to indicate conditions favourable to policy initiation and steps a Minister may take to perform his role. No assumption is made that Ministers ought to attempt to be policy initiators or that ministerial initiatives are in some way preferable to initiatives proposed by civil servants or pressure groups. Policy initiatives can misfire and lead to measures which produce undesirable or unintended consequences, or which are simply unenforceable. Furthermore, if all Ministers attempted to be policy initiators, the administrative burden on government departments would be overwhelming; as we noted earlier, the platitude that a period of reform needs to be followed by a period of consolidation still holds good. Nevertheless, once all caveats have been registered, it is probably true to say that policy initiation is not only the most difficult ministerial role but also the one that past Ministers whom one thinks of as outstanding – Peel, Gladstone, Cross, Lloyd George, Addison, Bevan – all performed outstandingly.

Chapter 10

Executive Ministers

'There is broad agreement about the manager's main functions. First
he must plan: set objectives, forecast, analyse problems and make
decisions – that is, formulate policy. Secondly, the manager organ-
ises: he determines what activities are necessary to achieve the objectives, he classifies the work, divides it and assigns it to groups and
individuals. Thirdly, a manager motivates: that is he inspires his staff
to contribute to the purposes of the organisation, to be loyal to its aims
and to pull their weight in achieving them. . . . Fourthly, the manager
controls what is done by checking performance against plans.'[1]

In British government it is not normally expected that all these
functions will be performed by the same individual. Most Ministers
claim to be mainly concerned with the first function, policy formulation. The managing director of the department, they say (defining
management more narrowly), is the Permanent Secretary. It is his job
to 'organise', 'motivate' and 'control'.

Executive Ministers are atypical in that, while still regarding policy
formulation as important, they also attach high priority to other
management functions. Thus, of the three Executive Ministers whose
performance in office is discussed in this chapter, Henry Brooke,
Conservative Minister of Housing and Local Government 1957-61
and Home Secretary 1962-4 believed in the importance of 'inspiring
his staff to contribute to the purposes of the organisation'. His
success may be gauged, in part, by the record amount of legislation
he placed on the statute book. Denis Healey, Labour Minister of
Defence 1964-70, gave a great deal of attention to the organisation of
his department and to checking and controlling the use of resources
through the introduction of modern management techniques. Last,
Peter Walker, Secretary of State for the Environment 1970-72, was

---

[1] Rosemary Stewart, *The Reality of Management* (London: Pan Books, 1967),
pp. 71-2.

also been concerned with questions of organisation, and particularly with running his department according to a management team concept, with his seven subordinate Ministers involved in decision making to a quite unusual degree.

HENRY BROOKE, MINISTER OF HOUSING AND LOCAL GOVERNMENT 1957-1961, HOME SECRETARY, 1962-1964.[1]

Henry Brooke was an unusual type of politician. He appeared to have no interest in being newsworthy and his speeches were lucid, logical expositions of complicated problems but completely devoid of striking phrases. Nor was he concerned to pass far-reaching reforms. Instead, he was the type of executive, or organisation man, who enjoyed getting things done and, as a Minister, he steered an enormous amount of useful but unspectacular legislation through the government machine and on to the statute book. As the head of a large department he prided himself on expediting the process of policy formation and on 'getting the optimum output of work from his department'. He believed that a Minister should encourage his officials by taking an interest, not just in the more politically sensitive matters, but in all aspects of the department's work. To Brooke man management, the exercise of effective leadership in his department, was an important aspect of his job.

In an interview in the summer of 1969, Brooke said that his greatest source of satisfaction as a Minister had come from 'being responsible for more needed legislation than any other Minister between 1957 [when he first became head of his own department] and 1964'. Day by day he derived satisfaction from 'not getting in arrears' with his paper work and over the long haul he was pleased to have 'reduced the backlog of legislation' in his department. He thought one important test of a Minister was his ability to pilot legislation through standing committees of the House of Commons. It was necessary in committee to display a mastery of detail and inspire confidence in legislation, otherwise amendments were likely to be tabled by the Government's own supporters and abstentions or absences might occasionally remove the Government's majority.

The quantity of legislation sponsored by the Ministry of Housing and Local Government (MHLG) and the Home Office while Brooke was Minister is certainly imposing. He and his junior Ministers introduced in the House of Commons (gave a first reading to) thirty-two MHLG bills and thirty-one Home Office bills. However, these two departments legislate heavily in every parliamentary session and, in order satisfactorily to test the hypothesis that Brooke was a particu-

[1] Now Lord Brooke of Cumnor.

larly prolific legislator, we have to compare his output with the output of other Ministers who held the same posts. Table 10.1 makes this comparison in respect of Ministers in the 1951-64 Conservative Government. Bills are attributed to the Minister in office when they received their first reading rather than to the Minister in office when they received the royal assent and became law. Also bills actually sponsored in the Commons by junior Ministers are attributed to the senior Minister as having overall responsibility.

It can be seen from Table 10.1 that Brooke 'outlegislated' the other three Ministers who were Home Secretary and the other four Ministers of Housing and Local Government.

Table 10.1 *Legislative Output of Home Secretaries and Ministers of Housing and Local Government 1951-1964*

Home Secretaries		Ministers of Housing	
Minister	*Average number of bills per session*[a]	*Minister*	*Average number of bills per session*
H. Brooke (1962-4)	15.5	H. Brooke (1957-61)	8.0
R. A. Butler (1957-61)	14.0	D. Sandys (1954-7)	7.7
Sir D. Maxwell-Fyfe (1951-4)	12.7	Sir K. Joseph (1962-4)	7.5
		C. Hill (1961-2)	6.0
G. Lloyd-George (1945-57)	9.0	H. Macmillan (1951-4)	6.0

[a] Bills are attributed to the Minister who was head of department when they received their first reading in Parliament.

At the Home Office he averaged 15.5 bills per parliamentary session, his closest 'rival' being Mr R. A. Butler with 14.0 bills per session. At MHLG he averaged 8.0 bills per session, closely followed by Mr Duncan Sandys and Sir Keith Joseph with 7.7 and 7.5 bills per session respectively. Of course not all bills are of equal importance or equally controversial. Brooke himself came close to conceding that much of his legislation was in the useful and worthy category, rather than in the innovative and world-shaking category. He was, as he said, concerned about 'reducing the backlog of legislation' in his department and cannot have expected to set the world alight with such measures as the National Parks (Amendment) Act, the Caravan Sites and Control of Development Act, or the Protection of Animals (Anaesthetics) Act. The most controversial measure which received the royal assent during his period in office at Housing and Local Government undoubtedly was the Rent Act 1957,[1] and this had been

[1] See M. J. Barnett, *The Politics of Legislation: The Rent Act, 1957* (London: Weidenfeld and Nicolson, 1969).

inherited from his predecessor, Mr Duncan Sandys. The Local
Government Act, 1958, under which the Exchequer would make over
money to local authorities in the form of block grants instead of ear-
marking it for specific purposes, and his New Towns Acts of 1958
and 1959, which kept the future management of new towns out of
the hands of local authorities and in the hands of central government,
both aroused the ire of the Labour Opposition but were only briefly
front page news. At the Home Office his most controversial measures
involved not new legislation but individual deportation orders;
notably the order to deport the Nigerian exile Chief Enahoro to
stand trial in his own country for treason. This provoked a censure
debate and calls for Brooke's resignation which were perhaps more
vehement than convention demanded.[1]

It has already been noted that a management function Brooke
believed important was that of maintaining the morale of civil servants.
He criticised his ministerial predecessors for concentrating too much
on housing (Macmillan) and planning green belts (Sandys) and whenever time permitted, so one of his officials claimed, he would ask to
see civil servants dealing with issues which rarely came before Ministers, in order to assure them of his interest and to encourage them in
their work. He also attempted to boost the morale of non-Whitehall
personnel who had some connection with his department. While he
was Home Secretary he and his junior Ministers visited every prison
in Britain and 40 per cent of the visits were made by Brooke himself.[2]
As Minister of Housing and Local Government he even opened a
new type of sewage works built by a Rural District Council, because
he thought it 'courteous to commend them on their enterprise'.

Not surprisingly Brooke won the admiration of his officials and
became popular in the departments he served in. A civil servant, who
had served in his Private Office at the Ministry of Housing and Local
Government, described him as a tremendous 'master and mover of
paper with a very orderly mind' and found him 'a pleasure to work
for'. He also approved of Brooke's 'realistic acceptance' of the fact
that urgent decisions often have to be taken on the basis of incom-
plete evidence and that big organisations must generally follow
precedents. He attributed this realism to the fact that Brooke had
previous experience of executive decision making as a director of
companies and as chairman of Southern Railways. An official who
had served at the Home Office also admired Brooke but noted that
there was another side to the picture. He contrasted the Minister's
popularity within the department ('probably the most popular Home
Secretary with officials since the war') with the reputation for harsh-

[1] *Parliamentary Debates* (Commons), 675, cols 1287-378.
[2] Information given by Lord Brooke in an interview with the author.

ness and bureaucratic rigidity that he acquired in some outside circles. At the Home Office his tendency to uphold the law as it stood, to follow precedent and stick to his brief, was sometimes a liability. It was a fair guess, so this official believed, that his more flexible and politically sensitive predecessor, R. A. Butler, would have avoided the parliamentary storms provoked by such decisions of Brooke's as to deport Chief Enahoro and, on another occasion, a Jamaican girl, Carmen Bryan, for petty shoplifting, to bar the American 'sick' comedian Lenny Bruce from the country and to let two journalists, who had been imprisoned for refusing to reveal their sources of information to a court, serve their gaol sentences. In truth, as a *Sunday Times* correspondent once wrote, Brooke was something of a political lightning conductor.[1]

Henry Brooke was an ideal Minister to appoint to a legislating department in a period of consolidation. As Minister of Housing and Local Government he followed two innovative Ministers (Macmillan and Sandys) and passed an enormous amount of amending and uncontroversial legislation. His capacity to encourage civil servants, expedite policy formulation and pass legislation was also displayed at the Home Office. But he was probably a less successful Minister there because his talents as an Executive Minister were not combined with political sensitivity and flexibility.

DENIS HEALEY, MINISTER OF DEFENCE, 1964-1970

The Ministry of Defence was not a happy hunting ground for Conservative Ministers in the 1951-64 Government. There were nine Ministers in thirteen years and the period was marked by costly failures.[2] Major difficulties arose because of inter-Service rivalry, which was mirrored in the federal structure of the Ministry. The Minister of Defence was supposed to act as overlord and co-ordinator of the demands pressed on him by the three Service Ministers: the Secretary of State for Air, the First Lord of the Admiralty and the Secretary of State for War. However, the evaluation of weapons systems is a highly technical business and the impression grew that Ministers and senior officials were being blinded by military science into agreeing to the manufacture of weapons which duplicated each other's capabilities, or which would soon need replacing.[3] The Ministry of Defence – like the US Pentagon – appeared to be, if not unmanageable, at least

[1] 'Lightning Conductor', *The Sunday Times* (23 April 1963).
[2] See Chapter 13.
[3] For a critical account of defence policy and defence organisations see William P. Snyder, *The Politics of British Defence Policy* (Columbus: Ohio State University Press, 1964).

desperately in need of a Minister with a high degree of managerial and organisational ability. The Pentagon got its McNamara and the Ministry of Defence its Healey.

Healey had long specialised in foreign and defence policy. From 1945 to 1952 he was Secretary of the International Department of the Labour Party, justifying Foreign Secretary Ernest Bevin's policies in a series of publications (*Cards on the Table*, *The Curtain Falls*, *European Unity* etc.) which were controversial in Labour Party circles as being too right wing and anti-Soviet. In 1956 he became the Labour Party's deputy to Aneurin Bevan as foreign affairs spokesman in the House of Commons. When Bevan died, he was briefly chief Opposition spokesman before being transferred to Commonwealth affairs and then, in February 1963, to the post of Shadow Defence Secretary. From 1948-60 he was a councillor of the Royal Institute of International Affairs and in 1958 was instrumental in founding and raising funds for the Institute of Strategic Studies. He was almost certainly the only Defence Secretary since 1945 who, at the time of his appointment, was already familiar with the (mainly American) writings on defence strategy and had a wide acquaintance with British, American and Western European academics and journalists concerned with defence questions. He had himself lectured and written widely on foreign policy and defence and, until 1964, contributed a regular column sold to a large number of foreign newspapers.[1]

Healey explicitly recognised the importance of efficient management at the Ministry of Defence. In an interview in August 1969 he said,

'Some Ministries are political, some managerial, some are both. This one is both. . . . There are three sides to the Ministry: the officers (many of whom regard MOD as a sabbatical – it is hard to recruit good people), scientists and civil servants. The only co-ordinator is the Minister and under a weak Minister there is no co-ordination.'

He proposed to ease problems of co-ordination by instituting organisational changes and modern management techniques. As far as the reorganisation of the Ministry was concerned, the process had been started by the Thorneycroft-Mountbatten reforms announced in the White Paper *Central Organisation for Defence* in 1963.[2] The separate Service departments were abolished and a unitary Ministry of Defence created.[3] At cabinet level the Defence and Overseas Policy

---

[1] Geoffrey Williams and Bruce Reed, *Denis Healey and the Policies of Power* (London: Sidgwick and Jackson, 1971), p. 73.

[2] Cmnd 2087 (London: HMSO, 1963).

[3] The merger dates from 1 April 1964.

Committee was set up and, within the Ministry, policy making was to be the responsibility of the Defence Council consisting of the Secretary of State, Ministers of State, Chiefs of Staff, the Chief Scientific Officer and the Permanent Under-Secretary. This gave the department an unusual advisory structure, in that, in order to improve co-ordination, military personnel and a scientist were made co-equal advisors with the Permanent Under-Secretary. Healey carried integration further. Separate Service Ministers were replaced by a Minister of Defence for Administration and a Minister of Defence for Equipment.[1] The remits of these Ministers covered all three Services and Healey claimed that, in the interests of efficient management, he delegated wide powers to them. Integration at ministerial level was matched by continuing integration on the military side. A unified Defence Staff (under the Chief of Defence Staff) and a unified Defence Operational Requirements Staff were created.[2]

Healey introduced a number of other organisational changes. He set up a four-man Programme Evaluation Group (PEG) to co-ordinate the different advice coming up from the military, scientists and permanent officials. The head of the PEG described it as serving a function similar to a French ministerial cabinet[3] and Healey stated that, although military staff had been given the right to refer issues to it, in practice he was the only person who did so.[4] Healey believed that the PEG served its purpose well but his biographers claim that it was regarded as a fifth column by the Chiefs of Staff and some officials and was on occasion denied information necessary for its work.[5]

Healey also strengthened his Private Office so that it could 'filter', organise and manage the mass of information pouring from the machine'.[6] An Assistant Secretary was put in charge (instead of a Principal) in the belief that an official of this rank would have enough seniority to deal on equal terms, and explain the Minister's thinking and requests, to top military and civilian personnel. By 1970 Healey had five officials engaged in Private Office work as against three at the time of his appointment.[7]

The Programme Evaluation Group and the enlarged Private

[1] From 1 April 1964 there had been separate Ministers of State for the three Services.
[2] The Defence Signals Staff and the Defence Intelligence Staff were also integrated. See *Central Organisation for Defence*, p. 6.
[3] See Williams and Reed, *Denis Healey and the Policies of Power*, p. 249.
[4] This statement was made in an interview with the author.
[5] Williams and Reed, *Denis Healey and the Policies of Power*, p. 250.
[6] ibid., p. 247.
[7] One of these officials, who dealt with parliamentary business, was not actually located in the Private Office. See ibid., p. 248.

Office were designed to help the Minister on immediate issues. Healey also took steps to improve long-range thinking on defence policy. Defence planning was separated from operational and contingency planning and became the responsibility of a section known as DS22 under Peter Nailer, now a professor at the University of Lancaster.[1] More use was made of the Defence Operations Analysis Establishment at Byfleet and a University Defence Lecturers Scheme was set up at five universities.[2] Naturally, Healey kept in touch with staff at the Royal Institute of International Affairs and the Institute of Strategic Studies, whom he had long regarded as colleagues.

One of Healey's main aims as an Executive Minister was to improve central resource management and 'get the best value for every pound spent on defence'.[3] His first White Paper argued that the Conservative expenditure proposals he had inherited 'would mean imposing an increasing burden on the British people which none of our competitors in world trade are carrying'.[4] The 1966 White Paper went a stage further and set the specific target of keeping expenditure down to £2,000 million at 1964 prices in 1970.[5] This target was 16 per cent lower than proposed in the 1964 estimates and its achievement meant that defence spending in 1970 was $5\frac{1}{2}$ per cent of GNP, rather than over 7 per cent as in the early 1960s.[6] The reduction was partly achieved by abandoning bases and commitments east of Suez but also by the introduction of management techniques which had already been tried in the US Pentagon.[7] Healey personally pressed for the introduction of these techniques while conceding that changes which had occurred in Washington would probably have come to Whitehall eventually, even if he had not been Secretary of State.

Programme budgeting was introduced in 1965.[8] This meant that the cost of each existing defence commitment, or 'output' (nuclear and conventional defence in Europe, counterinsurgency operations in the Far East, 'police' operations in the Persian Gulf etc.) was analysed separately instead of being partially obscured by the presentation of the budget in terms of 'inputs' (manpower, maintenance, material etc). Of perhaps greater significance was the introduction of cost-effectiveness analysis. This type of analysis

[1] Williams and Read, *Denis Healey and the Policies of Power*, pp. 277-8.
[2] ibid., p. 277.
[3] *The Times* (17 October 1964).
[4] *Statement on the Defence Estimates*, Cmnd 2592 (London: HMSO 1965).
[5] ibid., Cmnd 2592 (London: HMSO, 1966).
[6] ibid., Cmnd 4290 (London: HMSO, 1970).
[7] See Williams and Reed, *Denis Healey and the Policies of Power*, pp. 265-78.
[8] *Statement on the Defence Estimates* (1965).

involves asking the question, 'Which strategy (or type of military force, or weapon system) offers the greatest amount of military effectiveness for a given outlay?'[1] Wherever possible the effectiveness of a weapon (its explosive power, the probability of its hitting the target etc.) as well as its cost is quantified. The analysis enables decision makers to select weapons which, without necessarily being the most devastating on the market, inflict the most damage for every pound of expenditure incurred. Thus the 1965 Defence White Paper implied that cost-effectiveness analysis had helped the Ministry to avoid developing weapons which were extremely expensive, and unnecessarily sophisticated, for the type of military operations they were likely to be used in.[2] Last, increasing use was made in Healey's period in office of the exotic sounding techniques developed by systems analysts for inventing as well as evaluating weapons systems: contingency analysis, break-even analysis, sensitivity analysis, *a fortiori* analysis and the rest.[3]

Healey's great strength lay in his capacity to see foreign and defence policy in relation to economic policy. Ends must be adjusted to means as well as means to ends. He constantly asserted that the use of more sophisticated management techniques and the consequent cancellation of expensive projects, like the P-1154, HS-681 and TSR-2 aircraft and the CVA-01 aircraft carrier, could not save enough money to reduce Britain's defence expenditure to the level of its West European trading competitors. It was up to the Foreign Office to re-examine commitments:

'The Foreign Office were compelled to take decisions on priorities. Until Labour got in I don't think there was ever a serious attempt to cost foreign policy, of which defence costs are a very important part. In some ways I think this forced the Government to take decisions on priorities they'd always managed to avoid in the past.'[4]

Healey would have to concede though, that the single biggest decision on defence made by the Labour Government was not taken after a careful re-examination of commitments.[5] The decision to leave bases

[1] See C. J. Hitch, *Decision Making from Defence* (Berkeley: University of California Press, 1965), ch. 3.
[2] *Statement on the Defence Estimates* (1965).
[3] For an explanation of these techniques see E. S. Quade and W. I. Boucher (eds), *Systems Analysis and Policy Planning* (New York: American Elsevier Publishing Co. Inc, 1968).
[4] Williams and Reed, *Denis Healey and The Policies of Power*, p. 214.
[5] An account of the process by which this decision was reached, which makes a virtue out of muddle, is given by P. Gordon Walker, *The Cabinet* (London: Jonathan Cape, 1970), ch. 8.

east of Suez and concentrate on defence in Europe was inflicted on the Government by the need to cut public expenditure following devaluation of the pound in November 1967. Healey came close to resignation over the concomitant decision to cancel the F111A aircraft, which he had hitherto held out as a substitute both for the TSR–2 and for aircraft carriers.[1]

His biographers conclude that, 'Healey was able to play his part in the implementation of policy through the unique grasp of detail that virtually made him a superior permanent official.'[2] It is interesting to note, however, that his reputation as a specialist, and his well-known managerial, efficiency orientated approach to his job, were sometimes held against him and thought to diminish his prospects of higher office. *The Sunday Times* reported that he was seen as a '*Ministre-Fonctionnaire* on the French model, a brilliant technician . . . but with a strange lack of passion',[3] and the *Guardian* under the heading 'Thoroughly Competent Denis' quoted Healey in his own defence against the charge of being a soulless technocrat:

'I'm always rather amused when I hear that, because usually the assumption is that, if you have to run a big machine, you should run it incompetently rather than competently . . . The fact is that modern government is an immensely complicated administrative job and the task of making it work is a very difficult one. The tasks are infinitely more difficult than those which faced Ministers thirty or fifty years ago. . . . The problem of government is to try to identify the areas where you can intervene usefully and then to develop the techniques for intervening efficiently. So you come back again to the question of competence.'[4]

PETER WALKER, SECRETARY OF STATE FOR THE ENVIRONMENT, 1970-1972

Peter Walker's inclusion as an Executive Minister results from his devotion to a 'management team' concept of running his department and, more specifically, to the use he made of subordinate Ministers in his management team.[5] In the past, the tendency in Whitehall has been to regard junior Ministers as too unimportant to be assigned major tasks, or even to be regularly consulted by the senior Minister.

[1] Williams and Reed, *Denis Healey and the Policies of Power*, pp. 238-47.
[2] ibid., p. 276.
[3] 'Profile: Denis Healey', *The Sunday Times* (30 January 1966).
[4] 'Thoroughly Competent Denis', *Guardian* (3 April 1970).
[5] I have used the phrase 'subordinate Ministers' to include the Ministers for Housing and Construction, Transport Industries and Local Government and Development as well as the four Parliamentary Under-Secretaries in the DOE.

But, as Sir Richard Clarke has pointed out, senior Ministers in the new 'giant' unitary departments are going to be hopelessly over-worked if they fail to make fuller use of their ministerial subordinates: 'The ability to run his team of departmental Ministers, some only just below him in rank and party standing and some only just up from the backbenches, is thus becoming one of the main qualifications for a Cabinet Minister in charge of a 'giant' department.'[1]

Walker's background lies in insurance, unit trusts and banking. According to standard newspaper profiles, he is supposed to have set himself up in business following the advice of a former Conservative Cabinet Minister, Leo Amery, that he should become financially independent before going into politics.[2] He started out with £200 borrowed capital, selling insurance to policemen in the evenings, and by 1957 had done well enough to set up Unicorn with Edward du Cann (later chairman of the Conservative Party) with £40,000 capital. The lucrative concept of linking unit trusts with life assurance in a plan they christened Equitas was apparently Walker's. Then in 1963 the London *Evening News* ran a series on successful men under forty years of age. One of the articles was on Peter Walker, who promptly invited the other promising under-forties to join him in forming a dining club. Through this dining club he met Jim Slater with whom he founded the Slater-Walker investment bank. By the time he became a Cabinet Minister at the age of thirty-eight, he was a millionaire, having followed Leo Amery's advice unerringly.

As a businessman Walker may be said to have shown a talent for picking his associates. Cabinet Ministers are not generally in a position to do this. However, in an interview in 1969 Walker explained that as Opposition spokesman on transport, and later housing and local government, he had an excellent team of junior spokesmen and hoped to get at least some of them as subordinate Ministers.[3] His plan, he said, would be to 'delegate everything', to divide up all areas of the department's business among his sub-ordinate Ministers, and himself act in a co-ordinating and forward thinking role. In the event, he was able to get the Prime Minister to appoint three members of his Opposition team as Ministers in the Department of the Environment (DOE). Mr Graham Page, who in Opposition had worked on housing and land questions, was assigned responsibility for local government and development. Under Page, as Parliamentary Under-Secretary, was Mr Michael Heseltine who had been in the Opposition team as a transport spokesman. The third

---

[1] Sir R. Clarke, *New Trends in Government* (London: HMSO, 1971), p. 4.
[2] See, for example, 'Walker: Go-getter Who Got There', *Glasgow Herald* (18 October 1970).
[3] Interview with the author.

member of the Opposition team who received ministerial office was Mr Paul Channon, who became Parliamentary Under-Secretary in the housing and construction section of DOE, while retaining some responsibility for his Opposition subjects, 'arts and amenities'. The remaining ministerial members of the department (who had not worked with Walker in Opposition) were Mr John Peyton in charge of transport industries, assisted by Mr Eldon Griffiths as Parliamentary Under-Secretary, Mr Julian Amery in charge of housing and construction and Lord Sandford who, with Heseltine, was a Parliamentary Under-Secretary on the local government and development side.

In running the DOE Walker relied a great deal on the collective judgement of his management team. The eight Ministers in the department – the largest complement in Whitehall – met at 9.15 every morning to discuss policy questions and also questions of tactics and presentation.[1] No officials were present. Walker regarded decisions which emerged from these ministerial meetings as likely to be better thought out and more politically defensible than decisions imposed by himself as senior Minister. It may be supposed that daily ministerial meetings also helped to prevent Ministers within the DOE, who were in charge of previously independent departments, from attempting to run their own empires and acting purely as pressure group leaders for housing, transport industries and local government. This would have defeated the purpose behind the creation of the unitary department, which was to improve co-ordination between related areas of government. The Ministers in the DOE were also expected to work as a team in publicising policies. When a £1,000 million road building programme was announced in 1971, for example, the announcement was made not only by Walker, but simultaneously by his colleagues in different parts of the country.[2] So far as one can judge, Walker was true to his belief, expressed in an interview while his party was still in Opposition, in letting subordinate Ministers share in the public praise or criticism resulting from the policies to which they have contributed.

As well as showing concern for the role of subordinate Ministers in his department, Walker took more interest in patronage appointments than most cabinet members. A *Times* correspondent wrote that,

'He has already appointed a score of people in their twenties to posts which before would never have gone to anyone under 40. An

[1] This account of Walker's working methods is based on Ronald Butt, 'The Undiscovered Side of Selsdon Man', *The Times* (15 July 1971), and John Clare, 'Peter Walker: Minister of Hope and Glory', *The Times* (10 May 1972).

[2] Butt, *The Times* (15 July 1971).

example was the naming of Mr Denis Stevenson to be chairman, at the age of 26, of the Peterlee and Newton Aycliffe Development Corporation. The Civil Service challenged it and Downing Street asked for details. Mr Walker provided them and promptly got an acknowledgement saying it was assumed that 26 was a mis-typing for 62.[1]

If the creation of 'giant' unitary departments requires a new type of Executive Minister running his department according to a management team concept, then Walker may come to be regarded as a trend setter whose deployment of subordinate Ministers was at least as significant as the policy changes he introduced in the fields of local government reorganisation, housing finance and the reorganisation of water authorities. It should also be recognised that, in addition to advantages in running his own department, a senior Minister who gives significant responsibilities to subordinate Ministers is providing valuable experience for potential future members of the Cabinet.

CONCLUSION

Executive Ministers, like executives in non-governmental organisations, do not all approach their jobs in the same way. However, the three men whose working methods have been analysed in this chapter have this in common: they all emphasised roles more usually associated with business executives than with politicians in ministerial office. All were concerned with management as well as with policy, with departmental organisation and efficiency, as well as with objectives and policy programmes. In interviews they expressed their belief in the importance of management roles and in office they acted accordingly.

Executive Ministers of the Brooke type, who expedite the flow of business by being personally quick to reach decisions and by motivating civil servants, have presumably always been welcome in Whitehall, particularly in the great legislating departments.[2] The roles emphasised by Healey and Walker, on the other hand, have become more important with the creation between 1964 and 1970 of five 'giant' unitary departments out of previously independent Ministries.[3] These departments (with the exception of the Foreign

[1] Clare, *The Times* (10 May 1972).

[2] The legislative output of departments is compared in Chapter 7.

[3] The Ministry of Defence, the Department of Health and Social Security, the Foreign and Commonwealth Office, the Department of Trade and Industry and the Department of the Environment.

and Commonwealth Office) have large budgets and a large staff, and most Ministers will presumably see it as one of their main roles to decide on the allocation of resources between competing policy objectives and programmes. It will only be possible to arrive at sensible decisions on the basis of accurate assessments of the costs and benefits of current policy programmes and forecasts regarding proposed programmes. In these circumstances it would seem appropriate that a Minister should concern himself, as Denis Healey did, with the introduction and refinement of techniques to improve central resource management in his department. Similarly, Peter Walker's desire to develop a ministerial management team would seem particularly relevant in 'giant' departments. As noted above, there are two rather opposite dangers that the management team may avoid. One danger is that subordinate Ministers in charge of hitherto separate departments may try to run their own organisation without co-ordinating with the senior Minister. The opposite danger is that the burden on senior Ministers will be too great if they continue, in the time-honoured manner, to treat subordinate Ministers as dogsbodies fit only to perform undemanding and unglamorous tasks.

Chapter 11

Ambassador Ministers

Ambassador Ministers attach high priority to public relations roles. They are concerned to publicise the policies and services of their department, or in some instances, to offer symbolic reassurance or sympathy to sections of the public. Their target public may, in fact, be very large – the entire population of Northern Ireland, for example,[1] – or restricted to the interest group clientele of their department. All politicians, perhaps, have something of the public relations man in them and Ambassador Ministers are always liable to be accused of being publicity hounds whose real motive is to glamorise and advance their own careers. A more comprehensively cynical view, of course, is that most Ministers are no more than public relations officers for their departments. This is a view that the evidence of previous chapters enables us to dismiss and it is often advanced only semi-seriously:

'One of the pleasanter amusements of politics-watching is seeing new Ministers start to talk the lingo of their departments. It does not take long; and maybe that is how many of them are best employed. A fresh-eyed writer on the constitution will completely overhaul Bagehot one day soon, and point out that most Ministers, like the Queen, belong to the theatrical part of the system.'[2]

Naturally Ministers themselves are aware of this cynical view and also of the tendency in Whitehall and Westminster to dismiss men who enjoy the glare of publicity as 'lightweights' or 'whiz-kids'. This may be the reason why there are fewer self-confessed Ambassador Ministers than policy initiators or policy selectors. It was noticeable, furthermore, that the three Ministers in the sample who were clearly identifiable as Ambassadors were quick to add, having

1 See p. 242.
2 'Observations', *New Society* (17 September 1970).

stressed the importance of public relations roles, that 'of course you must have something worthwhile to sell'. They did not want to give the impression that sales promotion was all important and the product irrelevant. It is perhaps unfortunate that Ministers feel obliged to be apologetic about public relations activities. Many policy programmes are not implemented by force of law; they require publicising to evoke the appropriate response from the sections of the community they are aimed at. House improvement grants and export services, for instance, are no use unless home owners and exporters are made aware of them and use them. It will also be suggested that particular departments, especially new departments, require a Minister with a flair for publicity 'to put them on the map', to let target publics know that they are in business, promoting certain objectives and offering certain services. The following case studies illustrate the methods and impact of Ambassador Ministers.

ERNEST MARPLES, POSTMASTER-GENERAL 1957-1959, MINISTER OF TRANSPORT 1959-1964

Superficially, Ernest Marples would appear to have had the background and role conception of an Executive Minister. One frequently read, during his period as Postmaster-General and later as Minister of Transport, that he was a self-made man who worshipped efficiency. He was born of working-class parents (his father was an engineer-foreman, his mother put bands on bowler hats), as a boy he sold ice-cream and soft drinks at football grounds, and before the age of thirty he made his million, converting Victorian buildings into flats and in civil engineering. An *Observer* profile of him said: 'He is an entrepreneur of a type very rare in ministerial office in this country – a political technocrat who derives all his satisfaction from making things work.'[1]

In practice, though, it was obvious to fellow politicians and civil servants that Marples's most definite characteristic was his desire and flair for attracting publicity.[2] The Post Office, normally a fairly dull department from a publicity viewpoint, gave him his first opportunity. On his first morning he accompanied postmen delivering mail and, having got his fingers caught in letter boxes, announced rather grandly: 'I shall have to ask the Council for Industrial Design to produce an efficient thief-proof box which will take large packages and then start a blitz on shops and firms to install it.'[3] Other

[1] 'Profile', *The Observer* (3 June 1960).
[2] See pp. 234-35.
[3] *Guardian* (26 January 1957).

publicity stunts included regularly ringing up telephone operators to check that they were polite and replacing Post Office fountain pens which blotted, with ball point pens that merely smudged. Trivial, perhaps, but as even the hostile *New Statesman* said, he 'helped to raise the morale of Post Office workers by making them feel that their work really was important'.[1]

The Ministry of Transport – and road safety campaigns in particular – provided Marples with excellent opportunities for attracting public attention. His success in doing so may be gauged by comparing the publicity he generated with the amount generated by his cabinet colleagues. Table 11.1 lists the number of articles in *The Times* in 1960 in which Conservative Ministers were mentioned.

Table 11.1   *Publicity Generated by Cabinet Ministers, 1960*[a]

Ministers[b]	Office	Number of articles[a]	Ministers[b]	Office	Number of articles[a]
H. Macmillan	Prime Minister	919	Sir D. Eccles	Education	114
R. Butler	Home Office	350	Lord Hailsham	Lord President	92
S. Lloyd	Foreign Office/ Treasury	257	E. Heath	Labour / Lord Privy Seal	84
E. Marples	*Transport*	*202*	Lord Kilmuir	Lord Chancellor	80
I. MacLeod	Colonial Office	188	J. Hare	Agriculture/ Labour	73
R. Maudling	Board of Trade	163	J. Maclay	Scottish Office	49
H. Brooke	Housing	156	C. Hill	Duchy of Lancaster	27
H. Watkinson	Defence	150			
D. Sandys	Aviation/Commonwealth	145	Lord Mills	Paymaster-General	21
Lord Home	Commonwealth Foreign Office	142			

[a] Source: *The Times* index, 1960.
[b] Christopher Soames and Peter Thorneycroft, who were in the Cabinet for less than half the year, being appointed respectively Minister of Agriculture and Minister of Aviation on 27 July, are not included in this table.

In fact, only the Prime Minister, the Home Secretary and Mr Selwyn Lloyd, who was successively Foreign Secretary and Chancellor of the Exchequer in 1960, were mentioned more often in *The Times* than Mr Marples. 1960 was the latter's first full year at the Ministry of Transport and he made a number of headline catching coups. He obtained parliamentary sanction for taking exceptional powers to control London traffic and introduced controversial new regulations,

[1] 'The Rise and Fall of Ernie Marples', *New Statesman* (4 June 1960).

including the 'pink zone'.[1] The first major 'don't drink and drive' campaign was inaugurated and the Minister himself took up commercial television advertising time at Christmas 1960 to warn against drinking and driving. A civil servant who by no means admired him nevertheless said, 'to be fair, he was the first Minister to spread the idea that driving required social responsibility and that an Englishman's car is not like his castle'.[2]

Other observers were less charitable and implied that Marples's publicity gimmicks frequently served no purpose other than self-promotion. One columnist wrote that:

'Now dressed in a diving suit he is inspecting underwater foundations in a Poplar power station; now dressed as a hiker he is addressing a Young Conservative meeting on the top of Snowdon; now trapped by a Swiss avalanche he skis ten miles to the nearest rail-head so that he may catch an important division in the House of Commons; now he is tramping with a postman on his humdrum rounds. Whatever he does, whether it is climbing the Matterhorn, living on water for thirty-six days, or chasing and catching a burglar, he is never too exhausted to ring up the press.'[3]

Fellow politicians also found him hard to take. Sir Anthony Eden, as Prime Minister, dropped him from the Government, despite what was generally regarded as an outstanding record as Parliamentary Secretary at the Ministry of Housing 1951–4,[4] and he later suffered well-leaked cabinet defeats over his proposal to introduce a breathalyser (alcoholic intake) test for motorists, and his replacement by the Paymaster-General, Lord Mills, as the Minister in charge of the reorganisation of the railways.[5] Conservative backbenchers publicly humiliated him by putting down a motion congratulating his predecessor, Mr Watkinson, after Marples had made what was interpreted as a self-glorifying speech when opening Britain's first motorway, the M1.[6] The most weighty attack, however, was delivered

---

[1] The 'pink zone' was the central area of London in which at Christmas 1959 car parking regulations were tightened up. Extra car parks for 6,000 vehicles were provided on the perimeter of the pink zone and special trains and buses were arranged so that the public could get to the car parks more conveniently. See Marples's statement in *Parliamentary Debates* (Commons), 614 (1959-60), 560-65.

[2] Interview with the author.

[3] *New Statesman* (4 June 1960).

[4] See Chapter 9.

[5] Cross-Bencher, 'End of the Road for Ernest', *Daily Express* (22 January 1961).

[6] Even more vaingloriously Marples stole the limelight at a lunch given for Dr Alan Bombard who had drifted alone across the Atlantic on a raft by announcing that he himself had once lived for thirty-six days on nothing but water.

in the House of Lords by the elder statesman, Lord Morrison of Lambeth:

'He does not appear to take the job seriously. Like fire, publicity is a good servant: it can do much good. But it can be a bad master. At the Ministry of Transport it is easy enough to get publicity. . . . But it seems to me the motive of personal publicity is master of the present Minister of Transport. . . . I would advise that publicity should be used for the purposes of leadership, guidance and good counsel to the public at large, including all classes of road user, and that in this publicity on the part of the Minister the use of the first person singular is less important than the merits of what he is trying to get done.'[1]

His critics, then, judged Marples extremely harshly and he certainly could at times be absurd ('I hope by next Christmas we'll know how to make sensible use of the motor car')[2] and unblushingly hypocritical (on taking charge of London Transport he said, 'I have made up my mind that whatever happens I am going to be unpopular').[3] Also many people must have grown tired of reading interviews in which he told reporters that he slept in a bed owned by Queen Caroline, was wakened each morning by an alarm clock which brewed tea, that his front door opened by remote control and that he was a gourmet cook who had called time and motion experts in to plan his kitchen. Nevertheless, the credit side of the account must also be examined. Publicity, as Lord Morrison conceded, can be a useful servant for Ministers and Marples's achievements in this area apparently improved departmental morale at the Post Office and undoubtedly gained necessary attention for the policy programmes of the Ministry of Transport. As an Ambassador Minister he was, arguably, in the right departments at the right time and his seventeen and a quarter hour working day, in which he did three and a half hours paper work between 5 and 8.30 a.m., at least meant that he had time for other activities besides grabbing newspaper headlines.[4]

ANTHONY WEDGWOOD BENN, MINISTER OF TECHNOLOGY 1966-1970

Probably the least apologetic Ambassador Minister of recent years was Anthony Wedgwood Benn. In an interview in 1969 he made his role conception clear: 'You've got to use a politician's ability to

[1] *Parliamentary Debates* (Lords), vol. 223 (1959-60), 308-16.

[2] *Guardian* (17 March 1960).

[3] *Daily Record* (11 December 1959).

[4] Ernest Marples, 'A Dog's Life at the Ministry', in Richard Rose (ed.), *Policy Making in Britain* (London: Macmillan, 1969), pp. 128-31.

inspire people, not just act as a second rate Permanent Secretary. On visits to factories and so forth, I have established a set pattern of always meeting people with a real job to do, including people on the shop floor'.[1] At the Ministry of Technology his main clients, the public he was trying to sell his department's services to, were businessmen. It was a question, he said, of,

'Developing personal links between the department and the leading industrialists from the major firms, which is a relationship that has got to be based on confidence and on regular contact so that one can simply lift the phone and they can do the same at any time. . . . The second thing [he went on] is to put yourself in a position to be of some assistance if necessary, as we did with the Shipbuilding Industry Board and the Industrial Reorganisation Corporation. Our support for the aircraft industry, also, is intervention.'[2]

Not only did Benn see himself as an Ambassador Minister, he was seen as such by colleagues. Prime Minister Harold Wilson, aware of Benn's methods, apparently appointed him with slight misgiving: 'I suggested to him that he should go easy on publicity until he had mastered the intricacies of this large and expanding Ministry . . . But with a new minister a period of quiet assimilation was needed.'[3] Further testimony about Benn's methods comes from a junior Minister who had formerly worked under Benn at Technology: 'The communications function of a Minister is also important. Benn was marvellous at this. He could not be dull if he tried. You say something to him and he immediately thinks how to communicate it to a wider audience.'[4]

Benn's success in securing publicity may be gauged in several ways. The first method – the same as was used for Ernest Marples – compares the number of articles in which he and his cabinet colleagues were mentioned in *The Times*; 1969 was taken as a sample year. The left hand column of Table 11.2 gives the 'scores' of Ministers in the 'inner Cabinet'. In the right hand column are the scores of second rank Ministers, including Benn, who were not in the 'Inner Cabinet'. Like Table 11.1, this Table illustrates that the Prime Minister and the heads of the most venerable departments of state are guaranteed a wide press (though the Chancellor of the Exchequer appears to

[1] Interview with the author.

[2] 'Integration and Joint Project Teams for New Ministry of Technology', interview with Anthony Wedgwood Benn, *The Times* (18 October 1969).

[3] H. Wilson, *The Labour Government* (London: Weidenfeld and Nicolson, and Michael Joseph, 1971), p. 245.

[4] Interview with the author.

Table 11.2 *Publicity Generated by Cabinet Ministers, 1969*[a]

Inner Cabinet	Office	Number of articles[a]	Other Ministers	Office	Number of articles[a]
H. Wilson	Prime Minister	441	A. Benn	Technology	108
M. Stewart	Foreign Office	216	E. Short	Education and Science	88
J. Callaghan	Home Office	212	R. Mason	Power / Board of Trade	74
R. Crossman	Health and Social Security	162	A. Crosland	Board of Trade /Local Government	72
B. Castle	Employment and Productivity	153	R. Marsh[b]	Transport	72
R. Jenkins	Treasury	139	A. Greenwood	Housing	69
D. Healey	Defence	101	J. Diamond	Chief Secretary	48
F. Peart	Lord President	40	C. Hughes	Agriculture	46
			Lord Gardiner	Lord Chancellor	36
			Lord Shackleton	Lord Privy Seal	33
			G. Thomson	Common Market (Foreign Office)	29
			W. Ross	Scottish Office	28
			P. Shore	DEA/Minister without Portfolio	27
			J. Hart[c]	Paymaster-General Overseas Development	24
			G. Thomas	Welsh Office	18

[a] Source: *The Times* index, 1969.
[b] Out of office, October 1969.
[c] Out of the Cabinet, October 1969.

have had a quiet year in 1969). At the other end of the scale, Ministers who lack a department to generate publicity and arrange 'visits' for them fare badly. The main point for the purposes of the present discussion, however, is that Mr Benn's speeches and activities were found to be considerably more newsworthy than those of his colleagues of similar cabinet standing. He was mentioned in 108 articles in *The Times* as compared with 88 mentions for the Secretary for Education, Mr Short. Mr Benn also outscored two members of the 'Inner Cabinet'. The ability to fill newspaper columns may not be everyone's ideal qualification for Ministers but it is worth noting that the Permanent Secretary of the Ministry of Technology thought Benn's public relations activities both valuable and successful:

'. . . There is no substitute for the speeches of Ministers and the normal day-to-day professional apparatus of public relations and publicity work. Mr Wedgwood Benn ranked this high and developed some original techniques for creating a better understanding in selected newspapers and other communications media of what the department was trying to do; and this had, I thought, some degree of success.'[1]

A second method of measuring Benn's impact as an Ambassador relates more specifically to his efforts to sell his department's services to industry. Table 11.3 reports on the growth of public expenditure between 1964-5 and 1968-9. By 1969 there was a formidable array of Ministry of Technology services and inducements to industry: investment grants, local employment grants in the development areas, advisory services for industry, launching aid for aircraft and aero-engine projects, support for shipbuilding and computer industries, development contracts in industry and subsidies for industrial research associations. The cost of these services, as Table 11.3 indicates, grew at 9 per cent a year between 1966 and 1969 and they constituted the greatest growth point in public expenditure; greater than the Labour Government's increases in educational and social service expenditure. The task of Benn and his department in selling the services and persuading businessmen to take advantage of them was, of course, made easier by the generous terms they had to offer. Critics were not slow to speak of 'hand-outs' and to assert, for example, that the investment grant system consisted of giving away eight shillings in the pound.[2] Be this as it may, Table 11.3 indicates that some Ministers are better at giving away eight shillings in the pound than others. Expenditure on commerce and industry grew much more rapidly after Benn's appointment. In his first full year in office, 1967-8, the outturn was £1,318 million, compared with £768 million the year before. This represents an increase of over 70 per cent in a single year and was followed by another increase of of 13 per cent in 1968-9.[3] In the face of this growth pattern *The Times* correspondent commented that, 'the danger to private enterprise and a free economy is to be found less in Mr Benn and his plans than in the eagerness of industry, large and small, to take

[1] Sir R. Clarke, *New Trends in Government* (London: HMSO, 1971), p. 30.

[2] In the 'development areas' (areas of high unemployment) 40 per cent of approved capital expenditure incurred by firms moving into the area was paid by the Government.

[3] But see Table 11.3 note b.

Table 11.3   *Public Expenditure by Groups of Programmes 1964-5 to 1968-9* [a]

	1964-5 outturn £m.	1965-6 outturn £m.	1966-7 outturn £m.	1967-8 outturn £m.	1968-9 provisional outturn £m.	Average annual increase per cent 1964-5 to 1968-9
At 1969 Survey prices						
Defence and external relations	2,856	2,912	2,933	2,977	2,772	−0.7
Commerce and industry [b] (Mainly Ministry of Technology)	634	634	768	1,318	1,498	9.0
Environmental services	2,684	2,834	2,946	3,172	3,223	4.7
Social services	5,801	6,278	6,515	7,028	7,317	6.0
Other services	641	702	750	822	843	7.1
Nationalised industries etc., capital expenditure	1,376	1,374	1,620	1,783	1,510	2.4
Debt interest	1,564	1,618	1,735	1,936	2,051	7.0
Relative price effect and other adjustments [c]	−472	−254	−59	177	381	—
At 1969-70 outturn price TOTAL	15,084	16,098	17,208	19,213	19,595	5.9
Annual increases per cent	3.8	6.7	6.6	9.0	1.6	—

[a] *Public Expenditure 1968-9 to 1973-4*, Cmnd 4234 (London: HMSO, 1969), p. 8.

[b] The figures for this group of programmes include £52 million for selective employment tax additional payments in 1966-7 and £520 million and £604 million for investment grants, regional employment premiums and selective employment tax additional payments in 1967-8 and 1968-9 respectively, which were not payable in 1964-5 and 1965-6. The annual percentage change in the last column for this group, and for the total, are calculated excluding these new expenditures.

[c] 'Relative price effect' is the term used to refer to the allowance that needs to be made for the fact that over a period of time a series of figures on a constant price basis will understate the share of national resources which public expenditure absorbs.

up Mr Benn's invitation to go into partnership with the state'.[1]

We have concentrated here on Benn's public relations activities as a Minister. He was (and is), however, a true believer in the general importance of 'communication' in politics. He is on record as favouring 'participatory democracy' and the spread of social action groups, among which he includes the student Left, Shelter, the play school movement and the nationalist parties.[2] While he was a Minister he also made considerable efforts to improve communications within his own department. He held meetings with officials every Friday, which he described as 'Maoist self-criticism' sessions, and he invited junior Ministers from other departments and also backbench Labour MPs to discuss future Ministry of Technology policy. Overall, he believed that a major failure of the Labour Government lay in not communicating and explaining its achievements and problems to its own supporters.

Not surprisingly Benn's concern with politics as communication made him more vulnerable than most Ministers to the charge of being a 'whiz-kid' and a 'lightweight'. An *Observer* profile put it this way:

'Yet his undoubted success story has been marred by one critical word which has dogged his career. . . . He is, they say or suggest, a lightweight. . . . He is above everything a communicator, a master of the presentational arts; and these are important political qualities which the weighty often lack.'[3]

ADDITIONAL EXAMPLES AND CONCLUDING POINTS

As noted above, many politicians have something of the Ambassador Minister in them and it is not hard to produce further examples of Ministers who, because of the requirements of a particular department or situation, gave high priority to public relations roles. Thus many Ministers who would reject the idea that public relations are invariably the most important aspect of their job, have nevertheless given overriding attention, at some stage of their office-bearing career, to problems of public presentation and to mobilising support for their department's proposals or activities. One would not, for instance, think of Sir Edward Boyle, who served as a junior Minister at Education from 1957 to 1959 and as Cabinet Minister in the same department from 1962 to 1964, as a prototypical Ambassador

---

[1] David Wood, 'Sandwiches with Benn', *The Times* (17 November 1969).

[2] 'One Way Ahead for Labour', *Guardian* (6 November 1968).

[3] 'Anthony Wedgwood Benn: A Question of Weight', *Observer* (12 October 1969).

Minister.[1] The following extract, however, comes from his conversations with Maurice Kogan:

KOGAN: 'We had a long discussion about what the Parliamentary Secretary in Education ought to do. I think that the analogy we both hit on was that of Sir Samuel Hoare in the early 1920s, who felt strongly that the Royal Air Force was going to be an important part of the defence system, and that the thing it lacked above all was ministerial backing, and reputation and status in the whole country. You felt that any Minister who could make known to the wider political community the merits, advantages, problems and policies of the education service would be doing an important job. And so you took upon yourself the task of going to the country, of extolling the virtues of the system, and of bringing it home to the people who helped to form opinion. Is that a correct account of how you saw at least part of your role as Parliamentary Secretary?'

BOYLE: 'Yes, absolutely correct. And I don't remember, if I could help it, ever refusing a request from a local authority to pay a visit.'[2]

Later, as a Cabinet Minister at Education, Boyle was more concerned with substantive decisions arising from major reports on the education service.[3] Mobilising support for the conclusions of these reports remained a crucial task, however:

'After 1963 it was hardly controversial to say that you had massive evidence of the numbers of boys and girls who were being allowed to write themselves off below their true level of ability. . . . Indeed I would like to think, if I contributed anything to education, or indeed anything at all during my twenty years in politics, I did something to bring "middle" opinion over to this side, to make it plain that the norm of opinion had shifted here and that middle opinion had just simply got to accommodate itself to this.'[4]

Another politician who found himself functioning as an Ambas-

[1] Boyle was Parliamentary Secretary at the Ministry of Education January 1957 to October 1959, Minister of Education from 1962 to April 1964 and Minister of State for Education responsible for higher education until October 1964.
[2] E. Boyle, A. Crosland and M. Kogan, *The Politics of Education* (Harmondsworth: Penguin, 1971), pp. 87-8.
[3] Central Advisory Council for Education (England), *Half Our Future* (Newsom Report) (London: HMSO, 1963); Committee on Higher Education, *Higher Education* (Robbins Report) (London: HMSO, 1963).
[4] Boyle, Crosland and Kogan, *The Politics of Education*, pp. 91-2.

sador Minister, both as Chancellor of the Exchequer and as Home Secretary, was James Callaghan. As Chancellor from 1964 to 1967 in Mr Wilson's Government he became the symbol of the pound at $2.80 and frequently travelled to the United States and to meetings of European financiers and bankers to reassure them that devaluation would not be contemplated. It was reported two years after he left that, 'Certainly the pound could not have had a better public relations officer – the Treasury staff still revere him for the pugnacity of his salesmanship of *their* policies.'[1] At the Home Office Callaghan's flair for public relations again came to the fore. His tour of Ulster, after a severe outbreak of sectarian rioting, moved *The Sunday Times* editorial writer to make a claim which later events in the province showed to be exaggerated: 'For good as well as ill, personalities do count in politics. Mr Callaghan has proved it by his tour of Ulster. It was a triumph of personality, and a different approach by a different personality could have had a lamentably different result.'[2] Callaghan's other public relations activities as Home Secretary perhaps had less to do with the requirements of his department, or the situations he faced, than with the rebuilding of his political career after his transfer from the Treasury following devaluation:

'As he began his recovery at the Home Office he showed how a skilful politician can make the best of the cards which are dealt him. . . . When he repudiated the Wootton Report on the drug cannabis, Callaghan was saving the nation not only from pot but from experts. It required his sort of genius to invent a distinction between "hard games" and "soft games" and thereby erect a standard whereby bingo was a harmless flutter while *chemin-de-fer* was wicked gambling. Another Home Secretary might have found more important things to do than appear after question time with a statement on football rowdyism, but James Callaghan knew on which side his career was buttered. From his new base in the Home Office he projected a clear colourful image of himself. Everyone knew where *he* stood, everybody knew Jim – tough on immigration but soft on race relations, tough on crime but soft on capital punishment, tough on drugs but soft on children: the note was exactly right: the British admixture of virtue and hypocrisy, tolerance and prejudice was epitomised in Sunny Jim, Grim Jim and Honest Jim Callaghan.'[3]

[1] Lewis Chester, 'Why Jim's Lot Is Still a Happy One', *The Sunday Times* (24 August 1969).
[2] Editorial, *The Sunday Times* (31 August 1969).
[3] P. Jenkins, *The Battle of Downing Street* (London: Charles Knight, 1970), pp. 82-3.

Another Labour Minister whose flair for publicity was, in general, an asset (thought it occasionally backfired) in the post in which he found himself was George Brown. The Department of Economic Affairs was a new department and a new department probably always requires an Ambassador Minister so that its potential clients know its aims, become aware of the services it offers and feel obliged to respond to its promptings. At the DEA Brown was credited with personally persuading a large number of industrialists and trade union leaders to make the Joint Declaration of Intent on Productivity, Prices and Incomes (1964) and, throughout his period in office, he concentrated heavily on the public relations orientated prices and incomes side of his job.[1] In his memoirs he concedes that he overdid it and that it would have been wiser to stress that 'in fact the major central theme of the DEA was economic expansion'.[2] By late 1966 Prime Minister Wilson disagreed with Brown's priorities but recognised the initial value to the new department of an Ambassador Minister. Thus, recalling the transfer of Brown to the Foreign Office and his replacement by Mr Michael Stewart, he wrote:

'He [Brown] had done the job he set out to do in creating DEA; it was running well and the transfer to other ministers of responsibility for individual price and wage cases had eliminated some of the late night explosions. DEA I felt needed now, not the inspiration of its creating genius, but a period of quiet and orderly administration and Michael Stewart, I was equally sure, had the temperament required.'[3]

While accepting the general point, it may be that Wilson's judgement about the needs of the department was premature. Under Michael Stewart it was generally regarded in Whitehall as being in decline and under the next incumbent, Peter Shore, who certainly could not be described as a successful Ambassador Minister, it literally died and its functions were taken over by the Treasury and the Ministry of Technology.

The appointment of a Minister specifically charged to concentrate on public relations activities can sometimes be a product of the electoral situation. During periods of mid-term unpopularity Governments are always liable to decide that what is wrong is not their policies but their failure to communicate their achievements to the

---

[1] S. Brittan, *Steering the Economy* (London: Secker and Warburg, 1969), pp. 202-5.
[2] George Brown, *In My Way* (London: Gollancz, 1971), p. 118.
[3] Wilson, *The Labour Government*, p. 272.

public. In 1957, for example, Lord Hailsham, a Cabinet Minister, was appointed party chairman with the task of reviving party and public faith in the Government. He set about this with gusto, ringing bells ('Let us say to the Labour Party: 'Seek not to inquire for whom the bell tolls'. It tolls for them')[1] and being photographed at the annual party conference taking an early morning swim. Thirteen years later, Mr Heath, as Prime Minister of another Conservative Government, came to office with the evident determination to downgrade public relations activities and present a stark contrast to what he regarded as the gimmickry of the previous Labour administration.[2] His influence was such that the Cabinet was remarkable for lacking any member who behaved as if he had an Ambassador Minister's conception of his job. By 1972, however, the public opinion polls indicated that the Government was losing electoral support. Mr Heath perhaps did not revise his ideas to the extent of believing, like Mr Wilson, that a Prime Minister personally should be able to 'dictate, without a deparmental brief, the main text of any speech he has to make, in Parliament, or in the country'.[3] However, he did take the unusual, if not unprecedented step of appointing two Cabinet Ministers to win back electoral support; Lord Carrington, the Defence Secretary, became chairman of the party and Mr James Prior, the Minister of Agriculture, was deputy chairman. The moral seems to be that a Prime Minister must either devote a great deal of time to acting as his own public relations officer, or else must assign the task to specific members of the Cabinet who are already fairly well known to the public and have a flair for headline catching.

In concluding, it is worth reminding ourselves that Ambassador Ministers, more than most Ministers, are dependent on their personal skills and abilities. A politician either succeeds in developing a flair for publicity or he does not, and there is only a limited amount his department, or its public relations officer, can do if he lacks flair. But ambassadorial skills are wasted unless a Minister has in hand policy programmes that need selling, in the sense that they cannot

---

[1] *Keesing's Contemporary Archives* (1957-8), 15864.

[2] See, for example, Mr Heath's foreword to the 1970 Conservative election manifesto *A Better Tomorrow* (London: Conservative Central Office, 1970). He wrote,

'During the last six years we have suffered not only from bad policies but from a cheap and trivial style of government. Decisions have been dictated simply by the desire to gain tomorrow's headlines. The short term gain has counted for everything; the long term objective has gone out of the window. Every device has been used to gain immediate publicity, and government by gimmick has become the order of the day.'

[3] Wilson, *The Labour Government*, pp. 44-5.

simply be legally enforced, and worth selling in that they are of significant benefit to some section of the community. As will be argued in the final chapter, it is up to the Prime Minister to see that Ambassador Ministers are appointed to departments where their skills are most required and to ensure, in other words, that the man and his time meet.

Part IV

The Consequences
of Ministers

Chapter 12

Selecting Cabinet Ministers
Some International Comparisons

The thrust of the argument in Part II of this study was that British politicians are better equipped to serve as policy selectors and Ambassador Ministers than as policy initiators and Exicutive Ministers. We found that the expectations of civil servants are not such as to encourage Executive Ministers and attitudes to ministerial policy initiators appear ambivalent. The same two types of Minister appear likely to run into difficulties in securing from either Whitehall or non-Whitehall sources the range and quality of advice necessary to act in accordance with their role conceptions. It is above all in terms of their own experiences and skills, however, that Ministers appear qualified to perform some roles more satisfactorily than others. As non-specialists they lack qualifications which many observers believe to be an asset – if not a pre-requisite – for policy initiation and as non-organisation men they are not obviously fitted to be Executive Ministers.

In this chapter we review the criteria by which Ministers are selected, and the skills they bring to office, in four other industrialised democracies: Canada, Australia, the Netherlands and the USA. This review will serve several purposes. At a minimum it will demonstrate that elsewhere Ministers with qualifications markedly different from those regarded as almost self-evidently right in Britain are appointed to office. Second, we shall try to indicate some social and constitutional factors and differences in political culture which explain cross-national variance in ministerial recruitment. Last, it is hoped that the discussion of 'the consequences of Ministers' in the concluding section will lend perspective to the attempt in Chapter 13 to suggest linkages between ministerial skills and the achievements and failures of post-war British government.

The methodology of this chapter is quite unsophisticated. The four countries to which our evidence relates are selected as representing polar, or ideal types in terms of ministerial selection criteria. Attention is focused on those selection criteria which, in a cross-national comparative context, are most striking and characteristic. It would be mistaken to draw the inference that Ministers in these countries are selected on the basis of a single criterion. The point is that these four countries provide a clear contrast to Britain and hence give us a data base from which to start our search for explanations of cross-national variance in ministerial recruitment and for linkages between ministerial skills and governmental performance. It should be clear that data are used to illustrate points and suggest hypotheses: a systematic analysis designed to *test* hypotheses would ideally take account of all industrialised countries and would pose problems of data collection which are beyond the scope of this chapter.

MINISTERIAL SELECTION CRITERIA: CROSS-NATIONAL VARIANCE

Canada: Ministers as sectional representatives

In the more socially heterogeneous Western democracies the representation of economic, religious, regional and ethnic interests is an extremely important criterion affecting ministerial recruitment. Canada is outstanding, however, in the extent to which the Cabinet reflects social divisions. As the Canadian political scientist R. McGregor Dawson has written:

'The most notable characteristic of the Canadian Cabinet is the representative nature of its membership: the Cabinet has become to a unique degree the grand co-ordinating body for the divergent provincial, sectional, religious, racial and other interests throughout the dominion. Cabinets in other countries as, for example, Great Britain and the United States, frequently exhibit similar tendencies, but not over as wide a field or in compliance with the same rigid requirements.'[1]

The most politically divisive cleavage in Canada lies between English speaking, Protestant Ontario and predominantly French speaking, Catholic Quebec. In the past, in a Cabinet of about twenty members, French speaking Quebec obtained at least three representatives and the English minority one. Within the province representation was invariably given to the areas around the cities of Quebec and Montreal and the English speaking constituencies (including the

[1] R. McGregor Dawson, 'Cabinet – Position and Personnel', in Orest Kruhlak, Richard Schultz and Sidney Pobihushchy (eds), *The Canadian Political Process* (Toronto: Holt, Rinehart and Winston, 1970), pp. 345-66.

eastern townships) formed another unit.[1] Ontario, with a larger population than Quebec, demanded at least an equal voice in the Cabinet
and normally had four or five members, with representation from the
northern and western parts of the province and often, also, from
Toronto.[2] In recent years the size of the Cabinet has increased markedly and the two major provinces have more than maintained their
quota. In the Pearson Cabinet formed in 1963 ten of the twenty-
four members were from Ontario and seven from Quebec and in
the 1968 Trudeau Cabinet there were ten members from each
province in a Cabinet of twenty-nine. It is noteworthy that, with the
resurgence of French nationalism, Quebec's proportion of members
in the Trudeau Cabinet is the highest since the Liberal Cabinet of
1926-30.[3]

Apart from Ontario and Quebec all other provinces are given at
least one representative in the Cabinet. This principle has been followed even when a province has failed to return a single supporter of
the governing party and even in the case of Prince Edward Island
which returns only four members of the Lower House.[4] To secure
representation of the western provinces, which have tended to support
parties other than the Liberals or Conservatives, it has been necessary
to draft in provincial Premiers, ex-Premiers and Cabinet Ministers
with no previous experience of politics in Ottawa.[5] These western
appointees normally head Ministries whose work particularly affects
their provinces. Thus the Department of the Interior used to go to a
westerner and its successor, the Ministry of Energy, Mines and Resources normally does so.[6] The Ministry of Agriculture is also given to
a westerner, while the Ministry of Fisheries is reserved for a representative of the maritime provinces.

At cabinet meetings Ministers are expected to act as spokesmen
not only for their own departments but also for their provinces. Further, a Minister who belongs to the same party as controls the government of his province is expected 'at Ottawa to use his good offices to

[1] ibid., p. 356.

[2] loc. cit.

[3] For lists of Canadian Cabinets since 1867 see Kruhlak, Schultz and Pobi-
hushchy (eds), *The Canadian Political Process*, Appendix. Biographies of all
Parliamentarians, including Ministers are given in J. K. Johnson (ed.), *The
Canadian Directory of Parliament 1867-1967* (Ottawa: Public Archives of
Canada, 1968).

[4] Dawson, 'Cabinet – Position and Personnel', p. 356. In 1921 Alberta returned
no Liberals to Ottawa. However, the Prime Minister, Mr Mackenzie King,
appointed a Liberal ex-Premier of the province to the Cabinet.

[5] John A. Porter, *The Vertical Mosaic: An Analysis of Social Class and Power
in Canada* (Toronto: University of Toronto, 1965), pp. 398-403.

[6] The Trudeau Cabinet formed in 1968 was an exception: the Minister of
Energy, Mines and Resources came from Ontario.

promote the requests which the provincial Government may make'.[1]
We may also note that before dominion appointments are made in a
particular province it is usual for the appointing Minister to consult
the Minister representing the province.

Only in regard to Protestant denominations could it be said that
the pressure to afford group representation is diminishing. In the past
it was usual to ensure that members of the Church of England, the
Presbyterian Church, the Methodists, the Congregationalists and the
Baptists were all represented in the Cabinet. Nowadays, although
'some balance of Protestant denominations is at least considered',
sectarian differences are less significant.[2] Last, we should note that
the economic or social class cleavage, which is of great political significance in most European countries, has in Canada not much affected ministerial appointments. Both major parties have a middle class,
pro-business outlook and the social background of their leaders reflects and reinforces this tendency. John A. Porter, the leading student
of the recruitment of Canadian elites, considers that, 'it is the homo-
geneity of political leaders in terms of education, occupation, and
social class which gives the political system its conservative tone'.[3]
In fact, nearly two-thirds of Ministers since World War II have been
lawyers and the next largest group, just under 20 per cent, have been
businessmen.[4] Industrial workers are almost unknown at cabinet
level and the only concession made to organised labour is the appointment of a Minister of Labour acceptable to the unions.[5]

Canadian political scientists have disagreed in evaluating the consequences of this pattern of ministerial recruitment. Dawson, while
recognising that insistence on sectional representation is bound to
mean that sometimes mediocrities are preferred to abler men, nevertheless believes that, 'a national party must take as its primary
purpose the reconciliation of the widely scattered aims and interests
of a number of areas'.[6] In his view, politicians who serve as brokers
for regional interests meet Canada's requirements. Dawson belongs
to the school of thought of Pendleton Herring and David Truman
which sees brokerage parties as being 'functional' to the political
system.[7] John A. Porter, on the other hand, adopts the Marxist view

[1] Dawson, 'Cabinet – Position and Personnel', p. 357.
[2] ibid., p. 358.
[3] Porter, *The Vertical Mosaic*, p. 391.   [4] ibid., p. 391.
[5] Dawson, 'Cabinet – Position and Personnel', p. 358. Dawson notes, rather
enigmatically, that: 'The Minister of Labour has usually been associated in a
theoretical or practical way with organised labour'.
[6] R. McGregor Dawson, *The Government of Canada* (Toronto: 1948), p. 508.
[7] Pendleton Herring, *The Politics of Democracy: American Parties in Action*
(New York: Norton, 1940); D. B. Truman, *The Governmental Process* (New
York: Alfred A. Knopf, 1962).

that economic or social class interests alone are fundamental and that representation of other interests and Canadian insistence on the merits of federalism merely serve to prevent the development of 'ideological' (i.e. class) parties and the emergence of 'creative' (i.e. radical) leaders.[1] Porter writes that 'a dissociative federalism is raised to the level of a quasi-religious political dogma and polarisation to right and left in Canadian politics is regarded as disruptive. Consequently the main focus of Canadian politics has been to the right and the maintenance of the *status quo*.'[2] More specifically, in relation to political leaders, he believes that the system has encouraged the emergence of 'administrative politicians' who 'depoliticise politics'.[3] He points out that the majority of Canadian Ministers spend less than half their working lives in politics and, on losing office, frequently leave politics without regret. Certainly there can be few places in the world where there would be nothing remarkable in an ex-Minister saying, 'Politics are [sic] a jealous mistress. If you aren't careful they will take up more of your time than you bargained for.'[4]

Canada is the limiting case of interest representation in the Cabinet. However, in other countries with large diverse populations and federal systems of government, ministerial appointments also have to be made with a view to representing and reconciling potentially conflicting interests. Thus, in the United States, representation of ethnic, regional and religious groups receives careful presidential consideration and in the Federal Republic of Germany religious, regional and social class loyalties demand recognition.[5] Even in some small countries, of which Belgium, the Netherlands and Switzerland are obvious examples, deep social cleavages mean that groups are sensitive to the risks of under-representation in the central government.[6]

At the other extreme are societies such as Britain, Sweden, and Denmark, which it would be wrong to describe as homogeneous, but in which social class is the only major division of political signifi-

[1] Porter, *The Vertical Mosaic*, pp. 368-9, 405-12.

[2] ibid., p. 369.

[3] loc. cit.

[4] Mr Ralph Campney, a former Liberal Minister, quoted in ibid., p. 411.

[5] On the USA see Richard F. Fenno, *The President's Cabinet* (Cambridge: Harvard University Press, 1959), pp. 67-87. On Germany see Gerhard Loewenberg, *Parliament in the German Political System* (Ithaca: Cornell University Press, 1967), ch. 5.

[6] For Belgium see K. Hill, 'Belgium' in S. Henig and J. Pinder (eds.), *European Political Parties* (London: Allen and Unwin, 1969), pp. 68-95; for the Netherlands see A. Lijphart, *The Politics of Accommodation: Pluralism and Democracy in the Netherlands* (Berkeley: University of California Press, 1968); for Switzerland see C. J. Hughes, 'Switzerland' in Henig and Pinder (eds), *European Political Parties*, pp. 365-85.

cance and in which, even then, class conflict is not normally bitter. In these countries class divides the parties rather than having to be accommodated at an intra-party level. Otherwise there are no objections to a Cabinet made up entirely of Protestants and agnostics and demands for regional and ethnic representation are easily met.

Australia: party political heavyweights and the maintenance of party cohesion

Australia provides an even more striking example than Britain of a country in which cabinet selection is largely governed by the desire to maintain party cohesion. Ministers are faction leaders and, indeed, they are held responsible to their factions for policy decisions. The close control exercised by parliamentary factions over Ministers – and by extra-parliamentary bodies over Parliamentarians – is at bottom a manifestation of the profound diistrust of politicians which is characteristic of the Australian political culture.[1] This distrust is particularly strong, as one might expect, on the Left and has been reinforced by episodes in the Australian Labour Party's (ALP) turbulent history.

The ALP split with the most far-reaching consequences for internal party organisation and power occurred in 1916. W. M. Hughes, as Prime Minister, introduced conscription, contrary to the wishes of most party supporters. A special inter-state conference was called and Hughes, the New South Wales ALP Premier, and all Parliamentarians who had supported Hughes were expelled from the party. To secure future obedience from Parliamentarians the balance of power in party executive committees and conferences was transferred from constituency branches to trade unions and, incidentally, from Protestants to Catholics.[2] A later Labour Prime Minister, Ben Chifley, reconciled the party to some extent to the view that it could not dictate policy decisions and that Ministers must also accept guidance from civil servants, but the degree to which, at all levels of the party, followers seek to control leaders remains exceptional.[3]

Of principal interest from the point of view of this chapter are the methods adopted by the Labour parliamentary party to ensure that Ministers in office remain responsive to its demands. Ministers are elected by a ballot of the entire parliamentary party and the Prime Minister retains only the discretion of deciding whom to appoint to

[1] See S. Encel, *Equality and Authority: A Study of Class, Status and Power in Australia* (London: Tavistock Publications, 1970), ch. 11, 'The Politicians We Deserve'.

[2] James Jupp, *Australian Party Politics* (London: Cambridge University Press, 1964), p. 59.

[3] L. F. Crisp, *Ben Chifley* (London: Longmans, 1963).

which department.[1] Candidates for office conduct informal campaigns and 'tickets' or slates of candidates are formed. The Australian Workers Union (AWU) is influential behind the scenes in sponsoring pro-union candidates and tickets are balanced by including representatives from all the states.[2] The caucus election method has been criticised as favouring the advancement of party hacks at the expense of abler men.[3] A more charitable way of making the same point is to say that Australian Labour Cabinets come close to being a mirror image of the party which sustains them. In addition to the states being represented almost exactly according to their proportion of members in the Lower House, it is also noteworthy that a higher proportion of Ministers of working class origin reach Australian Labour Cabinets than reach Cabinets formed by any other party outside the Communist bloc.[4] Overall, 42 per cent of Labour Ministers who have held office in this century were former manual workers.[5]

Once in office Labour Cabinets remain, by comparative standards, remarkably responsive to caucus. The prestige of the Prime Minister counts for a good deal in obtaining acquiescence, but cabinet decisions are debated by caucus and individual Ministers are obliged to justify their actions to the party factions that elected them.[6] This greatly weakens the application of the doctrine of collective cabinet responsibility and the British convention that disputes in Cabinet are kept secret is mainly honoured in the breach.[7] If Ministers become unpopular with caucus a 'spill' may occur. That is to say, backbenchers demand another election of Ministers and a few heads roll. Spills have occurred on several occasions at the federal level (notably in 1915 when W. M. Hughes replaced Andrew Fisher as Prime Minister), less frequently at state level.[8]

In their desire to ensure that Ministers will be responsive to the parliamentary party and the party outside Parliament the two non-Labour parties – the Liberals and the Country Party – have been increasingly influenced by Labour Party practice, as well as by the national distrust of political leaders. Thus James Jupp in his study of *Australian Party Politics* writes that, 'Labour is the most extreme advocate of parliamentary subservience to the machine, but the gap

[1] S. Encel, *Cabinet Government in Australia* (London: Cambridge University Press, 1962), ch. 12.
[2] ibid., p. 149.
[3] ibid., Chapter 12.
[4] Encel, *Equality and Authority*, pp. 235-36.
[5] loc. cit.
[6] K. West, *Power in the Liberal Party* (Melbourne: F. W. Cheshire, 1966), p. 245.
[7] Encel, *Cabinet Government in Australia*, pp. 285-93.
[8] ibid., chs 13, 14.

between it and its opponents has narrowed in the past fifty years.'[1]
In the same vein S. Encel remarks that,

'These composite Ministries [see below] operate along lines which are
no more to be interpreted by reference to British criteria than are the
workings of a Labour Ministry. As with Labour they are calculated
to enforce the responsibility of the government parties to the interest
groups that support them, to check the operation of collective responsibility and to temper the purely "governmental" or "administrative"
outlook which any government, whatever its political colour, is
bound to assume.'[2]

Jupp's and Encel's assessments of Liberal-Country Party control
over Ministers hold true despite the personal dominance exercised in
the Liberal Party during the long reign of its founder, R. G. Menzies.
Menzies was Prime Minister from 1949 until 1966 and was not sympathetic to extra-parliamentary control over the parliamentary party,
or to proposals to elect Ministers.[3] Even Menzies was obliged, however, to heed demands for representation of each state in the Cabinet
and to accept nominees to about one-quarter of cabinet seats from
the Country Party.[4] In retrospect, the Menzies era is likely to stand
out as the high water mark of leader dominance in Australian party
history. As D. W. Rawson has pointed out, the non-Labour parties
have in the past been even more prone than Labour to dump their
leaders unceremoniously:

'Every federal leader of the Liberal Party and its predecessors illustrates, in one way or another, the difficulties and dangers which the
political life involves. Hughes and Menzies (in 1941) were removed
from the leadership, Bruce fell from it, Cook and Latham were eased
out of it, Lyons was driven to an early death, Deakin became
deranged.'[5]

Since Rawson wrote, another Liberal leader, John Gorton, has
been forced out of office.
A further feature of Australian politics which reflects the importance of reponsiveness to party demands is the 'composite' Ministry.
The term 'composite' Ministry (rather than coalition Ministry) is

[1] Jupp, *Australian Party Politics*, p. 181.
[2] Encel, *Cabinet Government in Australia*, p. 196.
[3] Proposals to elect Ministers by caucus have been made at Liberal party
conferences but have always been rejected. See West, *Power in the Liberal Party*,
p. 245.
[4] ibid., pp. 245-6.
[5] D. W. Rawson, *Labor in Vain?* (London: Longmans, 1966), p. 30.

insisted on by the Country Party, which was in office in Canberra with the Liberals from 1949 to 1972. In a composite Ministry the parties retain their separate identity and Ministers are not bound by collective cabinet responsibility but report to and receive instructions from party caucus.[1] No member of the Country Party is permitted to accept office in a federal or state composite Ministry without the approval of the federal (or state) council of the party. The object is to ensure that party leaders do not accept personal advancement without gaining maximum policy concessions in return for their party's adherence to the Government.[2]

Australia is exceptional in the extent to which, even in periods of single-party government, responsiveness to party demands has been a crucial factor in ministerial selection. It should be remembered, though, that in most Western democratic systems coalition governments, not single-party governments, are the norm.[3] In selecting members of a coalition government a Prime Minister is inevitably constrained by the demands of his party's allies. If he is head of a 'grand coalition' of the two largest parties in the system (cf. Austria 1945-66 and Germany 1966-9) or of a coalition dominated by one party but with a minor party ally or allies (since World War II such coalitions have occurred in Denmark, Norway, Sweden, Belgium, Germany and Italy) he is likely to retain some effective choice at least over which of his own party's members to appoint. In the latter type of coalition, however, as Browne and Franklin have shown, smaller parties are able to use the threat of not joining the Government to obtain a share of appointments greater than the proportion of legislative seats they contribute to the coalition.[4] In multi-party coalitions which, since World War II, have been the norm in the Netherlands, Switzerland, and Finland and in Fourth Republic France, the head of Government has even less discretion. He simply has to appoint a few top leaders from each party, regardless of their qualifications in other respects.

This section has been concerned with political systems in which responsiveness to party demands and the requirements of intra- and inter-party cohesion are an important criterion affecting ministerial appointments. As ever, though, it would be mistaken to conclude a

[1] Encel, *Cabinet Government in Australia*, ch. 16.

[2] ibid., pp. 197-8.

[3] The only democracies which have had single party governments for a majority of years since World War II are Britain, the USA, Canada, Australia, New Zealand, Eire, Norway and Sweden. France has had single party government since the founding of the Fifth Republic in 1958.

[4] E. C. Browne and M. N. Franklin, 'Aspects of Coalition Pay-Offs in European Parliamentary Democracies', *American Political Science Review*, 67.2 (1973), 453-69.

comparison of political systems without drawing attention to cross-national variance. At the opposite pole from Australia is the United States in which the demands of party cohesion affect ministerial appointments only slightly. It is perfectly normal to appoint as a Cabinet Secretary one member of the opposite party and several men with no previous experience of political office. [1] The majority of cabinet members normally have no national political reputation and lack standing in their party. It may help the Administration with its legislative programme if a prominent Senator or Representative is in the Cabinet but such appointments are not made by all Presidents. [2]

Specialist Ministers: the Netherlands [3]

In the Netherlands it is apparently believed that the specialised and technical tasks of modern government require the appointment of specialist Ministers. Since about 1930 it has become increasingly common to appoint Ministers and Under-Secretaries (*staats-secretaris*) [4] whose careers in government and, occasionally, non-government posts have provided them with substantive knowledge of particular policy problems and the business of particular Ministries.

The most surprising finding from a British viewpoint is that roughly a quarter of Dutch Ministers are civil servants appointed as political heads of departments in which they have previously served as officials. Among these appointees, economists form a significant group (one in ten Ministers since 1945) [5] as do diplomats, civil servants trained in law and engineers. Thus approximately half the Ministers appointed to the Ministry of Foreign Affairs in this century have been diplomats who previously served in the Ministry. [6] Several Ministers of Finance and Under-Secretaries were former section heads in the Ministry and it has become almost *de rigueur* to appoint a Ministry of Justice official as political head of department. By the same token, it would be considered irresponsible not to put a civil servant with a training in engineering in charge of such 'technical' departments as the Minis-

[1] Fenno, *The President's Cabinet.*
[2] ibid., ch. 2.
[3] This section is largely based on M. Dogan and M. Schaffer-Van der Veen, 'Le Personnel Ministériel Hollandais', *Année Sociologique* (1957, 3rd ser.), 95-125; Lijphart, *The Politics of Accommodation: Pluralism and Democracy in The Netherlands*; H. Daalder, 'Cabinets and Party Systems In Ten Smaller European Democracies', *Acta Politica*, 6.3 (July 1971), 282-303.
[4] *Staats-secretaris* were first appointed in 1948. Before that date all Ministers were of cabinet rank.
[5] Dogan and Schaffer-Van der Veen, *Année Sociologique* (1957, 3rd ser.) 97.
[6] ibid., pp. 101-2.

try of Waterways and Forests and Ministry of Works. It would be mistaken, however, to infer that specialist appointees are drawn exclusively from the Civil Service. University professors have since 1945 been recruited in growing numbers to head departments whose business coincides with their academic specialisation and, in the past, military officers were often appointed to the defence departments. Indeed, since 1848, thirty-seven army officers have been appointed Minister of War and twenty-seven naval officers Ministers for the Navy.[1] In the case of the military departments, however, recent trends have been atypical in that non-specialists, or at any rate civilians, are increasingly being appointed.

A factor which to some degree reinforces the specialist knowledge of Dutch Ministers is the length of their tenure in office. Presumably, the longer a Minister remains in post the more thorough his knowledge of departmental business is likely to become. From this standpoint it is significant that between 1945 and 1965 there were only five Dutch Prime Ministers, five Finance Ministers, six Ministers of Internal Affairs and six Ministers of Foreign Affairs.[2] Thus, in these key posts, continuity in office has, at least by British standards, been remarkable. In lesser government posts, however, ministerial turnover is higher.[3]

What are the conditions which make it possible in the Netherlands to appoint so many specialist Ministers? First, the appointment of civil servants is facilitated by the fact that, unlike British officials, they are not expected to be political eunuchs. They are permitted to have open party affiliations, to campaign for their party, take part in its counsels and hence attain some degree of party standing and prominence. A second crucial factor is the relative unimportance of Parliament in Dutch political life. A constitutional 'incompatibility rule' prevents the simultaneous holding of legislative and executive office and, although Ministers are required to defend their actions before Parliament, they do not require, and are not primarily judged, on the basis of their speaking ability and aplomb at the despatch box. Only about one Dutch Minister in three has served in Parliament prior to his initial government appointment.[4]

The United States: executive skills and experience

It was remarked in Chapter 5 that one *prima facie* qualification for a Minister was previous experience in a top level decision-making post

[1] ibid., p. 101.
[2] Lijphart, *The Politics of Accommodation*, p. 75.
[3] Dogan and Schaffer-Van der Veen, *Année Sociologique* (1957, 3rd ser.) 123-5.
[4] ibid., p. 100.

in a large organisation. The country in which the highest proportion of Ministers appear to possess this qualification is the United States. Biographical studies of political executives, who have served from the time of President Franklin Roosevelt to the present day, indicate that they are, above all, experienced organisation men who have previously held responsible posts in the private sector as well as in government.[1] They are, to use Richard E. Neustadt's term, 'in-and-outers', men who are summoned to Washington to serve a particular President but who revert to private life with equal facility and enhanced income prospects when the President dispenses with them, or himself demits office.[2] Thus David T. Stanley and his co-authors found that 63 per cent of all appointees between 1932 and 1965 had previous experience in the executive branch of government but that 66 per cent did not list government service as their principal occupation.[3] Prior to his appointment the median political executive had served 5.2 years in government and about 25 years in the private sector.[4]

It is particularly interesting, from the point of view of comparison with Britain, that business executives form the largest single occupational group at the top levels of the American political hierarchy. Forty per cent of Cabinet Secretaries in the 1932-65 period, 56 per cent of Military Secretaries and 42 per cent of Under-Secretaries were businessmen.[5] Businessmen were particularly prominent in departments in which their prior experience of such matters as man management and resource control might be expected to be particularly valuable. They obtained 60 per cent of political appointments in the Department of the Navy, 57 per cent in the Treasury, 40 per cent in the Army Department, and 39 per cent in Defence.[6] Prior executive experience was not the only qualification of these appointees. Thirty-five per cent of all political executives and 40 per cent of Cabinet Secretaries had previously served at lower levels in the department to which they were posted.[7] In other words a fair proportion were selected for their substantive knowledge and experience, as well as their executive skills.

In two separate studies, attempts have been made to assess the

[1] David T. Stanley, Dean E. Mann, Jameson W. Doig, *Men Who Govern* (Washington: The Brookings Institution, 1967); Mann and Doig, *The Assistant Secretaries: Problems and Processes of Appointment* (Washington: The Brookings Institution, 1965). It should be noted that the political executives, whose careers are analysed in the above books, range in rank from Cabinet Secretaries to Deputy Administrators and Commissioners.

[2] Richard E. Neustadt, 'White House and Whitehall', *Public Interest*, II (1966), 55-69.

[3] Stanley, Mann and Doig, *Men Who Govern*, pp. 41-50.   [4] loc. cit.

[5] ibid., p. 34.   [6] ibid., p. 36.   [7] ibid., pp. 42-3.

performance in office of appointees from different backgrounds.[1] The assessments were somewhat crude in that no effort was made to distinguish between tasks and allow for the possibility that a particular incumbent might be successful in the performance of certain tasks, but avoid, or perform other tasks unsuccessfully. In principle, however, the attempt to relate performance to background is worthwhile and the findings of the studies were broadly in agreement. The business appointees who were rated as 'successful' by their colleagues and superiors were those who combined subject matter competence with prior experience in the Federal Government.[2] Businessmen who had only their previous experience in private enterprise to rely on, generally received low ratings.[3] One problem was that they found the life of politics frustrating.[4] Their instinct was to try to run their own department but much of their time was spent in inter-departmental consultation, or in accounting for their actions to Congress. Public accountability was one source of frustration; another was the difficulty in politics, in contrast to business, of defining objectives and measuring their attainment. Last, we may note that businessmen who had run their own small firms, or whose background was in banking and finance, were rated more favourably than executives from large corporations.[5] The probable explanation of this finding is that heads of small businesses, bankers and financiers are more accustomed to taking decisions on their own initiative and probably have to deal with a wider range of problems, and people from more diverse walks of life, than corporation executives, who take major decisions collectively and tend to have more closely defined areas of responsibility. Experience of dealing with diverse problems and clients, it is suggested, is an asset for holders of political office.

WHY MINISTERIAL SELECTION CRITERIA VARY CROSS-NATIONALLY

This chapter provides not a systematic cross-national analysis but illustrations of the point that the ministerial selection criteria and hence the skills and attributes of cabinet members differ from political system to political system. On the basis of illustrative evidence it would be mistaken to try to draw firm conclusions but it may be of some value, nevertheless, to put forward some fairly tentative propositions to explain the cross-national variance.

[1] Mann and Doig, *The Assistant Secretaries*; M. Bernstein, *The Job of The Federal Executive* (Washington: The Brookings Institution, 1958).

[2] Mann and Doig, *The Assistant Secretaries*, ch. 9.   [3] loc. cit.

[4] loc. cit.; Bernstein, *The Job of the Federal Executive*, pp. 26-37, 180-1.

[5] Mann and Doig, *The Assistant Secretaries*, p. 249.

It is obvious that the various skills and attributes we have described are not mutually incompatible. Any Cabinet may include some specialists, some sectional representatives, others who possess the attributes of professional party politicians and Parliamentarians and so forth. Occasionally, it may even be possible to find a paragon Minister who rates high in terms of all the skills we have reviewed. In general, though, certain combinations of skills and attributes are more likely than others. If, as in Australia, certain sectional interests are organised into factions within the parties and these factions are active in ensuring that their leaders receive ministerial appointments, then Ministers are likely to be competent both to serve as interest representatives and to play their part in maintaining party cohesion. The appointment of factional leaders will also provide a Cabinet in which most members have political weight, sound political judgement, parliamentary skills and the interpersonal, verbal and brokerage skills which the life of politics develops. On the other hand, there seems no reason for expecting that executive or specialist skills will be found in combination with any other *desiderata*.

The first crucial factor determining selection criteria and the attributes of Ministers is the number and severity of social cleavages dividing a society. The four main cleavages which have political consequences in industrialised countries are based on religious, class, regional and ethnic loyalties.[1] If, in a particular country, all four cleavages are politically significant (cf. Canada and the USA) then interest representation is likely to be high priority. Even if only two or three cleavages are significant, the intensity of feeling generated may still mean that interest representation is the paramount consideration. Thus, in Belgium, the ethnic-regional cleavage[2] and the class cleavage (particularly the former) are so severe that Ministers have to be selected primarily to represent social groups and accommodate their divergent interests.[3]

A second set of factors affecting ministerial skills are constitutional laws and conventions. A federal system is likely to promote (as well as reflect) regional, state, or provincial consciousness and increase the importance of territorial representation at the central government level. It is also likely to increase the number of appointees with

[1] See S. M. Lipset and S. Rokkan, *Party Systems and Voter Alignments* (New York: Free Press, 1967), Introduction; also Richard Rose and D. W. Urwin, 'Social Cohesion, Political Parties and Strains in Regimes', *Comparative Political Studies* 2.1 (April 1969), 7-67.

[2] Ethnic and regional lines do not quite coincide. Brussells is a mixed Flemish and French-speaking city set in a Flemish area.

[3] On social cleavages in Belgium see D. W. Urwin, 'Social Cleavages and Political Parties in Belgium: Problems of Institutionalisation', *Political Studies*, 17.3 (September 1970), 320-40.

executive skills, because politicians who have served in the executive branch of government at sub-national levels can be recruited to serve in the federal government. Constitutional provisions affecting executive-legislative relations also have significant consequences. An 'incompatibility rule', such as is in force in the USA and the Netherlands, prevents Ministers sitting in the legislature and somewhat downgrades the importance of parliamentary skills and experience as a criterion for appointment. This means that a greater number of non-legislators can be recruited and that men with executive or specialist skills are more likely to come to the fore. Another constitutional rule of some relevance here stipulates whether the head of government has fixed or uncertain tenure in office. An American (or French Fifth Republic) President is in office until the next presidential election and cannot be removed, as Prime Ministers can, by losing the support of his own party, or coalition allies, in the legislature. It follows that fixed term heads of government are likely to display relatively little concern for party cohesion and judge potential appointees more on the basis of their capacity to perform other tasks.

Last, cultural factors (including the political culture) influence ministerial recruitment. In the Western European democracies and in Australia and New Zealand, party loyalties are sufficiently intense that it is assumed that, when a Cabinet is formed, the great majority of members will be career politicians who have demonstrated their devotion to the cause by serving an apprenticeship in party offices and usually in the legislature. In the North American democracies, on the other hand, identification with parties is not so strong that it ranks as a betrayal if a number of Ministers who have not previously been full-time politicians are appointed. The pool of potential appointees is increased and men with skills not commonly found among Parliamentarians may be preferred. The skills and general intellectual ability of Ministers also depends on whether politics as a career attracts its share of a country's most able men. If the prestige of electoral politics is lower than, say, the prestige of business, or the professions, or the Civil Service, then even leading politicians may not be of the highest calibre. Thus, in Australia and Canada, able graduates prefer a career in the private sector.[1] In the Netherlands and Britain, on the other hand, politics is perceived as a worthwhile career and attracts extremely able men and women.[2] A further cultural

[1] On the unattractiveness of politics as a career in Canada see Porter, *The Vertical Mosaic*, pp. 405-12. For Australia see Encel, *Equality and Authority*, ch. 11.

[2] It is often alleged that the ability of politicians is declining in Britain. There seems no evidence for this. See Chapter 4 and the figures there on the number of contemporary Ministers who obtained First Class degrees. On Holland see Lijphart, *The Politics of Accommodation*, ch. 3.

factor influences not the general level of ability of Ministers but their more specific skills. Although, as we have noted, the skills of politicians are to some extent the skills required to perform their characteristic tasks – hence the omniprescence of lawyers and teachers with their verbal and interpersonal skills – it is also true to say that the skills of politicians are a reflection of the type of educational and occupational experience which is considered prestigious in the culture. If by a 'good education' is meant a general arts education, then leading politicians are likely to have had an arts education and to pride themselves on being generalists or intelligent laymen. But if the cult of the expert or the specialist has taken hold (as in the Netherlands and Germany), or if efficient, hard driving executives are television heroes (cf. the United States) then political appointments are likely to go, respectively, to specialists and men with executive experience.

THE CONSEQUENCES OF MINISTERS

In all the countries we are considering it is possible for Ministers to perform significant roles in their own departments, in Cabinet and in relations with the legislature (even if they are not members), their party, and outside publics and pressure groups. The purpose of this section is not to argue that, overall, the Ministers of some countries are better qualified than these of other countries to hold office, but to suggest linkages between ministerial selection criteria and skills, the performance of particular ministerial roles and dimensions of governmental performance. How are governmental institutions, national unity and policy affected by the skills Ministers bring to office? Our answers to this question are bound to be speculative but the 'need to know' is sufficiently great for it to be worthwhile to offer some suggestions.

First, the Cabinet: if a country's Cabinet is not filled by major politicians whose views must be heeded because they have a power base in their own parties, there is a likelihood that the institution will tend to be by-passed and partially replaced by other office-holders and institutions. This has occurred in Canada, the United States and the Netherlands where Ministers are relatively lacking in political weight. In the United States the President, and in Canada the Prime Minister, have increasingly built up their own staffs, taken their own policy initiatives and appealed over the heads of the Cabinet (and, incidentally, the legislature) to the people.[1] In the Netherlands the

[1] On the USA see Richard F. Fenno, *The President's Cabinet*, ch. 1. For Canada see Senator Maurice Lamontagne, 'The Influence of the Cabinet Minister', in F. Vaughan *et al.*, *Constitutional Issues in Canadian Politics* (Scarborough: Prentice Hall, 1970), pp. 159-65. Anthony Westell, Trudeau – New Style PM,

fact that Ministers are by no means all political heavyweights has contributed to the tendency for policy decisions to be arrived at not in Cabinet but in quasi non-political settings like the Social and Economic Council.[1] On the other hand, in Britain and Australia Ministers do have the political weight to ensure that the Cabinet remains of real significance in the policy process. Some observers believe that there has been a tendency towards prime ministerial government in these countries but the trend has gone nothing like so far as in Canada and the United States.[2]

The consequences of Ministers lacking the skills to perform their parliamentary roles are not particularly serious in the United States, Canada and the Netherlands. It is true that party unity as reflected in parliamentary divisions in these countries is less 'impressive' than in Australia and Britain. However, the disunity of parties in the Congress of the United States has many explanations unconnected with ministerial skills and the relative tendency towards party disunity in Canada and the Netherlands does not seem to have a high price in governmental instability. Probably more significant are the consequences of ministerial failures to perform public relations roles. Failures of conciliation and failure to promote values of national unity may be part of the explanation for the persistence in the United States of regional and ethnic conflicts. In Canada, similarly, the division between French and English speaking citizens might well have been more successfully healed had Ministers, in addition to being sectional representatives, also been capable of reconciling conflict and persuading their followers of the merits of the conciliatory policies which have consistently been pursued. In contrast to the North American countries, it is worth pointing out that in Australia and, again, Britain, where Ministers are more politically skilled and experienced, social divisions have produced less conflict and fewer separatist threats to the continued existence of the national community. The Netherlands provides an ambiguous case. Collectively, Ministers could not be said to possess political and public relations skills of a high order. They have, however, in co-operation with other leaders of the four social blocs (Catholic, Protestant, Liberal and Socialist) combined to gain acceptance for a series of policy decisions on religious and other issues which, potentially, could have torn the nation apart.[3] The Dutch achievement in this respect is widely recognised as

'Power and Politics' in Paul W. Fox (ed.), *Politics: Canada* (London: McGraw-Hill, 1970), pp. 326-35.

[1] See Lijphart, *The Politics of Accommodation*, ch. 7.

[2] For a selection of articles on the prime ministerial government controversy in Britain see A. King (ed.), *The Prime Minister: A Reader* (London: Macmillan, 1969). For Australia see Encel, *Cabinet Government in Australia*, pp. 249-56.

[3] Lijphart, *Politics of Accommodation*, chs 2, 3.

remarkable in view of the fact that mass public members of the four blocs avoid almost all types of social interaction from intermarriage to tuning in to the same television stations.[1] The Dutch experience illustrates that in the performance of public relations roles other community leaders can partially serve as substitutes for Ministers.

Next, we consider the consequences of Ministers' possessing or lacking skills required to perform departmental policy and management roles. Whether Ministers should concern themselves with departmental management is a question answered differently in different countries. One view is that Ministers should leave civil servants to 'run' government departments. On the other hand, if a radical overhaul of departmental organisation, or financial control and programme review procedures is called for, there is no doubt that a Minister with managerial ability can make major positive contributions. No one would suggest that, despite the background of many American political executives, official Washington represents a triumph of managerial efficiency. But individual Cabinet Secretaries with managerial experience, among whom the most notable recent example would be the former President of Ford Motor Company and Secretary for Defence, Robert McNamara, have demonstrated extraordinary capacity to reorganise and streamline their departments and make them suitable instruments for implementing new policies.[2] As a general proposition it is undeniable that many policy decisions have significant managerial implications. A Minister who lacks an executive background is in a weak position to make an independent assessment of such implications and so is likely to be over-reliant on the advice of civil servants who may themselves not be completely objective about changes affecting their own organisation, their relations with colleagues and their administrative methods. As we noted in a previous chapter, numerous studies have shown that officials in all large bureaucracies are most likely to resist those policy changes which also require changes in organisational structure.[3]

Last, what consequences flow from Ministers' providing or failing to provide policy leadership in their departments? In the absence of ministerial initiatives civil servants are always ready with proposals for new legislation and for changes in administrative procedures. To some extent these proposals are likely to reflect the views of pressure

[1] ibid., ch.2. For figures on the decline of inter-bloc intermarriage see p.191.

[2] For an assessment of McNamara's managerial achievements see C. J. Hitch, *Decision Making for Defence* (Berkeley: University of California Press, 1965).

[3] For a review of these studies see Anthony Downs, *Inside Bureaucracy* (Boston: Little, Brown, 1967), ch. 16. Downs defines a bureaucracy as an organisation whose performance is not subject to market (profit and loss) evaluation. His review therefore covers not only central government bureaucracies but public utilities, regulatory agencies, welfare and philanthropic organisations, etc.

groups which have the ear of officials. In general, though, it seems reasonable to believe that proposals initiated by officials without ministerial encouragement are not likely to be very radical and innovative. It is not for civil servants, acting without the prior encouragement of Ministers, to argue for radical change and face the controversy and opposition from diverse sources which such proposed changes generally arouse. It may be that civil servants in some countries are more willing to go out on a limb than their counterparts elsewhere, but it is interesting that the emerging view among students of French politics is that even French civil servants, often regarded as the most independent of Ministers and self-confidently *dirigiste* in Europe, generally avoid proposing major initiatives except in response to ministerial directives.[1]

If we accept the view that Ministers with some degree of specialised knowledge are more likely to act as policy initiators than laymen, we would expect a more innovative pattern of policy making in the Netherlands than in Britain, Australia and Canada.[2] It is, of course, a hazardous and subjective business evaluating the overall policy performance of governments but it is certainly possible to point to major policy innovations in the Netherlands. One thinks particularly of the Dutch Government's incomes policy, operated highly successfully in the post-war years long before incomes policies became fashionable, and its policy for settling immigrants from Indonesia following decolonisation.[3] The latter policy was intended to ensure that racial tensions would not arise and took the form of preventing the growth of non-white immigrant ghetto areas. Families were directed in which cities and districts to live and, although the policy was criticised as somewhat dictatorial, it has largely succeeded in its aims.[4] Dutch housing policy in general has been highly directive with the massive provision of new (post-war) public housing and regulations stipulating which types of houses shall be inhabited by families in different income brackets.

By contrast, the whole 'What's wrong with British government?' outpouring of books and articles in the 1960s was based on the perception that conservatism, orthodoxy and received wisdoms led

[1] See A. Diamant, 'Tradition and Innovation in French Administration', *Comparative Political Studies*, 1.2 (July 1968), 251-74; B. Gourney, 'Un groupe dirigeant de la Société française' (mimeo, 1969).

[2] The United States, in which rather over a third of senior political executives have some specialised knowledge based on previously having held lower ranking jobs in their departments, would be expected to be an intermediate case in terms of its rate of policy innovation.

[3] Lijphart, *Politics of Accommodation*, ch. 4.

[4] United Nations, *Major Long Term Problems of Government Housing and Related Policies* (New York: UN, 1966).

to the maintenance of anachronistic commitments and alliances and failure to take advantage of favourable opportunities to change course.[1] This literature as it applies to post-war economic, social, foreign and defence policy will be reviewed more fully in the concluding chapter. It is important to note here that it has its equivalents in Australia and Canada, the other two countries in our sample in which Ministers typically lack special knowledge of the subjects they are responsible for. In foreign affairs the Australian Government concentrated on relations with its British and American allies long after many observers believed it should have sought closer links with Japan and other potentially friendly Asian countries.[2] Its 'white Australia' immigration policy inevitably gave offence in Asia. In the defence field there was a failure to develop a small professional army of the kind required to support the Americans in wars against Communist insurgents in Asia.[3] The co-ordination of defence policy remained inadequate largely due to the existence of four separate defence departments.[4] In education policy criticism was 'directed at the traditions of imitating successful overseas reforms or of extending existing systems with the minimum disturbance of the status quo',[5] and in transport the incremental growth of federal and state regulations produced the absurd situation by which it was cheaper for long haul traffic to go by road and short haul traffic to go by rail.[6] In Canada concern at the conservatism and 'stand-pat' nature of the Liberal Government's policies – the party had been in office since 1935 – culminated in a landslide for the Conservatives in 1958 but not, it is generally agreed, in innovative policies from the Diefenbaker Government.[7] Criticism was particularly widespread of failure

---

[1] See, *inter alia* E. Devons, 'Government on the Inner Circle', *The Listener* (27 March 1958); Hugh Thomas (ed.), *The Establishment* (London: Anthony Blond, 1959); M. Shanks, *The Stagnant Society* (Harmondsworth: Penguin, 1961); A. Sampson, *The Anatomy of Britain* (London: Hodder and Stoughton, 1962); B. Chapman, *British Government Observed* (London: Allen and Unwin, 1963); M. Nicholson, *The System: The Misgovernment of Modern Britain* (London: Hodder and Stoughton, 1967); Ian Gilmour, *The Body Politic* (London: Hutchinson, 1969).

[2] See T. B. Millar, *Australia's Foreign Policy* (London: Angus and Robertson, 1968), especially ch. 13 'The Way Ahead'; Donald Horne *The Lucky Country: Australia Today* (London: Angus and Robertson, 1965) ch. 5 'Living with Asia'.

[3] Encel, *Equality and Authority*, pp. 444-6.

[4] Horne, *The Lucky Country*, ch. 5.

[5] J. R. Lawry, 'Education', in A. F. Davies and S. Encel (eds), *Australian Society* (London: Pall Mall, 1965), p. 80.

[6] Maxwell Newton, 'The Economy', in ibid., pp. 230-52.

[7] For particularly severe attacks on the record of Canadian post-war government and particularly Diefenbaker, see Peter C. Newman, *Distemper of Our Times* (Toronto: McClelland and Stewart, 1968); Newman, *Renegade in Power: The Diefenbaker Years* (Toronto: McClelland and Stewart, 1963). A similar

to replace piecemeal welfare programmes by more comprehensive schemes,[1] to halt the take-over of Canadian business by Americans and, more generally, to overcome problems of federalism which persistently prevented the development of coherent national policies.[2]

CONCLUSION

Ultimately, our concern as students of ministerial leadership lies in discovering what impact Ministers make on the performance of Governments. In the concluding chapter we focus again on British Ministers and their impact on post-war government and policy. It will be useful to keep the comparative perspective of this chapter in mind, however. What difference does it make to British government that Ministers are selected primarily on the basis of their party standing and parliamentary skills, rather than as specialists (the Netherlands), experienced executives (the USA) or sectional representatives (Canada)? How would Whitehall and Westminster be affected, and how would policy be affected if there were a tendency to move more towards, say, the Dutch or American pattern of ministerial recruitment?

assault on the Trudeau Government has been mounted in Walter Stewart, *Shrug: Trudeau in Power* (Toronto: New Press 1971).

[1] See a statement by the Canadian Welfare Council, *Social Policies for Canada* (Ottawa: Canadian Welfare Council, 1969); Stewart, *Shrug,* ch. 2.

[2] The literature on Canadian federalism is enormous. It is sampled in Vaughan *et al., Contemporary Issues in Canadian Politics*; Fox (ed.), *Politics: Canada*; and Kruhlak *et al., The Canadian Political Process.*

Chapter 13

The Consequences of Ministers

We normally assume that the heads of organisations – army generals, trade union bosses, managing directors – have considerable influence on the efficiency and effectiveness of their organisation and we reward them accordingly in terms of pay and status. If organisations perform effectively their heads receive the credit, if they perform poorly it is often assumed that the rot starts at the top. On this reasoning it would be extraordinary if the role conceptions and skills of Ministers, the expectations others have of their performance in office, the advice they receive and the specificity of their policy objectives did *not* have profound consequences for the performance of government. This chapter begins with an attempt to suggest linkages between ministerial performance and the performance of British government in the post-war years. What is gained and lost by having Ministers who are well equipped to serve as policy selectors and Ambassador Ministers (or, for that matter, as Minimalists) but less well equipped to be policy initiators or Executive Ministers?

In the second section of the chapter analysis gives way to prescription. We summarise the implications of our findings for individual Cabinet Ministers, for the Prime Minister appointing his ministerial team and for reform of the structure of government. Reform proposals are too often put forward, however, without its being clear what value judgements underlie them, what objectives they are meant to serve and what costs may be incurred in terms of failure to achieve other objectives. These errors will be avoided here if the relationship between the first and second parts of the chapter is borne in mind. If a reader deplores the consequences of, say Ambassador Ministers, or policy initiators, then he will naturally discount the value of proposals designed to improve the performance of these types of Ministers.

The final section of this chapter considers some implications of the present work for students of political leadership in the executive branch of government. What problems have we encountered in seeking to answer the basic questions about leadership posed in Chapter 1? On the basis of our findings, what factors ('variables') appear to require inclusion in a theory of political leadership?

MINISTERIAL ROLE PERFORMANCE: THE CONSEQUENCES FOR GOVERNMENT

Do the obstacles to ministerial policy initiation mean that policy objectives are not re-examined often enough and critically enough, or are there other participants in the policy process who perform these tasks? We noted in the previous chapter that the most obvious candidates as substitutes for Ministers might appear to be their Civil Service advisers. Like officials elsewhere, however, British civil servants do not normally regard it as their task to initiate major policy changes. A survey carried out for the Fulton Committee indicated that most administrators do not join the Service because of the opportunities it provides to influence public policy, nor is this one of their main sources of job satisfaction.[1] Furthermore, the anonymity and political neutrality of civil servants, and their official titles as mere *secretaries* to Ministers, encourage the belief that their role is simply to be responsive to ministerial (or other) initiatives. In reality, not all civil servants behave as if they were there only to respond to the demands of their political masters (one thinks of innovators like the late Derek Morrell of the Home Office who was widely known to have been the driving force behind the Children and Young Persons' Act 1969),[2] but the official orthodoxy exerts its influence none the less.

Given that politicians are not qualified and civil servants are not motivated to act as policy initiators, it is not surprising that specialists in different policy areas find evidence of lack of innovation and reluctance on the part of post-war British Governments to re-order their priorities. Thus in the field of economic policy commentators such as Andrew Shonfield, Samuel Brittan and the Brookings Institution have alleged that low post-war growth rate has partly resulted from a desire to preserve the pound's historic role as a reserve currency and the City's position as an international money

---

[1] R. A. Chapman, 'Portrait of a Profession', *The Civil Service* (Fulton Report), 3 (2), pp. 1-29.

[2] See the obituary to Morrell in *New Society* (18 December 1969), p. 968.

market.[1] Protecting the pound has meant protecting the balance of payments which in turn has required deflationary, anti-growth policies. In the fields of foreign and defence policy such writers as David Vital, William P. Snyder and Kenneth N. Waltz have alleged that an outmoded view of Britain's Great Power status led successive Governments not to participate in negotiations which resulted in the founding of the European Coal and Steel Community and the Economic Community, and to maintain an 'independent' nuclear deterrent and expensive world wide military commitments.[2] The Ministry of Transport has been criticised by C. D. Foster and others for failing to develop a coherent national transport plan which would lay down, on the basis of explicit social as well as profit criteria, what types of cargo should travel by what type of transport.[3] Foster described the Ministry as muddling along in a Micawberite manner: 'Annual income twenty pounds, annual expenditure twenty pounds, nought and six, result misery.'[4] D. V. Donnison has made somewhat similar criticisms of post-war housing policy.[5] He notes that Germany, France and several other West European countries prepare comprehensive forecasts of housing needs and supply, and also seek to ensure that, once accommodation is built, the people for whom it is intended can afford to rent or buy it.[6] British people have, historically, been comparatively well housed, and slum clearance, local authority building and the development of 'new towns' have accomplished a great deal, but Britain is well down the European league in terms of post-war houses built and Donnison considers that there has been 'no fundamental reappraisal of pre-war thinking' and no major innovations since the Town and Country Planning Act, 1947, and the start of the 'new towns' programme.[7] In the Industrial Relations field the Government remained unwilling (until the late 1960s) to legislate, with the result

[1] Andrew Shonfield, *Modern Capitalism* (London: OUP, 1961), especially chs. 6 and 7; S. Brittan, *Steering the Economy* (London: Secker and Warburg, 1969), especially Part II; Richard E. Caves *et al.*, *Britain's Economic Prospects* (Washington: Brookings Institution, 1968).

[2] David Vital, 'The Making of British Foreign Policy', *Political Quarterly*, 39.3 (Autumn 1968), 255-68; William P. Snyder, *The Politics of British Defence Policy* (Columbus: Ohio State University, 1964); Kenneth N. Waltz, *Foreign Policy and Democratic Politics* (Boston: Little, Brown, 1967).

[3] C. D. Foster, *The Transport Problem* (London: Blackie, 1963). Foster got his opportunity to press for reform in the Ministry of Transport under Mrs Castle 1965-8. See ch. 9.

[4] ibid., p. 3.

[5] D. V. Donnison, *The Government of Housing* (Harmondsworth: Penguin, 1967).

[6] ibid., ch. 3.

[7] ibid., p. 165.

that competing unions and customary collective bargaining procedures seemed designed to produce maximum friction.[1] Finally, one might mention that even the British concept of the welfare state, once considered advanced, is now often said to be out of date and ungenerous by observers familiar with Scandinavian, Dutch and German welfare programmes.[2] Not surprisingly, overviews of postwar policy performance lead to books with titles such as *The System: The Misgovernment of Modern Britain* and *The Stagnant Society*.[3]

Carrying the argument a stage further, Professor Richard Rose has pointed out that failure to re-examine policy objectives systematically, so as to adapt to contemporary conditions, does not necessarily mean that 'no change' policies are pursued. Instead, the pattern is one of 'government by directionless consensus'.[4] A rapidly changing environment ensures that incremental adaptations of policy will occur but the changes tend to be unco-ordinated and to occur only when a consensus has been reached by departmental advisory groups, professional associations and the like (as well as Ministers and civil servants) that 'something needs to be done'.[5] Even then change is likely to reflect only the lowest common denominator of agreement.

Rather more problematical than the consequences of Ministers being ill-equipped to serve as policy initiators are the implications of their lack of executive experience and skills. The fact is that government departments are directly responsible for managing such major undertakings as the welfare services, the postal service and the motorways. It makes little sense to decide policy objectives without at the same time concerning oneself with the management functions of 'organisation', 'motivation' and 'control'.[6] Objectives often need to be modified in the light of such factors as existing organisational structure and administrative procedures (adjust ends to means as

[1] See *Royal Commission on Trade Unions and Employers' Association* (Donovan Commission) (London: HMSO, 1968); also M. Shanks, *The Stagnant Society* (Harmondsworth: Penguin, 1961), especially ch. 4, 'Trade Unions in Trouble'.

[2] See, for example, R. M. Titmuss, *Essays on the Welfare State* (London: Allen and Unwin, 1963); and C. A. R. Crosland, *The Conservative Enemy* (London: Cape, 1962).

[3] M. Nicholson, *The System: The Misgovernment of Modern Britain* (London: Hodder and Stoughton, 1967); Shanks, *The Stagnant Society*.

[4] Richard Rose, 'The Variability of Party Government', *Political Studies*, 17.4 (December 1969), 442.

[5] Charles E. Lindblom's phrase 'disjointed incrementalism' gives an appropriate description of the pattern of change likely to be produced by British Governments. See his *The Intelligence of Democracy* (New York: Free Press, 1965).

[6] For a description of these functions see Rosemary Stewart, *The Reality of Management* (London: Pan Books, 1967), ch. 4.

well as means to ends), one's likely capacity to motivate members of
the organisation to work for their attainment and the availability of
control systems to check that resources are not being used ineffici-
ently. A failure on the part of Ministers to comprehend the managerial implications of their proposals may lead them to one of two
extremes. They may grandly tell their civil servants that, 'these are
our policy objectives, it is up to you to find a way of implementing
them'. This approach is likely to promote a divorce between ends
and means, between intention and reality. Alternatively, a Minister
without executive experience may tend to be over-impressed by
objections to proposals on the lines that, 'the department has tried
such measures before and found them impractical' or 'the department requires a period of consolidation before another set of reforms
can be put through'.

In the past, civil servants have probably not adequately com-
pensated for any tendency on the part of Ministers to disregard
management problems. The Fulton Committee was scathing about
the defects of management in Whitehall and about the inclination
of senior officials to see themselves primarily as policy advisers and
not also as managers of large complex organisations. The Committee
recommended major changes in departmental structure, with the
introduction of accountable management units working to specified
objectives. The control function of management, it was stated, also
needed to be performed more effectively and the adoption of more
up-to-date cost accounting procedures and methods of resource
allocation was called for.[1] Certainly it is possible to point to Whitehall deficiencies in the management field. The cases of the engineering
company, Ferranti, overcharging the Ministry of Aviation by at least
£1 million, the Swiss Company, Hoffman La Roche, overcharging the
Department of Health and Social Security for new tranquilliser drugs
and the spiralling cost of the Concorde airliner are the most notorious
examples in recent years of the control function being poorly performed;[2] but, in general, Whitehall does seem to have been slow to
adopt such techniques as programme budgeting and cost-benefit
analysis and to concern itself with planning the careers of its
personnel systematically, so as to ensure that future senior officials
acquire appropriate experience.[3]

So far we have discussed, in rather general terms, the consequences of Ministers lacking specialised knowledge and executive

[1] *The Civil Service* (Fulton Report), vol. 2, 'Report of a Management Consultancy Group'.

[2] For the Ferranti case see *Parliamentary Debates* (Commons), 699 (1963-4),
cols 1801-65. The Hoffman La Roche case is reviewed in 'Roche Victory Could
Shatter Monopoly Laws', *Guardian* (14 July 1973).   [3] See Chapter 5.

skills. However, one would expect that these deficiencies would matter less in some departments than others. Thus one would expect more Ministers to perform satisfactorily in departments in which the element of political judgement in decisions is at least as important as a judgement based on specialised or technical knowledge, and in departments with relatively small manpower and financial budgets, which present less complex management problems. To take three specific departments, one might hypothesise that more politicians would emerge with credit from the Home Office than the Treasury (a specialised department) or the Ministry of Defence (managerially complex). A reliable test of this hypothesis is difficult to obtain, if only because of the value judgements entailed in assessing the performance of Ministers. However, Ministers do have 'reputations' and, taking a stab at the matter, one may assert that, of the nine Home Secretaries who have completed terms of office since 1945,[1] four – Chuter Ede, R. A. Butler, Roy Jenkins and James Callaghan – would generally be considered to have enhanced their reputations by their performance in office. Of the remaining five, Sir David Maxwell-Fyfe, who went on to become Lord Chancellor (as Lord Kilmuir), was a formidable Parliamentarian and certainly did not lose standing and, as we saw in Chapter 10, Henry Brooke had an impressive legislative record, although he undoubtedly made himself unpopular in liberal circles. Gwilym Lloyd-George (1954-7) was probably appointed to attract Liberal voters, having been a Liberal MP from 1922 to 1924 and 1929 to 1950. He neither made nor lost a reputation at the Home Office. This leaves only two post-war Home Secretaries, Sir Frank Soskice and, more doubtfully, Reginald Maudling who lost standing while at the department.

By contrast, the reputations of few Chancellors of the Exchequer and Ministers of Defence[2] have survived their departure from office by more than a year or two. An initial point is that turnover in these offices has been remarkably high; itself probably an indication that Ministers were not perceived to be performing satisfactorily. Thus there have been thirteen Chancellors in the twenty-seven years since 1945 and fourteen Ministers of Defence. In the case of two Chancellors (H. Gaitskell and I. Macleod), and five Ministers of Defence (W. Churchill, H. Macmillan, S. Lloyd, Sir Walter Monckton and A. Head), their period in office was a year or less, making it hazardous to attempt any assessment of their performance. Of the remaining Chancellors only Sir Stafford Cripps, R. A. Butler, D. Heathcoat Amory and Roy Jenkins enjoy favourable retrospective

---

[1] The Home Secretary at the time of writing, Mr Robert Carr, is not included.

[2] The Minister of Defence became the Secretary of State for Defence when the defence Ministries were merged in 1964.

reputations in Whitehall.[1] Reginald Maudling was well thought of during his period in office (1962-4) and apparently had a thorough intellectual grasp of economic problems, but his 'growth experiment' was discredited by the £763 million balance of payments deficit in 1964.[2] Selwyn Lloyd's merits and demerits were rather the opposite of Maudling's. Policy initiatives taken during his Chancellorship led Samuel Brittan to write that 'his period at the Exchequer was the most eventful since Cripps'.[3] The National Economic Development Council (NEDC) was set up and introduced indicative planning to Britain. The Government accepted the idea of an incomes policy, five year 'forward looks' at public expenditure were inaugurated, economic regulators by which the Chancellor varied taxes between budgets were used for the first time, and there was a new policy towards nationalised industries which gave them commercial targets to aim for.[4] The other side of the coin was that Lloyd, unlike Maudling, did not give the impression of comprehending the intricacies of economic problems and may have depended overmuch on his advisers. The remaining four post-war Chancellors – Dalton, Macmillan, Thorneycroft and Callaghan – although able politicians who would generally be considered to have had successful terms in other departments, clearly did not enhance their reputations at the Treasury.[5]

Post-war Ministers of Defence are even harder to evaluate than Chancellors. As noted above, their average tenure in office has been remarkably short. If we exclude the post 1970 Ministers and Denis Healey, who headed the department for nearly six years, the remaining twelve Ministers lasted, on average, only nineteen months. Of those who lasted more than a year Clement Attlee was only part-time, since he was also Prime Minister. Attlee's successor, Lord Alexander of Hillsborough was 'not at home in the world of grand strategy'[6] and, according to Field-marshal Montgomery, provoked the Chiefs of Staff into reaching agreement for the only time during the Field-marshal's period as Chief of the Imperial

[1] The performance of past Chancellors of the Exchequer, as the most prominent members of the Government after Prime Ministers, was evaluated in an informal way by several of the civil servants interviewed for this study. There was surprising unanimity that the most 'successful' Chancellors were the four mentioned above.

[2] Brittan, *Steering The Economy*, ch. 7.

[3] ibid., p. 145.

[4] ibid., p. 146. Brittan actually lists seven important initiatives taken during Selwyn Lloyd's Chancellorship. Those not mentioned in the text were the raising of the surtax level on earned income from £2,000 to £5,000 and the reform of the Budget Accounts.

[5] The Chancellor at the time of writing, Mr Anthony Barber, is not included.

[6] *The Times* (12 January 1965), obituary.

General Staff. The agreement, which incidentally was broken, was to ask the Prime Minister for Alexander's removal.[1] The last Minister of Defence in the 1945-51 Government, Emmanuel Shinwell, was not considered a good appointment at the time,[2] having been removed from his previous cabinet post (the Ministry of Fuel and Power) on grounds of incompetence.[3] He was only at Defence for twenty months, however, and his relationship with his military advisers was eased by the increased funds available for defence during the Korean War. Of the four Ministers of Defence in the 1951-64 Conservative Government who lasted any time at all, Earl Alexander of Tunis was a famous General but lacked any enthusiasm for politics. *The Economist's* verdict was that under Alexander the Ministry 'became little more than a technical link – no doubt an efficient one – between the Prime Minister and the Chiefs of Staff.'[4] Mr Duncan Sandys (1957-9) was undoubtedly a Minister who imposed his own priorities on the department, but defence analysts are almost unanimously agreed that his drastic cuts in army manpower, and his decision to rely primarily on nuclear deterrence, were serious mistakes of strategy.[5] The last two Conservative Ministers prior to 1964 – Harold Watkinson and Peter Thorneycroft – probably emerged with most credit. Watkinson acquired the reputation of an efficient manager in his department[6] – he had a business career behind him – and Thorneycroft, in conjunction with Earl Mountbatten of Burma, began the reforms leading to the full integration of the defence Ministries. Despite these two relative 'successes', however, it is probably accurate to say that, of post-war Ministers, only Mr Denis Healey enhanced his reputation at Defence.

There are, of course, several other plausible explanations for post-war failure in the economic and defence fields, besides the inappropriateness of Ministers' skills. Making due allowance for the multiple factors involved, however, it still seems reasonable to suggest that the fact that Treasury Ministers by and large lacked more than a layman's understanding of economics and Defence

[1] ibid., loc, cit.

[2] See, for example, 'The New Cabinet', *The Economist* (4 March 1950), p. 469: 'Finally, the appointment of Mr Shinwell to the Ministry of Defence dooms the department to a further period of insignificance and impotence . . .'.

[3] F. Williams, *A Prime Minister Remembers* (London: Heinemann, 1961), pp. 220-2.

[4] 'A Politicians' Cabinet', *The Economist* (23 October 1954), p. 288.

[5] For a review of criticisms of Sandys's policies see W. P. Snyder, *The Politics of British Defence Policy* (Columbus: Ohio State University Press, 1964), pp. 156-9.

[6] See, for example, 'A Good Ally', *The Economist* (21 July 1962), p. 215.

Ministers lacked managerial experience and skills, is one significant and neglected explanation for the post-war record.

IMPLICATIONS OF FINDINGS FOR INDIVIDUAL CABINET MINISTERS, THE PRIME MINISTER AND THE STRUCTURE OF GOVERNMENT

Individual Ministers

Before considering how the performance of Ministers, and hence of British Government, might be improved, it is worth reminding ourselves of the basic parameters of the Minister's job. Time constraints make it impossible for Ministers to play a dominant role in relation to all the tasks that they, or outside observers, might think they should ideally perform themselves. Three tasks are, however, unavoidable, and a Minister must perform them with some success in order to be regarded as minimally satisfactory by his political and Civil Service colleagues. First, he must be able to defend himself at the parliamentary despatch box. There have been a few exceptions to the rule, but, in general, a Minister who attracts derision in the House is a party political liability and has to be dropped. Second, a Minister must be able to win a proportion of the crucial cabinet battles for Treasury money and parliamentary time. The exact proportion he may hope to win depends quite largely on which department he heads (the Chancellor, for instance, may win nearly 100 per cent of his battles, lesser Ministers must be content with crumbs of comfort) but a Minister who falls well below expectations rapidly loses all standing in the gossip-ridden, reputation-sensitive world of Whitehall. The journalists soon hear that Minister X lacks 'political weight' and his demotion, or elevation to the House of Lords, becomes only a matter of time. The third *sine qua non* is that a Minister be temperamentally capable of taking decisions (or legitimating his advisers' recommendations) quickly, even though an error judgement could damage his career or mean that a quite serious injustice was done. The Minister who vacillates, or persistently delays decisions is the greatest bogey of civil servants who constantly require a politician's sanction for their actions so that the business of government can be carried on.

Beyond attempting to perform these minimum tasks satisfactorily a Minister has a choice over which roles to give priority. One conclusion to be drawn from this study is that it is desirable that this be a conscious choice (rather than a choice made subconsciously on the basis of predispositions acquired in his previous career) because the way in which a Minister allocates his own time is likely to be the single most important decision he takes in office. One question which needs to be asked in this concluding chapter concerns the criteria a politician may reasonably employ in deciding whether to try to serve as a policy initiator, a policy selector, an Executive Minister or an Ambassador Minister.

Some Ministers probably decide which role to emphasise on orthodox constitutional grounds. They take the textbook view that their job is to 'decide policy'. The phrase 'decide policy' is ambiguous, however, and is interpreted by some Ministers as meaning that they should themselves define policy objectives and seek to ensure their achievement (a policy initiation role) and by others only as requiring that they should choose between alternative policy proposals formulated by civil servants (a policy selection role). But constitutional theory need not be the only guide. Two other criteria would appear useful. First, a Minister could decide which roles to give priority after assessing his own skills and aptitudes. Using this criterion he would at least be likely to perform his selected tasks competently. Alternatively, or additionally, he might decide his priorities after taking into account the needs of the department to which he was appointed and asking himself, 'What contribution can I most usefully make in this department at this time?'

Consideration of the skills criterion would lead a Minister to reflect on his previous occupational experience and substantive interests. Thus a former businessman might well be highly effective as an Executive Minister and a good many parliamentary politicians might immodestly decide that they have the personality, the verbal skills and flair for publicity of an Ambassador Minister. Alternatively, to make a useful contribution as a policy selector, a Minister would need to believe that, in Bagehot's words, he was 'a man of quite sufficient intelligence, quite enough various knowledge, quite enough miscellaneous experience, to represent effectually general sense in opposition to bureaucratic sense'.[1] Last, to be a policy initiator, a Minister requires, if not specialist knowledge of the subjects he is dealing with, at least sufficient understanding to define his objectives in operational terms and evaluate alternative policy programmes in respect of their probable efficacy in achieving those objectives.

Looking at the matter from the point of view of a department's needs rather than a Minister's skills, it is difficult to know how specific to be. On the one hand, one cannot simply make a list of Whitehall departments and next to each write down the type of Minister

[1] W. Bagehot, *The English Constitution* (New York: Dolphin, 1965; London: Fontana, 1965), p. 232.

it invariably requires. The same department is likely to benefit from different types of Minister at different times; as social psychologists have demonstrated, an effective leader in one situation is liable to be a menace, or liable to be replaced in another situation.[1] Thus a period of radical reform directed by a policy initiator may appropriately be followed by a period of consolidation under an Executive Minister who attempts to ensure that new policies are administered efficiently and, perhaps, also concentrates on the man management task of boosting (restoring?) departmental morale. Having registered this point, however, it is not necessary to use it as an excuse for avoiding any prescriptions whatever. There are *some* fairly stable similarities and differences between departments which have implications for the type of ministerial leadership that is likely to be required.

First, every department requires a ministerial policy initiator every five or ten years in order that its objectives be critically re-examined and its future priorities set. However, certain departments operate in an especially rapidly changing environment with the result that significant policy changes are almost constantly under consideration. It is probably true to say that the Treasury and the Foreign Office, as departments faced with rapidly changing economic and international environments, more frequently have need of a policy initiator than, say, the Department of Health and Social Security and the Department of Education and Science. Thus policy programmes undertaken by the Treasury, or the Foreign Office, may temporarily achieve some of their stated objectives but frequent adjustments and, indeed, reversals of policy are required as the economic or international situation changes. The Department of Health and Social Security and the Department of Education and Science on the other hand, operate in relatively stable environments and can forecast the future demand for, say, old age pensions and schools with some accuracy. There can be a reasonable expectation in these departments that long-term policy programmes will be carried through to completion.

The statement that policy initiation is frequently required in certain departments does not, however, mean that Ministers can readily provide it. As noted in Chapter 9, ministerial policy initiation is more readily achieved in departments in which it is feasible to isolate 'key issues' and treat them separately from the rest of the department's business. In the Treasury (the Foreign Office is a less clear-cut case) a key issues approach is rarely feasible. What is required is an economic *strategy* which recognises the interrelations

[1] See, for example, C. A. Gibb (ed.), *Leadership* (Harmondsworth: Penguin, 1969), Introduction.

and trade-offs between such objectives as economic growth, price stability, a high level of employment and maintaining the exchange rate of the currency.

An Executive Minister would seem most valuable in one of the new 'giant' departments with their huge financial and manpower budgets. The Departments of the Environment, Defence, Trade and Industry, and Health and Social Security present problems of resource and man management on a scale new to Whitehall and, as Sir Richard Clarke has forcefully argued, the traditional distinction between policy and administration is more than ever inappropriate. Ministers themselves should be concerned with management problems – 'organising', 'motivating' and 'controlling' – as well as deciding on policy objectives.

Departments which have the greatest need of an Ambassador Minister are, obviously enough, those which stand to gain most if their policies are widely publicised and well understood by relevant sections of the public and interest groups. Certain departments are highly consumer or service orientated and operate largely by persuasion (one might almost say by salesmanship) rather than by means of policy programmes which are legally binding, or otherwise easily enforced. The Ministry of Transport, for instance, in its concern for road safety is a department which welcomes a Minister who has a flair for publicising its measures.[1] A touch of gimmickry does not come amiss; nor does it matter if the Minister and his actions are loathed by the motoring public, so long as they are widely understood. Another department which stands to benefit from an Ambassador Minister is the Department of Employment at which Ministers are regularly called on to conciliate in industrial disputes and persuade employers and employees of the need to restrain wage and price inflation. The ambassadorial requirements of the Departments of Trade and Industry, on the other hand, are liable to vary over the years. It always maintains close contacts with its business clients, but benefits particularly from an Ambassador Minister during a period (like 1964-70) when new incentives and services to industry are being introduced.[2]

Last, there are departments in which the traditional Minister who serves as a policy selector and intelligent layman is likely to

[1] The Ministry of Transport in 1970 became part of the Department of the Environment.

[2] If the DTI ever, in practice, became less interventionist, and market forces were let loose on industry, its need for a Minister with ambassadorial skills would correspondingly diminish. Mr John Davies, Secretary of State 1970-2 spoke of adopting non-interventionist policies but, in the event, felt obliged to provide large government subsidies to industry both on an *ad hoc* basis and systematically under the terms of the Industry Act, 1972.

flourish. At least two departments – the Home Office and the Scottish Office – cover so wide a range of subjects and have so much legislation to bring forward that no Minister could possibly become an expert. What is required is a man who is capable of exercising sound judgement, including political judgement, in selecting which programmes to proceed with. At the Home Office it is also vital, in view of the number of emergency debates, censure motions and simulated Parliamentary crises with which he is likely to be faced, that the Minister be a more than averagely adroit performer at the parliamentary despatch box.[1]

As well as making a conscious choice about their priority roles, there are other decisions affecting their working methods which Ministers should take for themselves. Ministers have great formal authority in their departments but sometimes lack the self-confidence to exercise it. It is a bit puzzling for an outsider to hear complaints that the department 'controls every ten minutes of the Minister's day and night',[2] or that the Minister is worried that he is not seeing a wide enough range of policy options because too few officials and specialist advisers have direct access to him, or that he thinks a more creative role could be found for junior Ministers on departmental committees but hesitates to break with convention, or that he would like to strengthen his Private Office with outside appointees but fears the department would 'reject them like heart transplants'. Clearly Ministers would be at fault if they took no account of departmental established practices and morale, but they also need to remember that only they can organise their job from the perspective of their own priorities. If their priorities require rearranging their timetable (appointments, 'visits', etc.), or altering departmental procedures for formulating policy or transmitting advice, they should normally press ahead and exert their legitimate authority unless persuaded that quite specific and serious consequences would follow.

The Prime Minister

The implication of the above discussion from the point of view of Prime Ministers is that they should make a careful assessment of the needs of particular departments at particular times, and then try to appoint Ministers with appropriate role conceptions and skills. It goes without saying that, in the exercise of patronage powers, some weight is bound to be given to the maintenance of party unity

---

[1] The Foreign Office and the Treasury are also frequently caught in parliamentary storms. See Chapter 7.

[2] B. Castle, 'Mandarin Power', *The Sunday Times* (10 June 1973).

(appoint Ministers from all factions of the party) and the maintenance of the Prime Minister's own position (appoint colleagues loyal to self) but it is suggested that giving more weight to the specific requirements of departments would improve the performance of British government.

Prime Ministers should also think through all the implications before embarking on a ministerial reshuffle. It may not matter that Ambassador Ministers be regularly reshuffled (a good salesman can sell anything?) and presumably policy selectors/intelligent laymen lose their capacity to view departmental proposals sceptically, with an outsider's independent judgement, if they stay in the same post more than two or three years. Policy initiators, on the other hand, and Executive Ministers who intend to introduce significant organisational changes, or changes in methods of management, need to remain in office rather longer than has been customary in recent years. Three years, in fact, is often said in Whitehall to be the optimum period of ministerial tenure and the rationale presumably is that it takes about this time to guide a major set of proposals from the planning stage to the stage at which they are being administered in accordance with objectives.[1] However, the practice of Stanley Baldwin and some nineteenth century Prime Ministers of leaving most Ministers in the same posts throughout a Government's electoral term seems at least as sensible.[2] After all, if a Minister is reshuffled after three years, it means that his successor will only last one or two years before a general election which may remove his party from office.

At the risk of sounding naive, one might suggest that a further way in which a Prime Minister, or successive Prime Ministers, might improve the performance of government through the appointments process would be to plan the careers of Ministers so that they specialised to a greater degree. 'Planned career development' for Ministers has not been fashionable in the past but a Prime Minister who happened to believe, in company with many outside observers, that specialised knowledge and experience is a great asset to Ministers (particularly policy initiators) in some departments could take steps to provide the requisite experience. He could, for example, categorise some promising junior Ministers as economic and industrial Ministers, others as external affairs Ministers, and the rest as social policy Ministers.[3] These rising politicians would be appointed as Parliamentary Secretaries and Ministers of State to

[1] See Chapter 8.
[2] See Chapter 4.
[3] As noted in Chapter 5 the Fulton Committee on the Civil Service proposed that civil servants be trained either as 'social' or as 'economic' administrators.

departments in their area of specialisation. Thus future Chancellors of the Exchequer, Foreign Secretaries, and Secretaries of State for the Social Services, would be groomed for office rather than pitched in at a few hours' notice.

In general – and without greatly reducing the use of patronage as a means of maintaining party unity – Prime Ministers could make greater efforts to appoint departmental teams of Ministers with complementary skills. In recent years there has been a certain amount of 'double-banking' by which a senior Minister in the Commons was paired with a subordinate Minister in the Lords (or vice versa) in the expectation that the peer would be able to concentrate on the departmental side of his job.[1] It would also be feasible, though, to make paired appointments on the basis that a department required, let us say, one Minister with the capacity to serve as a policy initiator and another with ambassadorial skills, or an Executive Minister in harness with a skilful Parliamentarian.

The structure of British government

One of the main themes of this study has been that British politicians are better equipped to serve as policy selectors or Ambassador Ministers than as policy initiators or Executive Ministers. Whether one regards this situation with equanimity depends on value judgements about the desirability of an innovative rather than a purely incrementalist pattern of government, and of making a sharp distinction between 'policy' and 'management' rather than regarding the two as inseparable. The purpose of this section is to discuss means of increasing the supply, and improving the performance in office of policy initiators and Executive Ministers; the assumption being that this option is at least worth exploring.

The most important single reform which would assist Ministers to serve as policy initiators would be the expansion of the party Research Departments to the point at which, in Government and Opposition, they provided Ministers with a steady flow of policy proposals. These proposals would need to be reasonably accurately costed (with their opportunity cost made explicit), and based on clearly defined objectives and priorities. Both parties at present make some effort to formulate proposals and prepare for office while in Opposition – although the Labour party is desperately short of permanent research staff – but once these proposals have been enacted Ministers become highly dependent on their civil servants. The longer a Government remains in office the more severe this

[1] D. N. Chester, 'Double-Banking and Deputy Ministers', *New Society* (11 June 1964).

problem becomes, and Ministers who conceive of themselves as policy initiators but have nothing to initiate, are not at all rare.[1] The essential point, then, is that Ministers require sources of information and ideas beyond those they get from their department and its regular interest group clientele. A few Ministers, like Anthony Crosland (see Chapter 9) continue, while in office, to pick the brains of non-Civil Service experts they have known for years, but most Ministers require a more institutionalised source of outside advice.

A second possible reform to assist policy initiators would involve supplementing existing Private Offices with 'friends' of the Minister, who might be either politically sympathetic experts or congenial party colleagues (from party head office, for example). These 'friends' of the Minister would both help to transmit the objectives of the Minister and his party to the department and would offer him a politically sympathetic second opinion on proposals initiated by officials. In some cases they might actually help formulate proposals by serving on departmental committees and project teams.

The obvious ways to increase the supply of competent Executive Ministers would be either for constituency associations to recruit more Parliamentary candidates with executive experience, or for the Prime Minister to go outside the ranks of his parliamentary party when appointing Ministers. The Conservative Party prior to 1970 attempted the former approach, but without much success. The problem is partly that constituency associations jealously guard their autonomy and resent interference from Central Office, and partly that leading corporations are unwilling to release their bright young men for temporary political service. The latter approach might improve the management of those departments to which potential Executive Ministers were appointed but would entail certain costs. First, to the extent that the Prime Minister appoints 'outsiders' to ministerial office, he forgoes using his power of patronage to maintain party solidarity. Second, Ministers who are not 'House-trained' are rarely effective House of Commons performers and their despatch box failures depress government morale.

Once in office, the tasks of Executive Ministers would be made easier by a recognition on the part of civil servants that management is not exclusively a Whitehall responsibility and that there are strong arguments in favour of Ministers not treating policy and management as separate entities. In addition to this, Ministers would also benefit from being able to make a certain number of appointments in their departments without needing to haggle with the Establishment divisions of the Civil Service Department. Thus, if an Executive

[1] See Chapter 8.

Minister wanted to appoint advisers to assist him in introducing programme budgeting, or cost effectiveness techniques, then he might be permitted to do so on his own initiative. More important for Executive Ministers, however, is the continuation of the present trend for departments to be able to allocate their resources as they wish, provided they stay below their fixed expenditure ceiling and subject only to review by means of PAR/PESC returns. Resource management is more than ever a crucial activity in the 'giant' unitary departments, and it is frustrating for Ministers and civil servants to have obtained Treasury approval and possibly have their priorities queried. Any slight tendency not to economise which resulted from the removal of the more petty aspects of Treasury control would be likely to be more than counterbalanced by a more rational allocation of resources in terms of priorities. Finally, we should recall Sir Richard Clarke's proposal that management functions which are now performed by the Civil Service Department, the public sector divisions of the Treasury and the Central Policy Review Staff, should all be located in a single central management department. This would assist Executive Ministers, as well as their civil servants, by reducing the amount of consultation with the 'centre' that they are obliged to undertake.

Last, some proposals which affect junior Ministers. Junior Ministers would be better prepared for cabinet office if they were given wider responsibilities. Senior Ministers would still be bound to assess the abilities of their subordinates before delegating much authority, but it would help if the parliamentary convention that the senior Minister is responsible for everything were discarded. If junior Ministers were known to be responsible for particular subjects and answered to Parliament in their own name instead of replying on behalf of 'My Right Honourable Friend', then senior Ministers might be a little less conscious of damage to their own reputations from any errors that were made. It would also be valuable for junior Ministers if senior Ministers adopted the practice of meeting them once a week, or even every day, to review departmental business. Regular departmental ministerial *cabinets* would enable juniors to obtain an overview of a Cabinet Minister's work and see their possible future job in perspective. As it is, junior Ministers are all too often given miscellaneous dogsbody duties which, they complain, leave them cut off from the mainstream of policy making and politicking. A final source of valuable experience for junior Ministers would be tapped if they sat on Civil Service committees dealing with intrinsically important, or politically sensitive issues. They would have the opportunity to see major proposals at the crucial formulation stage and could also act as watchdogs for their senior Minister, with a brief to ensure that feasible policy options were not foreclosed at official level.

POLITICAL LEADERSHIP IN THE EXECUTIVE BRANCH OF GOVERNMENT

In Chapter 1 we posed the following three questions:

What roles do political leaders intend to perform? In so far as their priorities (or role conceptions) differ, what are the main types of leader?

What factors influence leaders' ability to perform their intended roles, and act in accordance with their role conceptions?

What are the consequences for government of variance in political leadership performance?

In concluding, it may be useful to discuss the extent to which our findings in regard to Cabinet Ministers are likely to be generalisable to other political leaders. We shall also try to assess, in the light of the present study, the research problems which students of political leadership have to confront.

Preparatory to answering the first of the above questions, we found it useful to list all the roles Ministers might conceivably perform and to outline a 'typical' working week. It seems fair comment that previous studies of political leadership in the executive branch of government have not adequately analysed the time constraints under which leaders operate.[1] Failure to do this has meant that the necessity of choice which leaders face in selecting their role priorities and key issues has not been fully appreciated. In this study an 'ideal type' classification of Ministers based on their stated role priorities has been proposed. It is hoped that the typology will have some general validity as a means of categorising political executives in other systems. We have suggested that there are two types of policy leader – policy initiators and policy selectors – and that a third category of leaders see themselves as top level managers of government departments. A fourth type of leader is public relations orientated (cf. the Ambassador Minister). He is concerned

---

[1] This is true even of Neustadt's *Presidential Power*. Several of Neustadt's prescriptions, notably his advice to Presidents to act as their own directors of intelligence and systematically create overlapping jurisdictions and personality clashes so as to avoid having decisional options foreclosed, show little recognition that time is a scarce presidential resource. See especially ch. 7.

to 'sell' his policies, his department and himself to target publics. Finally, Minimalists are concerned only with preserving their own position and avoiding political controversy.

It is recognised that a typology based on interview data is not entirely satisfactory and that, ideally, one wants detailed evidence of the actual behaviour of leaders in office. Analysis of appointments diaries may prove particularly useful especially if, as was not the case here, a large enough sample can be obtained to permit analysis of variance in the way leaders utilise their time. Even better data would be obtained if political leaders could be persuaded (as business managers have been)[1] to fill in self-administered diaries designed by researchers.

For the purpose of this study a list of factors, or 'variables' which it seemed plausible to assume influence political leadership performance was derived partly from social psychology findings on small group leadership and partly from Neustadt's *Presidential Power*. Leader performance was viewed as a function of leaders' own skills, the advice and expectations of other actors, situational factors and feasibility of policy objectives. On this basis it was possible to discuss, in fairly general terms, the extent to which different types of Ministers are able to perform their priority roles and to present case studies of role performance. Clearly, however, it is desirable to test hypotheses systematically and discover the relative explanatory power of independent variables. In order to do this it is necessary that both independent and dependent variables be operationally defined (i.e. defined in such a way that they can be measured).[2]

It will require some ingenuity to measure validly such variables as the skills of leaders and the expectations of other actors. The dependent variable, leader performance, is likely to present greater problems however, and we may illustrate these problems briefly by considering policy initiation and public relations roles. At a conceptual level it would have to be decided whether policy initiation meant actually achieving policy objectives, or merely enacting programmes intended to do so. The former definition might be regarded as preferable in principle, but it is exceptionally difficult to measure the extent to which policy objectives have been achieved. Reliable and valid indicators have to be developed, a time scale specified and allowance made for unintended consequences of policy. Whichever definition was adopted, it would still be necessary to decide whether to regard all policy initiatives as equally significant,

---

[1] See Stewart, *Managers and Their Jobs*.

[2] Independent variables are explanatory factors ('causes') and dependent variables are factors to be explained ('effects').

or whether to take the view that a leader who introduced a 'major' change in policy had registered a greater 'success' than a leader who introduced a 'minor' change. A policy initiative may be regarded as major or minor in several senses. Thus policy programmes vary in terms of their intrinsic importance (a programme designed to redistribute national wealth might be regarded as intrinsically more important than a reafforestation programme), the amount of political controversy they generate, and according to whether they represent a major or minor deviation from established departmental, or inter-departmental policy. Arguably, each of these dimensions should be taken into account in assessing a policy initiator's performance.

Next, public relations roles: in principle it would be possible to collect survey data on the increase or decrease in support for particular policies among target publics, resulting from a leader's public relations activities. A conceptual difficulty similar to that encountered with the policy initiation role would arise, however. It would have to be decided whether to distinguish between policy programmes which were 'easy' to sell and those which were 'hard' to sell. Presumably a programme is hard to sell if, like an incomes policy, it requires groups to display self-restraint and act contrary to their short term interests, and easy to sell if, like investment incentives, it offers tangible immediate benefits. It is also likely to be easier to win support for a policy if no active campaign is being waged (for instance by the Opposition, or the TUC) against it.

When conceptual problems had been resolved, the next step would be to collect data on leaders' role performance. Published evidence would not normally be sufficient. Thus there is no possibility, using published materials, of assessing the performance of Ministers in winning cabinet battles, or as policy selectors/intelligent laymen in their departments. One way around this difficulty would be to ask panels of judges to make assessments. Different panels would probably be needed for different roles. In the case of Ministers, for instance, newspaper lobby correspondents might assess their performance of parliamentary and party roles but civil servants, or other Ministers, would be required to judge performance of policy leadership, cabinet and public relations roles. Members of the panels would, of course, have to be quite clear on definitions of roles and on the criteria (standards of measurement) to use in making their assessments.

The third of the questions listed above, relating to the consequences of leaders for government, seems certain to be the most difficult of all to answer. In this study we limited ourselves mainly to drawing inferences about the effects of ministerial role performance on post-war British policy. The element of subjective judgement involved in making these inferences was admittedly high and the reader may regard them as more or less plausible. In subsequent studies it will be necessary to try to establish more direct linkages between the performance of specific leadership roles and dimensions of governmental performance. One would also want to discover a great deal more about the limitations of leadership; the extent to which policy programmes and other achievements of government are determined by situational factors beyond the control of politicians and their advisers.[1] If these tasks can be accomplished, important steps will have been taken towards the development of an adequate theory of political leadership. Ultimately, the goal of such a theory should be to specify the conditions under which different types of leader contribute, positively or negatively, to the performance of the tasks of government.

[1] An interesting attempt on these lines is made in Robert Eyestone, *The Threads of Public Policy: A Study in Policy Leadership* (Indianapolis: Bobbs-Merrill, 1970).

Interview Schedules

In the interviews with both Ministers and civil servants a number of standard questions were asked. The answers to most of these questions are tabulated in the text. If the respondent had further time available (and most did), the author then selected additional questions from those listed below.

1. MINISTERS

STANDARD QUESTIONS

What are the most important tasks a Minister has to perform? In other words, what is a good Minister actually good at doing?

What skills and types of ability do Ministers need to carry out these essential tasks?

Do the skills a Minister needs vary from department to department? What special skills are needed in your present department?

Would you single out any experiences in your own career which were particularly good preparation for being a Minister?

Are you generally satisfied with the range and quality of advice available in the department?

When you were first appointed to the Ministry of . . . did you have definite policy objectives in mind, or did you have to generate your own objectives at a later stage?

Additional questions

(*a*) *general*

What kind of things can one only learn by experience as a Minister? What kinds of mistakes do new Ministers tend to make?

Is there some aspect of your work as a Minister you wish you could spend more time on but can't due to pressure of work? Are there some things it is frustrating to have to spend so much time on?

(*b*) *departmental responsibilities and relations with civil servants*

In your experience what are the main kinds of difficulties that arise when a Minister comes to a department determined to make major policy changes?

In your time as Minister of . . . have you made any changes in the way the department is run, or the way advice is transmitted to you?

In general what kind of relationship should a Minister seek to establish with his senior civil servants?

What would you say are the characteristics of the ideal Minister from a Civil Service point of view?

Are you in favour of bringing in non-Civil Service advisers to assist the Minister?

Have you ever had reason to believe that feasible policy options are foreclosed as advice is transmitted up the hierarchy of civil servants?

(*c*) *the Cabinet and inter-departmental relations*

Are there any general comments or criticisms you would care to make about the Cabinet as a decision-making body?

What factors contribute to a Minister's influence in Cabinet?

Do you regard informal conversations with your colleagues in which you discuss policy questions as an important part of your work?

Is it your experience that certain Ministers tend to form alliances and support each other over a wide range of issues?

Have you ever had reason to believe that feasible policy options were foreclosed on inter-departmental official committees?

(d) Ministers, their party and Parliament

Do you feel that there is much danger of Ministers getting out of touch with backbench opinion?

Are (were) you yourself as a Minister able to keep in close touch with your own backbenchers?

How important is it to a Minister's career that he be effective and/or popular in the House?

What qualities do you believe that Prime Ministers look for in Ministers they want to promote?

2. CIVIL SERVANTS

STANDARD QUESTIONS

From the point of view of the department what tasks must the Minister perform reasonably well? What are the essential things that he must do?

What skills and types of ability would you say Ministers need to carry out these essential tasks?

Do the skills needed by a Minister vary from department to department? Are there any special skills a Minister needs in your department?

In your experience do senior Ministers generally have most of the necessary skills and abilities? What are their main strengths and weaknesses?

Additional questions

(a) general

Do you find that Ministers generally tend to neglect certain tasks and spend too much time on others?

Do you ever find that feasible policy options are foreclosed as advice is transmitted up the hierachy of civil servants?

What special skills or knowledge do politicians bring to the work of a Minister that a good civil servant, if he were made a Minister, would not have?

How long does it usually take a new Minister in your department to get to know his job? What mistakes do new Ministers tend to make? Do you think that by and large Ministers change departments too frequently? How long should a Minister ideally stay in the same department – assuming he is doing his job well?

Specifically, do Ministers generally have adequate administrative ability and application? To what extent would you say that departments are able to cope if a Minister is not a good administrator?

In your view is it desirable that Ministers should have some prior specialist knowledge of the work of your Ministry before they are appointed?

Do Ministers' political ambitions sometimes have a detrimental effect on the way they approach their departmental work?

In so far as any day is typical could you describe a Minister's typical working day?

(b) *relationships between Ministers and civil servants*

In general what kind of relationship should a Minister try to establish with his senior civil servants?

Do Ministers sometimes have misconceptions about the role of civil servants or about Minister-civil servant relationships?

What are the main functions his Private Office performs for a Minister? In your experience do Ministers sometimes fail to get the best out of their Private Offices?

Do you feel that civil servants generally adequately appreciate a Minister's requirements and difficulties?

Is there any truth, in your view, in the assertion sometimes made on the Left that civil servants are sometimes too ready with objections to a new proposal – or is it a myth?

Do you personally ever feel much tension between your own policy views and the Minister's, or do you find it relatively easy to be dispassionate and implement whatever policies the Minister decides on?

Are you in favour of Ministers' bringing in non-Civil Service advisers to assist them? (If 'Yes') What role do you think these advisers can most usefully play in the department? (Specific jobs or general progress chasing?)

In your department is advice to the Minister mainly channelled through the Permanent Secretary, or is there a collegiate advisory structure (cf. the DEA, MOD etc)?

Do you ever find that feasible policy options are foreclosed on inter-departmental official committees?

Are you in favour of Ministers' consulting relatively junior civil servants if they wish to? Or do you think it preferable that the Minister should rely principally on his most senior civil servants?

(c) *specific tasks and possible characteristics of Ministers*

Do some Ministers (most, all?) tend to concentrate on certain areas of the department's work and de-emphasise others? (If 'Yes') What consequences follow from this? Do civil servants dealing with matters the Minister is not very interested in tend to get demoralised?

Are Ministers generally rather good or not so good at the job of consulting with interest group representatives?

Does briefing a Minister for cabinet committees take up much time?

What are the consequences if a Minister lacks the support or full confidence of his ministerial colleagues, or if he is not well informed of relevant developments in other departments, or in the Cabinet?

Do Ministers generally require a lot of briefing for their Parliamentary duties (Questions, committee stage of bills etc.)?

What kinds of things in your observation get a Minister promotion? What tends to hurt a Minister's promotion prospects?

(d) junior Ministers

In general how would you describe the role of junior Ministers in your department? How much power do they have? Does their importance vary a great deal? What factors explain the variations?

Do you approve of the increase in the number of junior Ministers and particularly Ministers of State? Do you think that enough work is delegated to them – or too much perhaps?

Appendix II

The Samples of Ministers
and Civil Servants

1. MINISTERS

In order to obtain a sample of 50 Ministers it was necessary to write
to 72 potential respondents. In so far as the author was conscious
of the need to contact Ministers from different social and occupational backgrounds, with varying reputations for ability, and with
experience in all Whitehall departments, it is hoped that the final
sample was not unrepresentative in its views. It was not possible,
however, to interview all post-war Cabinet Ministers, or even a large
statistically representative (random or quota) sample. In the first
place, over 40 of the 137 Ministers who have served in the Cabinet since
1945 are dead and, secondly, it was foreseeable that the refusal-to-be-
interviewed rate would be sufficiently high to defeat an attempt to
achieve statistical representativeness. In any case, the total number of
Cabinet Ministers who could be interviewed was limited by considerations of time and money and the need to interview civil servants and
junior Ministers. Civil servants clearly had to be interviewed because
they are in the best position to assess the impact of Ministers on
government departments and policy and it seemed desirable to interview junior Ministers because the extent of their responsibilities tells
us a good deal both about the value of junior office as preparation for
cabinet office and about the burden on senior Ministers.

Most of the interviews were held in the summer of 1969. Labour
Ministers were, in most cases, interviewed in their offices in Whitehall, Conservative ex-Ministers, then in Opposition, were seen either
at their London homes, or at the House of Commons, or House of
Lords. With one or two exceptions Ministers were not sent lists of
questions in advance. The interviews were held on the understanding
that they were initially 'off the record', but that permission to quote
might be requested. The shortest interview lasted 20 minutes, the
longest over 4 hours, and the average time was between an hour and

an hour and a half. As explained in Chapter 1, potential quotes were noted at the time and full notes were taken as soon as possible after interviews were completed.

Post-war Ministers and the sample for this study

Number of post-war Cabinet Ministers	137
Number still living	92
Number of Cabinet Ministers interviewed	30[a]
Heads of departments not in the Cabinet	5
Ministers of State and Parliamentary Secretaries	15
	—
	50
	—

[a] Two of these Ministers achieved cabinet rank in 1970.

Characteristics of the sample

1. *Party:* 27 respondents were Labour Ministers, 23 were Conservatives.

2. *Ministerial experience* (Cabinet and junior office)

Years in office	Number of Ministers
10+	9
5–9	22
Under 5	19
	—
	50
	—

3. The current Minister, or at least one former Minister, in each Whitehall department was interviewed. Four former Chancellors of the Exchequer, four Home Secretaries, four Ministers of Defence and two Foreign Secretaries were included.

Refusal to be interviewed

Twenty-two Ministers who were contacted were not interviewed. Eighteen refused and in 4 cases a mutually convenient appointment could not be arranged. Refusals came disproportionately, as might have been expected, from Labour Ministers who were in the Cabinet in 1969. Five serving Cabinet Ministers were interviewed but eight declined. Junior Ministers currently in office were not hard to see.

2. CIVIL SERVANTS

Clearly, no claims at all can be made on behalf of the representativeness of the sample of 25 civil servants. Twenty-one respondents were career officials, 4 were temporary appointees in Mr Wilson's Government. It became clear that civil servants preferred to be sent lists of questions in advance and in some cases they had been kind enough to give prior thought to their answers and had made notes which they referred to during the interview. The average interview lasted about 2 hours. The same understanding regarding quotation applied with officials as with Ministers and the same procedure for recording interviews was adopted.

The ranks of the officials interviewed were as follows:[a]

7 Permanent Secretaries (6 retired)
5 Deputy Secretaries (1 retired)
2 Under-Secretaries (1 retired)
3 Assistant Secretaries
7 Principals (mainly Ministers' Private Secretaries)
1 Executive Officer (Private Secretary)

[a] For the purpose of this listing no distinction is made between Permanent Secretary and Permanent Under-Secretary, Deputy-Secretary and Deputy Under-Secretary etc. Temporary civil servants were assigned to the rank indicated by their salary, as given in the *Imperial Calendar*.

Bibliography

The literature relevant to a study of the roles of Cabinet Ministers is enormous and no attempt is made here to provide a comprehensive bibliography. The one which follows lists only works consulted in preparing this study and is divided into five sections:

1. Leadership in non-political settings: small groups, business organisations etc. (including problems of methodology).
2. Memoirs and biographies of post-war Ministers and civil servants.
3. Government documents.
4. British central government (secondary sources).
5. Political leadership in industrialised societies.

Excellent and up-to-date bibliographies on British governments are to be found in R. M. Punnett, *British Government and Politics* (London: Heinemann, 1968) and John P. Mackintosh, *The Government and Politics of Britain* (London: Hutchinson, 1970). Richard Rose (ed.), *Policy Making in Britain* (London: Macmillan, 1969) provides a valuable bibliography of articles, some of them in journals not regularly consulted by political scientists. The principal academic journals containing articles on politics in Britain are the *British Journal of Political Science, British Journal of Sociology, Government and Opposition, Parliamentary Affairs, Public Law, Political Quarterly, Political Studies* and *Public Administration*.

The fullest bibliography of works in English on political leadership is given in Lewis J. Edinger (ed.), *Political Leadership in Industrialised Societies* (New York: John Wiley, 1967). To bring this listing up to date it is necessary to consult such standard reference sources as *International Political Science Abstracts* (Oxford: Blackwell, 1951–   ) and *Books in Print* (New York: Bowker, 1948–   ).

1. *Leadership in non-political settings: small groups, business organisations etc.*

R. F. Bales and P. E. Slater, 'Role Differentation in Small Decision Making Groups' in T. Parsons and R. F. Bales (eds), *Family Socialisation and Interaction Process* (New York: Free Press, 1955), ch. 5.

Lewis A. Dexter, *Elite and Specialised Interviewing* (Evanston, Ill.: Northwestern University Press, 1970).

Peter F. Drucker, *The Practice of Management* (London: Heinemann, 1955).

F. E. Fiedler, *A Theory of Leadership Effectiveness* (New York: McGraw Hill, 1967).

C. A. Gibb (ed.), *Leadership* (Harmondsworth: Penguin, 1969).

C. A. Gibb, 'Leadership' in G. Lindzey and E. Aronson (eds), *The Handbook of Social Psychology* (Reading, Mass.: Addison-Wesley, 1969) IV, 205–82.

E. P. Hollander, *Leaders, Groups and Influence* (London: Oxford University Press, 1964).

James G. March (ed.), *Handbook of Organisations* (Chicago: Rand, McNally, 1965).

Theodore R. Sarbin and Vernon L. Allen, 'Role Theory' in Lindzey and Aronson (eds), *Handbook of Social Psychology*, I, 488–567.

Rosemary Stewart, *Managers and Their Jobs* (London: Macmillan, 1967).

Rosemary Stewart, *The Reality of Management* (London: Pan Books, 1967).

S. Verba, *Small Groups and Political Behaviour* (Princeton: Princeton University Press, 1961).

Sir G. Vickers, *The Art of Judgement* (London: Chapman and Hall, 1969).

2. *Memoirs and biographies of post-war Ministers and civil servants*

C. R. Attlee, *As It Happened* (London: Heinemann, 1954).

R. Bevins, *The Greasy Pole* (London: Hodder and Stoughton, 1965).

G. Brown, *In My Way* (London: Gollancz, 1971).

A. Bullock, *The Life and Times of Ernest Bevin* (London: Heinemann, 1960), vol. II.

R. A. Butler, *The Art of the Possible* (London: Hamish Hamilton, 1971).

Lord Chandos, *Memoirs* (London: Bodley Head, 1962).

H. Dalton, *High Tide and After* (Memoirs: vol. II) (London: Frederick Muller, 1962).

Sir A. Eden, *Full Circle* (Memoirs: vol. III) (London: Cassell, 1960).

M. Foot, *Aneurin Bevan* (London: MacGibbon and Kee, 1962).

Sir R. Harrod, *The Prof: A Personal Memoir of Lord Cherwell* (London: Macmillan, 1959).

Lord Hill, *Both Sides of the Hill* (London: Heinemann, 1964).

Lord Kilmuir, *Political Adventure: Memoirs* (London: Weidenfeld and Nicolson, 1964).

H. Macmillan, *Memoirs: Tides of Fortune 1945–55*, vol III (London: Macmillan, 1969); *Riding the Storm*, vol. IV (London: Macmillan, 1971).

G. Mallaby, *From My Level* (London: Hutchinson, 1965).

E. Marples, 'A Dog's Life in The Ministry' in Richard Rose (ed.), *Policy Making in Britain* (London: Macmillan, 1969).

H. Morrison, *An Autobiography* (London: Odhams, 1960).

Lord Salter, *Memoirs of a Public Servant* (London: Faber, 1961).

A. Sampson, *Macmillan: A Study in Ambiguity* (Harmondsworth: Penguin, 1967).

E. Shinwell, *Conflict without Malice* (London: Odhams, 1955).

Lord Strang, *Home and Abroad* (London: Deutsch, 1956).

Lord Swinton, *Sixty Years of Power* (London: Hutchinson, 1966).

Lord Wigg, *George Wigg* (London: Michael Joseph, 1972).

F. Williams, *A Prime Minister Remembers* (London: Heinemann, 1961).

H. Wilson, *The Labour Government 1964–70: A Personal Record* (London: Weidenfeld and Nicolson, and Michael Joseph, 1971).

Lord Woolton, *Memoirs* (London: Cassell, 1959).

3. *Government documents*

All the listed documents were published in London by Her Majesty's Stationery Office (HMSO).

Central Organisation for Defence (Cmnd 2097, 1963).

The Civil Service (Fulton Report, Cmnd 3638, 1968).

Civil Service Department Report, 1970–1 (1971).

Civil Service Training, 1967–8 (1969).

The Commission on the Third London Airport (Roskill Report, 1971).

The Committee on Local Authority and Allied Personal Services (Seebohm Report, Cmnd 3073, 1968).

Committee on Overseas Representation (Duncan Report, Cmnd 4107, 1969).

Committee on Public Participation and Planning (Skeffington Report, SBN 750128X, 1969).

Control of Public Expenditure (Plowden Report, Cmnd 1432, 1961).

Education and Science: Annual Reports of the Department of Education and Science 1967–9.

The Financial Objectives of the Nationalised Industries (Cmnd 1337, 1961).

First Report of the Civil Service Department, 1969 (1970).

Fuel Policy (Cmnd 2798, 1965).

Fuel Policy (Cmnd 3468, 1967).

John Garrett and S. D. Walker, *Management by Objectives in the Civil Service* (CAS Occasional Paper No.10, 1969).

Information and the Public Interest (Cmnd 4089, 1970).

In Place of Strife (Cmnd 3888, 1969).

Ministerial Control of the Nationalised Industries (Cmnd 4027, 1969).

'*The Reorganisation of Secondary Education*', Department of Education and Science (Circular, October 1965).

'The Organisation of Secondary Education', *Department of Education and Science* (Circular, June 1970).

Public Expenditure 1968–9 to 1973–4 (Cmnd 4234, 1969).

Public Expenditure, Planning and Control, (Cmnd 2915, 1966).

Railway Policy (Morris Report, Cmnd 3439, 1967).

The Royal Commission on Local Government in England (Redcliffe-Maud Report, Cmnd 4040, 1969).

The Shipbuilding Inquiry Committees 1965–6 (Geddes Report, Cmnd 2937, 1966).

Statements on the Defence Estimates, 1956–70

A. Williams, *Output budgeting and The Contribution of Micro-economics to Efficiency in Government,* (CAS Occasional Paper, No. 4, 1967).

4. *British central government*

(a) *Books:*

R. K. Alderman and J. A. Cross, *The Tactics of Resignation* (London: Routledge and Kegan Paul, 1967).

L. Amery, *Thoughts on the Constitution* (London: Oxford University Press, 2nd ed, 1964).

W. Bagehot, *The English Constitution* (New York: Dolphin, 1965; London: Fontana, 1963; 1st edn 1867).

A. Barker and M. Rush, *The Member of Parliament and His Information* (London: Allen and Unwin, 1970).

M. J. Barnett, *The Politics of Legislation: The Rent Act 1957* (London: Weidenfeld and Nicolson, 1969).

S. H. Beer, *Modern British Politics* (London: Faber, 1965).

E. Boyle, A. Crosland and M. Kogan, *The Politics of Education*, (Harmondsworth: Penguin, 1971).

J. Bray, *Decision in Government* (London: Gollancz, 1969).

Lord Bridges, *The Treasury* (London: Allen and Unwin, 1964).

Lord Bridges, *Treasury Control* (London: Athlone, 1959).

Sir H. Brittain, *The British Budgetary System* (London: Allen and Unwin, 1959).

S. Brittan, *Steering the Economy* (London: Secker and Warburg, 1969).

R. G. S. Brown, *The Administrative Process in Britain* (London: Methuen, 1970).

P. W. Buck, *Amateurs and Professionals in British Politics* (Chicago: University of Chicago Press, 1963).

D. E. Butler and Anthony King, *The British General Election of 1964* (London: Macmillan, 1965).

D. E. Butter and M. Pinto-Duchinsky. *The British General Election of 1970* (London: Macmillan, 1971).

R. Butt, *The Power of Parliament* (London: Constable, 1967).

B. Chapman, *British Government Observed* (London: Allen and Unwin, 1963).

D. N. Chester and N. Bowring, *Questions in Parliament* (Oxford: Clarendon, 1962).

D. N. Chester and F. M. G. Willson, *The Organisation of British Central Government* (London: Allen and Unwin, 1968).

Sir R. Clarke, *New Trends in Government* (London: HMSO, 1971).

B. Crick, *The Reform of Parliament* (London: Weidenfeld and Nicolson, 1964).

C. A. R. Crosland, *The Conservative Enemy* (London: Jonathan Cape, 1962).

R. S. H. Crossman, *Inside View* (London: Jonathan Cape, 1972).

H. Daalder, *Cabinet Reform in Britain, 1914–63* (Stanford: Stanford University Press, 1964).

H. E. Dale, *The Higher Civil Service in Great Britain* (London: Oxford University Press, 1941).

D. V. Donnison, *The Government of Housing* (Harmondsworth: Penguin, 1967).

H. Eckstein, *Pressure Group Politics* (Stanford: Stanford University Press, 1960).

Fair Deal at Work (London: CPC, 1968).

H. Fairlie, *The Life of Politics* (London: Methuen, 1968).

G. K. Fry, *Statesmen in Disguise* (London: Macmillan, 1969).

I. Gilmour, *The Body Politic* (London: Hutchinson, 1969).

W. L. Guttsman, *The British Political Elite* (London: MacGibbon and Kee, 1963).

Hansard Society, *Parliamentary Reform* (London: Cassell, 2nd ed, 1967).

D. Howell, *A New Style of Government* (London: CPC, 1970).

P. Jenkins, *The Battle of Downing Street* (London: Charles Knight, 1970).

R. Jenkins, *The Labour Case* (Harmondsworth: Penguin, 1959).

Sir W. Ivor Jennings, *Cabinet Government* (Cambridge: Cambridge University Press, 1961).

A. King (ed.), *The Prime Minister: A Reader* (London: Macmillan, 1969).

J. M. Lee, *Colonial Development and Good Government* (Oxford: Clarendon, 1967).

W. J. M. Mackenzie and J. W. Grove, *Central Administration in Britain* (London: Longmans, 1957).

John P. Mackintosh, *The British Cabinet* (London: Stevens, 1968).

John P. Mackintosh, *The Government and Politics of Britain* (London: Hutchinson, 1970).

G. Marshall and G. Moodie, *Some Problems of the Constitution* (London: Hutchinson, 1959).

H. Morrison, *Government and Parliament* (London: Oxford University Press, 1959).

M. Nicholson, *The System: The Misgovernment of Modern Britain* (London: Hodder and Stoughton, 1967).

A. Nutting, *No End of a Lesson* (London: Constable, 1967).

H. Parris, *Constitutional Bureaucracy* (London: Allen and Unwin, 1969).

Political and Economic Planning (PEP) *Advisory Committees in British Government* (London: Allen and Unwin, 1960).

PEP, *Renewal of British Government* (London: PEP, 1969).

J. Enoch Powell, *Medicine and Politics* (London: Pitman, 1966).

R. M. Punnett, *Front Bench Opposition* (London: Heinemann, 1973).

P. G. Richards, *Honourable Members* (London: Faber, 1959).

P. G. Richards, *Patronage in British Government* (London: Allen and Unwin, 1963).

J. J. Richardson, *The Policy Making Process* (London: Routledge and Kegan Paul, 1969).

J. H. Robertson, *Reform of British Central Government* (London: Chatto and Windus, 1971).

Richard Rose, *Class and Party: Britain as a Test Case* (Glasgow: Strathclyde University, 1968).

Richard Rose, *People in Politics* (London: Faber, 1970).

Richard Rose (ed.), *Policy Making in Britain* (London: Macmillan, 1969).

H. Roseveare, *The Treasury* (London: Allen Lane, 1969).

G. W. Ross, *The Nationalisation of Steel* (London: MacGibbon and Kee, 1965).

J. F. S. Ross, *Parliamentary Representation* (London: Eyre and Spottiswoode, 2nd ed, 1948).

A. Roth, *The Business Background of MPs* (London: Parliamentary Profile Services, undated).

P. Shore, *Entitled to Know* (London: MacGibbon and Kee, 1966).

C. H. Sisson, *The Spirit of British Administration* (London: Faber, 2nd ed, 1966).

K. B. Smellie, *A Hundred Years of English Government* (London: Duckworth, 1960).

C. P. Snow, *Science and Government* (London: Oxford University Press, 1961).

William P. Snyder, *The Politics of British Defence Policy* (Columbus: Ohio State University Press, 1964).

H. Thomas (ed.), *The Establishment* (London: Blond, 1959).

D. Vital, *The Making of British Foreign Policy* (London: Allen and Unwin, 1968).

P. Gordon Walker, *The Cabinet* (London: Jonathan Cape, 1970).

S. A. Walkland, *The Legislative Process in Great Britain* (London: Allen and Unwin, 1968).

D. C. Watt, *Personalities and Policies: Studies in the Formulation of British Foreign Policy in the Twentieth Century* (London: Longmans, 1965).

G. Williams and Bruce Reed, *Denis Healey and the Policies of Power* (London: Sidgwick and Jackson, 1971).

H. V. Wiseman, *Parliament and the Executive* (London: Routledge and Kegan Paul, 1966).

M. Wright, *Treasury Control of the Civil Service, 1854–74* (Oxford: Clarendon Press, 1969).

(b) *Articles:*

C. Adamson, 'The Role of the Industrial Adviser', *Public Administration*, 46 (Summer 1968), 185–91.

N. Annan, 'The Reform of Higher Education', *Political Quarterly*, 38.3 (July–September 1967), 234–52.

Sir William Armstrong, 'The Tasks of the Civil Service', *Public Administration*, 47.1 (Spring 1969), 1–11.

J. Bonnor, 'The Four Labour Cabinets', *Sociological Review*, 6.1 (1958), 37–48.

Sir E. Boyle *et al.*, 'Who Are the Policy Makers?', *Public Administration*, 43 (1965) 251–87.

S. Brittan, 'The Irregulars', *Crossbow* (October-December 1966).

C. Brocklebank-Fowler, 'The Selection of Candidates', *Crossbow* (July-September 1968).

A. H. Brown, 'Prime Ministerial Power', Part I, *Public Law* (Spring 1968), 28-52, Part II (Summer 1968), 96-118.

Sir A. Cairncross, 'The Work of an Economic Adviser', *Public Administration*, 47.1 (Spring, 1968) 1-12.

D. N. Chester, 'Double-Banking and Deputy Ministers', *New Society* 11 June, 1964).

Lewis Chester, 'What's a Manifesto Worth?', *The Sunday Times* (24 May, 1970).

'The Civil Service', *The Sunday Times* (1 October, 1967). Articles by seven retired Permanent Secretaries.

C. A. R. Crosland, 'Social Objectives for the 1970s', *The Times*, (25 September, 1970).

Sir C. Cunningham, 'Policy and Practice', *Public Administration*, 41 (1963), 229-38.

N. Deakin, 'Racial Integration and Whitehall: A Plea for Reorganisation', *Political Quarterly*, 39.4 (October-December 1968), 415-26.

Sir M. Dean, 'The Fulton Report: Accountable Management in the Civil Service', *Public Administration* (March 1969), 49-63.

S. E. Finer, 'The Individual Responsibility of Ministers', *Public Administration*, 34 (Winter 1956), 277-96.

G. K. Fry, 'Policy-Planning Units in British Central Government Departments', *Public Administration*, 50.2 (Summer 1972), 139-56.

L. Gunn, 'Ministers and Civil Servants: Changes in Whitehall', *Public Administration* (Australia, March 1967), 78-94.

A. H. Hanson, 'Ministers and Boards', *Public Administration*, 47.1 (March 1969), 65-74.

John S. Harris and T. V. Garcia, 'The Permanent Secretaries: Britain's Top Administrators', *Public Administration Review*, 26.1 (March 1966), 31-44.

D. J. Heasman, 'The Ministerial Hierarchy', *Parliamentary Affairs*, 15, (1961-2), 307-30.

D. J. Heasman, 'The Prime Minister and the Cabinet' in W. J. Stanciewicz (ed.), *Crisis in British Government* (London: Collier-Macmillan, 1967), 161-82.

H. Helco, 'Pension Politics', *New Society* (23 September, 1971).

D. Houghton, 'The Labour Backbencher', *Political Quarterly*, 32 (1969), 454-63.

R. Jenkins, 'In and Out of Power', *The Observer* (20 June, 1971).

R. Jenkins, 'The Reality of Political Power', *The Sunday Times* (17 January 1971).

D. Kavanagh, 'The Deferential English: A Comparative Critique', *Government and Opposition*, 6.3 (Summer 1971), 333-60.

A. King, 'Britain's Ministerial Turnover', *New Society* (18 August, 1966).

A. King, 'The Conservative Party and Policy', *New Society* (20 July, 1972).

A. King, 'Who Cares about Policy?', *Spectator* (10 January, 1970).

Harold J. Laski, 'The Personnel of the English Cabinet', *American Political Science Review*, 22.1 (February 1928), 12-31.

'Lobbyman, Richard Sharples, OBE, MC, MP', *Crossbow* (July-September 1968).

R. T. McKenzie and A. Silver, *Angels in Marble* (London: Heinemann, 1965).

E. Marples, 'A Dog's Life at the Ministry', in Richard Rose (ed.), *Policy Making in Britain* (London: Macmillan, 1969) pp. 128-31.

R. S. Milne, 'The Junior Minister', *Journal of Politics*, 12.3 (1950), 437-50.

D. Munby, 'An Assessment of Priorities in Public Expenditure', *Political Quarterly* (1968), 375-83.

A. Norman, 'Candidates from Industry', *Crossbow* (October-December 1968).

D. E. Regan, 'The Expert and the Administrator: Recent Changes in the Ministry of Transport', *Public Administration*, 44.2 (Summer 1966), 149-67.

Richard Rose, 'The Making of Cabinet Ministers', *British Journal of Political Science*, 1.4 (October 1971), 393-414.

Richard Rose, 'The Variability of Party Government', *Political Studies*, 17.4 (December 1969), 413-51.

Colin Seymour-Ure 'The Disintegration of the Cabinet', *Parliamentary Affairs*, 24.3 (1971), 196-207.

B. C. Smith and J. C. Stanyer, 'Administrative Developments in 1967: A Survey', *Public Administration*, 46.3 (1960), 239-80. Similar surveys have been undertaken by Smith and Stanyer for years subsequent to 1967 and these are published annually in *Public Administration*.

Sir Geoffrey Vickers, 'Planning and Public Policy', *Political Quarterly*, 38.3 (July-September 1967), 253-65.

F. M. G. Willson, 'The Routes of Entry of New Members of the British Cabinet, 1868-1958', *Political Studies*, 7.3 (1959), 222-37.

5. *Political leadership in industrialised societies (excluding Britain)*

James D. Barber, *The Lawmakers* (New Haven: Yale University Press, 1965).

James D. Barber (ed.), *Political Leadership in American Government* (Boston: Little, Brown, 1964).

James D. Barber, *Power in Committees* (Chicago: Rand, McNally, 1966)

M. Bernstein, *The Job of the Federal Executive* (Washington: Brookings Institution, 1958).

Joseph B. Board, *The Government and Politics of Sweden* (Boston: Houghton, Mifflin, 1970).

E. Browne and M. N. Franklin, 'Perquisites of Government', *American Political Science Review* (1973, forthcoming).

Z. Brzezinski and S. P. Huntingdon, *Political Power USA/USSR* (New York: Viking Press, 1963).

B. Chapman, *The Profession of Government* (London: Allen and Unwin, 1959).

R. McGregor Dawson, 'Cabinet – Position and Personnel' in O. Kruhlak, R. Schultz and S. Pobihushchy, (eds.), *The Canadian Political Process* (Toronto: Holt, Rinehart and Winston, 1970), pp. 345-66.

Alfred Diamant, 'Tradition and Innovation in French Administration', *Comparative Political Studies*, 1.2 (July 1968), 251-74.

M. Dogan and M. Scheffer-Van Der Veen, 'Le Personnel Ministeriel Hollandais', *Annee Sociologique* (1957, 3rd ser.), 95-125.

A. Dutheillet De Lamothe, 'Ministerial Cabinets in France', *Public Administration*, 43 (1965), 365-81.

Lewis J. Edinger (ed.), *Political Leadership in Industrialised Societies* (New York: John Wiley, 1967).

Lewis J. Edinger and Donald Searing, 'Social Background in Elite Analysis: A Methodological Inquiry', *American Political Science Review*, 61.2 (June 1967), 428-45.

S. Encel, *Cabinet Government in Australia* (London: Cambridge University Press, 1962).

S. Encel, *Equality and Authority: A Study of Class, Status and Power in Australia* (London: Tavistock Publications, 1970).

R. Eyestone, *The Threads of Public Policy: A Study in Policy Leadership* (New York: Bobbs-Merrill, 1971).

Richard F. Fenno, *The Power of the Purse: Appropriations Politics in Congress* (Boston: Little, Brown, 1966).

Richard F. Fenno, *The President's Cabinet* (Cambridge, Mass: Harvard University Press, 1959).

Lars Foyer, 'The Social Sciences in Royal Commission Studies in Sweden', *Scandinavian Political Studies* (1969), 183-203.

F. W. Frey, *The Turkish Political Elite* (Cambridge: MIT Press, 1965).

James Jupp, *Australian Party Politics* (London: Cambridge University Press, 1964).

N. Leites, *On the Game of Politics in France* (Stanford: Stanford University Press, 1959).

A. Lijphart, *The Politics of Accommodation: Pluralism and Democracy in the Netherlands* (Berkeley: University of California Press, 1968).

G. Loewenberg, *Parliament in the German Political System* (Ithaca: Cornell University Press, 1967).

John F. Manley, 'Wilbur D. Mills: A Study in Congressional Influence', *American Political Science Review*, 63.2 (June 1969), 442-64.

Dean E. Mann and Jameson W. Doig, *The Assistant Secretaries: Problems and Processes of Appointment* (Washington: Brookings Institution, 1965).

Dwaine Marvick, (ed.), *Political Decision Makers* (New York: Free Press, 1961).

Donald R. Matthews, *The Social Background of Political Decision Makers* (New York: Random House, 1954).

Hans Meijer,' Bureaucracy and Policy Formulation in Sweden', *Scandinavian Political Studies* (1969), 103-16.

Richard E. Neustadt, *Presidential Power* (New York: John Wiley, 1960).

Richard E. Neustadt, 'White House and Whitehall', *Public Interest*, II (1966).

John A. Porter, *The Vertical Mosaic: An Analysis of Social Class and Power in Canada* (Toronto: University of Toronto Press, 1965).

D. W. Rawson, *Labor in Vain?* (London: Longmans, 1966).

F. F. Ridley (ed.), *Specialists and Generalists* (London: Allen and Unwin, 1968).

F. F. Ridley and J. Blondel, *Public Administration in France* (London: Routledge and Kegan Paul, 1964).

G. Sartori, *Il Parliamento Italiano 1946-63* (Naples: Edizioni Scientifiche Italiane, 1963).

Joseph A. Schlesinger, *Ambition and Politics* (Chicago: Rand, McNally, 1966).

A. Shonfield, *Modern Capitalism* (London: Oxford University Press, 1965).

H. Gordon Skilling, *The Governments of Communist East Europe* (New York: Crowell, 1966).

David T. Stanley, Dean E. Mann and Jameson W. Doig, *Men Who Govern* (Washington: Brookings Institution, 1967).

Graham Tayar (ed.), *Personality and Power: Studies in Political Advancement* (London: BBC publications, 1971).

Kenneth N. Waltz, *Foreign Policy and Democratic Politics* (Boston: Little, Brown, 1967).

K. West, *Power in the Liberal Party* (Melbourne: F. W. Cheshire, 1966).

A. Wildavsky (ed.), *The Presidency* (Boston: Little, Brown, 1969).

Index of Names

THE
ICE
IN
THE
BEDROOM

1.

Feeding his rabbits in the garden of his residence, The Nook, his humane practice at the start of each new day, Mr. Cornelius, the house agent of Valley Fields, seemed to sense a presence. He had the feeling that he was not alone. Nor was he. A lissome form had draped itself over the fence which divided his domain from that of Peacehaven next door, its lips attached to a long cigarette holder.

"Ah, Mr. Widgeon," he said. "Good morning."

With its trim gardens and tree-shaded roads, Valley Fields, that delectable suburb to the southeast of London, always presents a pleasing spectacle on a fine day in June, and each of these two householders in his individual way contributed his mite to the glamour of the local scene.

Mr. Cornelius had a long white beard which gave him something of the dignity of a Druid priest, and the young man he had addressed as Widgeon might have stepped straight out of the advertisement columns of one of the glossier and more expensive magazines. The face as clean-cut as that of any Adonis depicted wearing somebody's summer suitings for the discriminating man, the shoes just right, the socks just right, the shirt and Drones Club tie just right. Criticisms had been made from time to time of Freddie Widgeon's intelligence, notably by his uncle Lord Blicester and by Mr. Shoesmith, the solicitor, in whose office he was employed, but nobody—not even Oofy Prosser of the Drones, whom he often annoyed a good deal—had ever been able to find anything to cavil at in his outer crust.

"Lovely weather," said Mr. Cornelius.

"Just like mother makes," assented Freddie, as sunny to all appearances as the skies above. "Cigarette?"

"No, thank you. I do not smoke."

"What, never?"

"I gave it up many years ago. Doctors say it is injurious to the health."

"Doctors are asses. They don't know a good thing when they see one. How *do* you pass the long evenings?"

"I work on my history of Valley Fields."

"You're writing a history of Valley Fields?"

"I have been engaged on it for a considerable time. A labor of love."

"You like Valley Fields?"

"I love it, Mr. Widgeon. I was born in Valley Fields, I went to school in Valley Fields, I have lived all my life in Valley Fields, and I shall end my days here. I make a modest competence—"

"Mine's a stinker."

"—and I am content with it. I have my house, my garden, my wife, my flowers, my rabbits. I ask nothing more."

Freddie chafed a little. His views on suburban life differed radically from those the other had expressed, and this enthusiasm jarred on him.

"Yes, that's all right for you," he said. "You're a happy carefree house agent. I'm a wage slave in a solicitor's firm, as near to being an office boy as makes no matter. Ever see a caged eagle?"

Oddly enough, Mr. Cornelius had not. He did not get around much.

"Me," said Freddie, tapping his chest. He frowned. He was thinking of the dastardly conduct of his uncle Lord Blicester, who, on the shallow pretext that a young man ought to be earning his living and making something of himself, had stopped his allowance and shoved him into the beastly legal zoo over which Mr. Shoesmith presided. He thrust the distasteful subject from his mind and turned to pleasanter topics.

"I see you're lushing up the dumb chums."

"Always at this hour."

"What's on the menu?"

"The little fellows get their lettuce."

"They couldn't do better. Rich in vitamins and puts hair on the chest." He studied the breakfasters in silence for a moment. "Ever notice how a rabbit's nose sort of twitches? I know a girl whose nose does that when she gets excited."

"A resident of Valley Fields?" said Mr. Cornelius, searching in his mind for nose-twitchers of the suburb's younger set.

"No, she lives down in Sussex at a place called Loose Chippings."

"Ah," said Mr. Cornelius, with the gentle pity he always felt for people who did not live in Valley Fields.

"She's got a job there. She's secretary to a woman called Yorke, who writes books and things."

Mr. Cornelius started as if, mistaking him for a leaf of lettuce, one of the rabbits had bitten him.

"Not Leila Yorke the novelist?"

"That's the one. Ever sample her stuff?"

A devout look had come into the house agent's face. His beard waggled emotionally.

"She is my favorite author. I read and reread every word she writes."

"Sooner you than me. I dipped into one of her products once, misled by the title into supposing it to be a spine-freezer, and gave up the unequal struggle in the middle of Chapter Three. Slush of the worst description it seemed to me."

"Oh, Mr. Widgeon, no!"

"You don't see eye to eye?"

"I certainly do not. To me Leila Yorke plumbs the depths of human nature and lays bare the heart of woman as if with a scalpel."

"What a beastly idea! It sounds like let-me-tell-you-about-my-operation. Well, have it your own way. If hers are the sort of books you like to curl up with, go to it and best of luck. What were we talking about before we got off on to the Yorke subject? Oh yes, about me being a caged eagle. That's what I am, Cornelius, and I don't like it. The role revolts me. I want to slide out of it. Shall I tell you how a caged eagle slides out of being a caged eagle?"

"Do, Mr. Widgeon."

"It gets hold of a bit of money, and that's what I'm going to do. I want the stuff quick and plenty of it. I want people to nudge each other in the street as I pass and whisper, 'See that fellow in the fur coat? Widgeon, the millionaire.' I want to wear bank notes next to my skin winter and summer, ten-pound ones in the chilly months, changing to fivers as the weather gets warmer."

It is always difficult to be certain when a man as densely bearded as Mr. Cornelius is pursing his lips, but something of the sort seemed to be going on inside the undergrowth that masked him from the world. It was plain that he thought these aspirations sordid and distasteful.

There was an unspoken Tut-tut in his voice as he said, "But does money bring happiness, Mr. Widgeon?"

"I'll say!"

"The rich have their troubles."

"Name three."

"I was thinking of my brother Charles."

"Is he rich?"

"Extremely. He left England under a cloud, I regret to say, many years ago, and went to America, where he has done well. In the last letter I received from him he said he had an apartment on Park Avenue, which I gather is a very respectable quarter of New York, a house on Long Island, another in Florida, a private airplane and a yacht. I have always felt sorry for Charles."

"Why's that?"

"He does not live in Valley Fields," said Mr. Cornelius simply. He brooded for a moment on his brother's hard lot. "No," he continued, "the wealthy are not to be envied. Life must be a constant anxiety for them. Look at your friend Mr. Prosser, of whom you were speaking to me the other day."

This puzzled Freddie.

"Old Oofy? What's he got to worry him? Apart, of course, from being married to Shoesmith's daughter and having to call Shoesmith 'Daddy'?"

It seemed to Mr. Cornelius that his young friend must

have a very short memory. It was only the day before yesterday that they had been discussing the tragedy which had befallen the Prosser home.

"You told me that Mrs. Prosser had been robbed of jewelry worth many thousands of pounds."

Freddie's face cleared.

"Oh, that? Yes, someone got away with her bit of ice all right. The maid, they think it must have been, because when the alarm was raised and the cops charged in, they found she had gone without a cry. But bless your kind old heart, Cornelius, Oofy doesn't care. It happened more than a month ago, and the last time I saw him he was as blithe as a bird. He'd got the insurance money."

"Nevertheless, occurrences of that nature are very unpleasant, and they happen only to the rich."

It was Freddie's opinion that the house agent was talking through his hat. He did not say so, for the other's white hair protected him, but his manner, as he spoke, was very firm.

"Listen, my dear old lettuce-distributor," he said, "I see what you mean, and your reasoning is specious, if that's the word, but I still stick to it that what you need in this world is cash, and that is why you may have noticed that I've been looking a bit more cheerful these last days. The luck of the Widgeons has turned, and affluence stares me in the eyeball."

"Indeed?"

"I assure you. For the first time in years Frederick Fotheringay Widgeon is sitting on top of the world with a rainbow round his shoulder. You could put it in a nutshell by saying that Moab is my washpot and over wherever-it-was will I cast my shoe, as the fellow said, though what casting shoes has got to do with it is more than I can tell you. Do you know a chap called Thomas G. Molloy? American

6

bloke. Lives at Castlewood next door to me on the other side."

"Yes, I am acquainted with Mr. Molloy. I saw him only yesterday, when he came to my office to give me the keys."

Freddie could make nothing of this.

"What did he want to give you keys for? Your birthday or something?"

"The keys of the house. He has left Castlewood."

"What?"

"Yes, Castlewood is vacant once more. But I anticipate very little difficulty in disposing of it," said Mr. Cornelius (nearly adding from force of habit, "A most desirable property, tastefully furnished throughout and standing in parklike grounds extending to upwards of a quarter of an acre"). "There is a great demand for that type of house."

Freddie was still perplexed. Saddened, too, for in his vanished neighbor he felt he had lost a friend. Thomas G. Molloy's rich personality had made a strong appeal to him.

"But I thought Molloy owned Castlewood."

"Oh no, he merely occupied it on a short lease. These three houses—Castlewood, Peacehaven and The Nook—are the property of a Mr. Keggs, who has lived at Castlewood for many years. It was sublet to Mr. Molloy when Mr. Keggs went off on one of those round-the-world cruises. He came into a great deal of money recently and felt he could afford the trip. Though why anyone living in Valley Fields should want to leave it and go gadding about, I cannot imagine. But you were speaking of Mr. Molloy. Why did you mention him?"

"Because it is he who has brought these roses to my cheeks. Entirely owing to that bighearted philanthropist, I shall very shortly be in a position to strike off the shackles of Shoesmith, Shoesmith, Shoesmith and Shoesmith. I thought I was in for a life sentence in the Shoesmith snake

7

pit, and the prospect appalled me. And then Molloy came along. But I'm getting ahead of my story. All back to Chapter One, when I got that letter from Boddington. Pal of mine in Kenya," Freddie explained. "Runs a coffee ranch or whatever you call it out there. He wrote to me and asked if I'd like to take a small interest in it and come and join the gang. Well, of course I was all for it. Nothing could be more up my street. Are you familiar with the expression 'the great open spaces'?"

Mr. Cornelius said he was. Leila Yorke's heroes, he said, frequently made for the great open spaces when a misunderstanding had caused a rift between them and the girls they loved.

"Those are what I've always yearned for, and I understand the spaces in Kenya are about as open as they come. I don't quite know how you set about growing coffee, but one soon picks these things up. I am convinced that, given a spade and a watering can and shown the way to the bushes, it will not be long before I electrify the industry, raising a sensational bean. Kenya ho! is the slogan. That's where you get the rich, full life."

"Kenya is a long way off."

"Part of its charm."

"I would not care to go so far from Valley Fields myself."

"The farther the better, in my opinion. I can take Valley Fields or leave it alone."

These words, bordering to his mind closely on blasphemy, caused Mr. Cornelius to wince. He turned away and offered a portion of lettuce to the third rabbit on the right in rather a marked manner.

"So you are accepting your friend's offer?" he said, when he had recovered himself.

"If he'll hold it open for a while. Everything turns on

that. You see, as always when these good things come your way, there's a catch. I have to chip in with three thousand quid as a sort of entrance fee, and I don't mind telling you that when I read that passage in the Boddington communiqué, I reeled and might have fallen, had I not been sitting down at the time. Because I don't need to tell you, Cornelius, that three thousand quid is heavy sugar."

"You mean that your funds were insufficient to meet this condition?"

"Very far short of sweetening the kitty. All I had in the world was a measly thousand, left me by a godmother."

"Unfortunate."

"Most. I asked an uncle of mine for a temporary loan of the sum I needed, and all he said was 'What, what, what? Absurd. Preposterous. Couldn't think of it,' which, as you will readily agree, left no avenue open for a peaceful settlement. Oofy Prosser, too, declined to be my banker, as did my banker, and I was just about to write the whole thing off as a washout, when suddenly there was a fanfare of angel trumpets and Molloy descended from heaven, the sun shining on his wings. We got talking, I revealed my predicament, and he waved his magic wand and solved all my problems. In return for my thousand quid he let me have some very valuable oil stock which he happened to have in his possession."

"Good gracious!"

"I put it even more strongly."

"What oil stock?"

"Silver River it's called, and pretty soon England will be ringing with its name. He says it's going up and up and up, the sky the only limit."

"But was it not a little rash to invest all your capital in a speculative concern?"

"Good heavens, I leaped at the chance like a jumping

bean. And it isn't speculative. Molloy stressed that. It's absolutely gilt-edged. He assures me I shall be able to sell my holdings for at least ten thousand in less than a month."

"Strange that he should have parted with anything so valuable."

"He explained that. He said he liked my face. He said I reminded him of a nephew of his on whom he had always looked as a son, who handed in his dinner pail some years ago. Double pneumonia. Very sad."

"Oh, dear!"

"Why do you say 'Oh, dear!'?"

But Mr. Cornelius's reasons for uttering this observation were not divulged, for even as he spoke Freddie had happened to glance at his wrist watch, and what he saw there shook him from stem to stern.

"Good Lord, is that the time?" he gasped. "I'll miss that ruddy train again!"

He sped off, and Mr. Cornelius looked after him with a thoughtful eye. If youth but knew, he seemed to be saying to himself. He had not been favorably impressed by Thomas G. Molloy, late of Castlewood, who, possibly because he, Mr. Cornelius, reminded him, Mr. Molloy, of a goat he had been fond of as a child, had tried to sell him, too, a block of stock in this same Silver River Oil and Refinery Corporation.

With a sigh he picked up a leaf of lettuce and went on feeding his rabbits.

2.

All season-ticket holders who live in the suburbs run like the wind, and Freddie had long established himself as one of Valley Fields's most notable performers on the flat, but today, though he clipped a matter of three seconds off his previous record for the Peacehaven-to-station course, he had given the 8:45 too long a start and had to wait for the 9:06. It was consequently with some trepidation that he entered the Shoesmith premises, a trepidation which the cold gray eye of Mr. Jervis, the head clerk, did nothing to allay. He had no need to look into a crystal ball to predict that there might be a distressing interview with Mr. Shoesmith in the near future. From their initial meeting and from meetings that had taken place subsequently he had been able to gather that the big shot was a stickler for punctuality on the part of the office force.

But it was not this thought that was clouding his brow as he sat at the desk at which he gave his daily impersonation of a caged eagle. He did not enjoy those chats with Mr. Shoesmith, whose forte was dry sarcasm, very wounding to the feelings, but custom had inured him to them and he was able now to take them with a philosophical fortitude. The reason melancholy marked him for its own was that he was thinking of Sally Foster.

If Mr. Cornelius had not been so intent at the moment on seeing to it that the personnel of his hutch got their proper supply of vitamins, he might have observed that at the mention of the girl whose nose twitched like a rabbit's a quick spasm of pain had flitted across the young man's face. It had been only a passing twinge, gone almost immediately, for the Widgeons could wear the mask, but it had been there. He had rashly allowed himself to be reminded of Sally Foster, and whenever that happened it was as though he had bitten on a sensitive tooth.

There had been a time, and not so long ago, when he and Sally had been closer than the paper on the wall—everything as smooth as dammit, each thinking the other the biggest thing since sliced bread and not a cloud on the horizon. And then, just because she had found him kissing that dumb brick of a Bunting girl at that cocktail party—the merest civil gesture, as he had tried to explain, due entirely to the fact that he had run out of conversation and felt that he had to do something to keep things going—she had blown a gasket and forbidden the banns. Take back your mink, take back your pearls, she would no doubt have said, if his finances had ever run to giving her mink and pearls. What she had actually returned to him by district messenger boy had been a bundle of letters, half a bottle of Arpege and five signed photographs.

Yes, he had lost her. And—which made it all the more bitter—here he was in London, chained to the spot without a chance of getting away till his annual holiday in November, while she was down in Sussex at Claines Hall, Loose Chippings. Not an earthly, in short, of being able to get to her and do a little quick talking, a thing he knew himself to be good at, and persuading her to forget and forgive. It is not too much to say that at the moment when Elsa Bingley, Mr. Shoesmith's secretary, touched him on the shoulder, bringing him out of the wreck of his hopes and dreams with a jerk, Frederick Widgeon was plumbing the depths.

"His nibs wants to see you, Freddie," said Elsa Bingley, and he nodded a somber nod. He had rather thought that this might happen.

In the inner lair where he lurked during business hours, Mr. Shoesmith was talking to his daughter Mrs. Myrtle Prosser, who had looked in for a chat as she did sometimes—too often, in Mr. Shoesmith's opinion, for he disliked having to give up his valuable time to someone to whom he could not send in a bill. At the mention of Freddie's name Myrtle showed a mild interest.

"Widgeon?" she said. "Is that Freddie Widgeon?"

"I believe his name is Frederick. You know him?"

"He's a sort of friend of Alexander's. He comes to dinner sometimes when we need an extra man. I didn't know he worked here."

"It is a point on which I am somewhat doubtful myself," said Mr. Shoesmith. "Much depends on what interpretation you place on the word *work*. To oblige his uncle Lord Blicester, whose affairs have been in my hands for many years, I took him into my employment and he arrives in the morning and leaves in the evening, but apart from a certain rudimentary skill in watching the clock, probably instinctive, I would describe him as essentially a lily of the field. Ah, Mr. Widgeon."

The lily of the field of whom he was speaking had entered, and, seeing Myrtle, had swayed a little on his stem. This daughter of Mr. Shoesmith who had married Alexander ("Oofy") Prosser—a thing not many girls would have cared to do—was a young woman of considerable but extremely severe beauty. She did not resemble her father, who looked like a cassowary, but suggested rather one of those engravings of the mistresses of Bourbon kings which make one feel that the monarchs who selected them must have been men of iron, impervious to fear, or else short-sighted. She always scared Freddie to the marrow. With most of the other sex he was on easy terms—too easy was the view of his late fiancée—but the moon of Oofy Prosser's delight never failed to give him an uncomfortable feeling in the pit of the stomach and the illusion that his hands and feet had swelled unpleasantly.

"Oh, hullo, Mrs. Oofy," he said, recovering his equilibrium. "Good morning."

"Good morning."

"Going strong?"

"I am quite well, thank you."

"Oofy going strong?"

"Alexander, too, is quite well."

"Fine. He was telling me about those bits and pieces of yours."

"I beg your pardon?"

"Your jewelry. Getting stolen and all that."

"Oh, yes."

"Bad show."

"Very."

"But you've got the insurance money, he tells me."

"Yes."

"Good show."

Mr. Shoesmith broke in on these intellectual exchanges. He was not a man who suffered Freddie Widgeon gladly, considering him what in an earlier age would have been called a popinjay. Their souls were not attuned, as Freddie would have been the first to concede, though with the proviso that it was very doubtful if his employer had a soul. He had been serving under his banner for some six months now, and not a sign of one so far.

"I wonder if you could spare me your attention for a moment, Mr. Widgeon."

By standing on one leg and allowing his lower jaw to droop Freddie indicated that he would be delighted to do so.

"You have no objection to me talking shop for a little while?"

None whatever, Freddie indicated by standing on the other leg.

"Mr. Jervis tells me you were late again this morning."

"Er—yes."

"This frequently happens."

"Yes, sir. These suburban trains, you know."

"Well, no doubt we should consider ourselves fortunate that we are given at least some of your time, but I must ask you in future to try to synchronize your arrival at the office with that of the rest of the staff. We aim as far as possible at the communal dead heat."

"Yes, sir."

"So do your best, Mr. Widgeon, even if it means taking an earlier suburban train."

"Yes, sir."

"Or two suburban trains. You see, when you fail to appear, we become nervous and jumpy. Some accident must have occurred, we whisper to each other, and these gruesome speculations, so bad for office morale, continue until some clear thinker like Mr. Jervis points out that it would be a far greater accident if you were ever on time. However, that was not primarily what I wished to see you about. If you can tear yourself away from your desk this afternoon, I should like to engage your services for a confidential mission."

"Yes, sir."

"I have here some documents requiring the signature of Miss Leila Yorke, whose name will probably be familiar to you. Take them to her, if you will be kind enough, after lunch. Her address is Claines Hall, Loose Chippings, Sussex. You book your ticket at Victoria and alight at Loose Chippings station. The Hall is within an easy walk. Have I made myself clear?"

"Yes, sir."

"Splendid," said Mr. Shoesmith. "Thank you, Mr. Widgeon, that is all."

Eminent solicitors very seldom pay much attention to the muscular twitchings of the minor members of their staff, and Mr. Shoesmith, issuing these instructions, did not observe that at the mention of Claines Hall, Loose Chippings, Sussex, his young subordinate had started; but he had, and violently. His master's voice had affected him like a powerful electric shock, causing the eyeballs to rotate and everything for an instant to go black. It was only by the exercise of the greatest care that he was able to remove himself from the presence without tripping over his feet, so profoundly had the thought that he was going to see Sally again stirred him. For the rest of the morning and all through his frugal lunch at the Drones he brooded tensely on the situation which had arisen, running, it would not be too much to say, the gamut of the emotions.

At the outset he had been all joy and effervescence, feeling that out of a blue sky Fate had handed him the most stupendous bit of goose and that all was for the best in this best of all possible worlds, but as the time went by doubts began to creep in. Was this, he found himself asking himself, a good show or a bad show? Would seeing Sally alleviate that yearning feeling which so often darkened his days, or—let's face it—would he merely be twisting the knife in the wound, as the expression was? The question was a very moot one, and it is not surprising that those of his clubmates who threw lumps of sugar at him during the meal commented on his lack of sparkle and responsiveness.

On the whole, though it was a close thing, he was inclined to think that the show's goodness outweighed its badness. Agony, of course, to see her face to face and think of what might have been, but on the other hand there was always the chance that Time the great healer might have been doing its stuff, softening her heart and causing better counsels to prevail.

His mood, in consequence, as he made his way to Victoria and bought his ticket, was on the whole optimistic. Many a girl, he told himself, who in the heat of the moment has handed her loved one the pink slip, finds after thinking it over in the privacy of her chamber in the course of sleepless nights that what she supposed to be a sound, rational move was in reality the floater of a lifetime. Remorse, in short, supervenes, and when the rejected one suddenly pops up out of a trap before her, her eyes widen, her nose twitches, her lips part, she cries "Oh, Freddie darling!" and flings herself into his arms, and all is gas and gaiters again.

The day was Friday, never a good day for traveling, and

the congestion in all parts of the station had extended itself to the train for Loose Chippings. It bulged at every seam with human sardines. Faced with a choice between compartments filled with outsize adults and those where the adults were more streamlined but were accompanied by children, he chose one of the former. Only standing room remained in the little Black Hole of Calcutta which he had selected, so he stood, and from this elevation was able to see his fellow travelers steadily and see them whole.

There were eight of them, three men who looked like farmers, three women who looked like farmers' wives, a man in black who might have been an undertaker in a modest line of business, and over in the far corner a small, trim girl who was reading a magazine. She immediately arrested Freddie's attention. There was something about her that reminded him of Sally. Extraordinarily like Sally she was, from what he could see of her, and the next moment he was able to understand why there was such a resemblance.

It was Sally. She looked up from her magazine as the train started, and her eyes met his.

They were, he noted, as blue as ever, and the nose, the one that twitched like a rabbit's, still tilted slightly at the tip. The mouth was as of yore a little wide. Of the teeth he could not judge, for she was not smiling, but what he could see of her hair remained that attractive copper color he had always admired so much. Her face, in short, taking it by and large, was exactly as he remembered it from, it sometimes seemed to him, a previous existence, and at the sight of it he was conscious of an elation so pronounced that if the three farmers, the three farmers' wives and the undertaker had not been present, he would have snorted like the warhorse which, we are told, though it seems odd, used to say "Ha, ha!" among the trumpets.

3.

"Loose Chippings," chanted the porter as the train sauntered into the little country station, and Sally pushed her way through the sea of legs between her and the door and stepped down onto the platform.

She was furious, and, she considered, justly. At the cost of much mental distress she had cast this man out of her life because prudence told her he was irresponsible and not to be trusted, and it was monstrous that he should come sneaking back into it like this, reminding her that she still loved him and reviving all the old emotions which she had hoped she had killed long ago.

She fortified herself for the coming encounter by the simple process of thinking of that fatal cocktail party when the scales had fallen from her eyes and she had seen him for what he was.

She had been warned. There had been a group of young men near the door at that cocktail party, and as she had been passing them she had heard one of them utter these frightful words: "I suppose if all the girls Freddie Widgeon has been in love with were placed end to end—not that one could do it, of course—they would reach from Piccadilly Circus to Hyde Park Corner. Further than that, probably, because some of them were pretty tall."

And it was as she had been passing through the door, not wishing to sully her ears any longer, that she had come upon the Widgeon-Bunting combination linked in a close embrace on the top landing.

The recollection made her strong again. She looked at him as he stood beaming by the penny-in-the-slot machine, and an imperious desire swept over her to wipe that silly smile off his face.

"Freddie," she said, speaking from between clenched teeth, "go home!"

"Eh?"

"I told you I never wanted to see you again. Didn't you understand?"

"Well, yes, I more or less grasped that."

"Then why have you followed me here?"

Freddie stiffened. He ceased to beam. It pained him to find that he had overestimated the potentialities of Time the great healer and that the platform of Loose Chippings station was not to be the scene of a tender reconciliation, but righteous wrath overcame pain. He was deeply offended at being accused for once in his life of something of which he was not guilty. The apologetic lover became the man of ice, and he, too, spoke from between clenched teeth.

"Who's followed who where?" he said haughtily. "I'm here on business."

"*You?*"

"Yes, me. I've come to see Miss Leila Yorke. I understand she hangs out at a joint called Claines Hall. Perhaps you would be good enough to direct me there."

"I'll take you there."

"You won't object to being seen in public with one of our leading underworld characters?"

"There's no need to be so pompous."

"Yes, there is. Every need. I feel pompous. Followed you here, forsooth! You could have knocked me down with a banana skin when I saw you on that train. What were you doing in London, anyway?"

"I had to see Miss Yorke's agent about something."

"Oh, was that it? Do you often get up to London?"

"Very seldom."

"You're lucky. Lousy place. Ruddy sink of a place. No good to man or beast. Not a soul in it except blighters with brief cases and blisters in bowler hats."

"What's happened to the girls? Have they all emigrated?"

"Girls! They mean nothing in my life."

"Says you!"

"Yes, says me. Don't you believe me?"

"No, I don't. You're like the leopard."

"I'm not in the least like a leopard. What particular leopard had you in mind?"

"The one that couldn't change its spots."

"I call that a most distasteful crack."

"I'm sorry. Shall we be starting for the Hall?"

"Just as you like."

They came out into the High Street of Loose Chippings. The town's "pop," as the guidebook curtly terms it, is

4,916, and at perhaps two hundred and four of these Freddie glared bleakly as they passed on their way. He would have glared with equal bleakness at the other four thousand seven hundred and twelve, had they been there, for he was in sullen mood. Here he was, with Sally at his side, and for all the good it was doing him she might have been miles away. Aloof, that was the word he was groping for. She was distant and aloof. Not a trace of the old Sally who in happier days had been such a stupendously good egg. For all the kick she appeared to be getting out of his society, she might have been walking with an elderly uncle. Since entering the High Street she had not spoken except to direct his attention to the statue erected in the Market square to the memory of the late Anthony Briggs, J. P., for many years parliamentary representative for the local division, and if ever in Freddie's jaundiced opinion there was a ghastly statue of a potbellied baggy-trousered Gawd-help-us, this statue was that statue.

Conversation was still flagging when after leaving Loose Chippings and its pop behind and passing down a leafy lane they arrived at massive iron gates opening on a vista of shady drive, at the end of which could be seen glimpses of a Tudor mansion bathed in the afternoon sunlight.

"This is it," said Sally. "Nice place, don't you think?"

"It'll do," said Freddie, who was still in the grip of dudgeon.

"It has a moat."

"Oh, yes?"

"And a wonderful park."

"Really? La Yorke does herself well. And can afford to, of course. Oofy Prosser tells me she makes a packet with her pen. He's got a lot of money in the firm that publishes her stuff."

"I know. He was down here seeing Miss Yorke the other day. Have you met him lately?"

"Oh, yes, he's generally in at the Drones for lunch. His wife had her jewels pinched not long ago."

"So I read in the paper. Were they very valuable?"

"Worth thousands, I should think. They looked that way to me."

"You've seen them?"

"I've been to dinner once or twice with the Oofys, and she had them all on. She glittered like a chandelier."

"And they haven't got them back?"

"No."

"Too bad."

"Yes."

"It must have upset her."

"I suppose so."

Sally's heart was aching. All this formality and stiffness, as if they were strangers meeting for the first time and making conversation. Her own fault, of course, but a girl had to be sensible. If she were not, what ensued? She found herself fetching up at the end of that long line stretching from Piccadilly Circus to Hyde Park Corner. On the stage on which Frederick Widgeon strutted, she told herself, there were no female stars, just a mob of extras doing crowd work.

She forced herself to resume the conversation as they walked up the drive.

"Where are you living now, Freddie? At the old flat?"

His face, already dark, darkened still further.

"No, I couldn't afford it. My uncle stopped my allowance, and I had to move to the suburbs. I'm sharing a house with my cousin George. You remember George?"

"Dimly."

"Beefy chap with red hair. Boxed for Oxford as a heavyweight. He's one of the local cops."

"He went into the police?"

"That's right. Said it was a darned sight better than being cooped up in an office all day, like me."

"Like you? You aren't in an office?"

"I am. A solicitor's. Shortly after we— Soon after I last saw you my foul Uncle Rodney bunged me into the firm of Shoesmith, Shoesmith, Shoesmith and Shoesmith of Lincoln's Inn Fields."

Sally, firm in her resolve to be sensible, had not planned to betray any human feeling during this painful encounter, but at these words she was unable to repress a cry of pity.

"Oh, Freddie! Not really?"

"That's what he did. He placed me in the hands of his solicitor."

"But you must hate it."

"I loathe it."

"What do you do there?"

"I'm a sort of 'Hey, you' or dogsbody like the chap in 'Old Man River.' "

"Lift that trunk?"

"Shift that bale. Exactly. Today, for instance, old Shoesmith gave me some documents to take to Leila Yorke to sign. Why he couldn't just have popped them in the post is a matter between him and his God, if any. Tomorrow I shall probably be running down the street to fetch someone a cup of coffee and the day after that sweeping out the office. I tell you, when I see George coming in off his beat with a face all bright and rosy from a health-giving day in the fresh air, while I'm pale and wan after eight hours in a stuffy office, I envy him and wish I'd had the sense to become a copper."

"How do you two manage, living all alone with nobody to look after you? Or have you a cook?"

Freddie laughed hackingly.

"You mean a chef? On our starvation wages? No, we have no chef, no butler, no first and second footmen, no head and under housemaids, and no groom of the chambers. George does the cooking, and pretty ghastly it is. But I mustn't bore you with my troubles."

"Oh, Freddie, you aren't."

"Well, I shall if I go on any longer. Change the subject, what? How do you get along with Leila Yorke?"

"Oh, splendidly. She's the top."

"In what respect?"

"In every respect."

"Not in her literary output. You must admit that she writes the most awful bilge."

"No longer."

"How do you mean, no longer?"

"She's giving up doing that sentimental stuff of hers."

"You're kidding. No more slush?"

"So she says."

"But it sells like hot cakes."

"I know."

"Then why? What's she going to do? Retire?"

"No, she's planning to write one of those stark, strong novels— You know, about the gray underworld."

"Lord love a duck! This'll be a blow to Cornelius."

"Who's he?"

"Fellow I know. He reads everything she writes."

"I wonder if he'll read her next one."

"How's it coming?"

"It hasn't started yet. She feels the surroundings at Claines Hall aren't right. She says she can't get into the mood. She wants to move somewhere where she can soak in the gray atmosphere and really get going. What's the matter?"

"Nothing."

"You sort of jumped."

"Oh, that? Touch of cramp. Has she found a place to go to yet?"

"No, she's still thinking it over."

"Ah!"

"Ah what?"

"Just Ah. Well, here we are at the old front door. What's the procedure? Do I charge in?"

"You'd better wait. I'll tell her you're here."

Sally crossed the hall, knocked on a door, went in and came out again.

"She wants you to go in."

There was a pause.

"Well, Freddie," said Sally.

"Well, Sally," said Freddie.

"I suppose this is the last time we shall meet."

"You never know."

"I think it is."

"You wouldn't care to dash in and have lunch with me one of these days?"

"Oh, Freddie, what's the use?"

"I see what you mean. Well, in that case Bung-ho about sums it up, what?"

"Yes. Goodbye, Freddie."

"Goodbye."

"Better not keep Miss Yorke waiting. She's been a little edgy since she made her great decision," said Sally, and she went off to the potting shed by the kitchen garden to have a good cry. She knew she had done the sensible thing, but that did not prevent her feeling that her heart was being torn into small pieces by a platoon of muscular wildcats, than which few experiences are less agreeable.

4.

Freddie's first sight of Mr. Cornelius' favorite novelist, author of *For True Love Only, Heather o' the Hills, Sweet Jennie Dean* and other works, had something of the effect on him of a blow between the eyes with a wet fish, causing him to rock back on his heels and blink. Going by the form book, he had expected to see a frail little spectacled wisp of a thing with a shy smile and a general suggestion of lavender and old lace. From this picture Leila Yorke in the flesh deviated quite a good deal. She was a large, hearty-looking woman in the early forties, built on the lines of Catherine of Russia, and her eyes, which were blue and bright and piercing, were obviously in no need of glasses. She wore riding breeches and was smoking a mild cigar.

"Hullo there," she said in a voice which recalled to him that of the drill sergeant at his preparatory school, a man who could crack windows with a single " 'Shun!" "You Widgeon?"

"That's right. How do you do?"

"Shoesmith phoned me that you were bringing those papers. I'll bet you left them in the train."

"No, I have them here."

"Then let's sign the blasted things and get it over with."

She scribbled her signature with the flowing pen of a woman accustomed to recording her name in autograph albums, offered him a cigar and disposed herself for conversation.

"Widgeon?" she said. "That's odd. I used to know a Rodney Widgeon once. Know him still, as a matter of fact, only he goes around under an alias these days. Calls himself Lord Blicester. Any relation?"

"My uncle."

"You don't say? You don't look like him."

"No," said Freddie, who would have hated to. There was nothing in the appearance of his Uncle Rodney that appealed to his aesthetic sense.

"Do you brim over with a nephew's love for him?"

"I wouldn't say 'brim over' exactly."

"No objection, then, to my calling him an old poop?"

"None whatever," said Freddie, warming to the woman as he seldom warmed to one of the opposite sex over the age of twenty-five. There was no question in his mind that he and Leila Yorke were twin souls. "As a matter of fact, your words are music to my ears. 'Old poop' sums him up to a nicety."

She blew a meditative smoke ring, her thoughts plainly back in the past.

"I was engaged to him once."

"Really?"

"Broke it off, though, when he started to bulge at every seam. Couldn't keep that boy off the starchy foods. I don't mind a poop being a poop, but I draw the line at a poop who looks like two poops rolled into one."

"Quite. Have you seen him lately?"

"Not for a year or so. Is he as fat as ever?"

"He came out top in the Fat Uncles contest at the Drones last summer."

"I'm not surprised. Mark you, I'd have broken the engagement any way, because soon after we plighted our troth Joe Bishop came along."

"Joe Bishop?"

"Character I subsequently married. We split up later, and I've been kicking myself ever since. Silliest thing I ever did, to let him go. You married?"

"No."

"What are you screwing up your face for?"

"Did I screw up my face?"

"I got that impression. As if in anguish."

"I'm sorry."

"Quite all right. It's your face. Well, well, it's strange to think that if Joe hadn't come into my life and your uncle had done bending and stretching exercises and learned the knack of laying off sweets, butter and potatoes, you might now be calling me Aunt Bessie."

"Leila, you mean."

"No, I don't. Leila Yorke's my pen name. I was born Elizabeth Binns. You can't write books if you're a Binns. But let's go on roasting your uncle. You don't seem very fond of him."

"Not at the moment. He has incurred my displeasure."

"How was that?"

Freddie quivered a little. He always quivered when he thought of his Uncle Rodney's black act.

"He sold me down the river to Shoesmith."

"Don't you like working for him?"

"No."

"I wouldn't myself. How is Johnny Shoesmith these days?"

Hearing the Frankenstein's monster who employed him alluded to in this fashion shook Freddie to his depths. A vision of himself calling that eminent solicitor Johnny rose before his eyes, and he shuddered strongly. It was only after some moments that he was able to reply.

"Oh, he's fizzing along."

"I've known him since we were both so high."

"Really?"

"He once kissed me behind a rhododendron bush." Freddie started.

"Shoesmith did?"

"Yes."

"You mean Shoesmith of Shoesmith, Shoesmith, Shoesmith and Shoesmith of Lincoln's Inn Fields?"

"That's right."

"Well, I'll be a son of a— I mean, how very extraordinary!"

"Oh, he was a regular devil in those days. And look at him now. All dried up like a kippered herring and wouldn't kiss Helen of Troy if you brought her to him asleep in a chair with a sprig of mistletoe suspended over her. He'd consider it a tort or a misdemeanor or something. That's what comes of being a solicitor—it saps the vital juices. Johnny doesn't even embezzle his clients' money, which I should have thought was about the only fun a solicitor can get out of life. How long have you been working for him?"

"Six months or so."

"You haven't dried up yet."

"No."

"Well, be careful you don't. Exercise ceaseless vigilance. And talking of drying up, you're probably in need of a quick one after your journey. Care for something moist?"

"I'd love it."

"I've only got whisky, brandy, gin, beer, sherry, port, curaçao and champagne, but help yourself. Over there in the 'fridge in the corner."

"Oh, thanks. You?"

"Why, yes, I think I might. I've been feeling a little nervous and fragile these last few days. Open a bottle of champagne."

"Right," said Freddie, doing so. "Nervous and fragile?"

"Got a lot on my mind, Widgeon," said Miss Yorke, draining her beaker and extending it for a refill, "I am standing at a woman's crossroads. Do you read my stuff?"

"Well—er—what with one thing and another . . ."

"No need to apologize. One can't read everything, and no doubt you're all tied up with your Proust and Kafka. Well, for your information, it's lousy."

"Really?"

"Pure treacle. Would you call me a sentimental woman?"

"Not offhand."

"I'm not. In the ordinary give-and-take of life I'm as tough an egg as ever stepped out of the saucepan. Did my butler show you in when you arrived?"

"No. I came with your secretary, Miss Foster. I met her on the train. We—er—we know each other slightly."

"Oh, yes, I remember it was Sally who told me you were here. Well, you ought to see my butler. Haughty? The haughtiest thing you ever met. I've seen strong publishers wilt beneath his eye. And yet that man, that haughty butler, curls up like a sheet of carbon paper if I look squiggle-eyed at him. That's the sort of woman I am when I haven't a pen in my hand, but give me a ball-point and what happens? Don't keep all that champagne to yourself."

"Oh, sorry."

"And don't spill it. The prudent man doesn't waste a drop."

"It's good stuff."

"It's excellent stuff. It's what Johnny Shoesmith needs to make him realize he isn't something dug out of Tutankhamen's tomb. Where was I?"

"You were saying what happens."

"What happens when what?"

"When you get a ball-point pen in your hand."

"Oh, yes. The moment my fingers clutch it, Widgeon, a great change comes over me. I descend to depths of goo which you with your pure mind wouldn't believe possible. I write about stalwart men, strong but oh so gentle, and girls with wide gray eyes and hair the color of ripe wheat who are always having misunderstandings and going to Africa. The men, that is. The girls stay at home and marry the wrong bimbos. But there's a happy ending. The bimbos break their necks in the hunting field and the men come back in the last chapter and they and the girls get together in the twilight, and all around is the scent of English flowers and birds singing their evensong in the shrubbery. Makes me shudder to think of it."

"It sounds rather good to me. I wouldn't mind getting together with a girl in the twilight."

"No, it's kind of you to try to cheer me up, Widgeon, but I know molasses when I see it. Or is it 'them'? The critics call my stuff tripe."

"No!"

"That's what they do, they call it tripe."

"Monstrous!"

"And of course it is tripe. But I'm not going to have a bunch of inky pipsqueaks telling me so. And I'm fed to the teeth with all these smart alecks who do parodies of me, hoping to make me feel like a piece of cheese. The worm has turned, Widgeon. Do you know what I'm going to do? I'm going to write a novel that'll make their eyes pop out. What some call an important novel, and others significant. Keep that champagne circulating. Don't let it congeal."

"But can you?"

"Can I what?"

"Write an important novel."

"Of course I can. All you have to do is cut out the plot and shove in plenty of misery. I can do it on my head, once I get started. Only the hell of it is that as long as I remain at Claines Hall, Loose Chippings, I can't get started. The atmosphere here is all wrong. Butlers and moats and things popping about all over the place. I've got to get away somewhere where there's a little decent squalor."

"That's exactly what Sally Foster was saying."

"Oh, was she? Nice girl, that. She ought to marry somebody. Maybe she will before long. I think she's in love."

"You do?"

"Yes, I've an idea there's someone for whom she feels sentiments deeper and warmer than those of ordinary friendship. Well, if so, I wish her luck. Love's all right. Makes the world go round, they say. I don't know if there's anything in it. Or if there's anything in that bottle. Is there?"

"Just a drop."

"Let's have it. What were we talking about?"

"You getting away somewhere where there was a spot of squalor."

"That's right. I thought I'd be able to swing it here by going the round of the local pubs and having the peasantry bare their souls to me. Thomas Hardy stuff. Not a hope. At the end of a week all I had discovered about these sons of toil was that they were counting the days to the football season so that they could start in on their pools again. Makes one sick. No help to a woman. Why are you looking at me like a half-witted sheep?"

"Was I?"

"You were."

"I'm sorry. It's just that when Sally Foster was telling me about this new binge you were contemplating, I had an idea."

"Beginner's luck."

"I believe I've got the very spot for you. Castlewood, Mulberry Grove, Valley Fields."

"Where's that?"

"Just outside London. I doubt if you could find a grayer locality. The man who lives next door to me keeps rabbits."

"Oh, you live in Valley Fields?"

"That's right. Castlewood's next door to me on the other side. And it's vacant at the moment and fully furnished. You could move in tomorrow. Shall I fix you up with the rabbit fancier? He's the house agent."

"H'm."

"Don't say 'H'm'!"

"I wonder."

"I wouldn't. Strike while the iron's hot is my advice."

But Miss Yorke insisted on relapsing into thought, and Freddie scanned her pensive face anxiously. On her decision so much depended. For he was convinced that if he could only get Sally on the other side of the garden fence that divided Peacehaven from Castlewood, he would soon be able to alter the present trend of her thoughts with the burning words and melting looks he knew he had at his disposal. He had lived in the suburbs long enough to be aware that the preliminaries of seventy per cent of the marriages that occurred there had been arranged over garden fences.

Leila Yorke came out of her reverie.

"I hadn't thought of the suburbs. What I had in mind was a bed-sitting-room in Bottleton East, where I could study the martyred proletariat and soak in squalor at every pore."

Freddie yelped like a stepped-on puppy.

"Bottleton East? You're off your onion— I mean, you have an entirely erroneous conception of what Bottleton East is like. It's the cheeriest place in England. I sang at a song contest there once, so I know. The audience was the most rollicking set of blighters you ever saw. Never stopped throwing vegetables. No, Valley Fields is the spot for you."

"Really gray, is it, this outpost of eternity?"

"Couldn't be grayer."

"Squalor?"

"It wrote the words and music."

"Gissing!" exclaimed Miss Yorke, snapping her fingers. Freddie shook his head.

"There's very little kissing done in Valley Fields. The aborigines are much too busy being gray."

"I didn't say kissing. I said Gissing—George Gissing. He wrote about the suburbs, and it's just the George Gissing sort of book I'm aiming at."

"Well, there you are. Didn't I tell you? You can't miss if you string along with George Gissing. Ask anybody."

"He was as gray as a stevedore's undervest."

"Very stark, I've always said so."

"Widgeon, I think you've got something."

"Me, too."

"The telephone's in the hall. Ring up that rat-catching friend of yours, the house agent fellow, and book me in at this Castlewood hovel, starting tomorrow. And—correct me if I'm wrong—I think this calls for another half bottle."

"Me also."

"Make a long arm," said Leila Yorke.

5.

In the whole of London there is no interior more richly dignified—*posh* is perhaps the word—than the lobby of Barribault's Hotel in Clarges Street, that haunt of Texas millionaires and visiting maharajahs. Its chairs and settees are the softest that money can provide, its lighting dim and discreet, its carpets of so thick a nap that midgets would get lost in them and have to be rescued by dogs. It is the general opinion of London's elite that until you have seen the lobby of Barribault's Hotel, you have not seen anything.

Some forty hours after Freddie Widgeon's visit to Loose Chippings, the quiet splendor of this beauty spot was enhanced by the presence of a superbly upholstered man of middle age who looked as if he might be an American senator or something of that sort. He had a frank, open face, fine candid eyes and a lofty brow rather resembling Shakespeare's. His name was Thomas G. Molloy, and he was waiting for his wife, who was due that morning to leave Holloway gaol, where she had been serving a short sentence for shoplifting.

He looked at his wrist watch, a little thing his mate had picked up at a Bond Street jeweler's while doing her Christmas shopping. The hands pointed to one-fifteen, and he began to feel worried, for, though he knew that she would be having a shampoo and a facial and possibly a perm after leaving her recent abode, he had expected her long before this. He was consulting the timepiece again some uneasy minutes later, when a voice behind him said "Hi, Soapy!" and he spun round. She was standing there, looking, it seemed to him, as if instead of in the deepest dungeon beneath Holloway gaol, she had been spending the last few weeks at some bracing seashore resort like Skegness.

Dolly Molloy unquestionably took the eye. She was a spectacular blonde of the type that is always getting murdered in its step-ins in mystery stories. Her hair was golden, her eyes hazel, her lips and cheeks aflame with color, and she carried herself with a challenging jauntiness. Wolf whistling is, of course, prohibited in the lobby of Barribault's Hotel, so none of those present attempted this form of homage, but quite a few of the visiting maharajahs looked as if they would have liked to, and it was plain that it was only by the exercise of the most iron self-restraint that the Texas millionaires were holding themselves in. You could see their lips puckering.

Soapy Molloy was devouring her with adoring eyes. Few

husbands more loving than he had ever cracked rocks in
Sing Sing.

"Baby! I didn't see you come in."

"I was back there, hiding behind a pillar. There was a
guy having a cocktail I didn't want to see me. Nobody
you know. Fellow by the name of Prosser."

"Not the one they call Oofy?"

"I don't know what his first name is."

"Guy with pimples?"

"That's right. Why? Do you know him?"

"Must be the same. Young Widgeon next door to Castlewood introduced me to him. I've something to tell you
about Prosser."

"Me, too, you, but it can wait. Let's eat, Soapy, I'm
starving."

"I'll bet you are."

"They don't overfeed you in the coop."

"That's what I found last time I was up the river, and I
guess it's the same over on this side. Too bad they got
you, baby. What happened?"

"I didn't let my fingers flicker quick enough. And I
didn't know the store dick was standing right behind me.
Oh well, that's the way the cookie crumbles. You can't
win 'em all."

"No, you can't win 'em all. That's what I told Chimp."
Dolly started.

"Chimp?"

"I ran into him the other day."

"And told him about me?"

"He'd already heard. These things get around."

"What did he say?"

"He laughed."

"*Laughed?*"

"Laughed his head off."

Dolly bit her lip.

"He did, did he?" she said, and an ingrained dislike of their old associate Chimp Twist became accentuated. Circumstances had made it necessary for them to take this dubious character into partnership from time to time, but her relations with him had never been anything but strained, and it comforted her a good deal to remember that at their last meeting she had hit him on the head with the butt end of a pistol. She would willingly have done the same at this moment.

"The little potato bug!" she said, her fine eyes clouding as that unsympathetic laughter at her expense seemed to ring in her ears. "Is he still running that private-eye racket of his?"

The question surprised Mr. Molloy.

"Why, of course he is, sweetie. Why wouldn't he be? It's only a month since you've been away."

"Well, a month seems a long time for Chimp Twist to stay out of the coop. How's he doing?"

"He didn't say, but I guess he doesn't bother much about clients. The J. Sheringham Adair Private Investigation Agency's just a front."

Dolly laughed bitterly.

"J. Sheringham Adair! What a name to call himself."

"Had to call himself something."

"Well, why not Heels Incorporated or Double-crossers Limited or sump'n'? I tell you, Soapy, whenever I think of that undersized boll weevil, I go hot all over, clear down to the soles of my shoes."

"Oh, Chimp's not so bad."

"Not so bad as what?"

Mr. Molloy, though trying to be tolerant, found this question difficult to answer. He changed the subject.

"Swell place, this."

"Yeah."

"Makes one sort of sad, though."

"Why's that?"

"Well, seeing all these rich guys that nature intended I should sell 'em oil stock, and I can't because I don't know them. Sitting waiting for you and watching them come in through the swinging doors, I felt like a big-game hunter with a stream of giraffes, gnus and hippopotamuses passing by him and he can't do nothing because he came out without his gun."

"I know what you mean. It's tough."

"But no use worrying about it, I guess. Let's go eat."

"You can't make it too soon for me. But somewheres else, not here."

"Why, what's wrong with Barribault's? Best joint in London."

"So I've heard. But I don't like the company. Prosser's in there."

"I don't dig this Prosser stuff. What's he got on you?"

"Oh, this and that."

Soapy forbore to press his questioning. A solution of the mystery had occurred to him. It was, he knew, his consort's practice, when not collecting knickknacks at the department stores, to swoon in the arms of rich-looking strangers in the public streets and pick their pockets as they bent to offer her assistance, and no doubt Oofy Prosser had been one of the parties of the second part in some such business deal. This would, of course, account for a sensitive woman's reluctance to resume their acquaintance.

"Let's go to the Ivy," he said. "More onteem there, and I've lots to tell you, baby."

6.

It was not till they were settled at a corner table that Soapy touched on any subject other than his loneliness in his mate's absence and the ecstasy he felt in having her with him once more. The glass partition that separated them from the driver of their taxi was closed, but one never knew that a rich, rolling voice like his might not penetrate glass, and what he had to relate was not for the ears of taxi drivers.

"And now," he said, as the shrimps on his beloved one's plate vanished like nylon stockings from the counter of a department store, "lemme tell you what I've been doing since you went away."

"Not been idle?"

"Busy as that famous one-armed paper hanger."

"That's my boy! Shrimps," said Dolly, finishing the last one and regarding her empty plate hungrily, "are all right as a starter, but they don't have what you'd call authority."

"Just scratch the surface?"

"That's right. What's coming?"

"Sole mornay, and some sort of chicken after that."

"That's what I like to hear. You're doing me proud, honey."

"It's a celebration, and I can afford to. How would you feel about a month or so in the south of France?"

"As good as that, is it?"

"Just as good as that. I've cleaned up."

"Tell me."

Soapy Molloy's substantial form seemed to expand. He knew he was going to be impressive.

"Well, to start with, I unloaded a thousand pounds' worth of Silver River on young Widgeon at Peacehaven."

"You didn't!"

"That's what I did."

"I wouldn't have thought he had a thousand pounds."

"He hasn't now."

"Well, that's swell. I don't wonder you're feeling pleased with yourself. A thousand's nice sugar."

"Ah, but wait. You ain't heard nothing yet. I then took another thousand off his uncle, guy by the name of Blicester."

"You're kidding!"

"And," said Soapy, delivering the punch line, "two thousand off your friend Prosser."

Dolly choked on her sole mornay, as any loving wife would have done in similar circumstances. Her look of admiration warmed his heart.

"Soapy, you're a marvel!"

"I'm not so bad. What I always say is Give me a nice smooth-working sucker and plenty of room to swing my arms around, and I could sell the Brooklyn Bridge."

"Why, we're rich!"

"Rich enough to have a vacation in the south of France. Or would you prefer Le Touquet? Just the right time for Le Touquet now, and I haven't been there in three years. I did well when I was there last. That was before we were married. There was a woman I met at the Casino I sold quite a block of Silver River to."

"I'm not surprised. You're so fascinating, my great big wonderful man!"

"Just so long as I fascinate you, baby," said Mr. Molloy. "That's all I ask."

The meal proceeded on its delightful course. Coffee arrived. Soapy lit a large cigar, and it was only after he had sat smoking it for some little time that it was borne in upon him that his wife, usually an energetic talker, had fallen into a thoughtful silence. He looked across the table, somewhat concerned.

"What's the matter, baby?"

"Matter?"

"You're kind of quiet."

"I was thinking."

"What about?"

She seemed to brood for a moment, as if debating within herself whether silence would not be best. Then she made up her mind to speak.

"Soapy, there's something I want to tell you."

"I'm listening."

"I hadn't meant to tell you till your birthday."

"What is it?"

"It's something you'll like. You'll turn handsprings."

Soapy stared, not precisely aghast but definitely uneasy.

He had never been a great reader, but he liked occasionally to dip into the cheaper type of novelette, and in all the novelettes he had come across words like these on wifely lips could mean only one thing.

In a low, quivering voice, quite unlike his customary fruity utterance, he said, "Tiny garments?"

"Huh?"

He choked on his cigar.

"You heard. Are you knitting tiny garments?"

"You mean—?"

"That's what I mean."

Dolly broke into a peal of happy laughter.

"For Pete's sake! Of course I'm not."

"You aren't . . . ? We aren't . . . ?"

"Going to have little feet pattering about the home? Not a patter."

Soapy breathed deeply. He was not a philoprogenitive man, and a considerable weight had been lifted from his mind.

"Gosh, you had me scared for a minute!" he said, dabbing a handkerchief on his fine forehead.

Dolly was now all sparkle.

"No, nothing of that kind. Not but what later on . . ."

"Yes, later on," agreed Soapy. "A good deal later on. Then what's on your mind?"

"I don't know but what I still ought to save it up for your birthday, but— Oh, well, here it comes. Soapy, do you remember when I told you a couple of months ago I was going to spend a week or two visiting friends in the country?"

"Sure."

"Well, I didn't spend any week or two visiting friends in the country. Do you know what I actually done?"

"What?"

"I got a job as maid to a dame. Name of Prosser."

Soapy leaped in his chair, and sat staring. Enlightenment had come to him like a levin flash. In addition to dipping into novelettes, he read the daily papers regularly, and the front-page story of Mrs. Prosser's bereavement had not escaped his eye. Beads of excitement stood out on his Shakespearean brow, and he upset a coffee cup in his emotion.

"Baby! You aren't telling me— You don't mean— You didn't . . .?"

"Yup, that's what I did. I got away with her ice."

There was nothing small about Soapy Molloy. He experienced no trace of chagrin at the thought that the triumphs of which he had been boasting so proudly a short while before had been demoted to the chicken-feed class by his wife's stupendous feat. Wholehearted admiration was all he felt. He gazed at her worshipingly, wondering what he could ever have done to deserve such a helpmeet.

"All those jools?" he gasped.

"Every last one."

"They must be worth the earth."

"They're not hay. Well, now you're hep to why I didn't want to meet Prosser."

"But why didn't you say anything about it before?"

"I told you. I was saving it up for your birthday."

Mr. Molloy breathed devoutly.

"Baby, there's no one like you."

"I thought you'd be pleased."

"I feel like dancing a skirt dance. Where are they?"

"Oh, they're tucked away somewhere quite safe." Dolly looked about her. "Everyone seems to have gone. We'd better be moving before they throw us out."

"What do you feel like doing now?"

"I thought I might look in at Selfridge's."

"I wouldn't, baby."

"I need some new stockings awful bad."

"But not this afternoon. Look, what I suggest is we go to Barribault's and—well, sort of loll around. We'll think of something to do."

"Where? In the lobby?"

"In my suite."

"In your *what?*"

"I've taken a suite there. You'll like it. It's got— What's the matter, baby? Why are you looking like that?"

He spoke anxiously, for into his wife's face there had come a look of horror and dismay, suggesting to him for a moment that the shrimps, the sole, the chicken, and the French pastry which had followed them had been too much for an interior enfeebled by prison fare. But this diagnosis was erroneous. It was not Dolly's internal mechanism that was troubling her.

"Soapy! You're not telling me you've left Castlewood?"

"Sure. I'm not saying the way I've cleaned up is anything like the way you've cleaned up, but I have cleaned up pretty good, and when you've cleaned up pretty good, you don't want to be horsing around down in the suburbs. You feel like splurging."

"Oh, my Gawd!"

"Why, what is it, sweetie?"

Dolly's face had a twisted look, as if she had swallowed something acid.

"I'll tell you what it is," she said, seeming to experience some difficulty in articulating. "The Prosser ice is at Castlewood."

"What!"

"On top of the wardrobe in our bedroom, that's what."

Soapy could understand now why his baby was looking

47

like that, as he had expressed it. He was looking like that himself.

"On top of the wardrobe?" he gurgled weakly.

"Seemed to me the safest place to put it. Yessir, there it is, and not a chance of getting at it, because by this time somebody'll have moved in."

"Not already."

"I shouldn't wonder. That fellow Cornelius, the guy with the full set of white whiskers, was telling me that houses like Castlewood never stay vacant for more than a day or two. Say, listen, go call him up."

"Cornelius?"

"Yeah. Ask him what the score is."

Mr. Molloy rose as if a bradawl had pierced the seat of his chair. He hurried out.

"You're right," he said lugubriously, returning some minutes later. "The joint's been rented."

"I thought as much."

"To Leila Yorke, the novelist. She clocked in this morning," said Soapy, and, beckoning a waiter, ordered double brandies for two. They both felt they needed them.

It was some time before either of them spoke. Then Dolly emerged from the fog of silent gloom which had been enveloping her. Women are more resilient than men.

"You'll have to go down there and see this dame and make a spiel."

"How do you mean, baby?"

"Why, tell her some story that'll make her let us have the house back."

"You think she would?"

"She might, if you're as good as you always were. Everyone says there's no one can pull a line of talk the way you can."

Mr. Molloy, though still far from being his usual hearty

self, became a little more cheerful. On the horizon of his mind there was shining a tiny spark of hope, like a lighted match seen at the end of a tunnel. Pulling a line of talk was a thing he knew himself to be good at.

"Worth trying," he agreed.

"Sure it is. We're not licked. Because don't forget that this dame writes books, and there never was an author yet who had enough sense to cross the street with. All these novelists are halfway around the bend."

Mr. Molloy nodded. There was, he knew, much in what she said.

7.

Leila Yorke was breakfasting in bed. Sally had boiled the eggs and toasted the toast and taken them up to her, still a good deal dazed by the swiftness with which she had been uprooted and transferred from the old home to this new environment. On Friday her employer had told her to pack, on Saturday they had driven off in the car with the Claines Hall butler staring after them like a butler who is at a loss to understand, and here it was only Sunday morning and they had been established at Castlewood some twenty-four hours. Leila Yorke was a woman who believed in doing it now, and though Sally was extremely fond of her, there were moments when she found herself wishing that she would less often model her behavior on that of those American hurricanes which become so impulsive on arriving at Cape Hatteras.

As she sat trying to relax, the front doorbell rang. She went to answer it and found on the step a venerable figure almost completely concealed behind a long white beard. He was carrying a large suitcase and a bundle of papers, and she wondered for a moment if he had come to stay.

"Good morning," said this bearded pard.

"Good morning," said Sally.

"My name is Cornelius. Can I see Miss Yorke?"

"She's in bed."

"Not ill?" said Mr. Cornelius, blenching.

"Oh, no, just having breakfast."

"And thinking lovely thoughts," said Mr. Cornelius, reassured. "Does she keep a pad and pencil by her bedside?"

"Not that I know of."

"She should. The lightest of her meditations ought to be preserved. I have thirty-two of her books here," said Mr. Cornelius, indicating the suitcase. "I was hoping that she would autograph them."

"I'm sure she will. If you will leave them—"

"Thank you, Miss . . ."

"Foster. I'm Miss Yorke's secretary."

"What a privilege!"

"Yes."

"She must be a delightful woman."

"Yes, very."

"Her books have always been an inspiration to me, and not only to me but to the little literary society we have here which meets every second Thursday. I was wondering if Miss Yorke could be persuaded to come and talk to us this week."

"I'm terribly sorry, but I don't think she would be able

to manage it. She's just planning out a new novel, and of course that takes up all her time."

"I quite understand. Then I will just leave the Sunday papers for her. I thought she might care to see them."

"How awfully kind of you, Mr. Cornelius. I know she'll want the Sunday papers."

"They are rather difficult to obtain in Valley Fields. They are not delivered, and one has to go to a tobacconist's near the station. I always get Mr. Widgeon's for him. He lives at Peacehaven next door, and one likes to be neighborly. Goodbye, Miss Foster," said Mr. Cornelius, and with a courtly waggle of his beard he melted away.

His parting words made Sally jump. For an instant she thought she had heard him say "Mr. Widgeon." Then she knew that she must have been mistaken. Coincidences are all very well—in her novels Leila Yorke went in for them rather largely—but there is a limit. It was absurd to suppose that by pure accident she had come to live next door to the man she had resolved never to see again. A simple explanation suggested itself. Owing to his obiter dicta having to be filtered through a zareba of white hair, it was not always easy to catch exactly what Mr. Cornelius said. No doubt the name had been Williams or Wilson or possibly Wigham. It was with restored equanimity that she started to go and see how Miss Yorke was getting on with her breakfast and met her coming down the stairs in a pink dressing gown.

There was a frown on Leila Yorke's brow, as if she had temporarily suspended the thinking of lovely thoughts and had turned to others of an inferior grade.

"You look peeved," said Sally, noting this.

"I'm feeling peeved," said Miss Yorke. "What was that bell I heard?"

"That was the County starting to call. A Mr. Cornelius. I don't know who he is."

"He's the house agent. Keeps rabbits."

"Oh, does he? Well, he likes to be neighborly, so he brought you the Sunday papers."

"Bless him. Just what I wanted."

"And thirty-two of your books, to be autographed."

"Curse him. May his rabbits get myx-whatever-it-is."

"And he wants you to give a little talk to his literary society which meets every second Thursday."

"Oh, hell!"

"Keep calm. I got you out of it. I told him you were thinking out a new novel."

Leila Yorke snorted bitterly.

"You did, did you? Then you wantonly deceived the poor man. How can I think out a George Gissing novel, in surroundings like these? I always thought the suburbs were miles and miles of ghastly little semi-detached houses full of worn-out women ironing shirts and haggard men with coughs wondering where the rent was coming from, and look at this joint we've fetched up in. A palace, no less."

"Would you say that?"

"Well, it's got a summerhouse and two birdbaths and an aspidistra in the drawing room, not to mention a reproduction of Millais's 'Huguenot' and a china mug with 'A Present from Bognor Regis' on it in pink sea shells, which I'll bet they haven't got at Windsor Castle. I ought to have known it. That young hound was pulling my leg."

"What young hound?"

"You know him. Widgeon. You brought him along to see me, and we got along like a couple of sailors on shore leave. We split a bottle of Bollinger and got kidding back and forth about his Uncle Rodney and Johnny Shoesmith and what have you, and in a weak moment I confided in him about this novel of squalor I'm trying to write, and he told me that if I wanted a place where I could absorb squalor by the gallon, I ought to come to Valley Fields. He said if I played my cards right, I could get this Castlewood house, and like a chump I told him to phone Cornelius and fix it up. And here I am, stuck in a luxury suburb about as inspirational as Las Vegas. For all the gray atmosphere I'm likely to find here, I might just as well have stayed where I was. Shows how unsafe it is ever to trust anybody in a solicitor's office. Twisters, all of them."

Twice during these remarks, as the perfidy of Frederick Widgeon was made clearer and clearer to her, Sally had gasped—the first time like a Pekingese choking on a bone of a size more suitable to a bloodhound, the second time like another Pekingese choking on another bone of similar dimensions. She was stunned by this revelation of the Machiavellian depths to which the male sex can descend when it puts its mind to it, and Leila Yorke looked at her oddly, puzzled by the expression on her face.

"Why," she asked, "have you turned vermilion?"

"I haven't."

"Pardon me. You look like a startled beetroot. This means something. Good Lord!" said Leila Yorke, inspired. "I see it all. Widgeon loves you, and he talked me into taking this blasted house so that he could be next door to you and in a position to tickle you across the fence. Shows character and enterprise, that. I see a bright future for the boy, if only I don't murder him with a blunt instrument for letting me in for this Valley Fields jaunt. I may or may not. I haven't decided. Yes, we have established that important point, I think. Love has wound its silken fetters about Widgeon."

If Sally had been a character in one of Leila Yorke's books, she would have ground her teeth. Not knowing how to, she sniffed.

"It would be odd if it hadn't," she said bitterly. "He loves every girl he meets."

"Is that so?" said Leila Yorke, interested. "I knew a man once who had the same tendency. He was a chartered accountant, and all chartered accountants have hearts as big as hotels. You think they're engrossed in auditing the half-yearly balance sheet of Miggs, Montagu and Murgatroyd, general importers, and all the time they're writing notes to blondes saying, 'Tomorrow, one-thirty, same place.' I wouldn't let that worry you. It doesn't amount to anything. Men are like that."

"I don't want a man like that."

"You want Widgeon, whatever he's like. I've been watching you with a motherly eye for some time, and I've noted all the symptoms—the faraway, stuffed-frog look, the dreamy manner, the quick jump like a rising trout when spoken to suddenly. My good child, you're crazy about him, and if you've any sense, you'll tell him so and sign him up. I'm a lot older than you, and I'll give a piece of advice. If you love a man, never be such an ass as to let him go. I'm telling you this as one who knows, because that's what I did, and I've never stopped regretting it. Were you engaged?"

"Yes."

"Broke it off?"

"Yes."

"I was married. Much worse, because it hurts more that way. You've so much more to remember. But a broken engagement's nothing. You can stick it together again in a couple of minutes, and if you'll take my advice, you'll attend to it right away. You'll probably find him in his garden, rolling the lawn or whatever they do in these parts on a Sunday morning. Pick up your feet, kid, and go and tell him what you really think of him."

"I will," said Sally, and set forth with that resolve firmly fixed in her mind. She was breathing flame softly through the nostrils.

8

Freddie was not rolling the lawn when she came out into the garden; he was seated in the shade of the one tree that Peacehaven possessed, reading the Sunday paper which Mr. Cornelius had so kindly brought him, and Sally, reaching the fence, paused. The problem of how to attract his attention had presented itself. "Hi!" seemed lacking in dignity. "Hoy!" had the same defect. And "Freddie!" was much too friendly. What she would really have liked, of course, would have been to throw a brick at him, but the grounds of Castlewood, though parklike, were unfortunately lacking in bricks. She compromised by saying "Good morning," in a voice that lowered the balmy temperature of the summer day by several degrees Fahrenheit, and he looked up with a start and having looked up sat for an instant spellbound, the picture of a young man in flannels and an Eton Ramblers blazer who is momentarily unable to believe his eyes. Then, rising acrobatically, he hurried to the fence.

"Sally!" he gasped. "Is it really you?"

"Yes," said Sally, and once more the temperature dropped noticeably. A snail that was passing at the time huddled back into its shell with the feeling that there was quite a nip in the air these mornings and would have slapped its ribs, if it had had any.

"But this is the most extraordinary thing that ever happened," said Freddie. "It takes the breath away. What are those things they have in deserts? I don't mean Foreign Legions. Mirages, that's the word. When I looked up and saw you standing there, I thought it was a mirage."

"Oh?"

"Well, I mean, you can't say it isn't remarkable that I should look up and see you standing there. It—how shall I put it—it took the breath away."

"Oh?"

There is something about the monosyllable "Oh?" when uttered in a cold, level voice by the girl he loves that makes the most intrepid man uneasy. Freddie had been gifted by nature with much of the gall of an army mule, but even he lost a little of his animation. However, he persevered.

"Don't tell me you've come to live at Castlewood?"

It was practically impossible for Sally to look colder and prouder than she had been doing since the start of this interview, but she did her best.

"Do you need to be told?"

"Eh?"

"I've heard the whole story from Miss Yorke."

Freddie gulped. This, an inner voice was whispering, was not so good.

"The whole story?"

"Yes."

"She spilled the beans?"

"She did."

"You know all?"

"I do."

"Then in that case," said Freddie, suddenly, brightening as a man will when he has found a good talking point, "perhaps you'll get it into your nut how much I love you. I will conceal nothing from you."

"You won't have the chance."

"I did lure the Yorke here, and I'd do it again. I'd lure a thousand Yorkes here. It was imperative to have you within easy talking distance so that I could plead my cause and get you to stop being a little fathead."

"I am not a fathead."

"Pardon me. You appear to be under the impression that my love isn't sincere and wholehearted and all that sort of thing. Therefore you stand revealed as a fathead."

"And you stand revealed as a cross between a flitting butterfly and a Mormon elder," said Sally with spirit. "You and Brigham Young, a pair."

This silenced Freddie for a moment, but he continued to persevere.

"I beg your pardon?"

"You make love to every girl you meet."

"It's a lie."

"It is not a lie."

"It is a lie, and actionable, too, I shouldn't wonder. I must ask Shoesmith. Really, to come here flinging around these wild and unwarrantable accusations—"

"Unwarrantable, did you say?"

"That was the word I used."

"Oh? Well, how about Drusilla Wix?"

"Eh?"

"And Dahlia Prenderby and Mavis Peasemarch and Vanessa Vokes and Helen Christopher and Dora Pinfold and Hildegarde Watt-Watson?"

This rain of names plainly shook Freddie. He seemed to shrink within his Eton Ramblers blazer in much the same way as the recent snail had shrunk within its shell, and like the snail, he had the momentary illusion that Valley Fields was in the grip of a cold wave.

In a voice that gave the impression that he had tried to swallow something large and sharp, which had lodged in his windpipe, he said, "Oh, those?"

"Yes, those."

"Who told you about them?"

"Mr. Prosser."

"Oofy?"

"I told you he came to see Miss Yorke one day. I showed him round the place and we got talking and your name came up and he said you were always in love with every girl you met and proved it by supplying details. Those were the only names he mentioned, but I have no doubt he could have added hundreds more."

Freddie was stunned. He stammered as he spoke. He had seldom been so shocked.

"Oofy! A fellow I've practically nursed in my bosom! If that's his idea of being a staunch pal, then all I can say is that it isn't mine."

"He was merely passing on information which is generally known to all the young thugs of your acquaintance. It is common knowledge that if all the girls you've loved were placed end to end, they would reach from Piccadilly Circus to Hyde Park Corner."

It seemed to Freddie that Castlewood, a solidly built house, though of course, as in the case of most suburban houses, it was unsafe to treat it roughly by leaning against the walls or anything like that, was doing an Ouled Naïls stomach dance. With a strong effort he mastered an inclination to swoon where he stood. He found speech and movement, and not even Mr. Molloy, when selling oil stock, could have waved his arms more vigorously.

"But, dash it, don't you understand that those were just boyish fancies? You're different."

"Oh?" said Sally, and if ever an "Oh?" nearly came out as "Ho!" this one did.

Freddie continued to act like an emotional octopus. The speed at which his arms were gyrating almost deceived the eye.

"Yes, of course you're different. You're the real thing. You're what I've been hunting around for ever since I went to my first kindergarten. And all those girls you've mentioned had popped in and out of my life long before I met you. Oh, Sally darling, do get it into your loaf that you're the only damned thing in this damned world that matters a damn to me."

In spite of herself Sally found herself wavering. She had planned to be firm and sensible, but it is not easy for a girl to remain firm and sensible when such melting words are proceeding from the lips of the only man she has ever really loved. And a disturbing, weakening thought had floated into her mind—to wit, that she herself had not the unimpeachable record which she was demanding from this opposite number of hers. She had never revealed the fact to him, for a girl likes to have her little secrets, but she, too, had had her experiences. There had been quite a troupe of Bills and Toms and Jimmys in her life before Frederick Widgeon had come into it, and what did they amount to now? They had gone with the wind, they meant nothing to her, she did not even send them Christmas cards. Could it be that the Misses Wix, Prenderby, Pease-march, Vokes, Christopher, Pinfold and Watt-Watson ranked equally low in the estimation of Freddie Widgeon?

As she stood debating this point, a voice spoke from behind her. "Hullo there, Widgeon."

"Oh, hullo, Miss Yorke. Welcome to Valley Fields."

"Welcome to Valley Fields, my foot. I'd like a word with you some time about Valley Fields and its gray squalor."

"Any time that suits you."

"That was a nice trick you played on me, was it not? Still, we can go into that later. For your information, I'm inclined to take a lenient view."

"Good show."

"Now that I learn that it was love that drove you on. Love conquers all."

"You betcher."

"If you're in love, you're in love."

"You never spoke a truer word."

"Well," said Leila Yorke, who was always direct in her methods and seldom beat about bushes, "how's it coming? Have you kissed her?"

"Not yet."

"For heaven's sake! Are you man or mouse?"

"Well, you see, there's a snag. I'm not so dashed sure she wants me to. The thing's what Shoesmith would call sub judice."

"Of course she wants you to."

"You really feel that?"

"It's official."

Freddie drew a deep breath.

"How's chances, Sally?"

"Pretty good, Freddie."

"That's better. That's more the stuff. That's the sort of thing I like to hear," said Leila Yorke, and wandered off, thinking what Mr. Cornelius would have called lovely thoughts. The situation reminded her a little of the getting-together of Claude Hallward and Cynthia Roseleigh in her *Cupid, the Archer.*

"Woof!" said Freddie some moments later.

"Oh, Freddie!" said Sally. "I've been so miserable, Freddie."

"Me, too. Plunged in gloom."

"Do you really love me?"

"Like billy-o."

"You'll always love me?"

"Till the sands of the desert grow cold."

"Well, mind you do. When I'm married, I want my husband to stay put, not go flitting from flower to flower."

"That shall be attended to."

"I don't want you ever to speak to another girl."

"I won't."

"And don't—"

"I know what you're going to say. You would prefer that I didn't kiss them. Right ho. Never again. It's just a mannerism."

"Correct it."

"I will. I'll be like Johnny Shoesmith. He wouldn't kiss Helen of Troy if you brought her to him asleep on a chair with a sprig of mistletoe suspended over her. And now hop across that fence, and I'll show you round Peacehaven."

Leila Yorke, meanwhile, after doing the setting-up exercises with which she always began the day, had gone back to her bedroom to dress. She had just completed her toilet when the front doorbell rang. With a brief "Oh, hell!"— for this, she supposed, would be Mr. Cornelius playing a return date with another suitcaseful of books to be auto-graphed—she went to answer it.

It was not Mr. Cornelius. It was a snappily dressed man of middle age with a frank, open face, and a lofty brow resembling Shakespeare's, who gazed at her with fine, candid eyes as if the sight of her had just made his day.

"Miss Leila Yorke?"

"Yes."

"Good morning, Miss Yorke. This is a wonderful moment for me. I am one of your greatest admirers. That must be my excuse for this unceremonious call. Could I speak to you for a few minutes, if I am not interrupting your work? It would be a great privilege."

9.

Sunday, with the marts of trade closed and no chance of going out and doing a little shopping, was always a dullish day for Dolly Molloy, and after the departure of Soapy for Castlewood she had found the time passing slowly. She did her nails, tried her hair a different way, changed her stockings three times and experimented with a new lipstick, formerly the property of a leading department store, but she was unable altogether to dispel ennui, and it was with relief that as the hour approached when one would be thinking about a bite of lunch she heard a key turning in the door.

"I thought you were never coming, honey," she cried happily, bounding up to greet the warrior back from the front.

But her happiness was short-lived. One glance as he came into the room was enough to tell her that here was not a man bringing the good news from Aix to Ghent but one who had a tale of failure to relate. There was a cloud on Soapy's brow, and his eyes were somber. His whole appearance conveyed the suggestion that in the not distant past he had undergone some spiritual experience which he had found disturbing. Only too plainly he was in the grip of that grief—void, dark and drear, which finds no natural outlet, no relief, in word or sigh or tear—which in the early eighteen hundreds had depressed the poet Coleridge.

He sank into a chair and wiped his forehead with a silk handkerchief which his helpmeet had picked up at Harrod's one afternoon last fall and given him for Christmas.

"Gosh!" he said in a voice that might well have come from a tomb.

Dolly was a good wife. Though quivering with curiosity and burning to ask questions, she knew that first things must come first. Some quarter of an hour ago Room Service had deposited on a side table a tray containing ice and glasses, and she hurried to a cupboard and extracted from it gin, vermouth and a shaker. A musical tinkling broke the silence that had fallen on the room, and presently Soapy, after he had had one quick and had got started on another rather slower, gave evidence of being sufficiently restored to be able to render his report.

Dolly, observing these improved conditions, felt that the need for restraint was past and that questions were now in order.

"What happened, Soapy? Did you go there? Did you see her? What's she like?"

Soapy winced. The question had touched an exposed nerve. As had been the case with Freddie Widgeon, he had expected to find in Leila Yorke a frail little wisp of a thing who would be corn before his sickle, and right from the start her personality had intimidated him. He had found those bright, piercing blue eyes of hers particularly disturbing, and later, when she had produced that shotgun . . . He shivered at the recollection. He was a man not easy to disconcert—if you make your living selling stock in derelict oil wells, you learn to present a confident, even a brassy, face to the world—but Leila Yorke had done it.

"She's a tough egg," he said, drying his forehead again. "You remember Soup Slattery?"

"Of course." That eminent safeblower had been one of their intimate circle in the old Chicago days. "But what's Soup got to do with it?"

"She's a little like him. Better-looking, of course, but that same way of giving you the cold, glassy eye that Soup has when you're playing poker with him and he's got the idea that it's not all according to Hoyle. Those eyes of hers sort of go through you and come out the other side. The moment I saw her, I knew it wasn't going to be easy, but I never dreamed things were going to turn out the way they did. No sir, it never occurred to me."

Nothing is more irritating to a woman of impatient habit, wanting to get the news headlines quickly, than to try to obtain them from a man who seems intent on speaking in riddles, and a less affectionate wife than Dolly might well at this point have endeavored to accelerate her husband by striking him with the cocktail shaker. It is to her credit that she confined herself to words.

"What way? How do you mean? What *happened?*"

Soapy marshaled his thoughts. He had finished that second martini now and was feeling calmer. The knowledge that seven miles separated him from Leila Yorke had done much to restore his composure. And he was reminding himself, as Dolly had reminded him yesterday, that you can't win 'em all. It was a comforting reflection. He was not entirely his old hearty self as he began his story, but he had shaken off that dizzy feeling which comes to the man who pays a social call and suddenly finds his hostess jabbing a shotgun into his diaphragm.

"Well, sir, I got to Castlewood and rang the bell. The front doorbell. I rang it. Yes sir, I rang the front doorbell."

Though accustomed to her loved one's always deliberate methods as a raconteur, Dolly could not repress a sharp yelp of exasperation. She needed her lunch, and it looked as though this was going to take some time.

"Get on, get on! I didn't think you blew a bugle."

This puzzled Soapy. Except when he was selling oil stock, his mind always moved rather slowly.

"Bugle?"

"Get on."

"Why would I blow a bugle?"

"Skip it. Let it go."

"I didn't have a bugle. Where would I get a bugle?"

"I said skip it. Do concentrate, honey. We left our hero ringing at the door. What happened then?"

"She opened it."

"*She* did?"

"Yes."

"Hasn't she a maid?"

"Didn't seem to have."

"No help at all?"

"Not that I could see. Why?"

"Oh, nothing. I was just thinking."

The thought that had floated into Dolly's mind was that if the garrison of Castlewood was so sparsely manned, it might be possible to drop in one evening with a sandbag and do something constructive. She had always been a woman who liked the direct approach. But Soapy's next words showed this to be but an idle dream.

"All she's got is a secretary and a shotgun."

"A *shotgun?*"

"That's right. One of those sporting guns it looked like."

Dolly did not often touch her hair when she had done it to her liking, but she clasped it now with both hands. She was finding her mate's story difficult to follow. The shotgun motif perplexed her particularly.

"Tell me the whole thing right from the beginning," she said, reckless of the fact that this might involve another description of how he rang the doorbell.

Soapy asked if there was a dividend. There was, and he drank it gratefully. Then, as if inspired, he plunged into his narrative without more delay.

"Well, like I say, she opened the door, and there we were. 'Miss Leila Yorke?' I said. 'That's me, brother,' she said. 'You'll forgive me for butting in like this, Miss Yorke,' I said, 'but I am one of your greatest admirers. Can I talk to you for a moment?' I said, and then I went into my spiel. It was a swell spiel. If I say it myself, I was good."

"I'll bet you were."

"The line I took was that I was one of these rugged millionaires who'd made my money in oil, and I sketched out for her the sort of conditions you live in when you're starting out after oil—the barren scenery, the wooden shacks, the companionship of rough and uneducated men, the absence of anything that gives a shot in the arm to a guy's cultural side. I gave all that a big build-up."

"I can just hear you."

" 'For years,' I said, 'I went along like that, starved for intellectual sustenance, and it was getting so that my soul was withering like a faded leaf in the fall, when one day I happened on a tattered copy of one of your books.' "

"Did she ask you which one?"

"Sure she did. Having looked her up in *Who's Who*, I was able to tell her. It was one of the early ones. I said it kind of seemed to open a whole new world to me, and as soon as I was able to raise the money from my meager earnings I bought the whole lot and read them over and over, each time learning something new from them. I said I owed her more than I could ever repay."

"That must have tickled her."

"You'd have thought so, but it was just then that I noticed she was looking at me in that odd, Soup Slattery kind of way, sort of narrowing her eyes as if there was something about my face she didn't like."

"If she didn't like your face, she must be cuckoo. It's a swell face."

"Well, I've always got by with it, but that was the way she was looking. 'So you feel you owe me a lot, do you?' she said, and I said 'I do indeed,' and she said, 'That's just how I feel.' "

"Kind of conceited," said Dolly disapprovingly.

"That's how it struck me. These authors, I said to myself. Still, I didn't hold it against her, because I knew they were all that way. I went into my sales talk. I said money was no object to me, and I wanted to buy this house of hers, no matter what it cost, and keep it as a sort of shrine. I wasn't sure, I said, if I wouldn't have it taken down and shipped over to America and set up on my big estate in Virginia. Like William Randolph Hearst used to do."

"But Castlewood doesn't belong to her. She's only renting it, same as we did."

"Yes, I knew that, of course, but I was just leading up to the big moment. She told me the place belonged to Keggs and he was in Singapore or somewhere on his round-the-world cruise, and I said Well, that was too bad, because I'd set my heart on getting it and this was going to be a great disappointment to my friends on the other side, who were all great admirers of hers, same as me. 'But you won't mind me just rambling about and taking a look at this shrine where you live and work?' I said, and was starting to head for the bedroom when she said, 'Excuse me.' "

"Went to powder her nose?"

"No, she went to get this shotgun of hers. She came back with it, and pointed it at my wishbone. 'Listen, rat!' she said. 'Your kind attention for a moment, please. You have just three seconds to get out of here.' "

"For Pete's sake! Why?"

"The very question I asked her. And she said, 'So you made your money out of oil, did you? I'll say you did, my rugged millionaire, and a thousand pounds of it was do-nated by me. Le Touquet three years ago—remember?' Baby, she was the dame in the Casino I told you about, the one I sold that Silver River to. Naturally I hadn't placed her. When we did our deal, she was wearing dark glasses, and one meets so many people. But she remem-bered me all right. 'I shall count three,' she said, 'and if by the time I say -ee you aren't halfway back to America, you'll get a charge of shot in the seat of the pants.' Well, I can take a hint. I didn't stand loitering about. I left. So there you are, honey. Ninety-nine times out of a hundred that line of talk of mine would have dragged home the gravy, but this was the one time it didn't. Too bad, but nobody's to blame."

Dolly was all wifely sympathy.

"I'm not blaming you, sweetie. You did all that a man could do . . . unless . . . You couldn't have beaned her with a chair, I suppose?"

"Not a hope. If I'd made a move or so much as stirred a finger, I wouldn't be sitting down like this. I'd be lying on my face with you picking shot out of me with your eyebrow tweezers. She meant business," said Soapy, and he stirred uneasily in his chair as he thought of what might have been. He was a high-strung man, and vivid mental pictures came easily to him.

Dolly sat frowning thoughtfully. A lesser woman would have been crushed by this tale of disaster, but she never allowed a temporary setback to make her forget the lesson of the story of Bruce and the spider. Like the poet, she held it truth with him who sings to one clear harp in divers tones that men—or, in her case, women—can rise on steppingstones of their dead selves to higher things.

"We must have another try," she said, and Soapy started as if Leila Yorke and her shotgun had materialized themselves before him.

"You aren't suggesting I go to Castlewood again?"

"Not you, sweetie. Me."

"But what sort of spiel can you give her?"

"Ah, that wants thinking out. But I'll dig up something. The thought of all that ice laying there on top of that wardrobe, when at any moment someone might get the idea of dusting there and put their hooks on it, goes right against my better nature. Come on, honey, let's lunch. You need some nourishing food inside you after going through that— What's the word?"

"Ordeal," said Mr. Molloy, whose life work had given him a good vocabulary. "When you're up against a dame with glittering eyes and one finger on the trigger of a shotgun, that's an ordeal, and don't let anyone tell you different."

There is something about lunch at a place like Barribault's that raises the spirits and stimulates the brain. The hors d'oeuvres seem to whisper that the sun will some day shine once more, the cold salmon with tartare sauce points out that though the skies are dark the silver lining will be along at any moment, and with the fruit salad or whatever it may be that tops off the meal, there comes a growing conviction that the bluebird, though admittedly asleep at the switch of late, has not formally gone out of business. These optimistic reflections did not occur to Soapy, who remained downcast and moody throughout, but Dolly had scarcely taken two bites out of her pêche Melba when she uttered a glad cry.

"Soapy, I've got it!"

Mr. Molloy, who was toying with a strawberry ice, jerked a spoonful into space. It fell to earth, he knew not where.

"Got what, baby? Not an idea?"

"Yeah, and a darned good one."

The gloom which had been enveloping Soapy lightened a little. He had a solid respect for his wife's ingenuity.

"Look, honey, you told me there was no help at Castlewood. Well, look, this Yorke dame and the secretary have got to go out some time, haven't they? To do the shopping and all that."

"I guess so."

"So the place'll be empty. Well, what's to stop me going down there and hanging around till the coast's clear and slipping in? The Widgeon guy goes off to his office in the morning, so I can wait in the front garden of Peacehaven till I see them leave."

"Suppose they don't leave?"

"For heaven's sake, they've got to do it some time or other. As a matter of fact, I think the balloon'll go up tomorrow, because I read a thing in the paper about how Leila Yorke was due to speak at some luncheon or other, and I guess she'll take the secretary with her. Even if she doesn't, the secretary's sure to play hooky when she's not around. Ask me, the thing'll be handed to us on a plate. I'll go there tomorrow right after breakfast. Unless you'd rather?"

Mr. Molloy, shuddering strongly, said he would not rather.

"All right, then, me. I don't see how it can fail. The back door won't be locked. I can just slip in. Any questions?"

"Not a one. Baby," said Mr. Molloy devoutly, "I've said it before and I'll say it again. There's no one like you."

10.

The function at which Leila Yorke had committed herself to speak was the bimonthly lunch of the women's branch of the Pen and Ink Club, and she had completely forgotten the engagement till Sally reminded her of it. On learning that the curse had come upon her, she uttered one of those crisp expletives which were too sadly often on her lips and said that that was what you got for letting your guard down for a single moment with these darned organizing secretaries. Iron, unremitting firmness was what you needed if you were not to be a puppet in their hands.

"They're cunning. That's the trouble. They write to you in December asking you to do your stuff in the following June, and you, knowing that June will never arrive, say you will, and blister my internal organs if June doesn't come around after all."

"Suddenly it's spring."

"Exactly. And you wake up one fine morning and realize you're for it. You ever been to one of these fêtes that are worse than death, Sally?"

"No, I'm not a member of the Pen and Ink. Mine has been a very sheltered life."

"Avoid them," Leila Yorke advised, "especially the all-women ones. Yes, I know you're going to argue that it's better to be confronted with a gaggle of female writers in ghastly hats and pince-nez than a roomful of male writers with horn-rimmed glasses and sideburns, but I disagree with you. The female of the species is far deadlier than the male. What am I to say to these gargoyles?"

" 'Good afternoon, gargoyles'?"

"And then sit down? Not a bad idea. I don't think it's ever been done. Well, go and get the car out. I've some shopping to do, so we'll make an early start."

"We?"

"Oh, I'm not going to drag you into the lunch. One has one's human feelings. I want you to go and see Saxby and tell him of the change of plans about the new book. As my literary agent, I suppose he's entitled to be let in on the thing. Break it to him gently. Better take a flask of brandy with you in case he swoons."

"He'll be upset, all right."

"And so will my poor perishing publishers. I've a contract for six books with them, and if I have my strength, those books are going to get starker and starker right along, and the starker they become, the lower will those unhappy blighters' jaws drop. But what the hell? Art's art, isn't it? Suppose they do lose their shirts? Money isn't everything."

"You can't take it with you."

"Exactly. After seeing Saxby, look in on them and tell them that. It'll cheer them up. But do you know who's going to howl like a timber wolf about this?"

"The whole firm, I should say. They rely on you for their annual holiday-at-Blackpool expenses."

"Prosser, that's who. He's got a wad of money in the business, and when he finds I'm putting it in jeopardy, he'll hit the ceiling. Oh well, we can't help Prosser's troubles. Into each life some rain must fall. Go and get the car."

Sally got the car and, as they drove off and were passing Peacehaven, startled her employer by uttering a sudden exclamation.

"Now what?" said Leila Yorke.

"Nothing," said Sally.

But it had not been nothing. What had caused her to exclaim had been the sight of a spectacular blonde leaning on the Peacehaven front gate, as if, so it seemed to her jaundiced eye, the place belonged to her. The last thing a girl likes to see leaning in this manner on the gate of the man she loves, especially when she knows him to be one of the opposite sex's greatest admirers, is a blonde of that description. Even a brunette would have been enough to start a train of thought in Sally's mind, and she passed the remainder of the short journey to the metropolis in silence, a prey to disturbing reflections on the subject of leopards and spots and the well-known inability of the former to change the latter. It was only when the car had been housed at a garage near Berkeley Square and she and Leila Yorke had parted, the one to do her shopping, the other to go and ruin the morning of Mr. Saxby, the literary agent, and of the Messrs. Popgood and Grooly, Miss Yorke's poor perishing publishers, that there came to her a consoling recollection—to wit, that Freddie had told her that he shared Peacehaven with his cousin George, the sleepless guardian of the law. Policemen, she knew, have their softer side and like, when off duty, to sport with Amaryllis in the shade. No doubt the spectacular one was a friend of George's. As she entered the premises of the Saxby literary agency, Freddie having thus been dismissed without a stain on his character, she was feeling quite happy.

So, as she leaned on the gate of Peacehaven and watched the car disappear round the corner, was Dolly Molloy. Everything, as she envisaged it, was now hunky-dory. There remained only the task of walking a few yards, slipping in through a back door, mounting a flight of stairs, picking up a chamois leather bag and going home, a simple program which she was confident would be well within her scope. And she was opening the gate as a preliminary to the first stage of the venture, when from immediately behind her a voice spoke, causing her to skip like the high hills and swallow the chewing gum with which she had been refreshing herself.

"Oh, hullo," it said, and turning she perceived a tall, superbly muscled young man, at the sight of whom her hazel eyes, which had been shining with a glad light, registered dismay and horror. This was not because she disliked tall, superbly muscled young men or because the Oxford accent in which he had spoken jarred upon her transatlantic ear, it was due to the circumstance that the other was wearing the uniform and helmet of a policeman, and if there was one thing a checkered life had taught her to shrink from, it was the close proximity of members of the force. No good, in her experience, ever came of it.

"You waiting for Freddie Widgeon? I'm afraid he's gone up to London."

"Oh?" said Dolly. It was all she found herself able to say. The society of coppers, peelers, flatfeet, rozzers and what are known in the newest argot of her native land as "the fuzz" always affected her with an unpleasant breathlessness.

"He works in an office, poor devil, and has to leave pretty soon after the morning repast. Around six P.M. is the time to catch him. Is there anything I can do for you? I'm his cousin George."

"But—" Dolly's breath was slowly returning. The lack of menace in her companion's attitude had reassured her. Too many policemen in the past, notably in the Chicago days, had shown her their rather brusquer side, generally starting their remarks with the word Hey! and she found the easy polish of this one comforting. She was, of course, still in something of a twitter, for the conscience of a girl who has recently purloined several thousand pounds' worth of jewelry is always sensitive, but she had ceased to entertain the idea that her personal well-being was in danger.

"But you're a cop," she said.

"That's right. Somebody has to be, what?"

"I mean, you don't talk like one."

"Oh, that? Oh, well, Eton, you know. Oxford, you know. All that sort of rot, you know."

"I didn't know the bulls over here went to Oxford."

"Quite a few of them don't, I believe, but I did. And when I came down, it was a choice between going into an office or doing something else, so I became a flattie. Nice open-air life and quite a chance, they tell me, of rising to great heights at Scotland Yard, though they were probably pulling my leg. What I need to set my foot on the ladder of success is a good pinch, and how that is to be achieved in Valley Fields is more than I can tell you, for

of all the unenterprising law-abiding blighters I ever saw
the locals take the well-known biscuit. It discourages a
chap. But I say, I'm awfully sorry to be gassing about myself like this. Must be boring you stiff. Did you want to
see Freddie on some matter of import? Because, if so,
you'll find him at Shoesmith, Shoesmith, Shoesmith and
Shoesmith in Lincoln's Inn Fields, if you know where that
is. They're a legal firm. Freddie works for them. At least,"
said Cousin George, appearing to share the doubts expressed on a previous occasion by Mr. Shoesmith, "he goes
there and sits. Head for Fleet Street and ask a policeman.
He'll direct you. Our police are wonderful."

"Oh, no, it's nothing important, thanks. I just wanted
to say Hello."

"Then I'll be off, if you don't mind. We of the constabulary mustn't be late at the trysting place, or we get
properly told off by our superiors. Pip-pip, then, for the
nonce. Oh, there's just one other thing before I go. You
wouldn't care to buy a couple of tickets for the annual
concert of the Policemen's Orphanage, would you?"

"Who, me?"

"Sounds silly, I know, but the men up top issue bundles
of the beastly things to us footsloggers, and we're supposed to unload them on the local residents."

"I'm not a local resident."

"They come, nicely graded, to suit all purses—the five-
shilling, the half-crown, the two-shilling, the shilling and
the sixpenny—only the last-named means standing up at
the back. Anything doing?"

"Not a thing."

"Think well. You'll never forgive yourself if you miss
hearing Sergeant Banks sing 'Asleep in the Deep,' or, for
the matter of that, Constable Bodger doing imitations of

footlight favorites who are familiar to you all. So, on re-flection shall we say a brace of the five-bobs?"

Dolly was firm. The thought of doing anything even remotely calculated to encourage the police went, as she would have said, against her better nature.

"Listen, brother," she said, her voice cold and her eyes stony. "If you are open to suggestions as to where you can stick those tickets of yours, I can offer one."

"No need. I take your point. Not in the market, what? Then I don't have to go into my patter. There's a regular recitation they teach us, designed to stimulate trade, all about supporting a charitable organization which is not only most deserving in itself but is connected with a body of men to whom you as a householder—not that you are, but if you were—will be the first to admit that you owe the safety of your person and the tranquillity of your home. The rozzers, in short. Still, if you're allergic to Policemen's Orphanages, there is nothing more for me to add but—"

" 'Pip-pip.' "

"I was about to say 'Toodle-oo.' "

"Toodle-oo, then. Nice to have met you. Keep your chin up and don't arrest any wooden nickels," said Dolly, and Cousin George went on his way, his manner a little pensive. He was thinking that Freddie, though unques-tionably a picker as far as looks were concerned, had some odd friends. Charming girl, of course, his late companion, and one of whom he would willingly have seen more, but definitely not the sort you brought home and introduced to mother.

As for Dolly, she remained where she was for some moments, still a little unstrung, as always after she had been talking to policemen. Then, having shaken off most of the ill effects of the recent encounter, she hurried down the road and received further evidence that this was not, as she had at one time supposed, her lucky day. In the Castlewood front garden there was a gate similar to that of Peacehaven. On this Mr. Cornelius was leaning with folded arms and the general appearance of one who planned to be there for some considerable time. Courteous as always to tenants, he greeted her with a friendly waggle of his white beard, seeming much more pleased to see her than she was to see him. Of Thomas G. Molloy, as we have seen, he disapproved, but he had always admired Dolly.

"Why, good morning, Mrs. Molloy. It is a long time since we met. Mr. Molloy told me that you had been away."

"Yup, visiting friends," said Dolly, though feeling that it was stretching the facts a little to apply this term to the authorities of Holloway gaol. "Quite a surprise it was to me when Soapy said he'd left Castlewood."

"To me, also, when he told me he was leaving."

"Well, that's how it goes. With all those big business interests of his, he found he had to be nearer the center of things, what I mean."

"I quite understand. Business must always come first."

"Kind of a wrench, of course, it was to him, having to move from Valley Fields."

"I am not surprised. I am sure it was. There is no place like it. When I think of Valley Fields, Mrs. Molloy, I am reminded of the words of Sir Walter Scott. I daresay you know them. They occur in his poem 'The Lay of the Last Minstrel,' where he says, 'Breathes there the man, with soul so dead, Who never to himself hath said, This is my own, my native land? Whose heart hath ne'er within him burned, As home his footsteps he hath turned, From wandering on a foreign strand?'" said Mr. Cornelius, thinking of the day trip he had once taken to Boulogne.

Reduced to the status of a captive audience, Dolly found her already pronounced impatience increasing. Mr. Cornelius had recited this well-known passage to her soon after her arrival in Valley Fields, and she knew that, unless he was nipped in the bud, there was a lot more of it to come.

"Yeah," she said. "No argument about that. But what I came about—"

" 'If such there breathe,' " proceeded the house agent smoothly, " 'go, mark him well; For him no minstrel raptures swell; High though his titles, proud his name, Boundless his wealth as wish can claim—Despite those titles, power and pelf—' "

"What I came about—"

" '—The wretch, concentred all in self, Living, shall forfeit fair renown, And, doubly dying, shall go down To the vile dust from whence he sprung—' "

"I just wanted—"

" '—Unwept, unhonored and unsung,' " concluded Mr. Cornelius severely, putting the anonymous outcast right in his place. "Those words, Mrs. Molloy, will appear on the title page of the history of Valley Fields which I am compiling."

"Yes, so you told me, a couple of months ago."

"It will be printed at my own expense and circulated privately. I thought of a binding in limp leather, possibly blue."

"Sounds swell. Put me down for a copy."

"Thank you. I shall be delighted. It will not be completed, of course, for some years. The subject is too vast."

"I can wait. Say, listen. What I came about was that lucky pig of mine."

"That— I beg your pardon?"

"Little silver ninctobinkus I wear on my bracelet. I've lost it."

"I am sorry."

"Hunted everywhere for it and then suddenly remembered I'd had it last in the bedroom down here when I was dressing. Put it down somewheres and forgot about it."

"These lapses of memory frequently occur."

"Yeah. Well, do you think whoever's got the house now—"

"Miss Leila Yorke, the novelist," said Mr. Cornelius reverently.

"No, really? Is that so? I'm one of her greatest admirers."

"I, also."

"Swell stuff she dishes out. Knocks spots off all competitors."

"Indeed yes," said Mr. Cornelius, though he would not have put it in quite that way.

"Well, do you think she would mind if I just popped up to the bedroom and had a look around?"

"I am sure she would readily give her consent, if she were here, but she has left for London. That, I may say, is the reason for my presence. She asked me to keep an eye on the house. It seems that Miss Yorke received a visit yesterday from a most suspicious character, who tried to insinuate himself into Castlewood on some pretext or other, with the intention, no doubt, of returning later and burgling the place."

"Well, of all the ideas! Sounds cuckoo to me."

"I assure you that sort of thing is frequently done. I was speaking of this man to Mr. Widgeon's cousin, who is in the police and who had had the story from Mr. Widgeon, who had had it from Miss Foster, who had had it from Miss Yorke, and he told me it was a well-known practice of the criminal classes. 'Casing the joint,' it is called, he says. He expressed some chagrin that the exigencies of walking his beat would take him away from Castlewood so that, when the man returned, he would not be there to make what he described as a pinch. He is a most zealous officer."

"I'll bet he is. We want more of his sort around."

"Very true."

"Well, anyway, I'm not casing any joints. All I want is to mosey up to that bedroom and see if my pig's there. I'll prob'ly find I dropped it behind the dressing table or something. Miss Yorke won't mind me doing that?"

"I feel convinced that she would have no objection, but what you suggest is, I fear, impracticable, for before leaving she locked her bedroom door."

"What!"

"On my suggestion," said Mr. Cornelius rather smugly.

Dolly stood silent. Six separate blistering observations had darted into her mind like red-hot bullets, but she remembered in time that she was a lady and did not utter them. Contenting herself with a mere "Oh, is that so? Well, pip-pip." She turned and walked away, giving no indication of the vultures that gnawed at her bosom.

At the corner of the road that led to the station she caught a Number Three omnibus, and this in due season deposited her in Piccadilly Circus. Partly because the day was so fine and partly because she hoped with exercise to still the ferment in her blood, she walked along Piccadilly and turned up Bond Street, and it was as she did this that out of the corner of her eye she observed a well-dressed man behind her.

It has already been stated that the sight of a well-dressed man in her rear often called to Dolly to put into effect the technique which years of practice had bestowed on her. A moment later, she was swooning in his arms, and a moment after that withdrawing the hand that had crept toward his pocket. She had seen his face and knew that there would be little in that pocket to reward the prospector.

"Why, hello, Mr. Widgeon," she said.

11.

Until the moment of impact, Freddie had been in the best of spirits, feeling, like the gentleman in *Oklahoma!* that everything was coming his way. As he started to walk up Bond Street, he was not actually singing "Oh, What a Beautiful Morning!" but it would not have required a great deal of encouragement to induce him to do so. Few things so brace up a young man in springtime as a reconciliation with the girl he loves, and the thought that he and Sally, so recently a couple of sundered hearts, were once more on Romeo-and-Juliet terms would alone have been enough to raise him to the heights and, as we say, bring him to the very brink of bursting into song.

But in addition to this there was the uplifting reflection

that he had in a drawer at Peacehaven scrip of the Silver River Oil and Refinery Corporation which he would shortly be selling for ten thousand pounds and, to set the seal on his happiness, someone at the office, just before he left, had dropped a heavy ledger on the foot of Mr. Jervis, the head clerk, causing him a good deal of pain, for he suffered from corns. In the six months during which he had served under the Shoesmith banner Freddie had come to dislike Mr. Jervis with an intensity quite foreign to his normally genial nature, and he held very strongly the view that the more ledgers that were dropped on him, the better. His only regret was that it had not been a ton of bricks.

All in all, then, conditions, where he was concerned, could scarcely have been improved on, and joy may be said to have reigned supreme.

But the sudden discovery that his arms had become full of totally unforeseen blondes occasioned a sharp drop in his spirits. There had been a time when, if females of this coloring had fallen into his embrace, he would have clasped them to him and asked for more, but that had been in the pre-Sally days. Sally had changed his entire spiritual outlook. And, thinking of her, as he was now doing, he found himself entertaining a chilling speculation as to what she would say if she knew of these goings-on, to be succeeded by the more soothing thought that, being seven miles away in Valley Fields, she would not know of them. And when Dolly spoke and he realized that this was not some passing stranger who had taken a sudden fancy to him, but merely his next-door neighbor Mrs. Molloy, he was quite himself again. His acquaintance with Dolly was not an intimate one, but her husband had introduced them one afternoon and they had occasionally exchanged Good mornings across the fence, so if she had tripped over something and clutched at him for support, there was really nothing in the whole episode that even Emily Post could shake her head at.

When, therefore, she said "Why, hello, Mr. Widgeon," it was with a completely restored equanimity that he replied, "Why, hullo, Mrs. Molloy. Fancy bumping into you."

"Bumping is right. Hope I didn't spoil the sit of your coat. I kind of twisted my ankle."

"Oh, really? Those high heels, what? Always beats me how women can navigate in them. You're all right?"

"Oh, sure, thanks."

"Not feeling faint or anything?"

"A bit sort of shaken up."

"You'd better have a drink."

"Now that's a thought. I could certainly use one."

"In here," said Freddie, indicating the Bollinger bar, outside of which they happened to be standing. "There's no better place, so the cognoscenti inform me."

If at the back of his mind, as they passed through the door, there lurked a shadow of regret that he had not steered his guest to one of the many Bond Street tea shoppes for a quick cup of coffee, instead of giving his patronage to an establishment where, he knew, they charged the earth for an eye-dropperful of alcoholic stimulant, he did not show it. The chivalry of the Widgeons would alone have been enough to keep him from doing that, and when the thought stole into his mind, it was immediately ejected by the reflection that it was to the husband of this woman that he owed the prosperity that in the near future would be his. If a man out of pure goodness of heart has put thousands of pounds in your pocket, the least you can do when you find his wife all shaken from a near fall in Bond Street is to bring her back to midseason form with a beaker of the right stuff, even if her taste inclines to champagne cocktails.

Dolly's taste did, and he bore the blow to a purse ill adapted to the receipt of blows like a Widgeon and a gentleman, not even paling beneath his tan when she drained her first one at a gulp and asked for a refill. Nothing could have been more apparently carefree than his demeanor as he opened the conversation.

"Funny us meeting like this. What are you doing in these parts? Shopping?"

"No, just strolling along. I'm meeting my husband for lunch at Barribault's. We're living there now."

"Really?" said Freddie, impressed. "Nice place."

"Yeah. We're got a very comfortable suite."

"Bit of a change from Valley Fields. It came as quite a surprise when Cornelius told me you had left Castlewood."

"I guess we did move kind of quick, but that's Soapy all over."

"Oh, is it? Who's Soapy?"

"I call Mr. Molloy that. On account of he made his first million in soap. It's a sort of little joke between us."

"I see. Very droll," said Freddie, though he had heard more hilarious pleasantries in his time. "You'll never guess who's got the house now."

"Is it rented again already?"

"Went off right away. New tenant's a terrific celebrity. Leila Yorke, the novelist."

"You don't say? What's she doing in Valley Fields? I was reading a piece in a women's paper, where it said she owned one of those stately homes of England you hear about."

"Yes, Claines Hall, Loose Chippings, down in Sussex.

But she's got the idea of doing a book about the suburbs. Do you read her stuff?"

"I don't, no. I've heard tell of it, but it sounds too mushy for me. What I like is something with plenty of blood and lots of mysterious Chinamen in it."

"Me, too. But you haven't heard the latest. She's changing her act. Her new book's going to be strong and stark and full of grayness and squalor, the sort of thing George Gissing used to write, and she's gone to Valley Fields to get what they call local color. I think myself she's a sap to do it, because her usual bilge sells in vast quantities, and I don't suppose anyone'll buy a copy of this one. Still, there it is. She's got this goofy urge to do bigger and better things, and she means to go through with it."

"Won't her publishers let out a holler?"

"I should imagine a fortissimo one. And poor old Oofy's going to suffer fifty-seven pangs. He put a lot of money in the business, and losing money always cuts him to the quick."

"Oofy?"

"Nobody you know. Fellow clubman of mine. Chap called Prosser."

"Prosser? That name seems to ring a bell. Didn't a Mrs. Prosser have a lot of jewelry snatched not long ago?"

"That's right. Oofy's wife. She turned her back for a moment, and when she looked round the sparklers were gone."

"I read about it in the papers. They think the maid did it, don't they?"

"That's the general idea. When the hue and cry was raised, she had vanished."

"And I must vanish, too, or I'll be late for lunch, and Soapy hates waiting for his eats."

"I'll put you in a taxi," said Freddie, greatly relieved

that no more champagne cocktails were going to flow like water.

He put her in a taxi, and she drove off, waving a slender hand. Freddie waved his in courteous return, and was thinking what a delightful woman Mrs. Molloy was and wishing he had seen more of her during her stay at Castlewood, when his meditations were interrupted by a voice at his elbow, a soprano voice with a nasty tinkle in it.

"Mr. Brigham Young, I believe?" it said, and he jumped perhaps six inches. Sally was standing beside him, and he was quick to note that in her eyes was that unmistakable look which creeps into the eyes of idealistic girls when they see their betrothed helping blondes into taxis and waving after them with, it seems to them, far too much warmheartedness.

"Good Lord, Sally!" he said. "You gave me a start."

"I'm not surprised."

"What on earth are you doing here?"

"I've been seeing Leila Yorke's publishers about her change of plans regarding the next book. Their offices are just round the corner. Didn't you hear them screaming? Well?"

"How do you mean, 'Well?'"

"You would prefer I made myself clearer? All right, then, put it this way. Who was that lady I saw you coming down the street with?"

"Oh, the beazel who was here just now?"

"That is the beazel to whom I refer."

There is probably nothing so stimulating to a young fiancé in circumstances such as these as the knowledge that he has got his story ready and that it will be impossible for the most captious critic to punch holes in it. Where a young man less happily situated would have shuffled his feet and stammered sentences beginning with "Er—,"

Freddie stood firm and foursquare, and his voice, when he spoke, came out as clear and unhesitating as that of Mr. Cornelius when reciting his favorite passage from Sir Walter Scott's "Lady of the Lake."

"That was Mrs. Molloy."

"Ah, a new one."

Freddie's manner became cold and dignified.

"If you mean by that what I think you mean, you're missing your pitch and are very much off on your downbeat. Correct this tendency of yours to allow a diseased imagination to run away with you and make you say things which can only lead to bitter remorse. Ever seen driven snow?"

"I know the sort of snow you mean."

"Well, that's what I'm as pure as. That, I was saying, was Mrs. Molloy, and I was about to add, when you interrupted me, that she is the wife of Thomas G. Molloy, who resided at Castlewood before Miss Yorke took over. She twisted her ankle as she was walking along the street—"

"Lucky she had you at her side."

"She didn't have me at her ruddy side, not the way you mean. If you will be good enough to keep your trap shut for just half a minute, I will explain the circumstances and explain them fully. She was not walking along the street with me, but far otherwise, I was walking along the street, as it might be here, and she was walking along the street, as it might be there, quite distinct and separate, and suddenly she twisted this ankle of which I spoke. I saw her stumble—she was just in front of me—and very naturally grabbed her."

"Ah!"

" 'Ah' does not enter into it. If you see a female, and one to whom you have been formally introduced by her husband, about to take a toss, there is no course open to you but to lend her a hand. Chivalry demands it. So when you accuse me of licentious behavior in the middle of Bond Street, you are, as you will readily appreciate, talking through the back of your foolish little neck."

"I didn't accuse you of licentious behavior."

"You were going to when you got around to it. Well, having grabbed her, I thought she might be feeling faint after her unpleasant experience, so I took her into the Bollinger for a quick tissue restorer. And," said Freddie with feeling, "the prices they charge in that thieves' kitchen are enough to whiten your hair from the roots up. I was the one who was feeling faint when the waiter brought the bad news. I thought for a moment he must have added in the date."

"But it was worth the expense?"

"What do you mean by that?"

"Oh, nothing."

"I should hope not. It's no pleasure to me to pay out large sums, which I can ill afford, for champagne for women who are comparative strangers."

"Then why did you do it?"

Something that was almost a pang shot through Freddie as he thought how silly this girl was going to look in about fifty seconds or so. No man of fine sensibilities can ever really enjoy bathing the woman he loves in confusion and bringing home to her with a wallop what a priceless ass she has been making of herself with her baseless suspicions and cracks about Brigham Young and "new ones," but sometimes it has to be done. One must have discipline. He crushed pity down and spoke.

"I'll tell you why I did it. Because I was under a great obligation to her husband, Thomas G. Molloy, who recently out of pure goodness of heart let me have some oil stock which I shall be selling shortly for a matter of ten thousand quid."

"Freddie!"

"You may well say 'Freddie!' If anything, the word understates it. Yes, those are the facts, and I took the view that as Molloy had done the square thing by me in so stupendous a fashion, the least I could do in return was to lead his stricken wife into the Bollinger and tell the man behind the bar to fill her up, even with champagne cocktails costing a king's ransom, and she knocked back two of them and there was a moment when I thought she was going to order a third."

He had been right in supposing that his revelation of the inside story would have a powerful effect on the party of the second part.

"Oo!" said Sally.

"Ten thousand *pounds!*" said Sally.

"Oh, *Freddie!*" said Sally.

He pressed his advantage like a good general.

"Now perhaps you understand why I mentioned driven snow."

"Of course."

"No more baseless suspicions?"

"Not one."

"In short, sweethearts still?"

"You take the words out of my mouth."

"Then come along to some fairly cheap hostelry, and I'll give you lunch. And while we revel I'll tell you about Kenya and the bit of luck that's shortly going to happen to the coffee industry out there."

The operative word in Freddie's concluding remarks had been the adjective "cheap," so it was not to Barribault's that he escorted Sally for the midday meal. Had he done so, they might have observed Mr. and Mrs. Molloy seated at a table against the wall, in which event the animation of the latter would not have escaped their notice. Dolly, who had depressed her husband over the smoked salmon with a description of her misadventures in Valley Fields, was now, with the chicken in aspic, about to bring the sunshine into his life again.

"It's all right, Soapy," she was saying. "We aren't licked yet."

"Who says so?" inquired Mr. Molloy morosely. The tale to which he had been listening had turned the smoked salmon to ashes in his mouth, and he was not expecting better things of the chicken in aspic.

"Me, that's who, and I'll tell you why. On my way here I ran into young Widgeon in Bond Street, and he told me something that gave me an idea that's going to fix everything. You know the Yorke dame."

Soapy quivered a little.

"We've met," he said in a hushed voice.

"I mean, you know the sort of junk she writes?"

"No, I don't. What do you think I am? A bookworm?"

"Well, it's that mushy stuff that sells like hot dogs at Coney Island, and she's got a million fans over here and in America, too, but I guess she's got fed up with dishing out the marshmallow and chocolate sauce, because her next book's going to be one of those strong, stark things, so Widgeon tells me, quite different from her ordinary boloney."

"So what?" said Mr. Molloy, still morose.

"Well, that's news, isn't it? That's the sort of thing that's going to interest a whole lot of people, isn't it? So what'll seem more natural to her than having *Time* or *Newsweek* or someone—I mean some American magazine, that's got a London office—call her up and say can they send along one of their dames to get the low-down and find out why she's making the switch. So this dame goes down to Castlewood and asks her what the hell and all that, and then she says she needs some photographs of the house, including the bedroom, on account of their readers are always interested in bedrooms, and there you are, we're in."

Mr. Molloy, as has been indicated, was not a very quick-thinking man except when engaged in his professional activities, but even he could see that there was much in what she said. He had been raising a segment of chicken to his lips, and he paused spellbound with the fork in mid-air. He was no longer morose.

"Baby," he said. "I believe you've got it."

"You can say that again. Can't slip up, far as I can see. I'll call her after lunch and make the date."

A flaw in the setup occurred to Mr. Molloy.

"But you haven't got a camera."

"That's all right," said Dolly. "I'll pick one up at Selfridge's this afternoon."

12.

While entertaining Sally at lunch (shepherd's pie and an apple dumpling) at a pub he knew around the corner, Freddie had enjoined strict secrecy upon her in the matter of the Silver River Oil and Refinery Corporation, just as Mr. Molloy when letting him have that stock had enjoined it on him. Mr. Molloy, he explained, was planning to buy up all the outstanding shares and very naturally wanted to secure them at a low price, which he would not be able to do if people went around shooting their heads off about what a terrific thing it was. The principle, he said, was the same as when someone gives you a tip on a fifty-to-one outsider straight from the mouth of the stable cat and tells you to keep it under your hat so as not to shorten the odds. He was conscious as he spoke of a slight feeling of guilt as he remembered that he had not pursued this sealed-lips policy when chatting with Mr. Cornelius a few days ago, but too late to worry about that now, and anyway Mr. Cornelius, immersed as he was in house agenting and rabbits, was not likely to spread the news.

So when Sally rejoined Leila Yorke and started homeward with her in the car, it was not of the coming ten thousand pounds that she spoke, but of the Pen and Ink Club luncheon and Miss Yorke's speech.

"How did it go?" she asked. "Were you in good voice?"

"Oh, yes."

"What did you say?"

"The usual applesauce."

"How many gargoyles were there?"

"About a million."

"What were their hats like?"

"Nothing on earth," said Leila Yorke.

Her manner was not responsive, but Sally persevered.

"I saw Mr. Saxby."

"Oh?"

"He took it big, as anticipated. So did Popgood and Grooly. At least, Grooly. I didn't see Popgood. Grooly turned ashy pale, and said you ought to have your head examined."

"Oh?"

"I left him ringing up Mr. Prosser, to tell him the bad news."

"Oh, yes?" said Leila Yorke, and she relapsed into a silence that lasted till the end of the journey.

Sally, as she put the car away, felt concerned. Taciturnity on this scale was quite foreign to her usually exuberant employer. It might, of course, be merely the normal letdown which results from sitting through a women's luncheon, but she felt it went deeper than that. Even after two hours of looking at members of the Pen and Ink Club, Leila Yorke ought to be cheerier than this.

It seemed to her that what was needed here was a nice cup of tea. She had never herself attended one of these literary luncheons, but she knew people who had and had gathered from them that all the material, as opposed to intellectual, food you got at them was half a tepid grapefruit with a cherry in it, some sort of hashed chicken embedded in soggy pastry and a stewed pear. No doubt Leila Yorke's despondency was due to malnutrition, and this could be corrected with tea and plenty of buttered toast. She prepared these lifesaving ingredients and put them on a tray and took them out into the garden, where Miss Yorke was sitting gazing before her with what in her books she liked to describe as unseeing eyes.

The listlessness with which she accepted the refreshment emboldened Sally to speak. In the months which she had spent at Claines Hall she had become very fond of Leila Yorke, and she hated to see her in this mood of depression.

"What's the trouble?" she asked abruptly.

She was aware that she was exposing herself to a snub. It would have been quite open to the other, thus addressed by a humble secretary, to raise a cold eyebrow and reply that she failed to understand her meaning or, more probably, seeing that it was Miss Yorke, to ask her what the hell she thought she was talking about. But the question had come at a moment when the novelist needed to unburden her mind. There is something about grapefruit with a cherry in it, hashed chicken in pastry and stewed pears that breaks down reserve and inspires confidences.

She did not raise her eyebrows. She said, quite simply,

as if she was glad Sally had asked her that, "I'm worried about Joe."

Sally knew who Joe was, Leila Yorke's mystery husband, who had passed into the discard some years previously. There had been occasional references to him during her tenure of office, the latest only yesterday, and she had often wondered what manner of man he had been. She always pictured him as a large, dominant character with keen eyes and a military mustache, for she could not imagine anything less hardy entering into matrimony with so formidable a woman. Yes, big and keen-eyed and strong and, of course, silent. He would have had to be that, married to someone as voluble as Miss Yorke.

"Oh, yes?" was all she found herself able to say. It was not the best of observations, but it seemed to encourage her companion to proceed.

"I saw him this afternoon."

This time Sally's response was even briefer. She said, "Oh?"

"Yes," said Leila Yorke, "there he was. He looked just the same as he always did. Except," she added, "for a bald spot. I always told him his hair would go, if he didn't do daily hair drill."

Sally had no comment to make on the bald spot. She merely held her breath.

"Gave me a shock, seeing him suddenly like that."

On the point of saying she didn't wonder, Sally checked herself. Silence, she felt, was best. There was something in all this a little reminiscent of a deathbed confession, and one does not interrupt deathbed confessions.

"Hadn't seen him for three years. He was still living with his mother then."

Sally's interest deepened. So Joe had gone back to his mother, had he. This was, she knew, a common procedure with wives, but rarer with husbands. She found herself revising the mental picture she had made. A man like the Joe she had imagined would have taken his gun and gone off to the Rocky Mountains to shoot grizzly bears.

"That mother of his! Snakes!" said Miss Yorke unexpectedly.

"Snakes?" said Sally, surprised. She felt that a monosyllable would not break the spell, and she wanted to have this theme developed. She was convinced that the word had not been a mere exclamation. A strongly moved woman might ejaculate "Great Snakes!" but surely not "Snakes!" alone.

"She kept them," explained Miss Yorke. "She was in vaudeville—Herpina, the Snake Queen—and she used them in her act. When," she added with some bitterness, "she could get bookings, which wasn't often." She sighed, or, rather, said "Oh, hell!" which was her way of heaving a sigh. "Did I ever tell you about my married life, Sally?"

"No, never. I knew you had been married, of course."

"You'd have liked Joe. Everybody did. I loved him. Still do, blast it. His trouble was he was so weak. Just a rabbit who couldn't say 'Boo!' to a goose."

Sally knew that the number of rabbits capable of saying "Boo!" to geese is very limited, but she did not point this out. She was too busy making further revisions in the mental portrait.

"So when his mother, one of the times when she was 'resting,' suggested that she should come and live with us, he hadn't the nerve to tell her she wasn't wanted and that the little woman would throw a fit if she set foot across the threshold. He just said 'Fine!' And as he hadn't the nerve to tell me what he'd done, the first inkling I got of what was happening was when I came home all tired out from a heavy day at the office—I was a sob sister then on one of the evening papers—and found her in my favorite chair, swigging tea and fondling her snakes. A nice homecoming that was, and so I told Joe when I got him alone. He had the gall to say that he had thought she would be such nice company for me when he was away on tour."

"Was he an actor?"

"Of a sort. He never got a part in the West End, but he did all right in the provinces, and he was always going off to play juvenile leads in Wolverhampton and Peebles and places of that kind. So Mother and snakes dug themselves into the woodwork, and that," said Miss Yorke, again unexpectedly, "was how I got my start."

Sally blinked.

"How do you mean?"

"Perfectly simple. Everyone who's on a paper is always going to do a novel when he gets time, and I had often thought of having a bash at one, because if you're a sob sister, you accumulate a whole lot of material. This was where I saw my opportunity of buckling down to it. Instead of spending my evenings listening to Mother saying how big she had gone at the Royal, Wigan, and how it was only jealousy in high places that had kept her from working her act in London, I shut myself up in my room and wrote my first novel. It was *Heather o' the Hills*. Ever read it?"

"Of course."

"Pure slush, but it was taken by Popgood and Grooly, and didn't do too badly, and they sent the sheets over to Singleton Brothers in New York, who turn out books like sausages and don't care how bad they are, so long as they run to eighty thousand words. They chucked it into the sausage machine and twiddled the handle and darned if it wasn't one of the biggest sellers they had that season.

What's known as a sleeper. And they asked me to come to New York and lend a hand with the publicity, autograph copies in department stores and all that. Well, Joe was still on tour with half a dozen more towns to play, and I thought I'd only be over there a few weeks, so I went. And of course the damned book was bought for pictures and I had to go out to Hollywood to work on it, and when I'd been there a couple of months I sent Joe five thousand dollars and told him this looked like being a long operation so he must come and join me. And what do you think?"

"What?"

"He wrote back thanking me for the five grand and saying he couldn't make it, as his mother didn't want him to leave her. Said she had palpitations or something. It made me so mad that I did what I can see now was the wrong thing. I said to myself, All right, Joe, if you can do without me, I can do without you, and I stayed on in America six solid years. By that time I suppose we had both taken it for granted that the marriage was washed up."

"You didn't get a divorce?"

"Never occurred to me. I'm a one-man woman. I wouldn't have wanted to marry anyone, after having Joe. I just let things drift. Three years ago I ran into him in the street and we talked for a while. I asked him if he was all right for money, and he said he was. He had written a play that was being taken on tour, he said, and I wished him luck and he wished me luck, and I asked after his mother and he said she was living with him and still had the snakes, and I said that was fine, and I came away and cried all night."

It cost Sally an effort to break the silence which followed. Speech seemed intrusive.

"And you saw him again today?"

"Yes," said Leila Yorke. "He was one of the waiters at the luncheon."

Sally gasped. "A waiter!"

"That's what I said. They always get in a lot of extra waiters for these affairs, and he was one of them."

"But that must mean—"

"—that he's absolutely broke. Of course it does, and I've got to find him. But how the devil do you find an extra waiter in the whole of London?"

Inside the house, as they wrestled with this problem, the telephone began to ring.

"Answer it, will you, Sally," said Leila Yorke wearily. "If it's that man Cornelius, say I'm dead."

"It's somebody from *Time*," said Sally, returning. "They want to interview you about your new book."

"Tell them to go and— No, better not. Male or female?"

"Female."

"All right, tell the pest she can come tomorrow at five," said Leila Yorke. "That gives me twenty-four hours. Perhaps by then she'll have been run over by a bus or something."

13.

Tuesday began well for Freddie's cousin George. Leaning over the Nook-Peacehaven fence as the other fed his rabbits, he not only sold Mr. Cornelius two of the five-shilling tickets for the forthcoming concert in aid of the Policemen's Orphanage but received from him the information that Castlewood was now occupied by a famous female novelist, a piece of news that stirred him like a police whistle. All female novelists, he knew, were wealthy beyond the dreams of avarice, and he was convinced that if this one were to be properly approached, with just the right organ note in the voice, business could not fail to result. Before starting out on his beat, accordingly, he gave his uniform a lick with the clothes brush, said "Mi, mi," once or twice to himself in an undertone and, clumping over to Castlewood in his official boots, rang the bell.

Sally opened the door to him, and he gazed at her with undisguised admiration. Being betrothed to a charming girl who was something secretarial in a shipping office, a Miss Jennifer Tibbett, he took, of course, only an academic interest in the appearance of such others of her sex as he encountered, but his eye was not dimmed and he was able to see that here was something rather special in the way of nymphery. He approved wholeheartedly of this exhibit's trim little figure, her slightly tiptilted nose, her copper-colored hair and the blue eyes that gazed into his. The last-named seemed to him to be shining like twin stars, as he believed the expression was, and he was not mistaken in thinking so. Sally, while preparing breakfast for her employer, had been meditating on Freddie and how much she loved him, and thoughts of that nature always give the eyes a sparkle.

"Oh, hullo," he said. "I mean what ho. I mean good morning."

The subject being one that he considered too sacred to be discussed with cousins, especially cousins who, he knew from experience, had a tendency to greet his tales of love with uncouth guffaws, Freddie had not mentioned Sally to George. He shrank from having his idyll soiled by ribald criticism, and something told him that ribald was what George would inevitably be if informed that he, Freddie, had found the real thing at last. Intimate with the last of the Widgeons since their kindergarten days, George knew how volatile were his affections. It had, indeed, though Sally was not aware of it, been he who at that cocktail party had uttered those words about Piccadilly Circus and Hyde Park Corner which she had found so disturbing.

All that George knew of Sally, therefore, was what he had learned from Mr. Cornelius—to wit, that Miss Yorke in her descent on Valley Fields had been accompanied by a secretary. A rather attractive girl, the house agent had said, and to George, drinking her in, this seemed an understatement of the first water. She was, in his opinion, a grade-A pippin, and he could see Freddie, if and when he made her acquaintance, straightening his tie, shooting his cuffs and, like the horse to which allusion was made earlier, saying "Ha, ha" among the trumpets.

"I say," he proceeded, "do take a lenient view of this unwarrantable intrusion, as I've sometimes heard it called. I live next door, and I thought it would be neighborly if I looked in and passed the time of day."

"Oh?" Sally's smile was of such a caliber that, if he had not been armored by his great love for Miss Tibbett, it would have gone through him like a bullet through blancmange. As it was, it made him totter for a moment. "You're Freddie's cousin, the policeman. He was telling me about you."

George was conscious of a feeling of awed respect for his kinsman's enterprise. He had always known that he was a quick worker, never letting the grass grow beneath his feet in his dealings with the young and beautiful, but in not only introducing himself to but in getting to be on such familiar terms with a girl who hadn't been around for more than about twenty-four hours, he had, in George's opinion, excelled himself. "Freddie" already! Quick service, that. Why, in his own case it had been a matter of three weeks before he had got past the surname stage. It was a gift, of course, and Freddie had it and he hadn't.

"That's right," he said. "Great chap, Freddie. Always reminds me of one of those fellows who bound on stage with a racquet at the beginning of a play and say 'Tennis, anyone?' "

Sally stiffened.

"He isn't in the least like that."

She spoke coldly, and George saw that he had said the wrong thing. He hastened to correct himself.

"I only meant he's not a beefy bird like me, but slim and graceful and all that."

"Yes, you're right there."

"Svelte, shall we call him?"

"If you like."

"Fine," said George, relieved. "We pencil Freddie in as svelte. And now, for I shall have to be popping off in a moment to discourage the local crime wave, could I have a word with Miss Leila Yorke?"

"She's breakfasting in bed. Can I give her a message?"

George fingered his chin.

"Well, it might work that way," he said dubiously, "but I had hoped to come face to face with her and give her the old personality, if you understand what I mean. You see, I'm trying to sell tickets for the annual concert in aid of the Policemen's Orphanage, to be held at the Oddfellows Hall in Ogilvy Street next month, and my chances of success are always much brighter if I can get hold of the prospect by the coat button and give him—or, as in this case, her—all that stuff about supporting a charitable organization which is not only most deserving in itself but is connected with a body of men to whom he—or she—as a householder will be the first to admit that he or she owes the safety of his or her person and the tranquillity of his or her home—in other words, to cut a long story short and get right down to the nub, the police. There's a lot more of it, but you will have got the idea."

"Yes. I've got it. Did you think all that up by yourself?"

"Good Lord, no. It's written out for us by the big shots, and we memorize it. All over Valley Fields and adjoining suburbs at this moment a hundred flatties are intoning it in the ears of the rate-paying public."

"It must sound heavenly. Will it be a good concert?"

"Sensational."

"How much are the tickets?"

"They vary. The five-shilling ones are five shillings, the half-crown ones half a crown, the two-shilling ones—"

"Two shillings?"

"You guessed it right off," said George, regarding her with an increase of his previous admiration, as if stunned by this blending of brains and beauty. "And the shilling ones are a shilling and the sixpenny ones sixpence. The last named, those at a tanner, I don't recommend very highly, because all they draw is standing room. They are traditionally reserved for the canaille and the under-privileged, the poor slobs who can't afford anything better."

Sally had made a discovery.

"You do talk beautifully," she said.

"I do, rather," George agreed.

"And just like Freddie."

"Better than Freddie, I should have said. Well, will you toddle off like a dear little soul and see if you can work Miss Yorke up to the five-bob standard? A woman of her eminence ought to be in the first three rows."

Sally went upstairs and found Leila Yorke sipping tea and looking moody. Her air was that of one who is thinking of extra waiters.

"Did I hear the front doorbell?" she asked.

"Yes, it was a caller."

"Cornelius?"

"Not this time. It was Freddie's cousin George, the cop.

He's selling tickets for the concert in aid of the Police-men's Orphanage."

"Oh, a touch?"

"On a very modest scale. Ten bob will cover it, and you will be supporting a charitable organization which is not only most deserving in itself—"

"Oh, all right. Look in my bag. On the dressing table."

Leila Yorke had spoken listlessly, but now she suddenly sat up and became animated.

"Did you say this bird was a policeman?"

"Complete with helmet and regulation boots. Why?"

"Wouldn't a policeman know all about private eyes?"

"Oh! You mean—?"

"To look for Joe. Go back and ask him if he can recommend somebody for the job."

It was an idea, but to Sally's mind not a very good one.

"Do you think a private detective could do anything? I know they make inquiries and all that, but wouldn't it be rather like looking for a needle in a haystack?"

"Well, that's what private eyes are for. Go and ask him. I've got to find Joe, and this is the only way."

"I suppose it is," said Sally, and she returned to the front steps, where George was standing like a large blue statue, thinking, apparently of absolutely nothing, unless, of course, as it may well have been, his mind was on Miss Jennifer Tibbett. Tapped on the arm and hearing the words "Hi, officer!" he came out of his coma and the light of hope flashed into his face.

"Any luck?"

"Two of the five-bob."

"You're terrific! Was it a fearful struggle? Did you have to twist her arm?"

"Oh, no, she was a cheerful giver. Well, fairly cheerful.

She's a bit down at the moment because she's lost her husband."

George clicked his tongue sympathetically.

"I say, rather a bad show, that. Enough to give any woman the pip. Not but what we've all of us got to go some time. What is it they say all flesh is as? Grass, isn't it?"

"Oh, he isn't dead, he's an extra waiter."

"I'm not sure I quite got that. An extra what?"

Sally explained the position of affairs, and George said Oh, he saw now. For a moment, he added, he had not completely grasped the gist.

"And she asked me to ask you," said Sally, "if you knew any private eyes."

"You mean shamuses?"

"That's right."

"I don't, and I don't want to. Frightful bounders, all of them, from what I've heard. Always watching husbands and wives and trying to get the necessary evidence. We of the force look down on them like anything. Does Miss Yorke want to scoop one in to try and find her husband?"

"That's the idea."

"He'll have his work cut out for him."

"So I told her."

"He'll be looking for a needle in a haystack."

"I said that, too."

"Well, I wish I could help you. I'll tell you what I think her best plan would be. She ought to ask her solicitor."

"Why, of course. A solicitor would probably know dozens of private detectives."

"I think so. Solicitors always have oodles of shady work to be done—documents stolen from rival firms, heirs kidnaped, wills pinched and destroyed, and so on. Trot along and put it up to her. And now, if you'll excuse me," said George, "I must be buzzing off on my official duties, or heaven knows what the denizens of Valley Fields will be getting up to in my absence. Awfully nice to have seen you."

Sally returned to Leila Yorke, who had finished her breakfast and was enjoying one of her mild cigars.

"He says he doesn't know any private eyes, but he thinks a solicitor would."

"I wonder."

"It's worth trying."

"I suppose so. All right, go and see Johnny Shoesmith."

"Very well. I'd better wait till the afternoon. There are a lot of supplies to be got in, and if I'm not here to cook lunch for you, you'll try to do an omelet and make a frightful hash of it. Remember last time? I can't think why you never learned to cook. Didn't you have to get your own meals when you were a sob sister?"

"Me? You are speaking of the time when I was young and beautiful and men lined up in queues to feed me. Your Freddie's Uncle Rodney alone was good for six or seven dinners a week. And when I married, Joe did the cooking. He could cook anything, that boy. We had a little flat in Prince of Wales's Mansions, Battersea, and every night—"

A tear stole into Leila Yorke's eye, and Sally left the room hastily. Taking her shopping bag, she went out into Mulberry Grove and met George, who was emerging from the gate of Peacehaven. He had postponed his grappling with the criminal element of Valley Fields in order to return home and get his cigarettes, one, or possibly more, of which he hoped to be able to smoke when the sergeant's eye was not on him.

"Hullo," he said. "We meet again."

"We do," said Sally. "I'm going shopping. Oh, by the

way, did you find your friend when you got back yester-day?"

George cocked an inquiring eye.

"What friend would that be?"

"I only caught a glimpse of her as I went by in the car. A tallish, fair girl. She was leaning on the gate of Peace-haven."

George's face cleared.

"Oh, ah, yes. I know the girl you mean. I met her and we chatted of this and that. But she was a friend of Fred-die's, not of mine. I had never seen her before in my life. She said she had come to see Freddie and say Hello, by which I took her to mean pick up the threads and all that sort of thing. Well, pip-pip once more," said George, and with a courteous salute he went on his way.

14.

The day which had turned out so well for Freddie's cousin George had proved less enjoyable for Mr. Shoesmith of Lincoln's Inn Fields. At breakfast a usually meticulous cook had served up to him boiled eggs which should have been taken from the saucepan at least a minute earlier and, not content with this tort or misdemeanor, had scorched the toast to the consistency of leather. At lunch at his club, the Demosthenes, he had been cornered by old Mr. Lucas-Gore, whose conversation was always a bleating mélange of anecdotes about Henry James, an author in whom the solicitor's interest had never been anything but tepid. Toward the middle of the afternoon the weather had become close and oppressive, with thunder threatening. And at four o'clock Leila Yorke's secretary had appeared, babbling of private detectives.

A wholesome awe of Leila Yorke, bred in him from the days of his youth, had kept him from throwing the girl out on her ear, as he had wished to do, but he had got rid of her as quickly as possible, and scarcely had she gone when his daughter Myrtle arrived, interrupting him at a moment when he had hoped to be free to attend to the tangled affairs of Freddie's uncle, Lord Blicester, who was having his annual trouble with the income tax authorities. It was almost, Mr. Shoesmith felt, as if Providence were going out of its way to persecute him, and he was reminded of the case of Job, who had been the victim of a somewhat similar series of misfortunes.

Myrtle was not looking her sunniest. Her eyes smoldered, her lips were drawn in a tight line and her general aspect resembled that of the thunderclouds which were banking up in the sky outside. She was a human replica of one of those V-shaped depressions extending over the greater part of the United Kingdom south of the Hebrides which are such a feature of the English summer, and Mr. Shoesmith gazed at her wanly. Knowing her moods, he could recognize the one now gripping her. She had a grievance, and experience had taught him that when she had a grievance she sat and talked for hours, taking up time which could have been more profitably employed on lucrative work such as the tangled affairs of Lord Blicester. Wrenched from these, he felt like a dog deprived of a bone.

"Ah, Myrtle," he said, resisting a temptation to strike his child with the Blicester dossier. "Take a chair. Unpleasant weather. How is Alexander?"

He was not really interested in the health of his son-in-law, whose only merit in his eyes was his colossal wealth, but one must start a conversation somehow.

Myrtle, who had already taken a chair and looked, to her father's anxious eyes, as if she had glued herself to it, sat for a space breathing tempestuously through her nose. Her resemblance to a thundercloud had become more noticeable.

"Alexander is very upset."

"I'm not surprised."

"Why, have you heard?"

"Heard what?"

"About that Leila Yorke woman."

"What about her?"

"So you haven't heard. Then why did you say you weren't surprised that Alexander is upset?"

What had led Mr. Shoesmith to do so had been his familiarity with Oofy's habit of starting the day with a morning hangover, but he felt that it would be injudicious and possibly dangerous to put this into words. He replied that he was aware how delicate his son-in-law's digestion was.

"Eaten something that disagreed with him?" he asked with as much sympathy as he could muster, which was not a great deal.

Myrtle's breathing took on a snorting sound.

"My dear father, you don't suppose I came all this way to talk about Alexander's digestion. He's upset about this frightful business of Leila Yorke. I think she must have gone off her head. You know Alexander owns the majority stock in Popgood and Grooly, who publish her books?"

"Yes, you told me. A very sound firm, from all I hear. Bessie alone—"

"Who is Bessie?"

Mr. Shoesmith assumed the manner which Freddie

Widgeon disliked so much, his dry, put-you-in-your-place manner.

"An old friend of mine who writes under the pseudonym of Leila Yorke. She was Bessie Binns when I first knew her, and it is pardonable of me, I think, to refer to her by her real name. But if you would prefer that I do not do so, your wishes are law. I was about to say when you interrupted me—we were speaking, if you remember, of the financial stability of the publishing house of Popgood and Grooly—that Leila Yorke alone must be worth a good many thousands of pounds to them annually."

A curious sound which might have been a hollow laugh escaped Myrtle.

"Yes, because up to now she has written the sort of . . ." She hesitated for a word.

"Bilge?" suggested Mr. Shoesmith.

"If you like to put it that way. I was going to say the sort of horrible sentimental stuff that appeals to women. There isn't an author in England who has a bigger library public. Women worship her."

Mr. Shoesmith cackled like a hen, his way of chuckling.

"I wonder what they would think of her if they met her. She certainly isn't like her work. But why do you say 'up to now'?"

"Because she's planning to do something quite different with her next book. Her secretary called on Mr. Grooly yesterday and told him that the novel she's working on now is going to be gray and stark and grim, like George Gissing."

"A fine writer."

"I dare say; but he didn't sell. Imagine the effect this will have on her public. She'll lose every reader she's got."

"So that is why Alexander is upset?"

"Isn't it natural that he should be? It means thousands

of pounds out of his pocket. I was in the room when Mr. Grooly telephoned to tell him the news, and he turned ashy pale."

An improvement, Mr. Shoesmith thought. He had never admired his son-in-law's complexion. Owing to a too-pronounced fondness for champagne, Oofy had always been redder than the rose, and Mr. Shoesmith preferred the male cheek to be more damask.

"Has she written the book?" he asked.

"She's thinking it out. She has gone down to the suburbs to get local color."

"It may turn out to be very good."

"But it won't be Leila Yorke. Can't you understand? When people see the name Leila Yorke on a novel, they expect Leila Yorke stuff, and if they don't get it, they drop her like a hot coal. How would you like it if you bought a book you thought was about company law and found it was a murder mystery?"

"I'd love it," said Mr. Shoesmith frankly.

"Well, Leila Yorke's public won't. This book will kill her stone dead. She won't have a reader left."

"I don't suppose she cares. She's been making twenty thousand pounds a year for the last fifteen years and saving most of it. It seems to me it's entirely her own affair if she spurns Popgood and Grooly's gold and decides to go in for art for art's sake. I don't understand the Popgood and Grooly agitation. If they don't want to publish the thing, they don't have to."

"But they do. She's got a contract for six more books."

"Then what on earth do you expect me to do?" said Mr. Shoesmith, trying not to speak petulantly but missing his objective by a wide margin. The conflict between Lord Blicester and the income tax authorities presented several points of nice legal interest, and he was longing to get back to them. Not for the first time he was regretting that his daughter had not married someone with a job out in, say, the Federated Malay States, where leave to come to England is given only about once every five years. "If she has a contract—"

"I've brought it with me." Myrtle was fumbling in her bag. "I thought you might be able to find something in it which would prevent her doing this insane thing."

"I doubt it," said Mr. Shoesmith, taking the document. He skimmed through it with a practiced eye and handed it back. "I thought so. Not a word even remotely specifying any particular type of book."

"But isn't it implied?"

"Isn't what implied?"

"That she's got to do the sort of thing she has always done."

"Certainly not. You don't imply conditions in contracts, you state them in black and white."

"Do you mean to say that if Agatha Christie had a contract with her publisher—"

"No doubt she has."

"—that she could suddenly decide to turn in something like *Finnegans Wake?*"

"Certainly."

"And the publisher would have to publish it?"

"If he had so contracted."

"That is the law?"

"It is."

"Then the law's idiotic."

"Dickens put it better. He said it was a hass. But even if you and he are right, there is nothing to be done about it."

Myrtle rose, a thing which Mr. Shoesmith had begun to

feel that she was incapable of doing. A new animation came into his manner.

"Are you leaving me?" he asked, trying to keep exhilaration out of his voice.

Myrtle gathered up bag and umbrella. Her face was set and determined.

"Yes, I am going to Valley Fields."

"Odd spot to choose for a jaunt. Why not Surbiton?"

"This is not a jaunt, as you call it. Leila Yorke is living in Valley Fields, and I am going to see her and talk to her."

"You think that that will accomplish something desirable?"

"I hope so."

"I wonder. From what I know of Bessie, she is not a woman lightly to be turned from her purpose. Still, 'try anything once' is always a good motto. Goodbye, my dear. Nice of you to have looked in. Give my regards to Alexander," said Mr. Shoesmith, and he was deep in the affairs of Lord Blicester, almost before the door had closed.

Dolly, meanwhile, down at Castlewood with her notebook and her new camera, was finding her hostess charming. Leila Yorke, though she raged, like the heathen, furiously and muttered things better left unmuttered when one of them announced his or her intention of coming to see her, was always at her best with interviewers. She put them at their ease—not that Dolly needed that—and made a social success of the thing, feeling, for she was essentially a kindly woman, that it was not the fault of these children of unmarried parents if their editors told them to go and make pests of themselves. In her sob sister days she had had to do a good deal of interviewing herself, and she could sympathize with them.

Dolly she found unexpectedly congenial. Hard things had often been said of the light of Soapy Molloy's life by those who knew her—Chimp Twist, trading as J. Sheringham Adair, private investigator, was always particularly vehement when her name came up in the course of conversation—but she was unquestionably good company, and Leila Yorke took to her from the start. They roamed the parklike grounds of Castlewood in perfect amity, and she was delighted with the intelligent girl's attitude toward the change she was proposing to make in her approach to the life literary. Dolly left no room for doubt that she thoroughly approved of it.

"Onward and upward with the arts," she said. "Can't always be giving them the same old boloney. Look at a guy I . . ." She paused. She had been about to say "know" but felt it would be more prudent to substitute a less compromising verb. "Look at a guy I heard about through working on papers, like you do hear about all sorts when you work on papers. Fellow named Easy-Pickings McGee, who had a business in Cicero, outside Chicago. Used to stick up filling stations and drugstores and all like that and made a good enough living for years, and then one morning he says to himself, 'I'm through with this small-time stuff. I've gotten into a rut. I ought to be striving for something bigger.' So he goes right out and sticks up a bank and from that moment never looked back. Got his own gang now, and is one of the most highly thought-of operators in Cook County. I know for a fact—because someone told me," she added hastily—"that he has fifty-six suits of clothes, all silk lined and custom made, and a different pair of shoes for every day in the year. Well, there you are. Ambition pays off."

Leila Yorke said she had an idea that Horatio Alger had written a story of success on much these lines, and Dolly said "Mebbe." She had not, she explained, read very deeply in her Horatio Alger.

"But you see what I mean. You're in the same kind of a spot he was. You're doin' all right for a mountain girl, as the song says, but you feel the time has come to show 'em what you can do when you spit on your hands and go to it. You just carry on, honey, the way you want, and if anyone makes a holler, tell 'em to drop dead."

This so exactly chimed in with Leila Yorke's sentiments that she beamed on her visitor and cordially allowed herself to be photographed in a variety of attitudes, though if there was one thing she disliked more than another about these interviews, it was being propped up against something and told to smile. And it was as she relaxed from the last pose—leaning with one hand on the birdbath and gazing brightly over her left shoulder— that the leaden sky, which had hitherto not spoken, suddenly burst into sound. Thunder roared, lightning flashed, and rain began to descend in the manner popularized by Niagara Falls.

Dolly, being nearest to the French window of the living room, was the first to reach it, with Leila Yorke a close second. They stood looking out on the downpour.

"This realm, this England!" said Miss Yorke bitterly.

"Yeah," Dolly agreed. "I'll bet that guy who returned here after wandering on some foreign strand kicked himself squarely in the derrière for being such a chump as to come back. I wish I had the umbrella concession for this darned country. Well, seeing we're indoors and no chance of getting anything more in the garden, how about some interiors? Tell you what I'd like to have," said Dolly, struck with an idea, "and that's a shot of your bedroom. Kind of intimate, sort of. Mind if I go up?"

"Certainly. Room on the left at the top of the stairs."

"I'll find it," said Dolly, and at this moment the front doorbell rang.

With an impatient grunt, for this, she supposed, could only be Mr. Cornelius again, Leila Yorke went to answer it, and Dolly, about to follow and mount the stairs that led to Eldorado, was frozen in mid-step by a voice she had no difficulty in recognizing.

"Miss Yorke?" said the voice. "Can I come in and speak to you on a matter of importance? My name is Mrs. Alexander Prosser."

It is inevitable, as we pass through life, that we meet individuals whom we are reluctant to meet again. Sometimes it is the way they clear their throats that offends us, sometimes the noise they make when drinking soup, or possibly they remind us of relatives whom we wish to forget. It was for none of these fanciful reasons that Dolly preferred not to encounter Myrtle Prosser, and for an instant, knowing that she was on her way in and that ere long there would be a recognition scene which could not fail to be painful, she stood transfixed. Then life returned to the rigid limbs, and she was her resourceful self again. There was a whirring sound as she dashed back into the living room, dashed through the French windows and dashed across the garden and over the fence that separated it from that of Peacehaven.

In Peacehaven, if the back door was not locked, she would find the hide-out which on an occasion like this is so essential to the criminal classes.

15.

Standing before the mirror in his bedroom at Peacehaven, George was brushing his ginger hair with unusual care and wondering whether a drop of Scalpo, the lotion that lends a luster, would not give it just that little extra something which stamps the man of distinction. He was wearing a blue flannel suit with an invisible stripe, and his shoes, so different from regulation boots, shone with the light that never was on land or sea, for he had wangled a night off from his official duties and was taking Jennifer Tibbett to dinner and a theater. It was not often that he was able to do this, and his heart was light and his attitude toward all created things kindly and benevolent. If a burglar were to enter Peacehaven at this moment, he felt, he would give him a drink and a ham sandwich and help him pack his sack.

And by one of those odd coincidences he became aware, just as this thought floated into his mind, that a burglar had entered Peacehaven. Down below, somebody had sneezed, and as Freddie would not be back from his office for at least another half hour this sneezer could only be an unauthorized intruder. Replacing the hairbrush on the dressing table, he went down, the milk of human kindness still surging within him, to play the host and was interested to discover in the living room the golden-haired young woman with whom he had had such a stimulating conversation on the previous day. The sight of her increased the respect he always felt for Freddie's ability to fascinate the other sex. Wherein lay his cousin's magic, he could not say, but he certainly acted on the beazels like catnip on cats. This girl obviously could not keep away from him, drawn as with a magnet. Like the moth and the candle, thought George.

"Oh, hullo," he said. "You popped in again? Want to see Freddie? He ought to be arriving shortly. Stick around, is my advice."

"I will, if you don't mind," said Dolly, fighting down the womanly tremor she always felt when in the presence of the police. She eyed him closely, taking in with some bewilderment the flannel suit, the neat red tie and the shining shoes. "You'll excuse me asking," she said, "but what are you made up for?"

"Just gentleman, English, ordinary, one. I'm off duty."

"That's good," said Dolly, breathing more freely. "I mean for you."

"Yes, it's nice to get away from the old grind once in a while. One needs an occasional respite, or the machine breaks down. Ask any well-known Harley Street physician."

"Who's attending to all the murders?"

"Oh, a bunch of the other boys. They'll carry on all right in my absence. I say," said George, making a discovery which Sherlock Holmes certainly and Scotland Yard in all probability would have made earlier, "you're wet."

His observant eye had not deceived him. The trip from Castlewood to Peacehaven, though not a long one, had been long enough for the rain to get in some pretty solid work, and Dolly had been exposed to it for some unforeseen extra moments owing to falling while climbing the fence. George, who was given to homely similes, thought she looked like a drowned rat. Being also somewhat deficient in tact, he said so, and Dolly bridled.

"Drowned rats to you, with knobs on," she said coldly. "You're no oil painting yourself."

"Why, yes, if you put it that way," said George, "I suppose you're right. Well, unless you want to get a nasty cold in the head, you'd better change."

"Into what?"

"Ah, that's rather the problem, isn't it. Into, as you say, what? I know," said George, inspired. "Nip up to Freddie's room and swipe a pair of his pajamas. I'd offer you mine, but they wouldn't fit you. Bedroom slippers can also be provided. Come along up, and I'll show you. There you are," he said a few moments later. "Pajamas and slippers, precisely as envisaged. Your kit'll be dry by the time you're ready to leave. Anything else I can do for you in the way of hospitality?"

"Will it be okay for me to make myself a cup of hot coffee?"

"Perfectly okay. This is Liberty Hall. You'll find all the

ingredients in the kitchen. And now I'm afraid I must tear myself away. I'm taking my betrothed to dinner," said George, and with a kindly smile removed himself, feeling like a Boy Scout. Doing this little act of kindness had just put the finishing touch on the mood of yeasty happiness that always uplifted him when he was going to watch Jennifer Tibbett eat lamb cutlets and mashed potatoes. It made him feel worthier of her.

His departure left Dolly a prey to mixed emotions. She liked George as a man and found him an entertaining companion, but she could not forget that for all his suavity and the sparkle of his conversation he represented the awful majesty of the Law and, were he to learn of her activities in the Prosser home, would have no hesitation in piling on the back of her neck and whistling for stern-faced colleagues to come and fasten the gyves to her wrists. Better, then, that they should part. His going had deprived her of the pleasure of listening to his views on this and that and wondering how he could talk the way he did without having a potato in his mouth, but she had also lost the unpleasant feeling that centipedes were crawling up and down her spine which always affected her when hobnobbing with the gendarmerie.

It did not take her long to remove her wet dress and slip into the something loose represented by Freddie's pajamas, and she was on the whole in reasonably cheerful mood as she went down to the kitchen for the cup of hot coffee which she had mentioned. A certain chagrin was inevitable after she had come so near to success in the object of her quest and failed, owing to an act of God at the eleventh hour, to achieve her aims, but hers was a resilient and philosophical nature, and she was able to look on the bright side and count her blessings one by one. She was short, yes, of Prosser jewelry, and that, she would have been the first to admit, was in the nature of a sock in the eye, but she had at least the consoling thought that she had made a clean getaway when for an instant all had seemed lost.

She did not, however, look forward to telling Soapy of this third expeditionary disaster. He would sympathize, he would be all that a loving and understanding husband should be, but he would not be able to conceal that this was a blow. "Where do we go from here?" he would ask, and her only answer would be that she was goshdarned if she knew. It seemed to her, as it would seem to him, that every stone had been turned and every avenue explored. She could not keep on getting bright ideas indefinitely, and Soapy, except when he was selling oil stock, never had any.

It was as she mused thus, sipping coffee and thinking hard thoughts of Myrtle Prosser, whom it would have been a genuine pleasure to her to dip, feet first, into a vat of molten lead, that Freddie, alighting from the 6:03 down train, arriving Valley Fields 6:24, started to walk to Peacehaven.

The rain had stopped, which was all to the good, for he had gone out that morning without his umbrella, and not even the thought that, George being away for the evening, he would have to cook dinner for himself was able to affect his mood of *bien être*. Sally loved him, and he would shortly have a cool ten thousand pounds in his hip pocket, and, as for dinner, there were always sardines. As he latch-keyed himself into Peacehaven, one would not be far wrong in saying that there was a song on his lips.

There was also, it was borne in upon him as he entered, a song on somebody else's lips, the somebody in question apparently being in the kitchen, for as he parked hat on hatstand he could hear a distinct rendition of a popular ballad proceeding from that direction. This struck him as odd, for he had supposed that his cousin George, wafted Londonward on the wings of love, would have left long ere this. Another aspect of the matter that puzzled him was why George's voice, normally a pleasant baritone, should suddenly have become a highish soprano.

The singing ceased. Dolly had been doing it merely to cheer herself up, and this object she had now succeeded in accomplishing. She finished washing her coffee cup and the knife with which she had cut herself a slice of seed cake, and came into the living room, giving Freddie much the same feeling of having had a bomb touched off under him as the ghost of Banquo on a memorable occasion gave Macbeth. In the days before his roving affections had centered on Sally he had had a good deal of experience of girls popping up at unexpected moments in unexpected places, but he had never seen one before wearing his pajamas. A perfect stranger, too, it seemed to him—which deepened the bizarre note.

Then Dolly, who felt that it was for her to open the conversation, said, "Hi, brother Widgeon! How's tricks?" and he recognized her as the wife of Mr. Molloy, his benefactor. He was conscious of a passing wish that this woman would not keep flitting into his life every hour on the hour like a family specter, but she was linked by marriage to the man who had set his feet on the ladder of affluence by letting him have that Silver River stock, so she must not be allowed to think that her presence was unwelcome.

Replacing his heart, which had bumped against his front teeth, he said, "Oh, hullo, there you are."

"Nice meeting you again."

"Nice of you to drop in. Beastly weather, what?"

"You said it."

"Seems to be clearing up a bit, though, now."

"That's good."

"Rain's stopped."

"Probably just biding its time."

"I shouldn't wonder. Care for a cup of tea?"

"I've had some coffee."

"Have some more."

"No, thanks. Well, I guess I ought to explain why I've butted in this way."

"Not at all. Any time you're passing."

"That's just what I was doing—passing. And that storm suddenly came on, and I was getting soaked, so I dashed in here."

"I get the idea. For shelter, as it were?"

"That's right. Nobody can say I haven't sense enough to come in out of the rain, ha, ha."

"Ha, ha," echoed Freddie, but not blithely. Once again he was thinking of what Sally would make of all this, were it to be drawn to her attention.

"I borrowed your pajamas on account of if I stuck around in a wet dress, I might get a cold."

"Or pneumonia. Quite right."

"You aren't sore?"

"No, no."

"I wish I could say the same of myself. Coming here in such a rush, I fell and scraped my knee, and it's kind of acting up."

"Good heavens!"

"Rubbed quite a bit of skin off it. Take a look."

"At your knee?"

"That's the knee I mean."

A wrinkle creased the smoothness of Freddie's brow. His devotion to Sally being one hundred per cent, if not more, it was wholly foreign to his policy to take a look at the knees of others of her sex, especially of those so spectacularly comely as Mrs. Thomas G. Molloy. A year ago he would have sprung to the task, full of the party spirit, but now he was a changed, deeper man who had put all that sort of thing behind him. However, he was also a host, and a host cannot indulge his personal feelings.

"Right ho," he said. "Let's have a dekko. Egad," he went on, having had it, "that doesn't look too good. You ought to see the tribal medicine man about it. Nasty flesh wound, might cause lockjaw. And you don't want that."

Dolly admitted that she had no great fondness for lockjaw.

"The only catch is that you can't very well go charging about Valley Fields, looking for doctors, in striped pajamas. I'll tell you what," said Freddie. "My cousin George has some iodine. I'll go and fetch it."

"Too bad, giving you all this trouble."

"No trouble, no trouble at all. And George won't mind. You haven't met him, have you?"

"Why, yes, I did run into him for a moment."

"Nice chap."

"Yeah. Not like most cops I know."

"Do you know a lot of cops?"

"Well, not socially, but I've seen them around. Over in the States they're kind of tough."

"I know what you mean. Not bonhomous."

"They don't know how to treat a lady, the flat-footed sons of bachelors."

"I'll bet they don't. Well, ho for the iodine. George keeps it in his room."

The window of George's room looked on the back garden, and if Freddie had happened to glance out of it, he would have observed a slim figure making its way to the back door of Castlewood. Sally—for, as Leila Yorke was fond of saying in her novels, it was she—had no latchkey and did not want to disturb her employer by ringing the front doorbell.

She entered the rear premises and reaching the living room found Leila Yorke reading a magazine.

"Sorry I couldn't get back earlier," she said. "Busy day. How did the interview go off?"

"Better than I had expected," said Leila Yorke. "Most interviewers in my experience are recruited from homes for the mentally afflicted, but this one was a nice bright girl. We got along like anything. But a curious thing happened. She suddenly disappeared."

"Faded away, you mean, like the Cheshire Cat?"

"As far as I can make out, she must have gone into the garden and left that way."

"In all that rain? Odd."

"That's what I thought, but I wasn't giving it much attention, as I was coping at the time with Mrs. Prosser."

"Oh, did she come? Freddie's friend Oofy's wife? To reason with you about the book, I suppose?"

"Yes, she talked for hours and would be talking still, if I hadn't edged her to the door and pushed her out. But I don't want to sit chewing the fat about Ma Prosser. Tell me what happened when you saw Johnnie Shoesmith."

"Well, I went in."

"Yes?"

"And he gave me a nasty look."

"Was that all?"

"No, he gave me several more in the course of our chat. Would you call him a very genial sort of man?"

"Johnnie can be the world's leading louse when he likes, and he seems to like all the time these days. Comes of being a solicitor. They get soured. Did he recommend a private eye?"

"Yes, I suppose you could call it that. He grabbed the telephone directory, looked at the classified section and picked the name at the top of the list, a man called Adair, J. Sheringham Adair."

"Nonsense. There isn't such a name."

"Well, that's what he says it is. I went to see him, and there it was in large letters on his door. He's got a dingy little office in a dingy little backwater called Halsey Court. It's in Mayfair, so I suppose he thinks of himself as a Mayfair consultant."

"What's he like?"

"A frightful little man with a face like a monkey and a waxed mustache."

"Is he any good, do you think?"

"He said he was. He spoke most highly of himself."

"I imagine all these private eyes are much alike. Oh, well, let's hope for the best."

"That's the way to talk. He's coming here to see you and get a photograph of your husband. Can you spare him one?"

"Dozens."

"Then, as you say, we'll hope for the best. And now, will you be wanting me for half an hour or so?"

"No. Why? Want to go to Peacehaven and see your Freddie?"

"That's the idea," said Sally. "Give him a nice surprise."

16.

Dolly's premonition that her tale of failure would remove the sunshine from Soapy's life and cause him to feel that it was hopeless to struggle further was amply fulfilled. Melancholy marked him for its own not only over the pre-dinner cocktails but at the meal that followed them and at next day's breakfast. A student of the classics, watching him eat eggs and bacon, would have been reminded of Socrates drinking the hemlock, and though it meant a lonely morning for her, she experienced a sense of relief when he exchanged his bedroom slippers for a pair of serviceable shoes and announced that he was going to take a walk and think things over. She found the spectacle of his drawn face painful.

It was a considerable time before he returned, and when he did she was amazed to observe that his face, so far from being drawn, was split toward the middle by a smile so dazzling that she blinked at the sight of it. His opening remark, that everything was now as smooth as silk and that they were sitting pretty, deepened her bewilderment. She loved him dearly and yielded to no one in her respect for his ability to sell worthless oil stock to the least promising of prospects, but, except for this one great gift of his, she had no illusions about his intelligence. She knew that she had taken for better or worse one who was practically the twin brother of Mortimer Snerd, and she liked it. It was her view that brains only unsettle a husband, and she was comfortably conscious of herself possessing enough for the two of them.

"Sitting pretty?" she gasped. It seemed incredible to her that the briskest of walks could have given her loved one anything even remotely resembling an idea. "How do you figure that out?"

Soapy sank into a chair and took off his left shoe.

"Got a blister," he announced.

It was no time for wifely sympathy. When pain and anguish wring the left foot, a woman ought, of course, to be a ministering angel, but Dolly's impatience temporarily unfitted her for the role.

"How do you mean, we're sitting pretty?"

"Rustle up the lifesavers, and I'll tell you. The thing's in the bag."

Dolly rustled up the lifesavers, and he became even brighter at the sight of them.

"Gee!" he said, regarding her fondly between sips. "You look like a new red wagon, baby."

"Never mind how I look," said Dolly, though pleased by the compliment. "What's happened?"

"You mean the blister? It came on when I'd been walking about half an hour," said Soapy, massaging his foot, "and I felt as if I had a red-hot coal in my shoe. You ever had a blister?"

A dangerous look crept into Dolly's face.

"Get on," she said. "Tell me in a few simple words what's given you this idea that we're sitting pretty?"

She spoke quietly, but Soapy had been married long enough to know that a wife's quiet tones are best respected. He embarked on his narrative without further preamble.

"Well, sir, just after I got this blister, who do you think I met? Chimp."

Dolly sniffed. As has been stated, Chimp Twist was no favorite of hers. Circumstances in the past had sometimes led to their being associated in business deals, but he ranked in her affections even lower than Mrs. Alexander Prosser.

"Must just have made your day, seeing that little weasel," she said acidly, and Soapy's smile became broader.

"It did," he said, "because what do you think he told me?"

"If it was the time, I'll bet he lied about it."

"He told me Leila Yorke has engaged him to find her husband."

"Has she one?"

"Seems so, by all accounts, and she's hired Chimp to locate him."

"He's disappeared?"

"That's what he's done, and Chimp's got the job of looking for him."

"So what?"

Soapy's eyes widened in surprise. He had supposed his mate to be quicker at the uptake than this.

"So *what?*" he said. "Use your bean, baby. Why, can't you see, there he'll be, in and out of the house, having conferences and what not all the time, and don't tell me he won't find a chance sooner or later of getting up to that room and putting his hooks on the ice."

"But he doesn't know it's there."

"Sure he knows. I told him."

"What!"

A strong shudder had shaken Dolly from the top of her perm to the alligator shoes for which a leading department store had been looking everywhere since she had last paid them a visit. Her eyes bulged and her lips parted as if she were about to reveal to her mate just what she thought of this last stupendous act of folly. She did not do this because she loved him and knew that it was his misfortune rather than his fault that he was solid bone from the neck up, but the gasping cry she uttered was enough to make it clear to him that all was not well.

"You *told* him?"

Soapy was perplexed. His story was not going as well as he had expected.

"Well, I had to, baby, or he wouldn't have known where to look."

Again, Dolly's lips parted, and again she closed them. It is possible that she was counting ten, that infallible specific against reckless speech.

"He's going to see her this afternoon, he says. Why, for all we know, he might come back with that ice this evening. Beats me why you don't seem pleased, baby. Here we were, all washed up with no chance of getting the stuff, and along comes this wonderful bit of luck that solves everything. It isn't as if Chimp wants the earth. He said he would do it for ten per cent of the gross."

"And you believed him?"

"Sure I believed him. Why wouldn't I?"

"Because you know as well as I do that Chimp Twist is as crooked as a pretzel. What he hasn't learned about double-crossing you could write on a postage stamp. Shall I tell you what's going to happen, in case you're interested? Reach me down my crystal ball for a moment, and I'll peer into the future and give you the dope. Ha! The mists clear, and I see a little rat with a waxed mustache and a face that only a mother could love hurrying down to Valley Fields. He goes into Castlewood. He's sneaking up the stairs to the bedroom. He's looking on top of the wardrobe. What's that he's putting in his pocket? A bag of peanuts? No, by golly, it's the ice I got from Mrs. Prosser. You remember that ice? I was telling you about it the other day. And now what do I behold? Can he be heading for the nearest airport? Yeah, that's what he's doing. Now they're telling him to fasten his safety belt. Now the winged monster soars above the clouds, and unless it falls and he breaks his damn neck his next address'll be Box 243, rural free delivery, somewhere in South America. And who are these two poor slobs I can see, sitting watching and waiting and saying, 'Ain't he ever coming?' Their faces seem familiar somehow. Why, it's you and me! Yessir, that's who it is, it's us!"

Dolly paused, panting a little, and Soapy's lower jaw fell slowly like a tired flower drooping on its stem. He was not as a rule an easy man to explain things to, but on this occasion his wife's reasoning had been too lucid to allow of any misunderstanding. He had got the message.

"I never thought of that," he said.

"Give a mite of attention to it now."

"Gee!"

"Gee is right."

"What are we going to do if he hijacks the stuff?"

"Sue him," said Dolly, and even Soapy could discern that she spoke satirically. He fell into what would have been a thoughtful silence, if he had been capable of thinking. The best he was able to suggest at the end of several minutes was that he should telephone Leila Yorke and warn her to have nothing to do with J. Sheringham Adair, whose private-eye activities were a mere cloak or front for criminality of the lowest order.

"So then, if he comes trying to ooze into the house, she'll go into action with that gun of hers."

Dolly was not impressed.

"You think she'll have a lot of confidence in what you tell her, after that session you had with her about Silver River Oil and Refinery?"

"I could say I was Inspector Somebody speaking from Scotland Yard."

"With a Middle Western accent? Try again."

Soapy had finished his martini, but though agreeable to the taste and imparting a gentle glow, it brought no inspiration. He chewed his lip, and said it was difficult, and Dolly said Yeah, she had noticed that herself.

Soapy scratched his Shakespearean forehead.

"I don't know what to suggest."

"Make that double."

"We might . . . No, that's no good. Or . . . No, that's no good, either."

"Not so hot as your first idea. That first one seemed to me to have possibilities."

"If only," said Soapy wistfully, "there was some way of getting that dame out of the house!"

Dolly, who like a good wife had been refilling his glass,

paused with the shaker in mid-air, spellbound. She had not expected to hear so keen a summing-up of the situation from such a source. Out of the mouths of babes and sucklings, she seemed to be saying to herself.

"Get her out of the house? Soapy, I believe you've got something. When I was down there yesterday, she sort of gave me the impression that it wouldn't take a lot to make her pack up and leave. I got the idea she's kind of pining for that stately home of hers, where there's cooks and butlers and all like that. Nothing she actually said, but that's the way it struck me. Look, finish that up and go take a walk around the block."

"What, with this blister of mine?"

"Well, keep quiet, then. I want to think," said Dolly, and she walked to the window and stood looking out on London, while Soapy, scarcely daring to breathe lest he destroy thought at its source, lay back in his chair and gently massaged the sole of his left foot, his gaze fixed on her occipital bone as intently as if he could see the brain working behind it. The light of hope in his eyes was only faint, but it was there. Not once but many times in the past had his wife's little gray cells brought triumph out of disaster, and it might be that even the current problem, which, he freely admitted, was a lalapalooza, would not prove too much for her.

At length, Dolly spoke. "Soapy, come here. I want to show you something."

Soapy came as directed, and he too looked out on London. The portion of it that he saw was the back premises of Barribault's Hotel, for it was in that direction that the window faced. It was not a very exhilarating spectacle, mostly empty boxes and ash cans, and it did little to lighten the gloom in which he was plunged. Not that he would have derived any greater spiritual refreshment from it if the boxes had been the Champs Élysées in springtime and the ash cans the Taj Mahal by moonlight.

"See that cat?" said Dolly.

The cat to which she alluded was an animal of raffish and bohemian aspect, the sort of cat that hangs around street corners and makes low jokes to other cats as anti-social as itself. It was nosing about in the ash cans below, and Soapy regarded it without enthusiasm. He was not, he said, fond of cats.

"Nor's the Yorke dame," said Dolly. "One came into the garden while I was there and started stalking a bird, and she eased it out."

"With her shotgun?"

"No, she just hollered, and the cat streaked off, and then she told me she didn't like cats."

"And so?"

"Seeing that one down there gave me the idea."

Soapy was stirred to his depths.

"You haven't got an idea?" he said reverently.

"I have, too. Wait. Don't talk," said Dolly. She went to the ornate writing table with which all suites at Barri-bault's Hotel are provided and took pen and paper, frown-ing meditatively.

"How do you spell 'descriptions'?" she asked. "No, it's okay. I know."

"*D* as in *doughnut*—"

"All right, all *right*. I tell you I know. Is Castlewood *t-l-e* or *t-e-l*?"

"*T-l-e*. Why, honey? What is all this?"

Dolly waved him down impatiently, as authors will when interrupted with questions in the middle of an im-portant work, and for some moments concentrated tensely on whatever this literary composition of hers was, her forehead wrinkled and the tip of her tongue protruding a little. After what seemed an hour she rose and handed him a sheet of notepaper.

"How's this?" she said.

It was not a lengthy document. It read:

WANTED

CATS OF ALL DESCRIPTIONS

GOOD PRICES PAID

APPLY

CASTLEWOOD

MULBERRY GROVE

VALLEY FIELDS.

"It'll cost money," said Dolly, "on account of it's got to go in all the papers including the local ones down Valley Fields way. I know there's one called the *South London Argus* and there may be half a dozen more. That's up to you to find out. I want them in tomorrow morning, so you'll have to do some getting around, even if you do have a blister. But it'll bring home the bacon, believe me."

Soapy was examining the script with the puzzled eye of one who is not abreast.

"How do you mean, bring home the bacon, baby?"

"That's the way I figure it. I told you the Yorke dame wasn't any too strong for Valley Fields anyway, so what happens when hundreds of people come horning in on her with cats of all descriptions and prob'ly letting half of them loose in the garden? And if the cats don't do the trick, we can switch to something else. There's plenty of other things. I say she'll pack up and leave pronto. Am I right, or am I right?"

Soapy drew a long breath. Even to him all things had been made clear, and he was telling himself that he had known all along that the light of his life would find a way.

"Baby," he said, when emotion allowed him to speak, "there's no one—"

"Say, tell you something," said Dolly happily. "I'm beginning to think that myself."

17.

Tucked away in odd corners of the aristocratic Mayfair section of London there exist, like poor relations of the rich, certain alleys and byways which would be far more at home in the humbler surroundings of Whitechapel or Shoreditch. Halsey Court was one of these. Leila Yorke, on her way to the offices of the J. Sheringham Adair investigation agency two mornings after Dolly had put her plan of campaign into action, found it dark, dirty, dismal and depressing, and far too full of prowling cats. Circumstances had so arranged themselves on the previous day as to make her reluctant, if she lived to be a hundred, ever to see another cat again.

She mounted the three flights of stone stairs that led to

the dingy room where Chimp Twist passed his days and, with a brief nod, dusted a chair and sat down, eying him with the intentness of a woman who had come for professional advice and meant to get it.

He was not a very exhilarating spectacle. Sally, drawing a word picture of him for her benefit, had called him a frightful little man with a face like a monkey and a waxed mustache, and when he had come to Castlewood to obtain a photograph of her husband Leila Yorke had been struck by the accuracy of the description. But one does not engage an investigator for his looks. What counts is brain, and she had been favorably impressed by his obvious sagacity. Like Dolly, she would not have trusted him to tell her the right time, but she was not proposing to trust him. All she wanted from him was his trained assistance in tracking down the unknown hellhound responsible for the quite untrue statement that she was in need of cats of all descriptions.

"Hope I'm not interrupting you when you're busy on the mysterious affair of the maharajah's ruby," she said, "but I'd like a conference."

Chimp leaned back and put the tips of his fingers together.

"With reference to the matter we were discussing when I visited your residence, madam?" he said, assuming the manner and diction he always employed with clients. In private life he spoke in the vernacular and generally out of the side of his mouth, but in his official capacity he modeled his style on the more gentlemanly detectives in the books he read. "I can assure you that everything is being done to bring that to a successful conclusion. My whole organization is working on it. Half a dozen of my best men are busy on the investigation at this moment. Let me see, who did I put on the case? Wilbraham, Jones,

Evans, Meredith, Schwed—yes, fully half a dozen. They are scouring London from end to end. It is as if you had pressed a button and set in motion some vast machine. The Adair agency is like a kind of octopus, stretching its tentacles hither and thither and—"

Leila Yorke was not a patient woman. She banged the desk, causing a cloud of dust to rise, and Chimp's voice trailed away. Better men than he had fallen silent when Leila Yorke banged desks—Aubrey Popgood of her firm of publishers for one and Cyril Grooly, his partner, for another, and similar effects had been produced on headwaiters in restaurants when she banged tables. As she sometimes explained to intimate friends, it was all in the follow-through.

"In short," she said, "you're telling me you're good."

Chimp admitted that this was what he had intended to convey.

"Right," said Leila Yorke briskly. "So now we've settled that, perhaps you will let me mention what I've come about."

"*Not* the matter we were discussing when I visited your residence?"

"No. Cats."

Chimp blinked. "Did you say cats?"

"And dogs."

"I don't think I quite follow you, madam."

"You will," said Leila Yorke, and opening her bag she produced a wad of newspaper clippings. "Read those."

Chimp put on a pair of horn-rimmed spectacles. Seeing him in his normal state, one would have said that nothing could make him look more repulsive, but these glasses went far toward performing that miracle. Even Leila Yorke, though a strong woman, winced at the sight. He read the clippings and raised a surprised and inquiring eye.

"You are fond of cats, madam?"

"I like them in moderation, always provided they don't go for the birds, but you don't suppose I put those advertisements in the papers, do you? Somebody's playing a practical joke on me, and I want you to find out who it is, so that I can strangle him with my bare hands. Cats of all descriptions! I'll say they were. I don't know how many people there are living in South London, but they all called at Castlewood yesterday, and every damned one of them was carrying a blasted cat and wanted me either to buy it or pay him for the time I'd wasted telling him to bring it. I never saw so many cats in my life. I was up to my waist in them. Black cats, tabby cats, striped cats, cats with bits chewed out of their ears—it was like a mouse's nightmare. And more coming every minute. If it hadn't been for Widgeon's cousin George, they'd have been there still."

She paused, her eyes gleaming as she relived those testing moments, and Chimp asked who Widgeon's cousin George was.

"He's a policeman. He and Widgeon have got the house next door. He suddenly appeared and told the multitude to pass along, which they did, and I don't blame them. I'd have passed along myself if a man that size had told me to. Thank heaven for policemen, I say. Salt of the earth, those boys."

Chimp preserved a rather prim silence. He did not share her enthusiasm for the constabulary, with whom his relations both in his native country and in England had been far from cordial. Fewer and less vigilant officers were what both the United States and Great Britain needed, in his opinion, if they were to have any chance of becoming earthly Paradises.

"Very efficient, that Cousin George. Got lots of weight, and threw it about like a hero. I suppose he was grateful to me because I'd taken two of the five-shilling tickets for the concert in aid of the Policemen's Orphanage. Just shows it was right what the fellow said about casting your bread on the waters. He couldn't have been more zealous if I'd bought up the entire front row of orchestra stalls. Well, that ended the episode of the cats."

Chimp said that was satisfactory, and Leila Yorke corrected him.

"Not so darned satisfactory, because this morning there were the dogs, and he wasn't around to cope with them."

"Dogs, madam?"

"How many breeds of dogs are there?"

Chimp was unable to supply the information, but said he thought there were a good many.

"Well, representatives of every known breed were there this morning with the exception of Mexican Chihuahuas. I don't think I noticed any of them among those present, though I may be wrong. I'm fond of dogs, mind you, I've got six of them at home in the country, but—"

"Castlewood is not your home?"

"No, I only took the place because I was planning to write a book about the suburbs. I live at Loose Chippings in Sussex, and I'm beginning to wish I was back there. A little more of this, and Valley Fields will have seen the last of me. What's the matter?"

What had prompted the questions had been a sudden aguelike quiver which had run through her companion's weedy frame, causing his waxed mustache to behave like a tuning fork. Chimp Twist was, as has been indicated, astute, and a blinding light had flashed upon him. As clearly as if she had appeared before him and given him the low-down herself, he saw behind these unusual occurrences the shapely hand of Mrs. Thomas G. Molloy. His client had spoken of practical jokers. There was nothing of the practical joker about Dolly Molloy. She was strictly a businesswoman, actuated always by business motives. And Soapy, the dumb brick, had told him all about that ice, even to the very spot where it was hidden. It figured, he was saying to himself; yes, it certainly figured.

He stilled his vibrating mustache with a quick hand, and leaned forward—impressively, he hoped, though actually the impression he gave Leila Yorke was that he was about to have some sort of fit.

"Has it occurred to you, madam, that the person who inserted these advertisements may have been trying to force you to leave Castlewood because there is something there he wants to secure and will be able to secure if the house becomes unoccupied?"

Leila Yorke considered the suggestion, and after the briefest of moments placed it in the class of those she did not think much of. No doubt England's criminals included in their ranks a certain number of eccentrics, but she refused to believe that even these would go to so much trouble to obtain an aspidistra, a reproduction of Millais's "Huguenot" and a china mug with "A Present from Bognor Regis" on it in pink sea shells.

"What on earth is there in Castlewood for anyone to want?" she demanded.

"Possibly the object is buried in the garden."

"Not a bone, or those dogs would have got it."

Chimp's expression, though not losing the respectfulness due to a client, showed that he deplored this frivolity.

His manner became more portentous, his diction more orotund.

"If I am right in supposing that there is something of value concealed on the premises, it is to be presumed that it was placed there by some recent occupant of the house. It would be interesting to find out who was the tenant of Castlewood before you."

"I know that. Cornelius told me. It was someone called Molloy."

Chimp started dramatically. "Molloy?"

"So Cornelius said."

"An American?"

"Yes."

"A large man with a high forehead?"

"I don't know. I never saw him," said Leila Yorke, unaware that she had had that pleasure and privilege. "Why?"

"I am wondering if it can have been a dangerous crook known as Soapy Molloy. Who, by the way, is Cornelius?"

"The house agent."

"With your permission I will call him up. This cannot be a mere coincidence," said Chimp, rummaging in a drawer for the telephone book. "The name Molloy, and all these strange, one might say sinister, happenings. Suspicious, very suspicious. Mr. Cornelius?" he said. "This is the J. Sheringham Adair detective agency. We have been asked by Scotland Yard to assist them with some questions regarding a man named Molloy, who occupied a house called Castlewood until recently. Scotland Yard thinks this may be the same Molloy in whom they are interested. Could you describe him to me? . . . I see . . . Yes . . . yes . . . thank you." He hung up, and turned to Leila Yorke with an air of quiet triumph. "It is the same man, not a doubt of it."

"But who is he?" asked Leila Yorke, impressed. There

had been a period since she entered this office when its dustiness and dinginess had shaken her faith in its proprietor, but it was now quite solid again. What is a little dust, she was feeling, if the head it settles on contains a keen, incisive brain?

Chimp fondled his mustache.

"Soapy Molloy, though nothing has as yet been proved against him, nothing that would stand up in court, is known to be the head of an international drug ring which the police have been trying to smash for years, and I think we may take it as certain that he has buried a large consignment of the dope in the garden of Castlewood. No other explanation seems to meet the case. You must leave the house immediately, madam."

Leila Yorke's jaw tightened, and her blue eyes glowed with an offended light.

"What, let myself be chased out of my home by a blasted dope peddler?"

Chimp hastened to soothe her wounded pride.

"It is merely a ruse. Thinking the house is unoccupied, Molloy will act. But it will not be unoccupied. I shall be there."

"You?"

"What I suggest is this. You return to your home in Sussex tonight and tell this Mr. Cornelius that you are leaving. Molloy is certain to get in touch with him tomorrow or the day after to find out if his efforts to get rid of you have been successful. He will come to Castlewood, thinking the coast is clear, and I shall be waiting for him."

"You'd better borrow my shotgun."

"Unnecessary. I shall have some of my best men with me—Meredith certainly and possibly Schwed. Three of us will be enough to overpower this scoundrel."

"I thought Meredith and Schwed were looking for my husband."

"I shall take them off the case, but only for a few hours. I am expecting Molloy to make his move tomorrow night. We must oblige Scotland Yard."

"Why? I'm not worrying about Scotland Yard's troubles. I want to find Joe."

"We shall find him, madam. The Sheringham Adair Agency never fails. You will leave Castlewood tonight?"

"I suppose so, if you say so."

"Then that is settled. You will telephone me directly you are leaving?"

"Very well."

"And what did you say your address in the country was?"

"Claines Hall, Loose Chippings."

"I'll send my bill to you there," said Chimp, and having ushered his client to the door with a suavity of which those who knew him best would never have thought him capable, opened another drawer of the desk and produced the bottle of whisky without which, as is generally known, no detective agency can function. As he drank, a glow suffused him, due partly to the generous strength of the spirit but even more to the thought that he was about to slip a quick one over on the Mrs. Thomas G. Molloy who in the past had so often slipped quick ones over on him.

Leila Yorke, meanwhile, had groped her way out of the twilight dimness of Halsey Court and wandered into Bond Street to do a little window-shopping before lunch. She was thus enabled to encounter Freddie Widgeon, who was on his way to enjoy, if it could be called enjoying, the hospitality of his uncle Lord Blicester. An invitation, equivalent to a royal command, had reached him on the previous day.

Leila Yorke was delighted to see Freddie. She had been contemplating a solitary meal, and she disliked solitary meals.

"Hullo there, Widgeon," she said. "The hour has produced just the man I wanted."

Her interview with Chimp Twist had left her in excellent spirits. The prospect of getting away from Valley Fields, shocking as this would have seemed to Mr. Cornelius, elated her. She wanted to be back at Claines Hall, Loose Chippings, at her familiar desk, writing the same old tripe she had always written, and no more of this nonsense of being stark and gray and significant. It amazed her that she had ever dreamed of trying to top that gloomy historian of the suburbs, the late George Gissing. Even as she gazed into the jeweler's window, there had come into her head the germ of an idea for a story about a man named Claude and a girl called Jessamine who had gray eyes and hair the color of ripe wheat.

"Oh, hullo," said Freddie. He seemed to her distrait and out of tune with her joyous mood. "How have you been lately? Bobbing along? My cousin George tells me you've been having cat trouble."

"A spot," said Leila Yorke buoyantly, "the merest spot. I'll tell you all about it while you're giving me lunch."

"Frightfully sorry, but I can't give you lunch. I'm fixed up with my Uncle Rodney."

"Where?"

"Barribault's."

"I'll join you," said Leila Yorke.

18.

Catering as it does mainly to Texas millionaires who have just learned that another oil well has been discovered on their property and maharajahs glad to have got away from the pomp and ceremony of the old palace for a while, there is always an atmosphere of hearty—though never unrefined—gaiety about the lobby of Barribault's Hotel at the luncheon hour, and it was an atmosphere that fitted well with Leila Yorke's mood. Freed from the cloying society of the Castlewood cats and stimulated by her recent interview with J. Sheringham Adair, she had recovered all her normal exuberance. The dullest eye could discern that she was in the pink. Far too much so, Freddie considered, as he eyed her morosely. Wanting to be alone to brood on his

grief, preferably in some cemetery, he found her vivacit
hard to bear.

"Widgeon," she said, raising her glass and beaming wit
good will, "I would like you to join me in a toast, and n
heeltaps. To the fellow who first invented life, for h
started a darned good thing. What did you say?"

Freddie, who had said "Oh?" said he had said "Oh?'
and she proceeded.

"You see before you, Widgeon, a woman who, if suc
goings-on were allowed in this posh caravanserai, would b
clapping her hands in glee and dancing around on the tip
of her toes."

"Oh?" said Freddie.

"Today, and you may give this to the press, I am glad
glad, glad, like Pollyanna, and with good reason. I hav
seen the light and realize what a mug's game it was ever t
think of writing that stark novel of squalor I spoke to yo
about. I have abandoned the idea in toto."

"Oh?" said Freddie.

"There rose before me the vision of all those thousand
of half-witted women waiting with their tongues out fo
their next ration of predigested pap from my pen, and
felt it would be cruel to disappoint them. Be humane,
told myself. Who am I to deprive them of their simpl
pleasures, I soliloquized. Keep faith with your public, m
girl, I added, still soliloquizing."

"Oh?" said Freddie.

"And there was another aspect of the matter. Inasmuch
as these blighted novels of squalor have to be at least six
hundred pages long, hammering one out would have been
the most ghastly sweat, and the first lesson an author must
learn is how to make things as easy for himself as possible.
The ideal toward which one strives is unconscious cerebra-

ion. I look forward to a not distant date when I shall be able to turn out the stuff in my sleep."

"Oh?" said Freddie.

She gave him a sharp glance. Though preferring always to bear the major burden of any conversation in which she took part, she liked more give-and-take than this. A little one-sided this exchange of ideas was becoming, she felt.

"Aren't you saying 'Oh?' a good deal as of even date?" she said. "You seem distrait, Widgeon."

"I am a bit."

"What's eating you?"

Freddie laughed a mirthless laugh, the sort of laugh a lost soul in an inferno might have uttered, if tickled by some observation on the part of another lost soul.

"What isn't?"

"Hard morning at the office?"

"Well, I got fired, if you call that hard."

Leila Yorke was all warmhearted sympathy.

"My poor unhappy boy! What was the trouble?"

"Oh, nothing you'd understand. Technical stuff. I made a bloomer yesterday when copying out an affidavit, as the foul things are called, and when I arrived this morning— late again, because I'd been hanging round trying to get a word with Sally—Shoesmith sent for me and applied the boot. He said he had felt the urge for a long time and had struggled to fight against it, but this had made it irresistible. He gave me a month's salary in lieu of notice, saying it was well worth the money to get rid of me immediately. He added that this was the happiest day of his life."

"Didn't you plead with him?"

"Certainly not. I ticked him off. Remembering what you had told me about his murky past, I said that I might not be his dream employee, but at least I didn't kiss girls

behind rhododendron bushes. Oddly enough, I neve
have. Rose bushes, yes, but not rhododendrons. 'Kiss fewe
girls behind rhododendron bushes, Shoesmith,' I said, an
I turned on my heel and walked out."

"Very upsetting, I don't wonder you're feeling off you
oats."

"Oh, it isn't that. Being fired doesn't worry me, becaus
pretty soon I shall be making a vast fortune."

"How's that?"

"Sorry, I can't tell you," said Freddie, remembering Mr
Molloy's injunctions of secrecy. "It's just an investment o
sorts I'm going to clean up on. No, what I'm down among
the wines and spirits about," he went on, abandoning re
serve in his desire to unburden himself to a sympathetic
confidante, "is Sally. Has she told you what happened?"

"Not a word. What did happen?"

Freddie dipped his finger in his empty glass, secured
the olive and swallowed it with a moody gulp.

"If something's gone wrong between you and Sally, you
need another of those," said Leila Yorke maternally.

"You think so?"

"I'm sure of it. Waiter! Encore de martini cocktails.
Talking of waiters," she said, as the man withdrew, "my
missing husband's one."

"You don't say?"

"Saw him with my own eyes flitting to and fro with the
hashed chicken in pastry at the Pen and Ink Club luncheon. But don't let's get off on the subject of my affairs.
Everything's going to be all right as far as I'm concerned.
I have an octopus stretching its tentacles hither and
thither in search of him, and you know what these octopi
are like. They never fail. Forget me and tell me about you
and Sally. Have you really parted brass rags?"

"It looks like it."

"What did you do to the girl?"

"I didn't do anything."

"Come, come."

"It was my cousin George."

"The zealous officer who got into my ribs for ten of the best the other day for concert tickets? How does he come into it?"

Freddie scowled darkly at an inoffensive Texas millionaire who had seated himself at a nearby table. He had nothing specific against the man, but he was in the mood to scowl at anyone who came within his orbit of vision, and would have looked equally blackly at a visiting maharajah. When a Widgeon has lost the woman he loves, the general public is well advised to keep at a safe distance.

"I must begin by saying," he began by saying, "that of all the fatheaded, clothheaded half-wits that ever blew a police whistle, my cousin George is the worst. He's like that fellow in the poem whose name led all the rest."

"I know the fellow you mean. Had a spot of bother with angels getting into his bedroom in the small hours, if I remember rightly. So George is fatheaded, is he?"

"Has been from birth. But on this occasion he lowered all previous records. Oh, I know he has some sort of a story in . . . What's that word beginning with an *x*? It's on the tip of my tongue."

"Xylophone?"

"Extenuation. I know he can put up a kind of story in extenuation of his muttonheaded behavior. The woman was undoubtedly wet."

"You're going too fast for me. What woman?"

"This one who came to Peacehaven."

"Friend of yours?"

"I know her slightly."

"Ah!"

"Don't say 'Ah!' in that soupy tone of voice. Only th
other day I had to rebuke Sally for doing the same thing
That, of course," said Freddie, heaving a sigh that seemed
to come up from the soles of his shoes, "was when she and
I were on speaking terms."

"Aren't you now?"

"Far from it. This morning I saw her in your garden
and called to her, and she gave me the sort of look she
would have given a leper she wasn't fond of and streaked
back into the house. It was hanging round, hoping to
establish contact again, that made me late at the office
Mark you, I can understand her point of view. She was
unquestionably wearing my pajamas."

"Sally?"

"No, the woman."

"The one you know slightly?"

"Yes."

"Wearing your pajamas?"

"The ones with the purple stripe."

"H'm!"

Freddie raised a hand. Not even his cousin George,
when on traffic duty, could have put more dignity into the
gesture. On his face was a look rather similar to the one
Sally had given him that morning in the garden.

"Don't say 'H'm!' It's as bad as 'Ah!' I could explain
the whole thing so easily, if she'd only let me have a word
with her and not shoot off like a sprinter hoping to break
the hundred-yard record every time I open my mouth.
This woman got caught in the rain and barged into Peacehaven for shelter. She met George, and he saw she was
wet—"

"The trained eye! Nothing escapes the police."

"—and told her to go up to my room and get into my
pajamas before she caught a nasty cold. He then went off

to give his girl dinner, leaving her there, so when I got home, there I was, closeted with her."

"And Sally came in?"

"Not immediately. She entered at the moment when I was giving the woman a helping hand with her knee. She had fallen and scraped it, and I was putting iodine on it."

"On her knee?"

"Yes."

"Her *bare* knee?"

"Well, would she have been clad in sheet armor at such a moment?"

"H'm."

Freddie repeated the Georgelike gesture which had resulted from her previous use of this monosyllable.

"Will you *please* not say 'H'm!' The whole episode was pure to the last drop. Dash it, if a female has shaved about three inches of skin off her lower limbs and lockjaw is imminent unless prompt steps are taken through the proper channels, a fellow has to rally round with the iodine, hasn't he? You can't have women dying in awful agonies all over the sitting-room floor."

"Something in that. But Sally got the wrong angle?"

"She appeared to misunderstand the position of affairs completely. I didn't see her at first, because I was bending over the flesh wound with my back turned, but I heard a sort of gasping yip and looked round, and there she was, goggling at me as if shocked to the core. For an instant there was silence, broken only by the sound of a voice saying 'Ouch!'—iodine, stings like the dickens—and then Sally said, 'Oh, I beg your pardon. I thought you were alone,' and exited left center. And by the time I'd rallied from the shock and dashed after her, she was nowhere in sight. The whole thing's a pretty ghastly mess," said Freddie, and frowned blackly again, this time at a peer of the realm who, as peers of the realm so often did, had dropped in at Barribault's for a quick one before lunch and was sitting at a table across the room.

Leila Yorke was frowning, too, but the crease in her brow was a thoughtful crease. She was weighing the evidence and sifting it. A stern expression came into her face. She tapped Freddie on the arm.

"Widgeon, look me in the eye."

He looked her in the eye.

"And answer me one question. Do you intend to do right by our Nell, or are you regarding this innocent girl as the mere plaything of an idle hour, as Angela Fosdyke said to Bruce Tallentyre in my *Heather o' the Hills* when she found him kissing her sister Jasmine at the Hunt Ball. It would be interesting to know, for on your answer much depends."

Freddie, being sunk in one of Barribault's settees, than which none in London are squashier and more yielding to the frame, was unable to draw himself to his full height, but he gave her a cold, dignified look which made quite a good substitute for that maneuver. His voice, when he spoke, shook a little.

"Are you asking me if I love Sally?"

"I am."

"Of course I do. I love her madly."

"Satisfactory, as far as it goes. But one must bear in mind that you love every girl you meet."

"Where did you hear that?"

"Sally told me. I had it straight from the horse's mouth."

Freddie pounded the table passionately. Leila Yorke, a specialist at that sort of thing, liked his wrist work.

"Listen," he said, speaking thickly. "Sally's all wrong about that. She's judging me on past form, and there was a time, I admit, when I was a bit inclined to flit from flower to flower and sip, but I gave all that up when she came along. There's no one in the ruddy world for me but her. You know Cleopatra?"

"By name."

"And the Queen of Sheba?"

"Just to nod to."

"Well, lump them both together, and what have you got? Something I wouldn't cross the road for, if there was a chance of being with Sally. And you ask me if I love her. Tchah!"

"What did you say?"

"When?"

"On the cue, 'ask me if I love her.'"

"I said 'Tchah!' meaning to imply that the question is absurd, loony, incompetent, immaterial and irrelevant, as Shoesmith would say. Love her? Of course I love her. If not, why do you suppose I'm going steadily off my rocker because she won't speak to me and looks at me as if I were something more than usually revolting she had found under a flat stone?"

Leila Yorke nodded. His simple eloquence had convinced her.

"Widgeon, I believe your story. Many women wouldn't, for if ever there was a narrative that exuded fishiness at every pore, this is it. But I've always been a pushover for tales of love. Do you know what I'm going to do? I'm going to phone her and apprise her of the facts. I'll square you with her."

"You think you can?"

"Leave it to me."

"I absolutely can't tell you how grateful I am."

"Don't give it a thought."

"Do it now!"

"Not now. I want my lunch. And here comes our host,"

said Leila Yorke, as the portly form of Rodney, Lord Blicester, came through the swing door. "I wonder if he's heard about Johnnie Shoesmith easing you off the payroll."

Much of the light that had been illuminating Freddie's face faded away. The fact that he was in for a stormy interview with an uncle who on these occasions never minced his words had been temporarily erased from his mind.

"I expect so."

"Well, chin up. He can't eat you."

"He'll have a jolly good try," said Freddie. He had a momentary illusion that the spinal cord running down his back had been replaced by some sort of jellied substance.

19.

There are lunches which are rollicking from start to finish, with gay shafts of wit flickering to and fro like lightning flashes, and others where the going is on the sticky side and a sense of oppression seems to weigh the revelers down like a London fog. The one presided over by Lord Blicester at the restaurant of Barribault's Hotel fell into the second class.

It was in no festive mood that he had come to Barribault's Hotel. Calling on Mr. Shoesmith earlier in the morning to inquire how that income tax thing was working out and being informed by him that his nephew's services had been dispensed with, he had planned on meeting Freddie to speak his mind in no uncertain manner to that young blot on the London scene, and in the taxi on his way to the tryst he had been rehearsing and polishing his lines, substituting here a stronger adjective, there a more forceful noun. The discovery that what he had been looking forward to as a tête-à-tête was going to be a three-some gave him an unpleasant feeling of being about to burst. No one was more alive than he to what is done and what is not done, and in the matter of pounding the stuffing out of an errant nephew when there are ladies present the book of etiquette, he knew, was rigid.

Throughout the meal, accordingly, his obiter dicta were few and his demeanor that of a volcano biding its time. And as Freddie appeared to be in a sort of trance and Leila Yorke's conversation was confined for the most part to comments on his increased weight since she had seen him last, coupled with recommendations of dietary systems which could not fail to cut him down to size, the thing was not a great social success.

But even the weariest river winds somewhere safe to sea, and when after the serving of coffee his fair guest left the table, saying that she had a telephone call to make, he prepared to relieve what Shakespeare would have called his stuff'd bosom of its pent-up contents. Fixing his nephew with a baleful eye, he said, "Well, Frederick," and Freddie said, "Oh, hullo, Uncle Rodney," as if noticing for the first time that his relative was among those present. His thoughts had been with Leila Yorke at the telephone. Observing the bright, encouraging smile she had given him as she left, he knew she would pitch it strong, but would she pitch it strong enough to overcome Sally's sales resistance? So much hung on the answer to this question that he was understandably preoccupied.

Lord Blicester proceeded to arrest his attention. When moved, as he was now, he had an oratorical delivery not unlike that of a minor prophet of Old Testament days rebuking the sins of the people, and this he supplemented with appropriate gestures. The peer of the realm, who had finished his quick one and had come into the restaurant and was lunching at a table across the way, became immediately aware as he watched the drama with an interested eyeglass, that the thin feller over there was copping it properly from the fat feller, probably his uncle or something of that sort. His sympathies were with the thin feller. In his youth he, too, had known what it was to cop it from his elders. He belonged to a family whose senior members, when stirred, had never hesitated to dish it out.

It is one of the drawbacks to the historian's task that in recording dialogue between his characters he must select and abridge, giving merely the gist of their remarks and not a full stenographic transcript. It will be enough to say, therefore, that Lord Blicester, touching on his nephew's moral and spiritual defects, left nothing unspoken. The word "wastrel" occurred with some frequency, as did the adjective "hopeless." By the time he had rounded into his peroration, the conclusion anyone hearing it would have come to was that it was a mystery how such a despicable member of the human family as Frederick Fotheringay Widgeon had ever been allowed inside a respectable establishment like Barribault's Hotel.

The effect of this philippic on Freddie was to make him feel like somebody who had been caught in the San Francisco earthquake of 1906. He wilted visibly and was shrinking still further inside his well-cut flannel suit, when something occurred that stiffened his sinews, summoned up the blood and made him feel that it was about time he sat up and did a bit of talking back. Through the door of the restaurant two lunchers had entered and taken a table near the peer of the realm. One was Oofy Prosser, the other Soapy Molloy. They had been having an *apéritif* in Soapy's suite, and Oofy had just written out a check for a further block of Silver River stock, thanking Soapy with a good deal of effusiveness for letting him have it.

The sight of Soapy had an instant effect on Freddie's morale. The spate of injurious words proceeding from his uncle's lips had completely driven from his mind the thought that in a very short time he would be a rich man, on his way to Kenya to become still richer. It now came back to him, reminding him that there was absolutely no necessity for him to sit taking lip like this from an obese relation who, instead of saying offensive things to his nearest and dearest, would have been better employed having Turkish baths and going easy on the bread and potatoes.

He felt his calm, strong self again, and in the way he drew himself erect in his chair there was something suggestive of a worm coming out after a heavy thunderstorm. He knew himself to be more than equal to the task of telling a dozen two-hundred-and-fifty-pound uncles where they got off.

"That's all right, Uncle Rodney," he said briskly, "and there is possibly much in what you say, but, be that as it may, you don't know the half of it."

It would be erroneous to say that this defiant tone from one on whom he had been looking as less than the dust beneath his chariot wheels caused Lord Blicester to swell with indignation, for he had already swollen so far that a little more would have made him come apart at the seams. He had to content himself with glaring.

"I don't understand you."

"I'll make it clear to the meanest intelligence . . . That is . . . Well, you know what I mean. Let me begin by asking you something. You're all steamed up about Shoesmith taking the high road and me the low road and our relations being severed and all that, but how would you like being a sort of glorified office boy in a solicitor's firm?"

"The question does not arise."

"Yes, it does, because I've jolly well arisen it. The answer is that you wouldn't like it a bit. Nor do I. I want to go to Kenya and become a Coffee King."

"That nonsense again!"

"Not nonsense at all. Sound, practical move."

"You said you needed three thousand pounds to put into the business. You won't get it from me."

Freddie waved an airy hand. The peer of the realm, who was now eating *truite bleu,* paused in admiration with the fork at his lips. He had not thought the thin feller had it in him. Something seemed to have bucked the thin feller up, and good luck to him, felt the peer of the realm. He had just recognized Lord Blicester as a member of one of his clubs whose method of eating soup he disliked, and he was all for it if the thin feller was going to put him in his place.

"Keep your gold, Uncle Rodney," said Freddie, wishing too late that he had made it "dross." "I don't want it. I'm rolling in the stuff."

"What!"

"Literally rolling. Or shall be shortly. Turn the old loaf about ten degrees to the nor'-nor'east. See that bimbo at that table over there? Not the one with the pimples, the other one. Rich American financier."

Lord Blicester looked behind him.

"Why, it's Molloy!"

Freddie was surprised.

"You know him?"

"Certainly. He controls a stock in which I am interested."

"What's it called?"

"I fail to see what concern it is of yours, but its name is Silver River Oil and Refinery."

"Good Lord! You've got some of that?"

"I have."

"So have I."

Lord Blicester stared.

"You?"

"In person."

"How in the world did you obtain—"

"The wherewithal to buy it? My godmother left me some pieces of eight. Not a frightful lot, but enough to finance the venture. So now you know why I don't give a hoot for Shoesmith. In a month or so I shall have at least ten thousand quid laid up among my souvenirs. Molloy guarantees this. Shoesmith means less than nothing to me, and that goes for Shoesmith, Shoesmith and Shoesmith. Odd," mused Freddie, "the labels these solicitors' firms stick on themselves. I met a chap in a pub the other day who told me he worked for Hogg, Hogg, Simpson, Bevan, Murgatroyd and Merryweather, and when I said, 'Oh, yes? And how are they all?' he said they expired in the eighties, and the concern now was run by a fellow named Smith. I mean, it just shows how you never can tell, doesn't it?"

A distinct change for the better had come over Lord Blicester's demeanor. It would be too much, perhaps, to say that even now he was all sweetness and light, but he had ceased to eye Freddie as if the latter had been some-one with bubonic plague whom he had caught in the act of picking his pocket. The difference between the way an uncle looks at a nephew who has lost his job and whom there is a danger of his having to support and the way he looks at a nephew who has large holdings in a fabulously rich oil company is always subtle but well marked. Some indication of his altered outlook can be gathered from the fact that, though a thrifty man who seldom failed to watch the pennies, he asked Freddie if he would like a liqueur brandy with his coffee. He winced a little when Freddie said he would, for liqueur brandies cost money, but he continued amiable. The peer of the realm, who had been absorbing the proceedings with the goggle-eyed stare with which forty years ago he had watched silent motion pictures, realized that the drama was over and returned to his *truite bleu*.

"Well, I am bound to say this puts a different aspect on the matter," said Lord Blicester. "If you are a man of substance, you naturally do not wish to go on working for a small salary in Shoesmith's office, especially as you are bent on going to Kenya. You think you will like Kenya?"

"My pal Boddington speaks highly of it. The spaces are very great and open there, he tells me."

"There is money, no doubt, in coffee growing."

"Pots, I imagine. I know for a fact that Boddington smokes seven-and-sixpenny cigars."

"Yes, on the whole I think you are doing wisely. Not that I would care to go to Kenya myself."

"I know what you mean. Always the risk, of course, of getting eaten by a lion, which would be a nuisance, but one must expect a bit of give-and-take. I've given the thing a lot of thought, Uncle Rodney, and I'm convinced that Kenya's the place for me, always provided . . ." Freddie paused, and a faint blush mantled his cheek. "Always provided," he went on, "that Sally is by my side. I don't think I ever mentioned this to you, but I'm hoping to get married."

Lord Blicester gave a horrified gasp. Both in physique and mental outlook he was one of London's stoutest bachelors, and he never ceased to think gratefully of the guardian angel who had arranged a breaking-off of relations when years ago he had contemplated marrying Leila Yorke, née Bessie Binns.

"Are you engaged?" he asked anxiously. He was not particularly fond of Freddie, but one has one's human instincts, and he would have experienced concern for anyone on the brink of matrimony.

"That," said Freddie, "we shall know more certainly when Miss Yorke returns. Strictly in confidence, there has been something in the nature of a rift between self and betrothed."

"Ah!" said Lord Blicester, brightening, as a man will who feels that there is still hope.

"And Miss Yorke has gone to phone her and try to talk her round. The trouble was, you see, that when Sally popped in and found this woman in my pajamas— Ah, there she is," said Freddie, rising like a salmon in the spawning season. What, he was asking himself, would the verdict be?

Leila Yorke had the best of news.

"All set," she said briefly, as she reached the table. "You may carry on, Widgeon."

"You mean . . . ?"

"All's quiet along the Potomac. I've made your path straight. You can go ahead as planned. She's ordering the trousseau."

Lord Blicester was trembling a little.

"Do I understand you to say that this girl, whoever she is, is resolved to marry Frederick?"

"The moment he gets the license."

"Good God!" said Lord Blicester, as if he had heard a well-known Harley Street physician telling him that his nephew had but a month to live. He turned to Freddie, agitated. "Did you put anything in writing?"

"Lots."

"Specifically mentioning marriage?"

"Every other line."

"Waiter," Lord Blicester cried, reckless of the fact that Barribault's Hotel charged for this beverage as if it were liquid platinum, "bring me a brandy."

Freddie, though dizzy with relief, did not forget the courtesy due a woman standing by a luncheon table.

"Aren't you going to sit down?" he said.

"I haven't time."

"The day's yet young."

"I daresay, but I've just made a date with my hairdresser, and he can only take me if I get there in ten seconds flat. Thanks for the lunch, Rodney. Fine seeing you again. Just like the old days."

Lord Blicester shivered. He always did when reminded of the old days. But for the grace of God and the sterling staff work of that guardian angel, he was thinking, he would himself have been in his nephew Frederick's frightful predicament.

Leila Yorke had started to move away, but now, as if some basilisk had laid a spell upon her, she halted, rigid, her eyes narrowing. She was looking at the table where Soapy Molloy sat, doing himself well at Oofy's expense. Oofy as a rule was chary of spending his money on others, but when a man has let you have a large slice of so rich a melon as Silver River Oil and Refinery, it is almost obligatory to entertain him at lunch.

She drew a deep breath.

"I suppose one would be put on Barribault's black list if one were to throw a roll at a fellow customer," she said wistfully. "But it's a sore temptation. Look at the low, hornswoggling hound digging into the rich foods like a starving python. Not a thing on his conscience, you'd say.

If I weren't a poor weak woman, I'd step over and push his face in whatever it is he's gorging himself with."

Freddie was not abreast. To what hornswoggling hound, he asked, did she allude?

"Third table down, next to the man with the eyeglass. Fellow with a high forehead."

"You don't mean Thomas G. Molloy?"

"I don't know what his name is. I only met him twice, and we didn't exchange cards. The first time was at Le Touquet, when he swindled me out of a thousand pounds for some shares in a dud oil stock called Silver River, the second when he came to Castlewood one morning and I took a shotgun to him."

Freddie's bewilderment increased. His senses told him that she had applied the adjective "dud" to Silver River Oil and Refinery, but he could not believe that he had heard aright. Nor could Lord Blicester, who had come out of his thoughts and was staring with bulging eyes.

"What did you say?" Lord Blicester cried.

"I was speaking of this smooth confidence man and his Silver River oil stock, and how he talked me into buying it."

"But Silver River is enormously valuable!"

"I don't know who to, except somebody who's making a collection of waste paper. You'd be lucky if you got two-pence a share for it. I know, because I tried and found there was no market. The only offer I got was from a man who had a mentally arrested child. He said he thought the colors it was printed in would entertain the little fellow. And the maddening part of it is that I can't have the bounder arrested, because I made inquiries and found that there actually is a Silver River concern. It's in Arizona somewhere, and he bought it for fifty dollars, it having been worked out to the last drop in 1926. That lets him out and leaves him free to sell shares to innocent mugs like me without getting jugged for obtaining money under false pretenses. Just shows what a world this is," said Leila Yorke, and went off to keep her appointment at her beauty parlor.

She left an uncle and a nephew who looked as if they had been carved out of stone by a sculptor commissioned by a group of friends and admirers to make statues of them. The peer of the realm, who had finished his *truite bleu* and was starting in on a jam omelet, got the impression, as his gaze rested on them, that they must have been eating something that had disagreed with them. Not oysters, for the month was June, and not the *truite bleu*, for that had been excellent. More probably something in the nature of Hungarian goulash, always a dish to be avoided unless you had had the forethought to have it analyzed by a competent analytical chemist.

Lord Blicester was the first to move, and few who had only watched him waddling across the floor in his club smoking room to the table where the papers and magazines were, to get the current issue of the *Sketch* or *Tatler,* would have credited him with the ability to achieve such a turn of speed. In the manner in which he covered the space that separated him from Soapy there was a suggestion of a traveler by the railroad who, with his train due to leave in five minutes, dashes into the refreshment room at Victoria or Waterloo station for a gin and tonic.

Towering over Soapy, he placed a heavy hand on his shoulder and said, "You infernal crook!"

Soapy, whom the words had interrupted at a moment when he was swallowing a mouthful of filet steak medium rare, did not reply, for he was too fully occupied with choking. It was Oofy who undertook the role of straight man, so necessary on these occasions.

"What did you call him?"

"A crook."

"A *crook?* What do you mean?"

"I'll tell you what I mean. That Silver River stock he sold me isn't worth the price of waste paper. The man's a deliberate swindler."

Oofy's jaw dropped. His face paled beneath its pimples. "Are you serious?"

It was a question to which the accepted answer would have been "I was never more serious in my life," but Lord Blicester was beyond speech. His recent sprint had taken its toll. He merely nodded.

The nod was enough for Oofy. Where the other had obtained his information, he did not know, but not for an instant did he question its accuracy. Solid citizens like Lord Blicester do not make scenes in public places unless they have good grounds for them, and in Soapy's empurpled face he seemed to read obvious signs of guilt. Actually, Soapy had turned purple because of the piece of filet steak to which allusion was made earlier, but Oofy was not aware of this. The way he reasoned was that if a man is called a swindler and immediately becomes the color of a ripe plum, the verdict is in, and remembering that in his guest's wallet was a check for two thousand pounds, signed "A. Prosser," he acted promptly. Edging around the table, he flung himself on Soapy and in next to no time had begun to try to throttle him.

There are, no doubt, restaurants where behavior of this sort would have been greeted with a sympathetic chuckle or, at worst, by a mere raising of the eyebrows, but that of Barribault's Hotel was not one of them. Waiters looked at each other with a wild surmise, headwaiters pursed their lips, the peer of the realm said, "Most extraordinary!" and a bus boy was sent out to summon a police-man.

And in due season there arrived not one but two members of the force, and as each of the pair was built on the lines of Freddie's cousin George, they had no difficulty in intervening in time to save a human life, though Oofy, if asked, would have questioned the application of the adjective to the man on whose chest he was now seated. Taking Oofy into custody, they withdrew, and Barribault's restaurant settled back into its normal refined peace.

Freddie saw none of these things. He was sitting at his table with his head between his hands.

20.

It is unusual nowadays for people on receipt of good news to say "Tra-la," though it was apparently done a good deal in earlier times, and Sally, coming away from the telephone at the conclusion of her conversation with her employer, did not actually express herself in this manner. But she was unquestionably in a frame of mind to have done so, for her spirits had soared and life, a short while before as black and dreary as a wet Sunday in a northern manufacturing town, had become once again a thing of joy and sunshine, fully justifying the toast Leila Yorke had drunk to its originator. The word "Whoopee" perhaps best sums up her feelings.

But after happiness came remorse. She shuddered as she

recalled the unworthy suspicions she had entertained of a Frederick Widgeon who, as it now appeared, was about as close a thing to a stainless knight, on the order of Sir Galahad or someone of that sort, as you would be likely to find in a month of Sundays. She should have realized, she told herself, that anyone with a cousin like Freddie's cousin George was practically certain sooner or later to find pajama-clad blondes in his living room. With George at the helm and directing the proceedings, one was surprised that there had not been more of them.

Remorse was followed by gratitude to Leila Yorke for handling the role of intermediary so capably. It was she who, as she always made a point of doing in the novels she wrote, had brought about the happy ending, and it seemed to Sally that some gesture in return was called for. The only thing she could think of was to substitute an extra-special dinner for the chops and fried potatoes she had been contemplating. Putting on her hat, she went out in quest of the materials.

Valley Fields, though more flowers are grown and more lawns rolled there than in any other suburb south of the Thames, is a little short on luxury shops where the makings for a really breath-taking dinner can be procured. For these you have to go as far afield as Brixton, and it was thither that Sally made her way. It was not, accordingly, for some considerable time that she returned. When she did, she found Mr. Cornelius standing on the front steps of Castlewood.

"Oh, Miss Foster," said Mr. Cornelius, "here you are at last. I have been ringing and ringing."

"I'm sorry," said Sally. "I was shopping in Brixton, and my native bearer lost the way, coming home. Is something the matter? Nothing wrong with you, I hope?"

"Not with myself. I am in excellent health, thank you

very much. I always am," said Mr. Cornelius, who had a tendency to become communicative when the subject of his physical condition was broached, "except for an occasional twinge of rheumatism if the weather is damp. No, it is Mr. Widgeon who is causing me anxiety. He is sitting under the tree in the garden of Peacehaven, groaning."

"Groaning?"

"I assure you. I had gone to look at my rabbits, one of whom refused its lettuce this morning, a most unusual thing for it to do, for it is generally an exceptionally hearty eater, and I saw him there. I said, 'Good afternoon, Mr. Widgeon,' and he looked up and groaned at me."

"Didn't you ask him why?"

"I did not like to. I assumed that he had had bad news of some kind, and on these occasions it is always more tactful to refrain from questioning."

An idea occurred to Sally.

"You're sure he wasn't singing?"

"Quite sure. I have heard him sing, and the sound is quite different."

"Well, thank you very much for telling me, Mr. Cornelius," said Sally. "I'll go and see what's the matter."

She hurried into the house, deposited her supplies in the kitchen and went out into the garden. A theory which might cover the facts was forming itself in her mind. Freddie, she had learned from Leila Yorke in their telephone conversation, had been lunching at Barribault's Hotel at his Uncle Rodney's expense, and she knew that when young men accustomed to a cup of coffee and a sandwich at midday find themselves enjoying a free meal at a place like Barribault's, they have a tendency, in their desire to get theirs while the getting is good, to overdo things a little. As she reached the fence, she was hoping that a couple of digestive tablets taken in a glass of water would be enough to bring the roses back to her loved one's cheeks.

The hope died as she saw him. He had risen from his seat beneath the tree and had begun to pace the lawn, and one glance at his haggard face told her that this was no mere matter of a passing disturbance of the gastric mucosa. Even at long range it is easy to discern the difference between a man with an overwrought soul and one who is simply wishing that he had avoided the lobster Newburg at lunch.

"Freddie!" she cried, and he dragged himself to the fence and gazed at her over it with a lackluster eye.

"Oh, hullo," he said hollowly, and with a pang she saw that the sight of her and the fact that after that interlude of icy aloofness she was once more speaking to him had done nothing to lighten his gloom.

"Freddie, *darling!*" she wailed. It seemed inconceivable to her that he had not been informed that his story, fishy though, as her employer had rightly said, it was, had passed the censor. "Didn't she tell you that everything was all right?"

"Eh? Who?"

"Leila Yorke."

"Oh, ah, yes. She told me, and naturally it bucked me up like a weekend at bracing Bognor Regis. The relief was stupendous. That part of it was fine."

"Then what are you looking so miserable about?"

He brooded in silence for a moment. His aspect would have reminded a Shakespearean student, had one been present, of the less rollicking of the Hamlets he had seen on the stage at the Old Vic and Stratford.

"I wish I could break it to you gently."

"Break what?"

"This frightful thing that's happened."

"You're making my flesh creep."

"It'll creep a dashed sight more when you've heard the facts," said Freddie with a certain moody satisfaction. A man with bad news to tell takes a melancholy pleasure in the knowledge that it is front-page news. "I'm sunk!"

"What!"

"Ruined. Done for. I've had it."

"What do you mean?"

"Hang on to your hat while I tell you. You know that Silver River stock of mine?"

"Of course."

"It's no good."

"But I thought—"

"So did I. That's where I made my bloomer. That louse Molloy has turned out to be a hound of the first water. The fiend in human shape is a low-down swindler who goes about seeking whom he may devour. He devoured me all right. A thousand quid gone, just like that, for a wad of paper that would have been costly at twopence. Oh, by the way," said Freddie, remembering, "I've lost my job."

"Oh, Freddie!"

"Shoesmith drove me out into the snow this morning. One darned thing after another, what?"

Sally clung weakly to the fence. Freddie, as she stared at him, seemed to be flickering. Not that it made him look any better.

"The only bright spot is that he gave me a month's salary in lieu of notice, so I'll be able to take you out to dinner tonight. Okay with you?"

Sally nodded. She felt unable to speak.

"It'll be something saved from the wreck. We'll go to the Ritz, and blow the expense. We've still got each other. About all," said Freddie somberly, "we have got."

Sally found speech. "But what are you going to do?"

"Well, that's rather a moot point, isn't it? What *can* I do? Try for another job, I suppose. But as what? We Widgeons are pretty hard to place."

"You can't go to Kenya now?"

"Not if I don't raise three thousand pounds in the next day or two, and the chances of that seem fairly slim, unless I borrow a pickax and break into the vaults of the Bank of England. I had another letter from Boddington yesterday, saying he couldn't keep the thing open indefinitely and if I didn't want to sit in, he'd have to get someone else. No, it looks as if Kenya were off."

Sally started. A thought had occurred to her.

"Unless . . ."

"Unless what?"

"I was thinking of Leila Yorke."

"What about Leila Yorke?"

"Couldn't you get the money from her?"

Freddie stared.

"From Ma Yorke?"

"Yes."

"Three thousand of the best and brightest?"

"It would seem nothing to her. She's got more than she knows what to do with. Everything she writes sells millions of copies, and that last book of hers was sold to the movies for three hundred thousand dollars."

It would be idle to pretend that Freddie's mouth did not water at the mention of such a sum, but he was firm. A Leila Yorke hero, tempted with unclean gold by an international spy, could not have shown a more resolute front.

"No! No, dash it!"

"It would only be a loan. You would pay her back later."

Freddie shook his head. In many ways his ethics in the

matter of floating loans were lax, but on some points they could be rigid.

"It can't be done. Uncle Rodney, yes. Oofy Prosser, quite. If either of them showed the slightest willingness to co-operate and meet me halfway, I would bite his ear blithely. But nick the bankroll of a woman I've only known about a couple of days? Sorry, no. The shot's not on the board. The Widgeons have their self-respect."

And a lot of good it does them, Sally would have said, had she been capable of commenting on this nobility. With part of her mind she was in sympathy with the stern, strong, uncompromising man who had uttered these, she had to admit, admirable sentiments. With the other part, she was wishing she could hit him over the head with something solid and drive some sense into him.

A sudden conviction flooded over her that she was about to cry.

"I must go in," she said.

Freddie gaped.

"Go in?"

"Yes."

"But I need you by my side. We've a hundred things to thresh out."

"We can do that later. I've got to start cooking dinner."

"You're dining with me at the Ritz."

"I know, but Leila Yorke has to eat. I've bought her a guinea hen."

Freddie's emotion expressed itself in an overwrought gesture.

"Guinea hens at a moment like this! Well, all right. When will you be through?"

"She likes dining early. I ought to be ready to start at half-past seven."

"Right ho."

"Goodbye till then," said Sally, and she started for the house just in time. The tears were running down her face as she passed through the back door. She was not a girl who cried often, but when she did, she did it thoroughly.

She was in the bathroom, bathing her eyes, when the front doorbell rang. Wearily, for she assumed that this was Mr. Cornelius come seeking the latest news regarding his next-door neighbor's groaning, she went down and opened the door.

It was not Mr. Cornelius who stood on the steps. It was a tall, thin, seedily dressed man of middle age, whose face, though she was certain that she had never seen him before, seemed vaguely familiar. He was carrying a large wicker-work basket.

"Pardon me," he said. "Are you the lady of the house?"

"I'm her secretary."

"Is she at home?"

"I'm afraid not. But she ought to be back soon."

"I'll come in and wait, if I may," said the man. "I've come quite a long way, and I don't want to miss her."

He sidled round Sally in an apologetic, rather crushed way, and entered the living room. He placed the basket on the floor.

"I've brought the snakes," he said.

21.

There is nothing like a good facial and a new hairdo for freshening a woman up, and it was with an invigorating feeling of being at the peak of her form that Leila Yorke left the beauty parlor and started homeward in her car. Both physically and spiritually she was one hundred per cent. The Surreyside suburbs offer very little in the way of picturesque scenery, but they gave her quite a lift as she drove through them. She found much to admire in Clapham Common, and Herne Hill seemed to her particularly attractive.

Hers was a warm and generous nature. She liked everybody she met, except when tried too high by an occasional Thomas G. Molloy, and nothing gave her more pleasure than to ameliorate the lot of those around her. The thought that she had been able to bring the bluebird back into Sally's life was a very stimulating one, for she was extremely fond of her and on principle disapproved of young hearts being sundered, especially in springtime. She was looking forward to seeing the girl's face, now that all those foolish suspicions and misunderstandings, so like the ones in her novels, had been ironed out. Wreathed in smiles it would be, she assumed.

Her assumption was mistaken. Sally was in the front garden of Castlewood when she arrived, but her face, so far from being wreathed in smiles, had a careworn look. It was the look which always comes into the faces of girls who have just left a living room in which a strange man has been taking snakes out of a wickerwork basket, but Leila Yorke did not know this. The conclusion she drew was that there must have been another rift within the lute between the two young hearts in springtime, and for all her benevolence she could not check a twinge of annoyance. More work, she felt. She enjoyed bringing about reconciliations, but there is a limit. The besthearted of women does not like to have to be doing it every five minutes.

She felt her way into the thing cautiously.

"Hullo, Sally."

"Hullo."

"I've had a facial."

"It looks wonderful."

"Not too bad. Widgeon back yet?"

"Oh, yes."

"You've seen him?"

"Yes."

"Everything nice and smooth?"

"Oh, yes."

"Then why," said Leila Yorke, abandoning the cautious approach, "are you looking like a dyspeptic field mouse?"

Sally hesitated. A witness of her employer's emotional reaction to the recent cats, she shrank from informing her that these had now been supplemented by reptiles of which she knew her not to be fond. But there are times when only frankness will serve.

She said, "There's a man in there."

"Where?"

"In the living room."

"What does he want?"

Again Sally hesitated.

"He came in answer to the advertisement."

Leila Yorke's face darkened. She drew her breath in sharply.

"More cats?"

"No, not cats."

"Dogs?"

"No, not dogs."

"Then what?"

Sally braced herself, feeling a little like one of those messengers in Shakespeare's tragedies who bring bad tidings to the reigning monarch and are given cause to regret it.

"I'm afraid it's snakes this time," she said.

She had not erred in supposing that the words would affect her employer painfully. Leila Yorke seemed to swell like a well-dressed balloon. She was thinking hard thoughts of that unknown sinister Molloy, who stopped at nothing to attain his ends, and she was thankful that in J. Sheringham Adair she had an ally who could cope with him. She hoped that Meredith and Schwed, his assistants, were muscular young men who would spare no effort to show the scoundrel Molloy the error of his ways.

"Snakes?" She breathed strongly. "Did you say snakes?"

"He had them in a basket."

"In the living room?"

"They're all over the floor."

"You shouldn't have let him in."

"He went in."

"Well, if you watch closely, you'll see him going out."

The window of the living room opened on the front garden. With something in her deportment of a leopard on the trail, Leila Yorke went to it and looked in. She stooped, peered, and the next moment reeled back as if the sill on which her fingers had rested had been red-hot. Tottering to the front steps, she collapsed on them, staring before her with rounded eyes, and Sally ran to her, full of concern.

"What is it? What's the matter?"

Leila Yorke spoke in a whisper. Her words were hard to catch, but Sally understood her to say that this, whatever it was, was of a nature to beat the band.

"I might have guessed. Who else would have snakes?"

"You mean you know this man?"

"Do I know him!"

Sally gasped. She saw now why the visitor's face had seemed familiar. There were six photographs of him in her employer's bedroom.

"It isn't . . . ?"

"Yes, that's who it is. Looking just the same as ever. Of all the darned things! I want a drink."

"You're feeling faint?"

"I'm feeling as if some hidden hand had scooped out all my insides and removed every fiber of muscle from the lower limbs."

"There's some cooking sherry in the kitchen."

"Lead me to it. Ha!" said Leila Yorke some minutes

later, putting down her glass. "I think that was rat poison, but it's done me a world of good. I feel myself again. Let's go!"

She led the way to the living room, and paused in the doorway.

"Hullo, Joe," she said.

At the moment of her entry, the visitor had taken up one of the snakes with which the room was so liberally provided and was running it pensively through his fingers, like a man whose thoughts were elsewhere. Hearing her voice, he started violently and stood staring, the snake falling from his nerveless grasp.

"Bessie!" he cried.

Now that she was able to examine him more closely, Sally could see the justice in her employer's criticism of him as weak. His was a pleasant, amiable face, the sort of face one likes at first sight, but it was not a strong one. Weakness showed in the mild eyes, the slightly receding chin and the indecisive lines of the mouth. It would, as Leila Yorke had suggested, have had to be a very non-belligerent goose to which this man could have said "Boo!" and Sally found herself wondering, like everybody else on meeting an attractive woman's husband, why she had married him. Wherein lay the powerful spell he exercised on such a dominant character?

She sensibly reminded herself that it is fruitless ever to try to find the answer to a question of this sort. Love, as a thinker once said, is blind, and these things have to be accepted. She supposed that somebody like Rodney, Lord Blicester, would seek in vain for an explanation of why she loved his nephew Freddie.

Joe Bishop was still staring.

"Bessie!" he gasped again, and ran a finger round the

inside of his collar, as he must have done a hundred times when registering agitation on the stage. "Is it you?"

"It's me. Pick up those damned snakes," said Leila Yorke briskly. Sally, who had sometimes wondered what lovers say when meeting after long separation, felt that now she knew. "The same old faces!" said Leila Yorke, eying the reptiles with disfavor. "That one's Clarice, isn't it?"

"Yes, Bessie."

"And Rupert over there?"

"Yes, Bessie."

"Well, pick them up and put them back in their basket. They remind me of your mother. How is your mother, by the way?"

"She passed on last year, Bessie."

"Oh," said Leila Yorke, and it was so obvious that only with difficulty had she checked herself from adding the word "good" that for a moment there was an embarrassing silence. "I'm sorry," she said, breaking it. "You must miss her."

"Yes."

"Well, now you've got me."

Joe Bishop's spaniel eyes widened.

"But, Bessie, you don't want me back?"

"Of course I want you back. I've been pining away to a shadow without you. I've got octopi spreading their tentacles for you all over London. Why didn't you let me know you were hard up?"

"I didn't like to."

"You an extra waiter with half a dozen snakes to support, all wanting their hard-boiled eggs of a morning. It is hard-boiled eggs the beastly reptiles eat, isn't it?"

"Yes, Bessie."

"Runs into money, that. Took all your tips to foot the

bill, I should imagine. I do think you might have come to me."

"But, Bessie, I couldn't. We moved in different worlds. I was down and out, and you were rich and famous."

"Rich, yes, but as for famous, make it notorious. There isn't a critic in England who doesn't shudder at the sound of my name."

"I think your books are beautiful."

"Shows your bad taste."

"Do you know something, Bessie? I started to make a play of one of them."

"Which one was that?"

"Heather o' the Hills."

Leila Yorke frowned thoughtfully, a finger to her chin.

"There might be a play in that. How's it coming along?"

"I couldn't go on with it. I hadn't time."

"Well, you'll have plenty of time now. I'm going to take you down to Loose Chippings in my car right away. Five minutes for you to round up your snakes and ten for me to pack a bag, and we're off."

Sally uttered a cry of anguish.

"But the guinea hen!"

"What guinea hen would that be?"

"I was going to cook you one for dinner."

Leila Yorke was firm.

"It would take more than a guinea hen to make me stay another hour in this lazar house. Give it to the cats. There must be some of them still around. If they don't want it, you eat it."

"I'm dining with Freddie in London."

"Well, that's fine. Then what you do now is trot around to The Nook and tell Cornelius I'm leaving and he's at liberty to sublet Castlewood as soon as he likes. You stay on tonight and tomorrow close the place up and come to Claines with the bags and baggage. All clear?"

"All clear, Colonel."

"Then pick up your feet and get going. If Cornelius wants to know why I'm pulling up stakes, tell him I think this Valley Fields he's so fond of is a pain in the neck and I wouldn't go on living here if the London County Council came and begged me on their bended knees. He'll probably have an apoplectic fit and expire, but what of that? It'll be just one more grave among the hills. Well, Joe," said Leila Yorke, as the door closed behind Sally, "here we are, eh?"

"Yes, Bessie."

"Together again."

"Yes, Bessie."

"Gosh, how I've missed you all these years, Joe. Remember that flat in Prince of Wales's Mansions, Battersea? And now everything's all right. You can't give me anything but love, baby, but that just happens to be all I require. By the way, I hope I'm not taking things too much for granted when I assume that you do love me as of yore? Well, that's fine. I thought I'd better ask. Do you know what we're going to do, Joe? I'm going to take you for a Continental tour, starting in Paris and wandering around from there wherever the fancy takes us."

"Sort of second honeymoon."

"Second, my foot. We never had a first one. I couldn't leave my sob-sistering, and you were out touring the number two towns with some frightful farce or other."

"Mystery drama."

"Was it? Well, whatever it was, we certainly didn't have a honeymoon. It's going to be very different this time. You've never been abroad, have you, Joe?"

"Once, to Dieppe."

"Well, I've nothing against Dieppe. Swell spot. But wait till you see Marvelous Madrid and Lovely Lucerne, not to mention Beautiful Barcelona and Gorgeous Greece. And when we get back, you can start working on that play."

When Sally returned, she found the exodus well under way. Leila Yorke was at the wheel of her car, and her husband was putting her bag and the snake basket on the back seat.

"All set," said Sally. "I told him."

"How did he take it?"

"He seemed stunned. He couldn't grasp the idea of anyone wanting to leave Valley Fields."

Leila Yorke said it took all sorts to make a world and Mr. Cornelius was to be pitied rather than censured, if he was weak in the head, and the car drove off. It was nearing open country, when Joe Bishop uttered an exclamation.

"I believe I forgot to pack Mabel!"

"You talk like an absent-minded trunk murderer. Who's Mabel?"

"You remember Mabel. The green one with the spots."

"Oh, one of those darned snakes. Are you sure?"

"Not sure, but I think so."

"Well, never mind. She'll be company for Molloy," said Leila Yorke.

22.

At Mr. Cornelius's residence, The Nook, that night prevailing conditions were not any too good. A cloud seemed to have settled on the premises, turning what had been a joyous suburban villa equipped with main drainage, company's own water, four bed, two sit and the usual domestic offices into a house of mourning. Somber is the word that springs to the lips.

When Sally, speaking of Mr. Cornelius at the moment when she had informed him of her employer's abrupt departure, had described him as stunned, she had been guilty of no overstatement. The news had shaken him profoundly, dealing a heavy blow to his civic pride. It seemed scarcely credible to him that anyone having the opportunity of living in Valley Fields should wantonly throw that opportunity away. Leila Yorke was, of course, a genius who laid bare the heart of woman as with a scalpel, but even geniuses, he considered, ought to draw the line somewhere. As he sat with Mrs. Cornelius at their evening meal —a rather ghastly repast in which cocoa, kippered herrings and pink blancmange played featured roles—he was still ruffled.

Mrs. Cornelius, too, appeared to have much on her mind. She was a stout, comfortable woman, as a rule not given to strong emotions, but now she was in the grip of one so powerful that the kippered herring trembled as she raised it to her lips. Even Mr. Cornelius, though not an observant man, noticed it, and when later in the proceedings she pushed the pink blancmange away untasted, he knew that the time had come to ask questions. Only a spiritual upheaval on the grand scale could have made her reject what, though it tastes like jellied blotting paper, had always been one of her favorite foods.

"You seem upset, my dear," he said.

A tear stole into Mrs. Cornelius's eye. She gulped. It had been her intention to remain silent till a more suitable moment, but this solicitude was too much for her.

"I'm terribly upset, Percy. I'm simply furious. I hadn't meant to tell you while you were eating, because I know how little it takes to give you indigestion, but I can't keep it in. It's about Mr. Widgeon."

"Oh, yes? He was groaning in the garden, poor fellow."

"So you told me. Well, I've found out why. I was talking to his cousin, the policeman, before you came back from your office, and he told me all about it. That man Molloy!"

"Are you speaking of Mr. Molloy of Castlewood?"

"Yes, I am, and he ought to be Mr. Molloy of Wormwood Scrubs. He's nothing but a common swindler. Mr. Widgeon told his cousin the whole story. He persuaded Mr. Widgeon to put all the money he had into a worthless oil stock, and now Mr. Widgeon is penniless."

"You mean that Silver River of which he spoke so enthusiastically has no value at all?"

"None. And Molloy knew it. He deliberately stole Mr. Widgeon's money, every penny he had in the world."

Mr. Cornelius's brow darkened. His beard wagged censoriously. He was very fond of Freddie.

"I feared this," he said. "I never trusted Molloy. I remember shaking my head when young Widgeon was telling me about his selling him those oil shares. I found it hard to believe that an American businessman would have sacrificed a large financial gain merely because he liked somebody's face. Things look very bad, I'm afraid. Widgeon, I know, needs three thousand pounds to put into some coffee concern in Kenya. He was relying on a substantial increase in the value of these Silver River shares to provide the money."

"And he's engaged to that nice girl, Miss Yorke's secretary. But now of course they won't be able to get married. And you're surprised because I can't eat blancmange. I wonder *you* can."

Mr. Cornelius, who had been punctuating his remarks with liberal segments from his heaped-up plate, lowered his spoon guiltily, and a somewhat embarrassing silence followed. It was broken by the sound of the telephone ringing in the hall. He went to answer it, and came back breathing heavily. Behind his beard his face was stern. He looked like a Druid priest who has discovered schism in his flock.

"That was Molloy," he said. "He wanted to know if there was any chance of Miss Yorke vacating Castlewood, because, if so, he might like to take the house again. I gave him a very short answer."

"I should think so!"

"I told him that Miss Yorke had already left, and he expressed pleasure and said that he would let me know definitely about his plans in a day or two, and then I said that in no circumstances would I even consider his application. 'I know all, Mr. Molloy,' I said. 'Castlewood,' I said, 'is not for such as you.' I then proceeded to tell him just what I thought of him."

"And what did he say?"

"I seemed to catch something that sounded like 'Ah, nerts!' and then he hung up."

"How splendid of you, Percy! I wish I could have heard you."

"I wish you could."

There was a pause.

"I think I'll have a little blancmange, after all," said Mrs. Cornelius.

In holding the view that his denunciation of Soapy had been of a nature calculated to bring the blush of shame to the most hardened cheek, Mr. Cornelius had been perfectly correct. Only once in his life had he expressed himself more forcibly, on the occasion when he had caught the son of the family which had occupied Peacehaven in pre-Widgeon days, a bright lad of some nine summers, shooting with a catapult at his rabbits. But bitter though his words had been, they left Soapy, who had often been denounced by experts, quite unmoved. He was not a man who ever worried much about harsh words or even physical violence. The falling-out with Oofy Prosser at Barribault's restaurant, for instance, had seemed to him so trivial that he had scarcely mentioned it to his wife on his return from lunch. He classed that sort of thing under the heading of occupational risks, and dismissed it from his mind. All that had interested him in the house agent's observations was the statement that Leila Yorke had left Castlewood. Having replaced the receiver, he sat waiting eagerly for Dolly to return and hear the news. Finding herself short of one or two little necessities, she had gone out earlier to do some shopping.

"Baby," he cried, as at long last the door opened, "guess what. Great news!"

Dolly, who had been putting down her purchases, if one may loosely call them that, turned sharply.

"Don't tell me . . . ?"

"Yep!"

"She's gone?"

"Left this evening."

"Who told you?"

"That guy Cornelius. He's just been on the phone."

"So it's official?"

"That's right."

"Gee!" said Dolly with fervor.

She was feeling all the pleasurable emotions of a general who has seen his plan of campaign work out satisfactorily and knows that he will have something good to include in his memoirs.

"I thought those snakes would do it. Only thing I was afraid of was that there mightn't have been an answer to that advert, on account of it isn't everybody that's got snakes. But I thought it was worth trying, and it was. Well, I'd been hoping to take my shoes off and put my feet up and relax awhile, because let me tell you an afternoon's shopping's hard on the dogs and mine feel like they was going to burst, but we've no time for that. Let's go."

"Go? What's the hurry? We've all the time there is now. We've got it made."

As had so often happened in the course of their married life, Dolly found her consort's slowness of comprehension trying. She would have supposed that even Soapy would have seen what the hurry was. But where a less loving wife might have responded with some wounding reference to Dumb Isaacs who must have been dropped on their heads when babies, she merely sighed, counted ten and explained the situation.

"Look," she said. "You know the Yorke dame hired Chimp to find her lost husband. Well, when a woman's got a private eye working on an assignment like that, she don't cut herself off from the latest news bulletins. If she's checking out, she lets him know. She gets on the phone before she starts and says, 'Hey, I'm leaving for the country. Here's my forwarding address.' "

Soapy's jaw fell. As always, he had not thought of that.

"You think she told Chimp she was pulling out?"

"Of course she did. He may be on his way to Castlewood now."

"Gosh!"

"Only I've an idea he'd wait till it was later. These summer evenings there's generally people about in a place like Valley Fields, and Chimp's one of those cautious guys. Still, we don't want to sit around here, chewing the fat. We gotta move."

"I'm ready."

"Me, too. But let's not go off half-cocked. What'll we need? A torch—"

"Why a torch?"

Dolly counted ten again.

"Because when we get to Castlewood, we aren't going to switch on all the lights. On account we don't want to shout out to the neighbors 'Hey! You thought this house was empty, didn't you? Well, that's where you was wrong. The Molloys are here, come to pick up that Prosser ice.' "

"Oh, I see," said Soapy, taking her point. He could generally understand things, if you used short words and spoke slowly.

"So we'll need a torch. And, seeing that quite likely Chimp'll blow in while we're there, it wouldn't hurt," said Dolly, "to take along my blackjack."

Soapy nodded silently, his heart too full for speech. What a helpmeet, he was saying to himself. She thought of everything.

The journey from the metropolis to Valley Fields can be made by train, by omnibus and part of the way by tram, but if you are in a hurry and expense is no object, it is quicker to take a taxi. Soapy and Dolly did this, and were fortunate to get one of the newer and speedier kind, though to their anxious minds the vehicle seemed to be merely strolling. It was a silent ride. Light conversation is impossible at times like this. Only when they reached their destination and Castlewood's dark, deserted aspect heartened them, did either speak.

"Looks like he's not here yet," said Soapy.

"We'll know that better when we've scouted around some."

"How do you mean?"

"Well, if Chimp's come, he'll have broken a window or sump'n, or how could he get in?"

"Oh, I see."

"You go around that side. I'll go this."

They met at the back door.

"All straight my end," said Soapy.

"Same mine. I guess we're in time."

"You had me worried for a moment, baby."

"I wasn't feeling any too good neither myself," said Dolly. "Well, here goes."

Reaching in her dainty bag, she drew out the blackjack and with a firm hand broke the kitchen window. To Soapy, whose nervous system was not at its best, the sound of splintering glass seemed to ring through the silent night like the clashing of a thousand dishes coming apart in the hands of a thousand cooks, and he waited, breathless, for posses of policemen to come charging on the scene with drawn truncheons. But none appeared. Castlewood and its environs were part of Freddie's cousin George's beat that night, and at the moment of their illegal entry that able officer was standing behind a bush in the garden of a house some quarter of a mile distant, enjoying the cigarette to which he had been looking forward for the last two hours. To keep the record straight, he was also thinking tender thoughts of Jennifer Tibbett, his invariable custom when on night duty.

Standing in the kitchen, Dolly switched on her torch.

"I'm going up. Meet me in the living room."

"You taking the torch?"

"Sure I'm taking the torch. I want to see what I'm doing, don't I?"

"I'll bump into something in the dark."

"Well, bump," said Dolly indulgently. "Nobody's stopping you. This is Liberty Hall, as that cop said."

"Don't talk about cops, baby, not at a moment like this," begged Soapy nervously. "It does something to me. And don't be too long upstairs."

On her return, not even the sight of the chamois leather bag dangling from her fingers was able to restore his composure. He eyed it almost absently, his mind on other things.

"Say, look," he said. "Do you suppose this joint is haunted?"

"Shouldn't think so. Why?"

"I heard something."

"Some what sort of thing?"

Soapy searched for the *mot juste*.

"Sounded kind of slithery."

"How do you mean, slithery?"

"Well, slithery, sort of. I was feeling my way in here in the dark, and there was something somewhere making a kind of rustling, slithery noise. Just the sort of noise a ghost would make," said Soapy, speaking as one who knew ghosts and their habits.

"Simply your imagination."

"You think so?"

"Sure. You're all worked up, honey, and you imagine things."

"Well, if you say so," said Soapy dubiously. "It's all this darkness that gets you down. Beats me why a burglar doesn't go off his nut, having to go through this sort of thing night after night. It would reduce me to a nervous wreck. Could I use a drink!"

"Well, there's prob'ly something in the kitchen. Take the torch and go look."

"Won't you mind being alone in the dark, pettie?"

"Who, me? Don't make me laugh! Matter of fact, I guess it 'ud be safe enough to switch the lights on, if we draw the curtains. And I'll open the window a couple of inches at the bottom. Sort of close in here. If you find anything, bring three glasses."

"Three?"

"Just in case Chimp blows in."

"Oughtn't we to be moving out?"

"Not me! I want to see Chimp's face."

To anyone acquainted with Chimp Twist this might have seemed a bizarre, even morbid, desire, but Soapy followed her train of thought. He chuckled.

"He'll be sore!"

"He'll be as sore as all get out. Get moving, sweetie. Let's have some service."

When Soapy returned, bearing glasses and the bottle of champagne which Sally had been at such pains to buy for Leila Yorke's dinner, he found his wife looking thoughtful.

"Shall I tell you something, Soapy?"

"What, honey?"

"There *is* a slithery noise. I heard it. Like you said, sort of rustling. Oh, well, I guess it's just a draft or something."

"Could be," said Soapy, doubtfully, and would have spoken further, but before he could do so speech froze on his lips.

The front doorbell was ringing.

23.

The sound affected both the Molloys unpleasantly, throwing an instant damper on what had looked like a good party. Soapy, surprisingly agile for a man of his build, executed something resembling the *entrechat* to which ballet dancers are so addicted, while Dolly, drawing her breath in with a sharp hiss, sprang to the switch and turned off the lights. They stood congealed in the darkness, and not even a distinct repetition of the slithery sound which had alarmed him a few minutes before was able to divert Soapy's attention from this ringing in the night. He clutched the champagne bottle in a feverish grip.

"What was that?" he gasped.

"What did you think it was?" said Dolly. She spoke with an asperity understandable in the circumstances. No girl cares to be asked foolish questions at a moment when she is trying to make certain that the top of her head has not come off.

"Someone's at the front door."

"Yeah."

"I'll bet it's a cop."

Dolly had shaken off the passing feeling of having been the victim of one of those gas explosions in London street which slay six. She was herself again and, as always when she was herself, was able to reason clearly.

"No, not a cop. Want my guess, I'd say it was Chimp, wanting to find out if there's anyone home before he busts in. It's a thing he'd like to know."

She had guessed correctly. Chimp Twist, as she had said, was a cautious man. He thought ahead and preferred, before making any move, to be sure that there were no pitfalls in his path. Being in a hurry to get to her car and start shaking the dust of Valley Fields from its tires, Leila Yorke had made their telephone conversation a brief one, and in it had not mentioned whether or not she was being accompanied in her exodus by the secretary who had called at his office. It was quite possible that the girl had been left behind to do the packing.

This provided food for thought. Nothing is more embarrassing for a man who has entered an empty house through a broken window and is anxious for privacy than to find, when he has settled in and it is too late to withdraw, that the house is not empty, after all. This is especially so if he knows there to be shotguns on the premises. Soapy had told Chimp all about Leila Yorke's shotgun, and he shrank from being brought in contact with such a weapon, even if only in the hands of a secretary. So he rang the doorbell.

When he had rung it twice and nothing had happened, he felt he might legitimately conclude that all was well. He left the front doorstep and began to sidle round the house, and he was delighted to find that the very first window he came to had been carelessly left a few inches open at the bottom. It obviated the necessity of breaking the glass, a task to which, for his policy was to be as silent as possible and to avoid doing anything to arouse comment and curiosity in the neighbors, he had not been looking forward. To raise the window was with him the work of an instant, to slide over the sill that of another, and, well pleased, he was just saying to himself that this was the life, when a sudden blaze of light dazzled him. It also made him bite his tongue rather painfully and gave him the momentary illusion that he was in Sing Sing, being electrocuted.

The mists cleared away, and he saw Dolly. Her face was wearing the smug expression of a female juvenile delinquent who has just played a successful practical joke on another member of her age group, and her sunny smile, which Soapy admired so much, seemed to gash him like a knife. Not for the first time he was wishing that, if it could be done without incurring any unpleasant after-effects for himself, he could introduce a pinch of some little-known Asiatic poison into this woman's morning cup of coffee or stab her in several vital spots with a dagger of Oriental design. A vision rose before his eyes of Mrs. Thomas G. Molloy, sinking for the third time in some lake or mere and himself, with a sneer on his lips, throwing her an anvil.

It is never easy at times like this to think of the right

thing to say. What Chimp said was, "Oh, there you are," which he himself recognized as weak.

"Yes, we're here," said Dolly. "What are you doing in these parts?"

A lifetime spent in keeping one jump ahead of the law had given Chimp the ability to think quickly and to recover with a minimum of delay from sudden shocks.

"I came here," he said with a good deal of dignity, "to get that ice for Soapy, like I promised him I would."

"Oh, yeah?"

"Yeah."

"You was going to pick it up and hand it over to Soapy?"

"Yeah."

"For ten per cent of the gross?"

"That was the arrangement."

"Sort of a gentlemen's agreement, was there? Well, that's too bad."

"What's too bad?"

"That you should have had all this trouble for nothing. We've got that ice ourselves. It's over there on that table. And," said Dolly, packing a wealth of meaning into her words as she produced her blackjack from its bag and gave it a tentative swing, "you take one step in its direction, and you're going to get the headache of a lifetime."

Observations like this always cause a silence to fall on a conference. If a Foreign Secretary at a meeting of Foreign Secretaries at Geneva were to use such words to another Foreign Secretary, the other Foreign Secretary would for a moment not know what to say. Chimp did not. He fondled his waxed mustache in the manner of a baffled villain in old-time melodrama, and cast an appealing glance at Soapy, as if hoping for support from him. But

Soapy's face showed that he was in full accord with the remarks of the last speaker.

He decided to make an appeal to their better feelings, though long association with the Molloys, Mr. and Mrs., particularly Mrs., should have told him that he was merely chasing rainbows.

"Is this nice?" he asked.

"I like it," Dolly assured him.

"Me too," said Soapy.

"Yessir," said Dolly. "If there's one thing that gives me a warm glow, it's getting my hooks on a chunk of jewelry like this Prosser stuff. Must be worth fifty thousand dollars, wouldn't you say, Soapy?"

"More, pettie."

"Yup, prob'ly more. When we've sold it to our financial associates, I and Soapy thought we'd go to Paris for a while and walk along the Bois de Boulong with an independent air, like the man who broke the bank at Monte Carlo. We can afford it."

Chimp writhed. His fingers fell from his mustache. Usually, when he let them stray over it, he felt heartened, for he loved the unsightly little growth, but now no twiddling of its spiky ends could cheer him. He was blaming himself bitterly for not having had the sense to come to this house earlier, instead of lingering over his dinner. It had all seemed so smooth to him as he sipped his coffee and liqueur, never dreaming that time was of the essence, and now this had happened.

Although it was already abundantly clear to him that if Soapy and his helpmeet had any better feelings, they were in abeyance tonight, he persevered in appealing to them.

"I want a square deal. I'm entitled to my ten per."

"Oh, yeah? Why?"

"Because I'm Soapy's accredited agent, that's why. You coming down here ahead of me and getting the stuff has nothing to do with it. It's like the Yorke dame and her books. Do you suppose if she went and sold one of them herself, she could collar all the dough and not pay her accredited agent his commish? Sure she couldn't. He'd want his. Same here. And there's another thing. It was entirely owing to me that the Yorke dame lit out. She wanted to stay on, said she liked cats and couldn't have too many around the place, but I made her go. I told her there was a dangerous gang trying to get her out of the joint for some reason and she'd look silly if she woke up one night and found her throat cut. So if there's any justice in the world, if you've one spark of fairness in your— What did you call me?"

Dolly, who had called him a chiseling, double-crossing little hydrophobia skunk, repeated her critique.

"I wouldn't let you in on this for so much as a red cent," she said coldly. "Not even if the Archbishop of Canterbury was to come and beg me with tears in his eyes. You know as well as I do that you was planning to slip a quick one over on I and Soapy, and it was only because we got off to a fast start that you didn't do it. Ten per cent, my left eyeball! We'll give you sixpence to buy wax to put on your mustache, but that's our limit."

Chimp drew himself up. He had never really hoped. What you need when trying to soften the heart of a Dolly Molloy is someone next door starting to play some song on the gramophone that reminds her of her childhood. Either that or a good, stout club.

"Okay," he said. "If that's the way you feel, I have nothing more to say. Except this. What's to stop me walking out that door and calling a cop, and telling him I found you here with the Prosser ice?"

"I'll tell you," said Dolly in her obliging way. "The moment you made a move, I'd bean you. Matter of fact," she went on after a moment's thought, "it wouldn't be a bad idea to do it anyways."

"Now, pettie," said Soapy, always the pacifist, "there's no need for rough stuff," and Chimp said No, he liked women to be feminine.

"There'd be the satisfaction," Dolly pointed out. "Every time I see this little horror from outer space, I want to sock him with sump'n, and now seems as good a time as any."

Chimp backed an uneasy step. He had not forgotten the occasion when the butt end of a pistol in this woman's capable hands had connected with the back of his head, and left him knowing no more, as the expression was. The swelling had subsided, but the memory lingered on.

"Hey, listen!" he cried.

But Soapy and Dolly were listening to the slithery sound which had attracted their attention earlier. It had come again, and this time it was no longer a disembodied rustling. A large green snake was making its way across the carpet.

Joe Bishop's misgivings had been well founded. In saying that he had forgotten to pack Mabel, he had not erred. At the moment when he was gathering up his little flock, she had been overlooked, and for some time she had explored her new surroundings, broadening her mental outlook by taking in fresh objects of interest, and finally fallen into a light doze under an armchair. Waking now from this, she had started out on another sight-seeing tour. Dolly's foot engaged her notice, and she made for it at a speed highly creditable to a reptile with no feet, for she had begun to feel a little peckish. The foot might prove edible or it might not—time alone could settle the point—but it seemed to her worth investigation.

In the circles in which she moved Dolly Molloy was universally regarded as a tough baby who kept her chin up and both feet on the ground, and a good deal of envy was felt of Soapy for having acquired a mate on whom a man could rely. But there were weak spots in her armor, and at times she could be as feminine as even Chimp Twist could have wished. At the sight of Mabel all the woman in her awoke, and with a sharp cry she leaped for the sofa, the nearest object of furniture that seemed capable of raising her to an elevation promising temporary security. At the same moment Soapy, who shared her dislike of snakes, took to himself the wings of a dove and soared up to the top of the bookcase. Mabel, a little taken aback, looked from one to the other with a puzzled expression, not quite, as Freddie's cousin George would have said, having got the gist. Nothing like this had ever happened in the days when Herpina the Snake Queen and her supporting cast had come on next to opening at Wigan, Blackpool and other centers of entertainment.

There is, as a brother author of the present historian has pointed out, a tide in the affairs of men which, taken at the flood, leads on to fortune. It is doubtful if Chimp Twist was familiar with the passage, for he confined his reading mainly to paperback thrillers and what are known as scratch sheets, but he acted now as if the words had for years been his constant inspiration. Dolly's bound had been lissome, and that of Soapy still more so, but neither could compare in agility with the one that took him to the table where the chamois leather bag of jewelry lay, and not even Freddie Widgeon and his friend Boddington, with their liking for the open spaces, could have hastened toward them with a greater zest. Not more than a few seconds had elapsed before he was at the front gate of Castlewood, fumbling at the latch.

He had passed through, and was about to proceed to spaces still more open, when something loomed up before him, and he found himself confronting a policeman so large that his bones turned to water and his heart fluttered within him like a caged bird. He was allergic to all policemen, but the last variety he would have wished to encounter at such a moment was the large.

His immediate thought was that he must get rid of the chamois leather bag before this towering rozzer asked him what it was. Reaching behind him, he dropped it over the gate into the Castlewood front garden.

24.

Freddie's cousin George—for the government employee who had manifested himself from the darkness was he— was glad to see Chimp. A chat with something human— even if, like Chimp, only on the border line of the human—was just what he had been needing to break the monotony of his nocturnal footslogging. Walking a beat is a lonely task, and a man cannot be thinking of Jennifer Tibbett all the time.

"Nice evening," he said.

Chimp might have replied that it had been one until this meeting, but the prudent man does not bandy words with the police, so he merely nodded.

"The moon," said George, indicating it.

"Uh-huh," said Chimp, but he spoke without any real enthusiasm. He was, indeed, not giving the conversation his full attention, for his mind was occupied with thoughts of Soapy and Dolly. He could not believe that his departure had passed unnoticed by them, and he knew that ere long they must inevitably come leaping out in pursuit, modeling their movements on those of the well-known Assyrians who came down like a wolf on the fold. Their delay in doing so he attributed correctly to the magnetism of the snake Mabel, but he doubted if any serpent, however powerful its personality, would be able to detain two such single-minded persons for long. The result was that in the matter of moonlight chats he and George had different viewpoints. George liked them, he did not. He wanted to be up and away, to return for the chamois leather bag later, when conditions would be more favorable to the fulfillment of his ends and aims, and he was regarding George in much the same way as the wedding guest regarded the ancient mariner.

Something of his thoughts may have communicated itself to George, for he abandoned the subject of the moon, seeing that it had failed to grip.

"Been calling on Miss Yorke?" he said.

"That's right. Little business matter."

"She's left. Skinned out this evening."

"So that's why nobody answered the bell. Too bad. I came all the way from London to see her."

"You're not a resident of Valley Fields?"

"No."

"In fact, live elsewhere?"

"Yes."

"Still, you are a householder?"

"Oh, sure."

"Then," said George, falling easily into his stride, "you

will doubtless be willing and eager to support a charitable organization which is not only deserving in itself, but is connected with a body of men to whom you will be the first to admit that you owe the safety of your person and the tranquillity of your home. Coming, then, to the point, may I have the pleasure of selling you for yourself and wife—"

"I'm not married."

"—for yourself and some near relative—as it might be a well-loved uncle or a favorite aunt—a brace of the five-bob tickets for the annual Concert in aid of the Policemen's Orphanage, to be held at the Oddfellows Hall in Ogilvy Street next month. There are cheaper seats—one cannot ignore the half-crown and the two-bob—but the five-bobbers are the ones I recommend, for they admit you to the first three rows. If you are in the first three rows, people point you out to their friends as a man of obvious substance, and your prestige soars to a new high. Money well spent," said George, producing two of the five-bobbers from an inside pocket, for he was confident that his eloquence would not have been wasted.

He was right. Chimp Twist shared Dolly's rugged distaste for encouraging the police force and experienced a strong feeling of nausea at the thought of contributing to the upkeep of a bunch of orphans who would probably, when grown to man's estate, become policemen themselves, but he saw no alternative. Refusal would mean being rooted to the spot while this pestilential peeler renewed his sales talk, and if there was a spot to which he was reluctant to be rooted, with Soapy and Dolly due at any moment, it was the piece of stone paving outside the gate of the desirable villa Castlewood. He could not have been called, as Sally had called Leila Yorke, a cheerful giver, but he gave, and George beamed on him as on a public-minded citizen who had done the right and generous thing. He would have his reward, George told him, for only one adjective could be applied to the forthcoming concert, the adjective *slap-up*.

"No pains are being spared to make the evening an outstanding success. If you knew the number of throat pastilles sucked daily in all the local police stations, you would be astounded," said George, and with a courteous word of thanks he moved off in an easterly direction, while Chimp, anxious to be as far away from him as possible, set a westerly course.

He had proceeded some half dozen yards on this, when the door of Castlewood flew open and Dolly and Soapy emerged in the order named. A few moments earlier, observing that Mabel had turned in again under the armchair, they had felt at liberty to descend from their respective perches, and the hunt was on. But there was not much hope in their hearts. With the substantial start he had had, Chimp, they both felt, must by now have joined the ranks of those loved ones far away, of whom the hymnal speaks.

Their surprise at seeing him only a short distance down the road was equaled by their elation. No two bloodhounds, even of championship class, could have produced a better turn of speed as they swooped upon him, and George, who was nearing the corner of the street and had started thinking of Jennifer Tibbett again, paused in midstride, one regulation boot poised in the air as if about to crush a beetle. In the hitherto silent night behind him there had broken out what, had it not been that in the decorous purlieus of Valley Fields such things did not happen, he would have diagnosed as a fracas, and for an instant there surged within him the hope that he was about to make the pinch he had yearned for so long. Then he felt that he must have been mistaken. It was, he told himself, merely the breeze sighing in the trees.

But, he asked himself a moment later, did breezes in trees sigh like that? A country-bred man, he had had the opportunity of hearing a good many breezes sigh in trees, but he had never heard one with a Middle Western American accent calling somebody opprobrious names. He turned alertly, and having turned, stood gaping. Just as a gamester who has wagered his luck against a slot machine becomes momentarily spellbound on hitting the jack pot, so was he numbed by the spectacle that met his eyes. A large citizen appeared to be trying to strangle a small citizen, while in their vicinity there hovered a woman of shapely figure who looked as if she would have liked to join in the fray if she could have found room to insert herself. In other words, as clear and inviting an opportunity for a pinch as ever fell to the lot of a zealous constable.

He hurried to the scene of conflict with uplifted heart. This, he was saying to himself, was his finest hour. If he did not actually utter the words "My cup runneth over," he came very close to doing so. The expression he actually used was the one provided by wise high officials for the use of officers in circumstances such as these.

He said, "What's all this?"

It is a question which, if asked when the blood is hot, often goes unanswered. It did so now. Chimp was in no shape for speech, and Soapy was far too preoccupied with the task in hand. Instead of merely strangling his old associate, George noticed that he now appeared to be trying to pull his head off at the roots, and it seemed to him that the time had come to intervene. His method of doing so, in keeping with his character, was simple and direct. Wasting no time on verbal reasoning, he attached himself to the scruff of Soapy's neck, and pulled. There was a rending sound, and Chimp found himself free from that clutching hand, a thing he had begun to feel could never happen again in this world. For a brief moment he stood testing his breathing apparatus to make sure that it was still in working order; then, in pursuance of his policy of putting as great a distance as possible in as short a time as possible between himself and the Molloy family, he vanished into the night at a speed which Freddie Widgeon, racing of a morning to catch the 8:45 train, might have equaled but could never have surpassed.

George, in his patient, stolid way, was trying to get an over-all picture of the events leading up to this welcome break in the monotony of police work in Valley Fields. His original theory, that the large blighter to whose neck he was adhering had snatched the shapely lady's bag and that the small blighter, happening to be passing at the time, had interfered on her behalf, he dismissed. He had not seen much of Chimp, but he had seen enough to convince him that he was not the type that comes to the rescue of damsels in distress. More probably the small blighter—call him the human shrimp—had spoken lightly of a woman's name, and the large blighter, justly incensed, had lost his calm judgment and allowed his feelings to get the better of him.

Well, that was all very well, thought George, and one raised one's helmet in approval of his chivalry and all that, but you can't have fellows, no matter what the excellence of their motives, committing breaches of the peace all over the place, particularly in the presence of policemen who have been dreaming for weeks of making their first arrest. He tightened his grip on Soapy's neck, and with his other hand grasped the latter's wrist, placing himself in a position, should the situation call for it, to tie him in a reefer knot and bring back to him memories of old visits to the osteopath. And it was at this point that Dolly's pent-up emotions found expression.

"You big jug-headed sap!" she cried.

George started. He knew that this was in many ways a not unfair description of himself, for the fact had been impressed upon him both by masters at his school and, later, by superiors in his chosen profession. His sergeant, for one, had always been most frank on the subject. Nevertheless, the outburst surprised him. He peered over Soapy's head at the speaker and was interested to recognize in her an old acquaintance, might he not almost say friend.

"Why, hullo," he said. "You again? You do keep popping up, don't you? Did I hear you call me a jug-headed sap?"

"Yes, you did," rejoined Dolly with heat. "See what you've been and done, you clam. You've gone and allowed that little reptile to make a getaway and he's got something very valuable belonging to I and my husband."

George shook his head.

"You shouldn't have let him have it. Neither a borrower nor a lender be. Shakespeare."

"Plus which, you're giving my husband a crick in the neck."

"Is this your husband?"

"Yes, it is, and I'll thank you to take your fat hands off'n him."

"Release him, do you mean? Set him free?"

"That's what I mean."

Again George shook his head.

"My dear little soul, you don't know what you're asking. Goodness knows I'd do anything in my power to oblige one with whom I have passed such happy moments, but when you suggest releasing this bimbo, I must resolutely decline to co-operate. He was causing a breach of the peace. Very serious matter, that, and one at which we of the force look askance."

"Oh, applesauce!"

"I beg your pardon?"

"Why all this fuss and feathers about him choking an undersized little weasel that would have been choked at birth if his parents had had an ounce more sense than a billiard ball?"

George appreciated her point, but though as gallant a man as ever donned a uniform he could not allow her to sway him from his purpose.

"I get the idea, of course, and I'd fall in with your wishes like a shot, were the circumstances different, but you're overlooking a vitally important point. Have you any conception of what it means to a rozzer in a place like Valley Fields to be in a position to make a pinch? It's only about once in a blue moon that even so much as a simple drunk-and-disorderly comes along in this super-saintly suburb, so when you get a red-hot case of assault and battery . . ."

Words failed George, and he substituted action. Increasing the pressure on Soapy's neck, he propelled him along the road. Dolly, following, had fallen into a thoughtful silence and made no reply when George begged her to take the sporting view and to bear in mind how greatly all this was going to improve his relations with his sergeant. She was feeling in her bag for her blackjack, a girl's best friend. Experience had taught her that there was very little in this world that a blackjack could not cure.

Chimp Twist, meanwhile, his first instinct being to keep going and get away, had wandered far afield, so far that when at length he paused and felt it would be safe to return to Castlewood and its chamois leather bag, he became aware that he had lost himself. Valley Fields, while not an African jungle, is, like most London suburbs, an easy place for the explorer to get lost in, consisting as it does of streets of houses all looking exactly alike. But much may be accomplished by making inquiries of friendly natives, and after an hour or so of taking the first turn to the left and the second to the right and finding himself back where he had started, he won through to the railway station, and, from there to Castlewood was but a step. His spirits were high as he entered Mulberry Grove, but they became abruptly lowered when he came in sight of the house he sought.

It was not that the sight of the front gate brought back thoughts of George and the Molloys. What caused him to halt suddenly and to realize that Fate was still persecuting him was the spectacle of a young man and a girl standing at that gate, engaged in earnest conversation.

He turned away, with sinking heart. He knew what happened when young men and girls stood in earnest conversation on any given spot. They stayed fixed to it for hours.

25.

Freddie's dinner had been a great success. It had started, as was natural in the circumstances, in an atmosphere of some depression, and during the soup course it would not be too much to say that gloom had reigned. But with the fish there had come a marked change for the better, for it was then that Sally, using all her feminine persuasiveness, had prevailed on him to forget the self-respect of the Widgeons and agree to allow her to apply to Leila Yorke for a temporary loan. After that, everything had gone with a swing.

It was only as they stood at the gate of Castlewood that the jarring note crept back into their conversation. For some little time during the homeward journey Sally had noticed a tendency toward silence on her loved one's part, and now he revealed that, having thought things over a bit, he was not easy in his mind about this idea of appealing for help to Leila Yorke. His scruples had risen to the surface again.

"What I mean to say," he said, "can a Widgeon bite a woman's ear?"

"Oh, Freddie!"

"You can say 'Oh, Freddie!' till the cows come home, but the question still remains moot. Odd, this feeling one has about getting into the ribs of the other sex. It's like rubbing velvet the wrong way. I remember when I was a kid and went to dancing school, there was a child called Alice who had a bar of milk chocolate, and knowing how deep her love for me was I deliberately played on her affection to get half of it off her. I enjoyed it at the time, but now, looking back, I feel unclean. A thoroughly dirty trick I consider it, and I'm not sure this idea of sharing the wealth with Leila Yorke isn't just as bad."

"You won't be getting the money from her. I will."

"But I shall be getting it from you."

"Well, what's wrong with that?"

"Nothing actually *wrong*, but—"

Sally's patience gave out.

"Look here," she said, "do you want to marry me?"

"You betcher."

"Do you want to go to Kenya and make an enormous fortune, growing coffee?"

"Oh, rather."

"And do you realize that you can't do either of these things unless you get some money quick?"

"Yes, I see that."

"Then don't be an ass," said Sally.

Freddie saw her point. He nodded. Her clear feminine reasoning had convinced him.

"I see what you mean. After all, as you say, it's just a loan."

"Exactly."

"Once the coffee beans start sprouting, I shall be able to repay her a thousandfold."

"Of course."

"And you think she'll part?"

"I'm sure she will. She's the most generous person on earth."

"Well, I hope you're right, because I told you about that letter from Boddington, saying he couldn't hold his offer open much longer. The sands are running out, as you might say. You'll be seeing her tomorrow, I take it?"

"Yes, she told me to hire a car and drive down with the luggage. That shows you what she's like. Any other woman would have made me go by train."

"A sterling soul. I've always thought so. She—"

Freddie broke off. Out of the night a large figure in policeman's uniform had appeared and was standing beside them, breathing rather stertorously, as if it had recently passed through some testing spiritual experience.

"Hullo, Freddie," it said.

"Hullo, George."

"Hullo, Miss . . . I keep forgetting your name."

"Foster. But think of me as Sally."

"Right ho. I say," said George, "I've just been conked on the base of the skull with a blunt instrument."

"What!"

"Squarely on the base of the skull. And, what makes it even more bitter, it was a woman who did it. You remember that girl friend of yours who borrowed your pajamas, Freddie?"

"She wasn't my girl friend!"

George was in no mood to split straws.

"Well, your distant acquaintance or whatever she was. Hers was the hand that let me have it."

Sally squeaked incredulously.

"You mean Mrs. *Molloy* hit you?"

"Feel the bump, if you care to."

Freddie drew in his breath sharply. Since his betrothal to Sally, his views on dallying with the female sex, once broad-minded to the point of laxity, had become austere. He spoke severely.

"You have only yourself to blame, George. How you can do this sort of thing beats me. You are engaged to a sweet girl who loves and trusts you, and yet you go about the place forcing your attentions on other women, a thing which Sally knows I wouldn't do on a bet. You ought to be ashamed of yourself."

"What are you talking about?"

"Didn't you kiss Mrs. Molloy?"

"Certainly not. I wouldn't kiss her with a ten-foot pole."

"Then why did she sock you?"

"I was pinching her husband."

A thrill ran through Freddie's system. Anyone who pinched the hellhound Molloy had his sympathy and support.

"I found him causing a breach of the peace, and took him into custody, and we all marched off en route for the police station. The female Molloy had been pleading with me piteously to let the blighter go, and I might have done it, in spite of the fact that it was my dearest wish to make my first pinch and be fawned on by my sergeant and others, but it suddenly came home to me that she had kept referring to the accused as her husband, and I knew she was Mrs. Molloy, and I put two and two together and realized that this must be the bird who had done you down over those oil shares. After that, of course, I was adamant, and the upshot of the whole thing was that while my attention was riveted on Molloy, she hauled off and biffed me on the occipital bone with what I assumed to be a cosh. I don't know what girls are coming to these days."

Freddie clicked his tongue.

"So you let Molloy get away?"

"How do you mean, *let* him get away?" said George, with spirit. "I was temporarily a spent force. Everything went black, and when I came out of the ether I was sitting in the gutter with a lump on the back of my bean—you may feel it, if you wish—the size of an ostrich egg, and the Molloys had vanished into the night."

Sally squeaked again, this time in sympathy.

"You poor man! Does it hurt?"

"Lady, I will conceal nothing from you. It hurts like hell."

"Come on in and have a drink."

George shook his head, and a sharp yelp of pain showed how speedily he had regretted the rash act.

"Thanks, but sorry, no, afraid impossible. I'm on duty, and they have a nasty habit at headquarters of sniffing at one's breath. What I stopped for was to touch you for a cigarette, Freddie. Have you the makings?"

"Of course. I've also got a cigar, rather a good one, judging from the price."

"A cigar would be terrific," said George gratefully. "Add a match—I used my last one just before the affair Molloy—and I shall be set." And having expressed a wish that at some point in his patrolling he might once more encounter Mr. Molloy, he, too, vanished into the night.

His departure left a silence. Freddie broke it.

"Poor old George!"

"My heart bleeds for him."

"Mine, too. Must be very galling for an old Oxford box-ing blue, who may at any moment represent his country on the football field, to be put on the canvas by a woman and not to be able to wash it down with a drop of the right stuff. That suggestion of a nip of something to keep the cold out, by the way, strikes me as sound. Have you anything on the premises?"

"I've a whole bottle of champagne I bought for Leila Yorke's dinner."

"You may lead me to it."

They went into the house, and Sally passed on into the kitchen. When she joined Freddie some moments later in the living room, her face was a little pale.

"It isn't there," she said.

"No, it's here," said Freddie, pointing. "Wonder who brought it in? Three glasses, too. Odd."

"I'll tell you something odder. The kitchen window's broken. Somebody's been getting in."

"Burglars? Good heavens!" A grave look came into Freddie's face. "I don't like this."

"I don't like it myself."

"But what on earth would burglars want, breaking into a house of this sort?"

"Well, they evidently did, and what I'm asking myself is, Are they coming back?"

"You mustn't get the wind up."

"I'm jolly well going to. If you want to know how nervous anyone can be, watch me. I've got to sleep here all alone, and if you think that's a pleasant thought, with burglars popping in and out all the time, you're wrong."

Freddie waved a reassuring hand.

"Have no concern whatsoever. I shall be outside, keeping watch and something. Ward, that's the word I wanted. I'll be in the offing, keeping watch and ward. Don't let burglars weigh on your mind. I will be about their bed and about their board, spying out all their ways."

"No, you mustn't."

"Yes, I must."

"No. You need your sleep. I shall be all right," said Sally with sudden confidence. She had just remembered Leila Yorke's shotgun. There is nothing like a shotgun for putting heart into a girl.

Freddie pondered.

"You don't want me to keep watch and ward?"

"No. You're not to."

"Right ho," said Freddie agreeably. Though still a bachelor, he knew better than to argue with a woman. He kissed Sally fondly and left by the front door, and Chimp Twist, who had stolen cautiously to the gate and was about to open it, backed hastily and melted into the night again, thinking hard thoughts of the younger generation. The trouble with the younger generation, he was feeling bitterly as he removed himself, was that they were always round and about, popping up all the time where they were not wanted.

It was perhaps an hour later that he thought it would be safe to try again. He knew exactly where the chamois leather bag was, just behind where he had been standing, and it was with a bright anticipation of the happy ending that he approached the gate once more, only to find the same member of the younger generation leaning on it, his eyes raised to the moon and his general aspect that of one who was there for the night.

A man experienced in dealing with the female sex knows that the policy to pursue, when a woman issues an order, is not to stand arguing but to acquiesce and then go off and disobey it, and Freddie had wasted no time trying to persuade Sally to change her mind and allow him to patrol the grounds of Castlewood. He had simply gone and done it. For the last hour he had been, in defiance of her wishes, walking round and round the house like the better type of watchdog, his eye alert for nocturnal marauders. The complete absence of these had induced ennui and, like George, he was delighted to see Chimp. He would have preferred to pass the time of night with someone who looked a little less like something absent without leave from the monkey house at the zoo, but he knew that he was in no position to pick and choose. Valley Fields goes to bed early, and this at such an hour was the best it could provide.

"Nice evening," he said, though evening was hardly the right word.

Chimp wondered glumly how many people were going to make this quite untrue statement to him. Of all the evenings in his experience, not excluding the one in the course of which Mrs. Thomas G. Molloy had hit him with the butt end of a pistol, this had been the worst. His response to the observation was merely a grunt, and Freddie felt a little discouraged. Here, evidently, was no sparkling conversationalist who would enliven his vigil with shafts of wit and a fund of good stories.

However, he persevered.

"The moon," he said, indicating it precisely as George had done, with a movement of the hand designed to convey the impression that he thought well of it.

It was possible—not probable, perhaps, but still possible—that Chimp would have had something good to say about the moon, but it did not pass his lips, for at this moment, quite unexpectedly, the world came to an end. That, at least, was how it sounded both to Freddie and his companion. Actually what had occurred was that Sally, leaning out of an upper window, had discharged Leila Yorke's shotgun. For the last hour she had been listening in alarm to the sound of stealthy footsteps going round and round the house, and the sight of the two sinister figures standing plotting together at the front gate, evidently exchanging ideas as to how best to sneak in and loot the premises, had decided her to act. The shotgun was in Leila Yorke's bedroom. She proceeded thither, and having found it, took it to her own room, opened the window and pulled the trigger, aiming in the general direction of the moon, for she was a tenderhearted girl and averse to shedding even burglarious blood.

The effect on Freddie and friend was immediate. Chimp, able to understand now why Soapy disliked shotguns, after the first moment of paralysis which so often follows shots in the night, did not linger but was off the mark like a racing greyhound. George, who was enjoying his cigar in the front garden of Peacehaven, keeping his ear to the ground in case his sergeant happened along, got an impression of a vague shape whizzing by, and assumed it to be a flying saucer or something of that nature. Then, like the splendid fellow he was, he remembered that he was an officer of the peace and answering the call of duty hurried in the direction from which the shot had seemed to proceed. At the same moment Mr. Cornelius emerged from The Nook in a beige dressing gown and said, "What was that?" George said that that was precisely what was puzzling him, and Mr. Cornelius said that this sort of thing was most unusual for Valley Fields. They made their way to Castlewood together.

Freddie also was keeping his ear to the ground, and all the rest of him as well. This was because at the moment of the explosion he had flung himself to earth, remembering from Westerns he had seen that this was the thing to do on these occasions. He lay there breathing softly through the nose, and as he lay he became aware of something hard and knobbly pressing into his chest and rendering his position one of extreme discomfort. Cautiously, for when one is under fire the slightest movement is often fatal, he felt for it and pulled it from beneath him. It seemed to be a bag of some description, and appeared to be full of a number of hard substances. He had just slipped it into his pocket and was finding himself much more comfortable when George and Mr. Cornelius arrived. Emboldened by these reinforcements, he rose and accompanied them to the front door, which George banged with his truncheon.

A voice spoke from above.

"Go away, or I'll shoot again. Police!" added the voice, changing the subject. "Police!"

"We are the police, old thing," said Freddie. "At least, George is. For heaven's sake return that damned gun to store and come down and let us in."

"Oh, is that you, Freddie?"

"It is."

"Was that you I saw lying on the ground?"

"It was."

"What were you doing there?"

"Well, commending my soul to God, mostly."

"I mean, why weren't you in bed?"

"I was keeping ward and watch."

"I told you not to."

"I know, but I thought I'd better."

"Oh?"

In the brief interval of waiting for the door to open, Mr. Cornelius enlarged on his previous statement that episodes of this nature were far from customary in the

232

suburb he loved. Not that remarkable things did not happen from time to time in Valley Fields, he added, instancing the case of a Mr. Edwin Phillimore of The Firs at the corner of Buller Street and Myrtle Avenue, who in the previous summer had been bitten by a guinea pig. He was beginning what promised to be a rather long story about a resident named Walkinshaw who came back from London in a new tweed suit and, the animal being temporarily misled by the garment's unaccustomed smell, was chased by his dog onto the roof of his summerhouse, when Sally appeared. She was carrying the shotgun, just in case. She had had an enthralling conversation with someone purporting to be Freddie, but burglars are cunning and know how to imitate voices. They are notorious for it.

George was the first to speak.

"I say, you know! I mean to say, what?" he said, and Mr. Cornelius said, "Just so."

Sally saw their point.

"I know, but you can't blame me. I thought Freddie was one of the gang of burglars who have been in and out of here all night. I'm so sorry I woke you up, Mr. Cornelius."

"Not at all, Miss Foster, not at all. Actually, I was not asleep. I was downstairs, working on my history of Valley Fields."

"Oh, I'm so glad. How's it going?"

"Quite satisfactorily, thank you, though slowly. There is so much material."

"Well, you got some more tonight, didn't you? How's the head, George?"

"Better, thanks."

"But still throbbing?"

"A bit."

"You'd better have that drink, even if you are on duty."

"I think you're right."

"I've got a bottle of champagne."

"My God!"

"It's all ready in there. Freddie!"

"Hullo?"

"You're covered with dust. Come here and let me brush you. What on earth," said Sally, wringing her fingers, "have you got in your pocket?"

"Oh, this?" said Freddie, taking it out. "It seems to be a bag of sorts. I came down on it when I took my purler."

"What's inside it?"

"I don't know. Take a look, shall I? Well, Lord love a duck!" said Freddie. "Well, blow me tight! Well, I'll be a son of a whatnot!"

He was fully justified in speaking thus. From the table on to which he had decanted the bag's contents there gleamed up at them a macédoine of rings, both diamond and ruby, bracelets set with the same precious stones, and, standing out from the rest in its magnificence, an emerald necklace.

George, again, was the first to speak. The police, trained for emergencies, pull themselves together more quickly at times like this than the more emotional householder.

"The bounders dropped their swag!" he said, and Mr. Cornelius, unable to utter, endorsed the theory with a waggle of his beard.

Sally could not accept it.

"But those aren't Leila Yorke's. She hasn't any jewelry except a couple of rings."

"Are you sure?"

"She told me so."

"Then where on earth did the ruddy things come from?" said George, baffled.

A strange light was shining in Freddie's eyes. He had

taken up the necklace and was subjecting it to a close scrutiny. It made all things clear to him.

"I'll tell you where they came from," he said. "From *chez* Oofy. This is the Prosser bijouterie. And if you're going to ask me how I know, I've seen this horse collar on the neck of Myrtle P., née Shoesmith, a dozen times when I've been dining at their residence. She slaps it on even if there is only a Widgeon in the audience. Do you know what this means, Sally? It means that we've come to the end of the long, long trail, and our financial problems are solved. Tomorrow, bright and early, I seek Oofy out and, having restored the stuff to him and been thanked brokenly, I collect the huge reward he'll be only too delighted to bestow. It ought to run into thousands."

It is never easy to find the right words at a moment like this, but George did it. The police are wonderful.

"Open that champagne!" said George.

26.

Feeding his rabbits in the garden of The Nook, Mr. Cornelius, as he plied the lettuce, began to hum one of the catchier melodies from *Hymns Ancient and Modern* and would have sung it, had not the words escaped his memory. He was in the best of spirits. The events of the previous night had left him in a gentle glow, not unlike the one he got from cocoa, kippered herrings and pink blancmange. A kindly man, he wished all his neighbors well, particularly his next-door neighbor, Frederick Widgeon, for whom he had always felt a paternal fondness, and the thought that Freddie's troubles were now at an end, his prosperity assured, the joy bells as good as ringing and nothing for his friends to worry about except the choosing of the fish slicer for a wedding present, was a very heartening one.

A shadow fell on the grass beside him, and he looked up.

"Ah, Mr. Widgeon," he said. "Good evening."

Ever eager to catch the historian in a blunder, carpers and cavilers, of whom there are far too many about these days, will seize gleefully on that word "evening." Did not the historian, they will ask, state that it was in the morning that Mr. Cornelius fed his rabbits? To which, with a quiet smile, the historian replies, "Yes, he did, but this big-hearted animal lover also gave them a second snack around about five P.M., feeling that only thus could they keep their strength up." There was no stint at The Nook.

Mr. Cornelius was glad to see Freddie. A theory concerning last night's happenings had come to him, and he was anxious to impart it.

"I have been thinking a great deal, Mr. Widgeon, about the mystery of how Mrs. Prosser's jewelry came to be in the front garden of Castlewood, and I have come to the conclusion that under a mask of apparent respectability the man Molloy must have been one of these Master Criminals of whom one reads, a branch of his activities being the receiving of stolen goods. He was what I believe, though I should have to apply to your cousin for confirmation, is known as a fence."

"Oh, no, quite all right," said Freddie.

"I beg your pardon?"

"You said something about taking offense."

Mr. Cornelius was concerned. He saw that his companion's eyes were blank, his manner preoccupied. He had learned from Sally, with whom he had had a brief conversation as she was preparing to drive off to Claines Hall in her hired car, that Freddie had set out for London in the morning to restore the stolen jewelry to its owner and be lavishly rewarded by him, and he would have expected to see him on his return wreathed in smiles and feeling, as he had once described it, like one sitting on top of the world with a rainbow round his shoulder. Yet here he was, manifestly a prey to gloom. Exchanging glances with the rabbit nearest to him, he was frowning at it as he had frowned at the Texas millionaire in the restaurant of Barribault's Hotel.

"Are you feeling quite well, Mr. Widgeon?"

Dotted throughout this chronicle there have been references to occasions when Freddie Widgeon uttered mirthless laughs, but on none of these had he produced one comparable for lack of jollity with that which now passed his lips. It was a mirthless laugh to end all mirthless laughs, and sounded like a gramophone needle slipping from the groove.

"No," he replied, "I'm not. I'm feeling the way George must have felt last night when beaned by that cosh of Mrs. Molloy's. Do you know what, Cornelius?"

Mr. Cornelius said he did not.

"You don't know Oofy Prosser, do you?"

"We have never met. I have heard you speak of him, of course."

"Well, if you ever do meet him, you will be doing me a personal favor if you sit on his chest and skin him with a blunt knife. The louse has done me down."

"I don't understand."

"I went to see him this morning."

"So Miss Foster told me."

"Oh, did you see Sally? She got away all right?"

"Yes, I saw her off in her car. She had a snake with her, belonging, I understand, to Miss Yorke's husband. She was taking it to Claines Hall. It is a curious story. It appears— But you were telling me about your visit to Mr. Prosser."

Freddie raised a protesting hand.

"Don't call him Mr. Prosser, call him the hound Prosser or the Prosser disease. I went to his house in Eaton Square, and found him in sullen mood. He had just come from Bosher Street police court, where the presiding magistrate had soaked him for a fine of ten quid, telling him he was pretty dashed lucky not to have got fourteen days without the option."

"You astound me, Mr. Widgeon! Why was that?"

"Didn't I tell you he tried to murder Molloy at Barribault's yesterday? No? Well, he did, and the gendarmerie scooped him in and he spent last night in a prison cell. He was pretty sore about it, what embittered him chiefly being the fact that he was given a bath by the authorities. He wouldn't talk about anything else for the first ten minutes, but when I could get a word in edgeways, I handed him the bijouterie, and he said, 'What's this?' I explained that it was his better half's missing jewelry and said that, while I would not presume to dictate and would leave the matter of the reward entirely to him, I thought ten per cent of the value of the gewgaws would be fair to all parties concerned, and what do you think his reply was? He said he would be blowed if he gave me a ruddy penny, adding that if a few fatheaded buttinskys like me were to refrain from being so damned officious and weren't always meddling in other people's affairs, the world would be a better and sweeter place. It seems that he insured the stuff for about twice its proper value and got the money, and now he would have to give it back to the insurance people. He was very heated about it, so, seeing that my presence was not welcome, I came away. And I'd been counting on getting my three thousand quid from him," said Freddie brokenly, still gazing at the rabbit, but now as if seeking its sympathy.

He received none from that quarter, rabbits being notoriously indifferent to human suffering—lettuce, lettuce, lettuce, that is all that ever matters to them—but he got plenty from Mr. Cornelius. The house agent's beard quivered, as a bearded man's beard always will at the tale of a friend's distress. He became silent, seeming to be pondering on something or trying to come to some decision. At length he spoke.

"There *is* another source from which you can obtain the money you require, Mr. Widgeon," he said.

Freddie was surprised.

"Oh, did Sally tell you about her idea of trying to get the necessary funds from Leila Yorke? It looks like being our last chance, now that Oofy has declined to do the square thing. I phoned her from the Drones about Oofy letting me down, and though of course knocked slightly base over apex by the news, she speedily rallied and said everything was going to be all right, because she was sure that Leila Yorke would come through, she having a heart of gold and more cash than you could shake a stick at. Well, I wore the mask and said, 'Oh, fine!' or words to that effect, but I don't mind telling you, Cornelius, that I'm far from happy at the thought of letting a woman pick up the check. It jars my sense of what is fitting. True, as Sally keeps pointing out, it's merely a loan and it isn't as though she were kissing the stuff goodbye. Nevertheless—"

He would have spoken further, but at this moment a bell sounded, and he drew the fact to his companion's attention. A man of the other's age might well be hard of hearing.

"Your phone's ringing, Cornelius."

"Yours, I think, Mr. Widgeon."

"By jove, so it is," said Freddie, starting into life. "It must be Sally. Excuse me."

Left alone, Mr. Cornelius fell into a reverie. Rabbits twitched their noses at him, at a loss to understand why there had been this unexpected stoppage in the hitherto smoothly running lettuce supply, but he remained plunged in thought, not heeding their silent appeal. Minutes passed, and when at length Freddie came out of the back door of Peacehaven, a glance told Mr. Cornelius that he had not received good news. His aspect reminded the house agent of his brother Charles at the time when there was all that trouble about the missing cash from his employer's till. Charles, confronted with the evidence of his peculations, had looked as if something heavy had fallen on him from a considerable height, and so did Freddie.

Wasting no time on preambles, he said, "Well, that's torn it!"

"I beg your pardon?"

"I'm sunk!"

Again Mr. Cornelius begged his pardon, and Freddie forced himself to a semblance of calm. In order to get the sympathy he was seeking, he saw that he must be coherent.

"That was Sally on the phone, speaking from Claines Hall, Loose Chippings, and what do you think she told me? Leila Yorke has gone!"

"Dead?" said Mr. Cornelius, paling.

"Worse," said Freddie. "Legged it abroad with her husband on a sight-seeing jaunt, leaving no address but just a note saying that they were going to roam hither and thither about the Continent in the car, she didn't know where, and she didn't know when she would be back. In short, she has disappeared into the void, breaking contact with the human herd, and can't be located. You see what that means?"

"You will be unable now to apply to her for assistance in your financial emergency?"

"Exactly. I would have said that now we haven't an earthly way of touching her, but your way of putting it is just as good. And I have to give Boddington my decision in the next couple of days or so. Now you see why I said I was sunk. I see no ray of hope on the horizon."

It was stated earlier in this chronicle that the luxuriant growth of Mr. Cornelius's beard rendered it hard for the observer to see when he was pursing his lips. A similar difficulty presented itself when he smiled, as he was doing now. Freddie may have noticed a faint fluttering of the foliage, but nothing more. He continued in the same lugubrious strain.

"Leila Yorke was my last hope. Where else can I raise the needful?"

"Why, from me, Mr. Widgeon. I shall be delighted to lend you the money, if you will accept it. That was what I meant just now, when I spoke of an alternative source."

Freddie stared.

"You?"

"Certainly. It will be a pleasure."

There came to Freddie the feeling he had sometimes had when trying to solve a *Times* crossword puzzle, that his reason was tottering on its throne. There was nothing in the other's appearance to indicate that he had gone off his rocker, and still less to suggest that he was trying to be funny, but he could place no other interpretation on his words.

"Listen," he said. "Are you sure you've got this straight? It isn't a fiver till Wednesday week that I want, it's three thousand pounds."

"So I have always understood you to say."

"You mean you've actually *got* three thousand pounds?"

"Precisely."

"And you're willing to lend them to me?"

"There is nothing I would like better."

"But look here," said Freddie, his scruples troubling him again. "I'll admit that these doubloons would mean everything to me, and it's a great temptation to sit in on the project, because I honestly believe from what Boddington tells me that I should be able to pay you back in the course of time, but I don't like the idea of you risking all your life's savings like this."

Once more, Mr. Cornelius's beard stirred as if a passing breeze had ruffled it.

"These are not my life savings, Mr. Widgeon. I think I have spoken to you of my brother Charles?"

"The one who's living in America?"

"The one who was living in America," corrected Mr. Cornelius. "He passed away a few days ago. He fell out of his airplane."

"I'm sorry."

"I also. I was very fond of Charles, and he of me. He frequently urged me to give up my business and come and join him in New York, but it would have meant leaving Valley Fields, and I always declined. The reason I have brought his name up in the conversation is that he left me his entire fortune, amounting, the lawyers tell me, to between three and four million dollars."

"What!"

"So they say."

"Well, fry me for an onion!"

"The will is not yet probated, but the lawyers are in a position to advance me any sums I may require, however large, so you can rest assured that there will be no difficulty over a trivial demand like three thousand pounds."

"Trivial?"

"A mere bagatelle. So you see that I can well afford to lend you a helping hand, and, as I told you before, it will be a pleasure."

Freddie drew a deep breath. Mr. Cornelius, his rabbits and the garden of The Nook seemed to him to be executing a spirited version of the dance, so popular in the twenties, known as the shimmy.

"Cornelius," he said, "you would probably object if I kissed you, so I won't, but may I say . . . No, words fail me. My gosh, you're wonderful! You've saved two human lives from the soup, and you can quote me as stating this, that if ever an angel in human shape . . . No, as I said, words fail me."

Mr. Cornelius, who had been smiling—at least, so thought Freddie, for his beard had been in a constant state of agitation—became grave.

"There is just one thing, Mr. Widgeon. You must not mention a word of this to anyone, except of course Miss Foster, in whom you will naturally have to confide. But you must swear her to secrecy."

"I'll see that her lips are sealed all right. But why?"

"This must never reach Mrs. Cornelius's ears."

"Hasn't it?"

"Fortunately, no."

"You mean she doesn't know? You haven't told her about these pennies from heaven?"

"I have not, and I do not intend to. Mr. Widgeon," said Mr. Cornelius, graver than ever, "have you any conception of what would happen, were my wife to learn that I was a millionaire? Do you think I should be allowed to go on living in Valley Fields, the place I love, and continue to be a house agent, the work I love? Do you suppose I should be permitted to keep my old friends, like Mr. Wrenn of San Rafael, with whom I play chess on Saturdays, and feed rabbits in my shirt sleeves? No, I should be whisked off to a flat in Mayfair, I should have to spend long months in the south of France, a butler would be engaged and I should have to dress for dinner every night. I should have to join a London club, take a box at the opera, learn to play polo," said Mr. Cornelius, allowing his morbid fancy to run away with him a little. "The best of women are not proof against sudden wealth. Mrs. Cornelius is perfectly happy and contented in the surroundings to which she has always been accustomed—she was a Miss Bulstrode of Happy Haven at the time of our marriage— and I intend that she shall remain happy and contented."

Freddie nodded.

"I see what you mean. All that program you were outlining sounds like heaven to me, but I can understand that you might not get the same angle. Just depends how you look at these things. Well, rest assured that none shall ever learn your secret from Frederick Fotheringay Widgeon, or, for the matter of that, from the future Mrs. F. F. W. Her lips, as I say, shall be sealed, if necessary with Scotch Tape. I wonder if you'd mind if I left you for a space? I want to go and phone her the good news."

"Not at all."

"I won't be able to see it, but her little face'll light up like glorious Technicolor. Thanks to you."

"My dear Mr. Widgeon, please!"

"I repeat, thanks to you. And if ever there's anything I can do for you in return—"

"I can think of nothing. Ah, yes. Could you tell me how 'Rock of Ages' goes?"

"A horse? I don't think I have it on my betting list."

"The hymn."

"Oh, the hymn? Now I get your drift. Why, surely, tum tumty tumty tumty tum, doesn't it?"

"The words, I mean."

"Oh, the words? Sorry, I've forgotten, though I seem to recall the word 'cleft.' Or am I thinking of some other hymn?"

Mr. Cornelius's face lit up, as Sally's was so shortly to do.

"Why, of course. It all comes back to me."

"Well, that's fine. Anything further?"

"No, thank you."

"Then for the nonce, my dear old multimillionaire, pip-pip."

Freddie hurried into the house. Mr. Cornelius returned to his rabbits, who were feeling that it was about time.

"Oh, rock of ages, cleft for me," he sang.

The rabbits winced a little. They disapproved of the modern craze for music with meals.

Still, the lettuce was good, they felt philosophically. A rabbit learns to take the rough with the smooth.

P. G. WODEHOUSE *was born in Guildford, England, in 1881 and educated at Dulwich College, a school in the suburbs of London. He worked in the Hong Kong and Shanghai Bank for two years and then got a job writing a column in the* Globe. *He came to America in 1909 and has lived in the United States the greater portion of the time since. He has written over sixty books, as well as magazine serials and short stories beyond count. He has also been a highly successful collaborator on musical shows with Guy Bolton and Jerome Kern. It would be hard to name another writer whose work has held up steadily at top caliber over so long a period.*

Mr. Wodehouse is an Honorary D.Litt. of Oxford University. He became an American citizen a few years ago. He and his wife live the year round in Remsenburg, Long Island.